Fodor's

TORONTO

WELCOME TO TORONTO

Cultured and cosmopolitan, Toronto nevertheless manages to remain relaxed, livable, and fun all at the same time. Canada's center of the arts and media has plenty of pleasant tree-lined streets in Yorkville for window-shopping and wandering; a host of independent galleries in West Queen West with edgy works; big-name music festivals year-round; and an adventurous, constantly evolving food scene. Toronto's impressive sights may be what pull you in, but its vibrant neighborhoods, artistic happenings, and friendly locals will make you want to return.

TOP REASONS TO GO

★ **CN Tower:** Rising 1,815 feet in the air, this icon has stupendous panoramic views.

★ **Foodie Paradise:** Sophisticated restaurants, excellent ethnic spots, markets.

★ **Nonstop Shopping:** High-end designer flagships and a plethora of vintage shops.

★ **Festival City:** A star-studded film festival, the Nuit Blanche all-nighter, and more.

★ **Hip and Happening:** Urbanites flock to West Queen West, Old Town, and beyond.

★ **The Waterfront:** The Beach's boardwalk and car-free Toronto Islands help you unwind.

Fodor's TORONTO

Design: Tina Malaney, *Associate Art Director*; Erica Cuoco, *Production Designer*

Photography: Jennifer Arnow, *Senior Photo Editor*

Maps: Rebecca Baer, *Senior Map Editor*; Mark Stroud (Moon Street Cartography), David Lindroth, *Cartographers*

Production: Angela L. McLean, *Senior Production Manager*; Jennifer DePrima, *Editorial Production Manager*

Sales: Jacqueline Lebow, *Sales Director*

Business & Operations: Chuck Hoover, *Chief Marketing Officer*; Joy Lai, *Vice President and General Manager*; Stephen Horowitz, *Head of Business Development and Partnerships*

Writers: Rosemary Counter, Natalia Manzucco, Jesse Ship

Editor: Amanda Sadlowski

Production Editor: Carrie Parker

25th Edition

ISBN 978-1-101-88006-7

ISSN 1044–6133

All details in this book are based on information supplied to us at press time. Always confirm information when it matters, especially if you're making a detour to visit a specific place. Fodor's expressly disclaims any liability, loss, or risk, personal or otherwise, that is incurred as a consequence of the use of any of the contents of this book.

SPECIAL SALES

This book is available at special discounts for bulk purchases for sales promotions or premiums. For more information, e-mail specialmarkets@penguinrandomhouse.com.

PRINTED IN THE UNITED STATES OF AMERICA

10 9 8 7 6 5 4 3 2 1

CONTENTS

CONTENTS

ABOUT THIS GUIDE

Fodor's Recommendations

Everything in this guide is worth doing—we don't cover what isn't—but exceptional sights, hotels, and restaurants are recognized with additional accolades. Fodor's Choice★ indicates our top recommendations; and **Best Bets** call attention to notable hotels and restaurants in various categories. Care to nominate a new place? Visit Fodors.com/contact-us.

Trip Costs

We list prices wherever possible to help you budget well. Hotel and restaurant price categories from **$** to **$$$$** are noted alongside each recommendation. For hotels, we include the lowest cost of a standard double room in high season. For restaurants, we cite the average price of a main course at dinner or, if dinner isn't served, at lunch. For attractions, we always list adult admission fees; discounts are usually available for children, students, and senior citizens.

Hotels

Our local writers vet every hotel to recommend the best overnights in each price category, from budget to expensive. Unless otherwise specified, you can expect private bath, phone, and TV in your room. For expanded hotel reviews visit Fodors.com.

Top Picks
★ Fodor's Choice

Listings
⊠ Address
⊠ Branch address
☎ Telephone
🖷 Fax
🌐 Website
✉ E-mail
🎟 Admission fee
⊘ Open/closed times
Ⓜ Subway
⁎ Directions or Map coordinates

Hotels & Restaurants
🏨 Hotel
↪ Number of rooms
🍽 Meal plans
✗ Restaurant
🖎 Reservations
🏛 Dress code
💳 No credit cards
💲 Price

Other
⇨ See also
☞ Take note
🏌 Golf facilities

Restaurants

Unless we state otherwise, restaurants are open for lunch and dinner daily. We mention dress code only when there's a specific requirement and reservations only when they're essential or not accepted.

Credit Cards

The hotels and restaurants in this guide typically accept credit cards. If not, we'll say so.

EUGENE FODOR

Hungarian-born Eugene Fodor (1905–91) began his travel career as an interpreter on a French cruise ship. The experience inspired him to write *On the Continent* (1936), the first guidebook to receive annual updates and discuss a country's way of life as well as its sights. Fodor later joined the U.S. Army and worked for the OSS in World War II. After the war, he kept up his intelligence work while expanding his guidebook series. During the Cold War, many guides were written by fellow agents who understood the value of insider information. Today's guides continue Fodor's legacy by providing travelers with timely coverage, insider tips, and cultural context.

EXPERIENCE TORONTO

TORONTO TODAY

It can be hard to define a city like Toronto. It's culturally diverse, to be sure, but that's not exactly a unifying characteristic. So what exactly is Toronto all about? Americans call Torontonians friendly and the city clean, while other Canadians say its locals can be rude and egocentric. Toronto is often touted simply as a "livable" city, a commendable but dull virtue. Toronto might not be quite as exciting as New York City, as quaint as Montréal, as outdoorsy as Vancouver, or as historic as London, but instead it's a patchwork of *all* these qualities. And rest assured that Toronto *is* clean, safe, and just all-around nice. Torontonians say "sorry" when they jostle you. They recycle and compost. They obey traffic laws. For many, Toronto is like the boy next door you eventually marry after fooling around with New York or Los Angeles. Why not cut the charade and start the love affair now?

Diversity

Toronto is one of the most immigrant-friendly cities on the planet, and the city's official motto, "Diversity Our Strength," reflects this hodgepodge of ethnicities. More than half its population is foreign-born, and half of all Torontonians are native speakers of a foreign language.

(The "other" national language of French, however, is not one of the most commonly spoken languages here, trailing Chinese, Portuguese, Punjabi, and Tagalog.) In a few hours in Toronto you can travel the globe, from Little India to Little Italy, Koreatown to Greektown, or at least eat your way around it, from Polish pierogi to Chinese dim sum to Portuguese salt-cod fritters.

Neighborhoods

Every city has neighborhoods, but Toronto's are particularly diverse, distinctive, and walkable. Some were once their own villages, and many, such as the Danforth (Greektown), Little Portugal, and Chinatown, are products of the ethnic groups who first settled there. For the most part, boundaries aren't fixed and are constantly evolving: on a five-minute walk down Bloor Street West you can pass a Portuguese butcher, an Ethiopian restaurant, a hip espresso bar, and a Maltese travel agency. In the '70s and '80s, areas such as Yorkville and Queen West were transformed by struggling-artist types and have since grown into downright affluent, retail powerhouses. In the last decade once run-down neighborhoods including West Queen West and Leslieville, have

WHAT'S HOT IN TORONTO NOW?

After years of continuous condo construction and a recent building boom that included a bevy of luxury hotels, Toronto's distinctive skyline is becoming a blur of glossy high-rise buildings. The CN Tower still stretches above it all, making the loftiest

architecture appear pretty insignificant.

A newer addition to the ever-changing skyline is the L Tower, a curvaceous glass building located downtown by Union Station, where the UP Express train now runs

to Pearson International Airport—a much needed direct link from downtown to the city's main airport.

And speaking of airports and shoreline, the controversial Toronto Island Airport (also known as Billy Bishop Airport), blossomed into funky, boho areas with enviable shopping and eating options with housing prices to match. Barring a change in fortune, gentrification is set to continue to more areas.

Culture

The Toronto International Film Festival, the Art Gallery of Ontario, Canada's center for magazine and book publishing, national ballet and opera companies, the Toronto Symphony Orchestra—these are just a handful of the many reasons Toronto attracts millions of arts and culture lovers each year to live, work, and play. On any given day or night, you'll find events to feed the brain and the spirit: art gallery openings, poetry readings, theatrical releases, film revues, dance performances, and festivals showcasing the arts, from the focused Toronto Jazz Festival and the North by Northeast indie rock extravaganza to events marrying visual and performing arts, like Nuit Blanche and Luminato.

The Waterfront

Lake Ontario forms Toronto's very obvious southern border, but residents who live out of its view often forget it's there until they attend an event at the Canadian National Exhibition or the Harbourfront Centre. It's one of the city's best features, especially in the summer, providing opportunities for boating, ferrying to the Toronto Islands, or strolling, biking, or jogging beside the water. The lakeshore is more of an attraction than ever, with ongoing initiatives to revitalize the waterfront and create more parks, beaches, and walkways.

Food

There's no shortage of amazing restaurants in this city, and local and fresh produce is all the rage. Celebrity chefs like Lynn Crawford, Mark McEwan, and Jamie Kennedy give locavores street cred, while Toronto's cornucopia of cultures means you can sample almost any cuisine, from Abyssinian to Yemeni. Nowhere is the Toronto love of food more apparent, perhaps, than at St. Lawrence Market, where you can pick up nonessentials like fiddlehead ferns, elk burgers, truffle oil, and mozzarella *di bufala*. In warm weather, farmers' markets bring the province's plenty to the city.

squeezed between the edge of Toronto Island and the harborfront, is pushing to add more flights and bigger planes. That would provide local jet setters even greater convenience, but annoy the lakeshore's residents to no end. The subway is being extended into the northern suburbs where so many Torontonians live, and a light rail line is under construction along Eglinton, through uptown Toronto's cosmopolitan hub.

WHAT'S WHERE

1 Harbourfront, the Entertainment District, and the Financial District. Between the waterfront and Queen Street, the city's main attractions are packed in: the CN Tower, Harbourfront Centre, the Hockey Hall of Fame, and Ripley's Aquarium of Canada. Most of the lofty peaks in Toronto's skyline are in this epicenter of Canadian financial power, as well as the restaurants, theaters, and clubs of King Street West.

2 Old Town and the Distillery District. Stroll through the Old Town past Victorian buildings to the foodie paradise St. Lawrence Market. Farther east, the Distillery District offers great shopping and cafés.

3 Yonge-Dundas Square Area. The square hosts frequent performances in summer, and the surrounding neighborhood has Broadway-style theaters and department stores.

4 Chinatown, Kensington Market, and Queen West. Busy and bustling, the sidewalks here are overflowing. Wander through the much-loved hippy-punk hangout of Kensington Market and scoff dumplings in Chinatown. Don't miss the Canadian and contemporary art at the Art Gallery of Ontario (AGO).

5 **East and West of the City Center.** Here, the leafy residential streets and board-walk of the Beaches beckon, while funkified Leslieville offers boho shopping and great brunch spots. The Danforth is super lively in the evening with packed patios. And West Queen West steps up the city's hip quotient.

6 **Queen's Park, the Annex, and Little Italy.** Stately Queen's Park is home to the Ontario Legislature Building and the ivy-covered buildings of the University of Toronto. Farther west lies Little Italy, packed with cool cafés. North of the campus you'll hit the Annex, the city's academic and artsy haunt.

7 **Yorkville, Church-Wellesley, and Rosedale.** Yorkville itself is refined and classy, the narrow streets lined with chic cafés and high-end boutiques. North of here is the moneyed residen-tial neighborhood of Rosedale. A nudge east and south is Toronto's gay-friendly Church-Wellesley neighborhood.

8 **Greater Toronto.** Top attractions such as Canada's Wonderland theme park, the Ontario Science Centre, and the Toronto Zoo lure visitors from downtown.

TORONTO PLANNER

When to Go

Toronto is most pleasant from late spring through early fall, when there are outdoor concerts, frequent festivals, and open-air dining. On the other hand, some hotels drop their prices up to 50% in the off-season. Fall through spring is prime viewing time for dance, opera, theater, and classical music. The temperature frequently falls below freezing from late November into March, when snowstorms can wreak havoc on travel plans, although Toronto's climate is mild by Canadian standards, thanks to the regulating properties of Lake Ontario. Still, snow is substantial enough to lure skiing enthusiasts to the resorts north of the city. A few underground shopping concourses, such as the PATH in the Financial District downtown, allow you to avoid the cold in the winter months.

Getting Here

Most flights arrive and depart from Toronto Pearson International Airport (YYZ), about a 30-minute drive northwest of downtown. Cabs are a C$50–C$75 flat rate (varies by destination) for most downtown locations. The Toronto Transit Commission (TTC) operates the 192 Airport Rocket, a shuttle bus to Kipling subway station; the TTC fare of C$3.25 applies. The UP Express train to Union Station downtown began operating in June 2015, and connects with the Bloor-Danforth subway line near Dundas West station and also to Weston Station. The Billy Bishop Toronto City Airport (YTZ), better known as the Toronto Island Airport, right downtown, is served almost entirely by Porter Airlines, which flies to Chicago, Newark (New Jersey), Boston, Washington, D.C., and several cities in northern Ontario and in eastern Canada, including Montréal. Amtrak and VIA Rail trains pull into Union Station, at the intersection of Bay and Front streets.

Getting Around

Traffic is dense and parking expensive within the city center. If you have a car, leave it at your hotel. ■TIP→ **In the city, take taxis or use the excellent TTC subway, streetcar, and bus system.**

Car Travel. A car is helpful to access some farther-flung destinations, but it isn't necessary and can be a hassle. Street parking is sometimes difficult; garages and lots usually charge C$3–C$5 per hour or C$15–C$25 per day.

Taxi Travel. Taxis here are easy to hail, or you can call ☎416/829–4222 for pickup. The meter starts at C$3.25 and you are charged C25¢ for each additional 0.143 km (roughly 1/10 mile) after the first 0.143 km.

TTC Travel. The Toronto Transit Commission operates the subway, streetcars, and buses that easily take you to most downtown attractions. The subway is clean and efficient, with trains arriving every few minutes; streetcars and buses are a bit slower. A single transferable fare is C$3.25; day (C$12) and week (C$41.50) passes are available. A day pass covers up to two adults and four children on weekend days and holidays. Most systems operate from about 6 am to 1:30 am Monday through Saturday and 8 am to 1:30 am Sunday.

Getting Oriented

The boundaries of what Torontonians consider downtown, where most of the city sights are located, are subject to debate, but everyone agrees on the southern cutoff—Lake Ontario and the Toronto Islands. The other coordinates of the rectangle that compose the city core are roughly High Park to the west, the

DVP (Don Valley Parkway) to the east, and Eglinton Avenue to the north. A few sights beyond these borders make excellent half- or full-day excursions. An ideal way to get a sense of the city's layout is from one of the observation decks at the CN Tower on a clear day; the view is especially lovely at sunset.

Most city streets are organized on a grid system: with some exceptions, street numbers start at zero at the lake and increase as you go north. On the east–west axis, Yonge (pronounced "young") Street, Toronto's main north–south thoroughfare, is the dividing line: you can expect higher numbers the farther away you get from Yonge.

Making the Most of Your Time

Planning is the key to maximizing your experience. First, book a hotel near the activities that most interest you. If you're here to see a Broadway-style show, get the view from the CN Tower, stroll the lakefront, stomp your feet at a Raptors game, or soak up some culture at the ballet, opera, or symphony, go for a room in or near Harbourfront. If food, shopping, or museums are your passion, affluent Yorkville might be better suited (bonus: it's at the axis of both major subway lines). To live like a local, wandering neighborhood streets and patronizing funky cafés and shops, consider the Queen West boutique hotels.

In a short trip you can do a lot but not everything. Decide on your priorities, and don't overbook. Allow time for wandering. Schedule coffee (or Ontario microbrew) breaks. Be realistic about your sightseeing style. If you tend to scour every inch of a museum, you could spend an entire afternoon at the Royal Ontario Museum (ROM); if you're selective, you can breeze through in an hour.

Plan your days geographically. Kensington and Chinatown make an excellent combo; High Park and the Beaches, not so much.

Ditch the car and get a TTC day pass for unlimited travel on the subways, buses, and streetcars.

Visitor Information

Tourism Toronto.
☎ 800/363–1990, 416/203–2600
⊕ www.seetorontonow.com.

Savings Tips

■ Toronto CityPASS (www.citypass.com) saves money and time as it lets you bypass ticket lines. Admission fees to the CN Tower, Casa Loma, the ROM, the Ontario Science Centre, and the Toronto Zoo are included for a onetime fee of C$72 plus tax—a savings of more than C$50, valid for nine days.

■ Many events listed on the city's website (www.toronto.ca/events) are free. Harbourfront Centre (www.harbourfrontcentre.com) hosts numerous free cultural programs and festivals year-round.

■ Some museums and art collections have free (or Pay What You Can) admission all the time, including the Gallery of Inuit Art in the TD Centre and Harbourfront Centre's Power Plant gallery. But even the major museums, including the ROM, the Bata Shoe Museum, the Gardiner Museum, Textile Museum of Canada, and Art Gallery of Ontario, have one or two free, Pay What You Can, and/or half-price evening(s) per week, usually Wednesday or Friday, and usually beginning after 4 pm.

TORONTO
TOP ATTRACTIONS

CN Tower

(A) Since it opened as a communications tower in 1976, the CN Tower has defined Toronto's skyline and is the city's most iconic structure. Everyone has to step onto the glass floor, hovering more than 1,000 feet above the ground, at least once; you can sometimes even see Niagara Falls from the SkyPod. At nearly 1,500 feet it was the highest observation deck in the world for more than 30 years, until the Guangzhou Canton Tower in China crushed its record in 2009.

Historic Distillery District

(B) The 1832 Gooderham and Worts distillery was restored and revitalized in 2003 to create a pedestrian-only mini-village of cobblestone streets and brick buildings housing restaurants, shops, galleries, and theaters. The design perfectly incorporates the original Victorian industrial architecture, and the Distillery District is a great place to spend an afternoon or evening. Concerts and other events take place outdoors in the summer.

Hockey Sites

(C) To truly experience Canadian culture you should school yourself at the Hockey Hall of Fame and get a glimpse of the original 1892 Stanley Cup. The Maple Leafs are Toronto's National Hockey League team, and though they haven't won the Stanley Cup since 1967, fans are loyal and tickets are notoriously tough to get. ■ **TIP→ If you can't nab a Leafs ticket, head to the Ricoh Coliseum to catch the Marlies, Toronto's AHL team.**

Great Markets

(D) St. Lawrence Market is as much a destination for its brick 1846 building as for its city block of meats, cheeses, produce, and prepared foods inside. It's the quintessential place to grab one of the city's famed peameal bacon

sandwiches (we said "famed," not "gourmet"). Kensington Market is an entirely different beast with its several blocks of used-clothing stores, head shops, cheap ethnic and vegetarian eats, and shops selling spices, fish, and baked goods. The best—albeit busiest—time to go is when cars are prohibited, the last Sunday of every month between May and October.

Toronto Islands

(E)A short ferry ride from Harbourfront, the car-free islands are a relaxing respite from the concrete jungle. Take a picnic, lie on the beach, or ride a bicycle on the boardwalk. The kiddie amusement park on Centre Island attracts families. Don't forget your camera: the view of Toronto's skyline from here is unparalleled.

Top Museums

(F) Your first stop should be the Art Gallery of Ontario (AGO), with its collection of more than 90,000 works spanning almost 2,000 years of art. Then hit the ROM with its world-class Age of Dinosaurs gallery. And don't miss the changing exhibitions at the Design Exchange and the Bata Shoe Museum's staggering collection of footwear, as well as the Aga Khan Museum and Ismaili Centre, a groundbreaking, expansive cultural center dedicated to the Muslim world.

Queen West

(G) Many a visitor falls in love with Toronto after a foray to historically bohemian Queen Street West. Though the entire strip has spirit, the ragtag artist-forged businesses keep moving west. Begin with the spiffy chain stores near Spadina and see how the record shops, boutiques, cafés, bookstores, bars, and galleries change as you head west.

IF YOU LIKE

Wining and Dining

Those in search of haute cuisine are pampered in Toronto, where some of the world's finest chefs vie for the attention of the city's sizable foodie population. Toronto's range of exceptional eateries, from creative Asian fusion to more daring molecular gastronomy, offers wining and dining potential for every possible palate. Aromas of finely crafted sauces and delicately grilled meats emanate from eateries in Yorkville, where valet service and designer handbags are de rigueur, and the strip of bistros in the Entertainment District gets lively with theatergoing crowds. Weekdays at lunch, the Financial District's Bay Street is a sea of Armani suits, crisply pressed shirts, and clicking heels heading to power lunches to make deals over steak frites.

Sassafraz. The staff here is sure to be attentive—they're used to serving celebrities and power-wielding bigwigs who fill the Yorkville hot spot.

Bymark. An ultramodern and ultracool spot primed for the Financial District set; chef-owner Mark McEwan aims for perfection with classy contemporary fare.

Canoe. Toronto's most famous "splurge" place. Sit back, enjoy the view, and let the waiter pair your dish with a recommended local Ontario wine.

Colborne Lane. Star chef Claudio Aprile's venture is *the* place to sample cutting-edge creations that blur the boundary between dinner and science project.

The Hogtown Vegan. Popular, ultratrendy vegan nouvelle cuisine with a menu to rival any steak house.

Cool Neighborhoods

Toronto's coolness doesn't emanate from a downtown core or even a series of town centers. The action is everywhere in the city. Dozens of neighborhoods, each with its own scene and way of life, coexist within the vast metropolitan area.

West Queen West. As Queen Street West (to Bathurst Street or so) becomes more commercial and rents increase, more local artists and designers have moved farther west; it's also home to a burgeoning night scene and experimental restaurants.

Kensington Market. This well-established bastion of bohemia for hippies of all ages is a grungy and multicultural several-block radius of produce, cheese, by-the-gram spices, fresh empanadas, used clothing, head shops, and funky restaurants and cafés.

The Annex. The pockets of wealth nestled in side streets add diversity to this scruffy strip of Bloor, the favorite haunt of the intellectual set, whether starving student or world-renowned novelist.

The Beaches. This bourgeois-bohemian neighborhood (also called The Beach) is the habitat of young professionals who frequent the yoga studios and sushi restaurants along Queen Street East and walk their pooches daily along Lake Ontario's boardwalk.

Performing Arts

Refurbished iconic theaters such as the Royal Alexandra and Ed Mirvish theaters host a number of big-ticket shows in elegant surroundings. More modern venues such as the Princess of Wales Theatre highlight local and Broadway performances. The Four Seasons Centre is home to both the National Ballet of Canada and the Canadian Opera Company, which shares the music scene with the Toronto Symphony Orchestra and mainstream concerts at the Sony Centre and Massey Hall. Indie artists are attracted to the bars and grimy music venues on Queen Street West. (True theater buffs will also want to leave Toronto to hit the festivals of Stratford and Niagara-on-the-Lake.)

Massey Hall. Since 1894, this has been one of Toronto's premier concert halls. British royals have been entertained here and legendary musicians have performed: Charlie Parker, Dizzy Gillespie, George Gershwin, Bob Dylan, and Luciano Pavarotti, to name a few. Orchestras, musicals, dance troupes, and comedians also perform at this palpably historic venue.

Rivoli. In this multifaceted venue, you can dine while admiring local art, catch a musical act, or watch stand-up. Before they were famous, Beck, the Indigo Girls, Iggy Pop, Janeane Garofalo, and Tori Amos all made appearances here.

Elgin and Winter Garden Theatre Centre. These two 1913 Edwardian theaters, one stacked on top of the other, provide sumptuous settings for classical music performances, musicals, opera, and Toronto International Film Festival screenings.

The Second City. The comedic troupes here always put on a great performance. Photo collages on the wall display the club's alumni, including Mike Myers, Dan Aykroyd, and Catherine O'Hara.

Architecture

At one point, Toronto's only celebrated icon was the CN Tower, but architects have been working hard to rejuvenate the cityscape in the new millennium—at a dizzying pace. In the past decade, the city has unveiled the transparent-glass-fronted Four Seasons Centre for the Performing Arts (Jack Diamond), the ROM's deconstructed-crystal extension (Daniel Libeskind), the wood-and-glass Art Gallery of Ontario (Frank Gehry), and a redesign of the Sony Centre for the Performing Arts with attached residential 58-story, all-glass, swooping L Tower (Libeskind). A series of high-rises topping 50 stories—not the least of which is the 68-story, glass-spired Trump Tower—is changing the skyline of the city forever.

Philosopher's Walk. This scenic path winds through the University of Toronto, from the entrance between the ROM and the Victorian Royal Conservatory of Music, past Trinity College's Gothic chapel and towering spires. Also look for University College, an 1856 ivy-covered Romanesque Revival building, set back from the road across Hoskin Avenue.

ROMwalks. From May through October, free themed walks organized by the ROM tour some of the city's landmark buildings, such as the Church of the Redeemer, the St. Lawrence Market, and the Royal York Hotel.

Art Gallery of Ontario. The Frank Gehry–designed building and its wooden facades, glass roofs, and four-story blue titanium wing are spectacular to admire from the outside or within.

Sharp Centre for Design. Locals are split by Will Alsop's salt-and-pepper rectangle held aloft by giant colored-pencil-like stilts standing above the Ontario College of Art and Design (OCAD).

TORONTO WITH KIDS

Toronto is one of the most livable cities in the world, with many families residing downtown and plenty of activities to keep them busy. *Throughout this guide, places that are especially appealing to families are indicated by FAMILY in the margin.*

Always check what's on at **Harbourfront Centre**, a cultural complex with shows and workshops for all ages. On any given day you could find a circus, clown school, musicians, juggling, storytelling, or acrobat shows. Even fearless kids' (and adults') eyes bulge at the 1,465-foot glass-elevator ride up the side of the **CN Tower**, and once they stand on the glass floor, their minds are officially blown.

Kids won't realize they're getting schooled at the **ROM**, with its Bat Cave and dinosaur skeletons, or the **Ontario Science Centre**, with interactive exhibits exploring the brain, technology, and outer space; documentaries are shown in the massive OMNIMAX dome. Out at the eastern end of the suburb of Scarborough, the well-designed **Toronto Zoo** is home to giraffes, polar bears, and gorillas. Less exotic animals hang at **Riverdale Farm**, in the more central Cabbagetown: get nose-to-nose with sheep, cows, and pigs.

Spending a few hours on the **Toronto Islands** is a good way to decompress. The Centreville Amusement Park and petting zoo is geared to the under-12 set, with tame rides, such as the log flume and an antique carousel. Alternatively, pile the whole family into a surrey to pedal along the carless roads, or lounge at the beach at Hanlan's Point (warning: clothing-optional) or Ward's Island (clothes generally worn). The **Canadian National Exhibition (CNE)**, aka "the Ex," is a huge three-week fair held in late August with carnival rides, games, food, puppet shows, a daily parade, and horse, dog, and cat shows. Kids can also pet and feed horses at the horse barn or tend to chickens and milk a cow on the "farm." But the mother of all amusement parks is a half-hour drive north of the city at **Canada's Wonderland**, home of Canada's tallest and fastest roller coaster. In winter, **ice-skating** at the Harbourfront Centre is the quintessential family activity.

Young sports fans might appreciate seeing a **Blue Jays** (baseball), **Maple Leafs** (hockey), **Raptors** (basketball), or **Toronto FC** (soccer) game. To take on Wayne Gretzky in a virtual game and see the original Stanley Cup, head to the **Hockey Hall of Fame**.

Intelligent productions at the **Young People's Theatre** don't condescend to kids and teens, and many are just as entertaining for adults. The **TIFF Kids International Film Festival** takes place in April, with films for ages 3 to 13. Teens and tweens who aren't tuckered out after dark might get a kick out of a retro double feature at the **Polson Pier Drive-In**, right downtown.

For the latest on upcoming shows and events, plus an overwhelming directory of stores and services, go to the website Toronto4Kids (⊕ *www.toronto4kids. com*).

BEST TOURS IN TORONTO

General Tours

Tourism Toronto. Tourism Toronto can provide further tour information. ✉ *Toronto* ☎ *416/203–2600, 800/363–1990* ⊕ *www. seetorontonow.com.*

Boat Tours

If you want to get a glimpse of the skyline, try a boat tour. There are many boat-tour companies operating all along the boardwalk of Harbourfront.

Great Lakes Schooner Company. To further your appreciation for man-made beauty, this company lets you see Toronto's skyline from the open deck of the 165-foot three-mastered *Kajama.* Two-hour tours are available early June to the end of September. ✉ *Harbourfront* ☎ *416/203– 2322* ⊕ *www.greatlakesschooner.com* ✉ *From C$27.*

Bus Tours

For a look at the city proper, take a bus tour around the city. If you want the freedom to get on and off the bus when the whim strikes, take a hop-on, hop-off tour.

Toronto Bus Company. Two-hour guided tours are offered in 24-passenger buses. ✉ *Toronto* ☎ *416/945–3414* ⊕ *www. torontobusco.com* ✉ *From C$25.*

Gray Line Sightseeing Bus Tours. Gray Line has London-style double-decker buses and turn-of-the-20th-century trolleys. They also have tours of Niagara Falls. ✉ *610 Bay St., north of Dundas St., Dundas Square Area* ☎ *800/594–3310* ⊕ *www.grayline.ca* ✉ *From C$43.*

Special-Interest Tours

Toronto Field Naturalists. More than 150 guided tours are scheduled throughout the year, each focusing on an aspect of nature, such as geology or wildflowers, and with starting points accessible by public transit.

✉ *Toronto* ☎ *416/593–2656* ⊕ *www. torontofieldnaturalists.org* ✉ *Free.*

Toronto Bruce Trail Club. This hiking club arranges day and overnight hikes around Toronto and its environs. ✉ *Toronto* ☎ *416/763–9061* ⊕ *www.torontobruce- trailclub.org* ✉ *From C$23.*

Walking Tours

Heritage Toronto. To get a feel for Toronto's outstanding cultural diversity, check out one of about 56 walking tours offered from April to early October. They last 1½ to 2 hours and cover one neighborhood or topic, such as music history on Yonge Street or historical architecture downtown. ✉ *Toronto* ☎ *416/338–0682* ⊕ *www.heritagetoronto.org* ✉ *Free, some starting at C$20.*

Royal Ontario Museum. The museum runs 1½- to 2-hour ROMwalks on such topics as Cabbagetown, a now-trendy, heritage neighborhood with many houses dating to the 1850s. Several free walks are given weekly. ✉ *Toronto* ☎ *416/586–5799* ⊕ *www.rom.on.ca/en/whats-on/romwalks* ✉ *Free.*

A Taste of the World. Food, literary, and ghost-themed tours of various lengths are offered in several neighborhoods. Reservations are essential. ✉ *Toronto* ☎ *416/923–6813* ⊕ *www.torontowalks- bikes.com* ✉ *From C$25.*

TORONTO'S BEST FESTIVALS

Festivals keep Toronto lively even when cold winds blow in off Lake Ontario in winter. Themes range from art to food, Caribbean culture to gay pride. Most national championship sports events take place in and around Toronto.

Tourism Toronto. Tourism Toronto maintains an online calendar of nearly every event in the city. ☎ 416/203–2600, 800/363–1990 ⊕ www.seetorontonow.com.

January–February

Winterlicious. A winter culinary event offering discount prix-fixe menus at top restaurants as well as themed tastings and food-prep workshops. ☎ 416/395–0490 ⊕ www.toronto.ca/winterlicious.

April

TIFF Kids International Film Festival. Taking place in April, this children's film festival holds screenings for kids and teens aged (roughly) 3–13. ✉ Toronto ☎ 416/599–8433 ⊕ www.tiff.net.

April–November

Shaw Festival. Held from late spring until fall in quaint Niagara-on-the-Lake, this festival presents plays by George Bernard Shaw and his contemporaries. Niagara-on-the-Lake is a two-hour drive south of Toronto. ☎ 905/468–2172, 800/511–7429 ⊕ www.shawfest.com.

Stratford Festival. One of the best known Shakespeare festivals in the world, this event was created in the 1950s to revive a little town two hours west of Toronto that happened to be called Stratford (and its river called the Avon). The festival includes at least three Shakespeare plays as well as other classical and contemporary productions. Respected actors from around the world participate. ☎ 519/273–1600, 800/567–1600 ⊕ www.stratford-festival.ca.

April–May

Hot Docs. North America's largest documentary film fest, Hot Docs takes over independent cinemas for two weeks. ☎ 416/203–2155 ⊕ www.hotdocs.ca.

Scotiabank Contact Photography Festival. More than 200 art spaces and galleries mount photo exhibits by 1,500 different artists throughout the entire month of May at this photography festival. ✉ Toronto ☎ 416/539–9595 ⊕ www.scotiabankcontactphoto.com.

June

Luminato. For 10 days, this citywide arts festival combines visual arts, music, theater, dance, literature, and more in hundreds of events, many of them free. ☎ 416/368–3100 ⊕ www.luminatofestival.com.

North by Northeast (NXNE). Modeled after South by Southwest in Austin, Texas, this is a seven-day music and arts festival. ✉ Toronto ☎ 416/863–6963 ⊕ nxne.com.

Pride Toronto. Rainbow flags fly high during Pride Month, the city's premier gay and lesbian event. It includes cultural and political programs, concerts, a street festival, and a parade, and is centered around the Church–Wellesley corridor. ✉ Church–Wellesley ☎ 416/927–7433 ⊕ www.pridetoronto.com.

Toronto Jazz Festival. For 10 days this festival brings big-name jazz artists to city jazz clubs and other indoor and outdoor venues. ✉ Toronto ☎ 416/928–2033 ⊕ torontojazz.com.

July

Beaches International Jazz Festival. In the east-end Beach (aka Beaches) neighborhood, this event is a free, 10-day jazz, blues, and Latin music event and street festival. ⊠ *The Beach* ☎ *416/698–2152* ⊕ *www.beachesjazz.com.*

Honda Indy. At this summer fixture, cars speed around an 11-turn, 1.77-mile track that goes through the Canadian National Exhibition grounds and along Lake Shore Boulevard. ⊠ *Toronto* ☎ *416/588–7223* ⊕ *www.hondaindytoronto.com.*

Summerlicious. More than 220 restaurants in Toronto create prix-fixe menus—some at bargain prices—for this two-week culinary event. ⊠ *Toronto* ☎ *416/395–0490* ⊕ *www.toronto.ca/summerlicious.*

Toronto Fringe Festival. This 10-day event is the city's largest theater festival. It features new and developing plays by emerging artists. ⊠ *Toronto* ☎ *416/966–1062* ⊕ *www.fringetoronto.com.*

July–August

Toronto Caribbean Carnival. One of the largest carnival festivals in North America, the Toronto Caribbean Carnival (commonly called Caribana) is a three-week celebration of Carribean culture, with calypso, steel pan, soca, and reggae music; fiery cuisine; and plenty of revelry. The celebrations culminate in a massive parade on the first Saturday of August. ⊠ *Toronto* ☎ *416/391–5608* ⊕ *www.torontocaribbeancarnival.com.*

August

Canadian National Exhibition. With carnival rides, concerts, an air show, a dog show, a garden show, and a "Mardi Gras" parade, this 2½-week-long fair is the biggest in Canada. Also known as "The Ex," it's been held at the eponymous fairgrounds on the Lake Ontario waterfront since 1879. ⊠ *Harbourfront* ☎ *416/263–3330* ⊕ *www.theex.com.*

Rogers Cup. Founded in 1881, this is an ATP Masters 1000 event for men and a Premier event for women. It's held at Aviva Centre on the York University campus, with the men's and women's events alternating between Toronto and Montréal each year. ⊠ *Toronto* ☎ *416/665–9777,* ⊕ *www.rogerscup.com.*

Toronto International BuskerFest. No ordinary street festival, aerialists, fire-eaters, dancers, contortionists, musicians, and more perform here in Woodbine Park at the end of the summer. ⊠ *The Beach* ⊕ *www.torontobuskerfest.com.*

SummerWorks Performance Festival. Plays, concerts, and performances are mounted at local theaters during this 11-day festival. ⊠ *Toronto* ☎ *416/628–8216* ⊕ *www.summerworks.ca.*

September

Toronto International Film Festival. Renowned worldwide, this festival is considered more accessible to the public than Cannes, Sundance, or other major film festivals. A number of films make their world or North American premieres at this 11-day festival each year, some at red-carpet events attended by Hollywood stars. ⊠ *Toronto* ☎ *416/599–8433, 888/599–8433* ⊕ *tiff.net.*

October

Nuit Blanche. Concentrated in Toronto's downtown core, this all-night street festival has interactive contemporary art installations and performances. ⊠ *Toronto* ⊕ *www.nbto.com.*

November

Royal Agricultural Winter Fair. Held since 1922 at the Ex, this 10-day fair is a highlight of Canada's equestrian season each November, with jumping, dressage, and harness-racing competitions. ⊠ *Toronto* ☎ *416/263–3400* ⊕ *www.royalfair.org.*

SPORTS AND THE OUTDOORS

Toronto has a love–hate relationship with its professional sports teams, and fans can sometimes be accused of being fair-weather, except when it comes to hockey, which has always attracted rabid, sell-out crowds whether the Maple Leafs win, lose, or draw. In other words, don't count on getting Leafs tickets but take heart that sports bars will be filled with fired-up fans. It can be easier, however, to score tickets to Blue Jays (baseball), Raptors (basketball), Argos (football), and Toronto FC (soccer) games—depending on who they play.

StubHub. Ticket reseller StubHub is a good resource for sold-out games. ☎ 866/788–2482 ⊕ www.stubhub.com.

If you prefer to work up a sweat yourself, consider golf at one of the GTA's courses, ice-skating at a city rink in winter, or exploring the many parks and beaches.

Baseball

Toronto Blue Jays. Toronto's professional baseball team plays April through September. Interest in the team lagged since they won consecutive World Series championships in 1992 and 1993, but recent seasons have seen many young players make their mark. The spectacular Rogers Centre (formerly the SkyDome) has a fully retractable roof; some consider it one of the world's premier entertainment centers. ⊠ Rogers Centre, 1 Blue Jays Way, Harbourfront ☎ 416/341–1234 ticket line, 888/OK–GO–JAY toll-free ticket line ⊕ www.bluejays.com Ⓜ Union.

Basketball

Toronto Raptors. The city's NBA franchise, this team played its first season in 1995–96. For several years they struggled mightily to win both games and fans in this hockey-mad city, but the Raptors have finally come into their own, and games often sell out. Single-game tickets are available beginning in September; the season is from October through May. ⊠ Air Canada Centre, 40 Bay St., at Gardiner Expwy., Harbourfront ☎ 416/366–3865 ⊕ www.nba.com/raptors Ⓜ Union.

Football

Toronto Argonauts. The Toronto Argonauts Canadian Football League (CFL) team has a healthy following. American football fans who attend a CFL game often discover a faster, more unpredictable and exciting contest than the American version. The longer, wider field means quarterbacks have to scramble more. Tickets for games (June–November) are usually a cinch to get. ⊠ BMO Field, Harbourfront ☎ 416/341–2746 ⊕ www.argonauts.ca Ⓜ Union.

Hockey

Toronto Maple Leafs. Hockey is as popular as you've heard here, and Maple Leafs fans are particularly ardent. Even though the Leafs haven't won a Stanley Cup since 1967, they continue to inspire fierce devotion in Torontonians. If you want a chance to cheer them on, you'll have to get on the puck. ■TIP→ Buy tickets at least a few months in advance or risk the game's being sold out. No matter the stats, Leafs tickets are notoriously the toughest to score in the National Hockey League. The regular hockey season is October–mid-April. ⊠ Air Canada Centre, 40 Bay St., at Gardiner Expwy., Harbourfront ☎ 416/703–5623 Ticketmaster ⊕ www.mapleleafs.com Ⓜ Union.

Toronto Marlies. If you're keen to see some hockey while you're in town, go to a Toronto Marlies game at Ricoh Coliseum. The level of play is very high, and tickets are cheaper and easier to come by than those of the Marlies' NHL affiliate, the Toronto Maple Leafs. ⊠ *Ricoh Coliseum, 45 Manitoba Dr., Harbourfront* ☎ *416/597–7825* ⊕ *www.marlies.ca* Ⓜ *Union, then 509 Harbourfront streetcar west; or Bathurst, then 511 streetcar.*

Soccer

Toronto's British roots combined with a huge immigrant population have helped make the Toronto Football Club (TFC), the newest addition to the city's pro sports tapestry, a success. And during events like the FIFA World Cup, UEFA European Championship, and Copa América (America Cup), sports bars and cafés with TVs are teeming.

Toronto FC. Canada's first Major League Soccer team and Toronto's first professional soccer team in years, Toronto FC kicked off in 2006 in a stadium seating more than 25,000 fans. They get seriously pumped up for these games, singing fight songs, waving flags, and throwing streamers. Games sometimes sell out; single-game tickets go on sale a few days before the match. The season is March–October. ⊠ *BMO Field, 170 Princes' Blvd.* ☎ *855/985–5000 Ticketmaster* ⊕ *www.torontofc.ca* Ⓜ *Union, then 509 Harbourfront streetcar west; 511 Bathurst streetcar south.*

Golf

The golf season lasts only from April to late October. Discounted rates are usually available until mid-May and after Canadian Thanksgiving (early October). All courses are best reached by car.

Angus Glen Golf Club. This club has remained one of the country's best places to play since it opened in 1995, hosting the Canadian Open in 2002 and 2007 on its par-72 South and North courses, respectively, and the 2015 Pan Am Games. It's a 45-minute drive north of downtown. ⊠ *10080 Kennedy Rd., Markham* ☎ *905/887–0090, 905/887–5157 reservations* ⊕ *www.angusglen.com.*

Don Valley Golf Course. About a 20-minute drive north of downtown, this is a par-72, 18-hole municipal course. Despite being right in the city, it's a lovely, hilly course with water hazards and tree-lined fairways. ⊠ *4200 Yonge St., North York* ☎ *416/392–2465* ⊕ *www.toronto.ca/parks/golf.*

Glen Abbey Golf Club. This Jack Nicklaus–designed 18-hole, par-73 club is considered to be Canada's top course. It's in the affluent suburb of Oakville, about 45 minutes east of the city. ⊠ *1333 Dorval Dr., just north of QEW, Oakville* ☎ *905/844–1800* ⊕ *www.glenabbey.clublink.ca.*

Ice-Skating

Harbourfront Centre. This spacious, outdoor rink is often voted the best in the city due to its lakeside location and DJ'd skate nights. Skate rentals are C$8. ⊠ *235 Queens Quay W, Harbourfront* ☎ *416/973–4866* ⊕ *www.harbourfrontcentre.com* Ⓜ *Union.*

Toronto Parks, Forestry & Recreation Rink Hotline. The favorite city-operated, outdoor rinks are the forested, west-side **High Park** and the tiny **Nathan Phillips Square**, surrounded by towering skyscrapers in the heart of the Financial District. City rinks are free, and most don't have rental facilities, although the Nathan Phillips Square rink does. ⊠ *Toronto* ☎ *311 Toronto Parks, Forestry & Recreation rink hotline* ⊕ *www.toronto.ca/parks/skating.*

GREAT ITINERARIES

Five Days in Toronto

To really see Toronto, a stay of at least one week is ideal. However, these itineraries are designed to inspire thematic tours of some of the city's best sights, whether you're in town for one day or five. We've also included a two- to three-day escape to the Niagara region.

Day 1: Architecture and Museums

There's no better spot to begin your Toronto adventure than Finnish architect Viljo Revell's **City Hall,** at Queen and Bay, with its regal predecessor, **Old City Hall,** right across the street. Take a stroll through the **Financial District,** looking up to admire the skyscrapers above you, and then head west along Front Street. You'll see your next destination before you reach it: the spectacular **CN Tower.** Take a trip to the top to experience its glass floor and amazing views.

Next, grab a streetcar going east to Parliament, then head south toward the water to find the **Historic Distillery District,** filled with restored Victorian industrial buildings. Here's a great place to stop for lunch, with plenty of delicious restaurants and bistros.

After lunch, head to the **Royal Ontario Museum**—even if you just admire the still controversial modern Crystal gallery from the outside. Across the street is the smaller **Gardiner Museum,** filled with gorgeous ceramics, and down the street is a shoe-lover's dream, the **Bata Shoe Museum.**

Day 2: Shopping Around the World

Brave shoppers should begin in **Chinatown,** at the wonderfully chaotic intersection of Spadina Avenue and Dundas Street, for shops and stalls overflowing with exotic vegetables, fragrant herbs, and flashy Chinese baubles. Go all out with a heaping bowl of steaming noodles, or just grab a snack at an empanada stand in nearby **Kensington Market** (head west on Dundas to Augusta and turn right). Take your time browsing the market; quirky grocery stores, modern cafés, and funky clothing boutiques all beckon. Then grab the College streetcar across town to Coxwell street to see the **India Bazaar** and shop for some bejeweled saris and shiny bangles. Finish the day with a spicy madras curry washed down with a soothing mango lassi (yogurt drink).

Day 3: With Kids

Get an early start at the **Toronto Zoo,** where 700-plus acres of dense forests are home to 5,000 animals and 460 species, including two giant panda cubs—Canada's first pandas. Little science enthusiasts might prefer the equally exciting (and indoor air-conditioned) exhibits at the **Ontario Science Centre.** Sports fans can see the original Stanley Cup at the **Hockey Hall of Fame,** right downtown at Yonge and Front.

Kid-friendly adventures vary by season. In the sweltering summer, Harbourfront Centre is full of activities and performances along the cooler waterfront. In winter, bundle kids up for a skate on the Centre's ice rink. **Ripley's Aquarium of Canada** is a great way for kids to stay warm or stay cool in any season, and get to learn about 450-plus species of sea creatures.

Day 4: Island Life

Start with picnic supplies from **St. Lawrence Market** (closed Sunday and Monday) for a cornucopia of imported delicacies. It's a short walk from the market to catch the ferry, at the foot of Bay Street and Queen's Quay, to the **Toronto Islands.** There, besides a city skyline you can't get anywhere else, beaches include **Hanlan's Point** (infamous for its nudists, so be warned) and **Ward's Island,** with its sandy beach and shady patio at the Rectory Café. Island life has an alluring slow pace, but anyone who'd rather cover more ground can rent a bicycle at the pier on **Centre Island.** Winter options include cross-country skiing, snowshoeing, and skating on the frozen streams.

Day 5: Neighborhood Exploring

Window-shoppers should begin along the rows of restored Victorian homes of **Yorkville**—in the 1960s, a hippie haven of emerging Canadian artists like Joni Mitchell and Gordon Lightfoot. These days, the country's most exclusive shops and hottest designers have all moved in and spilled over onto Bloor Street West, between Yonge Street and Avenue Road, which is so swanky it's sometimes called Toronto's Fifth Avenue. But in traditional Torontonian style, walk a few blocks west for a stark contrast in the grungy shops along Bloor in crumbling turn-of-the-20th-century homes. Take a rest to recharge at **Future Bakery & Café,** a student favorite for affordable comfort food, or splurge on the more upscale **Bar Mercurio** on Bloor. In the evening, catch a play, concert, or comedy show downtown at **Second City.**

Days 6–7: Niagara Getaway

If you have a few days to spare, don't miss the glory of **Niagara Falls,** about 80 miles south of Toronto. It's easiest to get there by car, or else hop on a GO or VIA train from Union Station. Private buses (like Greyhound or Megabus) are also ample and affordable. When you arrive, see the Falls best via a ride on the **Maid of the Mist.** In the afternoon, and especially if you've got energetic kids to tire out, try the kitschy **Clifton Hill** for the skywheel and glow-in-the-dark mini putt. For a more relaxing day, try the **Botanical Gardens** or

White Water Walk along the scenic Niagara Parkway. Get dressed up for dinner at the Skylon Tower or another restaurant overlooking the falls and tuck in for a night at the slots. Look to the skies for fireworks at 10 pm every Wednesday, Friday, and Sunday from May to October from either your falls-view hotel room or the **Table Rock Center.** The next day, a good breakfast is essential to prepare for a day of wine-tasting and strolling in bucolic **Niagara-on-the-Lake.** You'll need a car to follow the beautiful Niagara Parkway north to Niagara-on-the-Lake's **Queen Street** for shopping. Wine and dine the day away along the **Wine Route,** which follows Highway 81 as far west as Grimsby. Dinner at one of the wineries or excellent area restaurants, then a night in a boutique hotel or luxurious B&B is a great way to end your trip. If you're lucky enough to visit during the **Shaw Festival,** running between April and October, be sure to book a theater ticket.

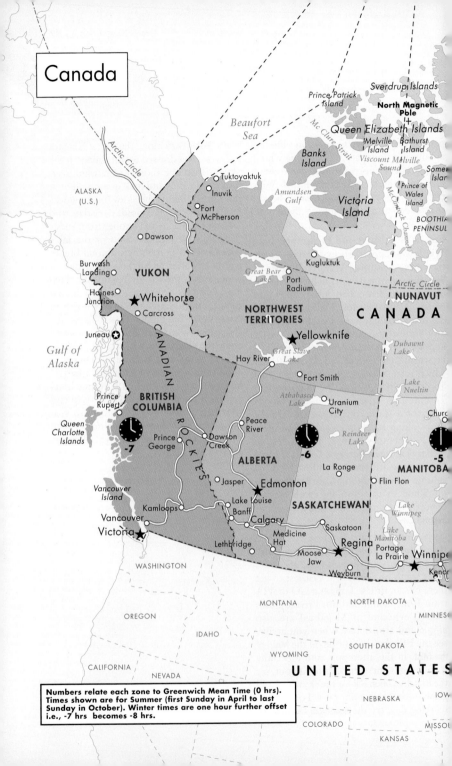

Canada

Beaufort
Sea

Arctic Circle

ALASKA
(U.S.)

Prince Patrick
Island

Sverdrup Islands

**North Magnetic
Pole**
+

Queen Elizabeth Islands

Melville
Island

Bathurst
Island

*Viscount Melville
Sound*

Mc Clure Strait

Banks
Island

*Amundsen
Gulf*

Somer
Islar

Prince
of
Wales
Island

Victoria
Island

McClintock Channel

BOOTHIA
PENINSUL

○ Tuktoyaktuk

○ Inuvik

○ Fort
McPherson

○ Dawson

Burwash
Landing ○

YUKON

*Great Bear
Lake*

○ Port
Radium

Arctic Circle

Haines ○
Junction

★ **Whitehorse**

○ Carcross

**NORTHWEST
TERRITORIES**

○ Kugluktuk

NUNAVUT

C A N A D A

Juneau ✪

*Gulf of
Alaska*

CANADIAN

★ **Yellowknife**

○ Hay River

*Great Slave
Lake*

*Dubawnt
Lake*

*Lake
Nueltin*

Prince
Rupert ○

**BRITISH
COLUMBIA**

ROCKIES

○ Fort Smith

*Athabasca
Lake*

○ Uranium
City

Churc

*Queen
Charlotte
Islands*

🕐
-7

○ Prince
George

○ Dawson
Creek

○ Peace
River

*Reindeer
Lake*

🕐
-6

🕐
-5

MANITOBA

*Vancouver
Island*

○ Jasper

ALBERTA

○ La Ronge

○ Flin Flon

Kamloops ○

★ **Edmonton**

○ Lake Louise
○ Banff

SASKATCHEWAN

*Lake
Winnipeg*

Vancouver ○

○ Calgary

○ Saskatoon

*Lake
Manitoba*

Victoria ★

○ Lethbridge

○ Medicine
Hat

○ Moose
Jaw

★ **Regina**

Portage
la Prairie ○

★ **Winnip**

○ Kenar

WASHINGTON

○ Weyburn

UNITED STATES

OREGON

MONTANA

NORTH DAKOTA

MINNES

IDAHO

SOUTH DAKOTA

CALIFORNIA

NEVADA

WYOMING

NEBRASKA

IOW

COLORADO

KANSAS

MISSOU

> **Numbers relate each zone to Greenwich Mean Time (0 hrs).
> Times shown are for Summer (first Sunday in April to last
> Sunday in October). Winter times are one hour further offset
> i.e., -7 hrs becomes -8 hrs.**

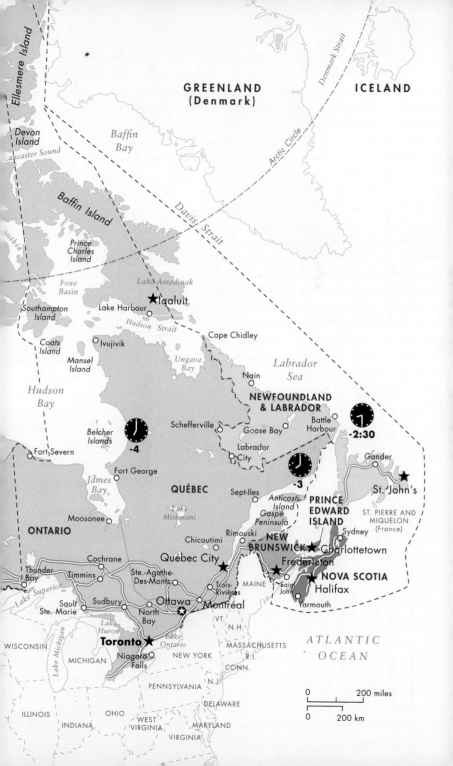

GREENLAND
(Denmark)

ICELAND

Ellesmere Island

Devon Island

Baffin Bay

Lancaster Sound

Arctic Circle

Baffin Island

Denmark Strait

Prince Charles Island

...thia

Davis Strait

Foxe Basin

Southampton Island

Lake Amadjuak

★Iqaluit

Lake Harbour

Coats Island

Hudson Strait

Cape Chidley

Ivujivik

Mansel Island

Ungava Bay

Labrador Sea

Nain

Hudson Bay

NEWFOUNDLAND & LABRADOR

Belcher Islands

Scheffervile

Goose Bay

Battle Harbour

🕐 -4

Fort Severn

🕐 -2:30

Labrador City

Gander

James Bay

Fort George

QUÉBEC

Sept-Iles

🕐 -3

St. John's

Moosonee

Lake Mistassini

Anticosti Island

Gaspé Peninsula

PRINCE EDWARD ISLAND

ST. PIERRE AND MIQUELON (France)

ONTARIO

Chicoutimi

Rimouski

Sydney

Cochrane

NEW BRUNSWICK

Charlottetown

Thunder Bay

Timmins

Ste.-Agathe-Des-Monts

Québec City★

Fredericton★

NOVA SCOTIA

Sault Ste. Marie

Sudbury

North Bay

Ottawa

Trois-Rivières

Saint John

Halifax

Lake Superior

MAINE

Yarmouth

WISCONSIN

Lake Huron

Toronto★

Lake Ontario

VT.

N.H.

ATLANTIC OCEAN

MICHIGAN

Niagara Falls

NEW YORK

MASSACHUSETTS

R.I.

Lake Michigan

CONN.

ILLINOIS

INDIANA

OHIO

WEST VIRGINIA

PENNSYLVANIA

N.J.

DELAWARE

MARYLAND

VIRGINIA

0   200 miles

0   200 km

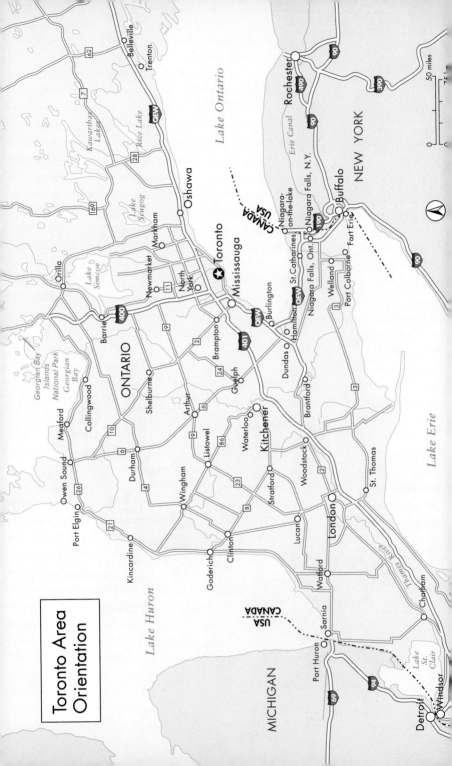

Toronto Area Orientation

EXPLORING
TORONTO

HARBOURFRONT AND THE ISLANDS

(above) Enjoying the skyline from one of Toronto's ferries. (top right) A performance of the Luminato Cirque du Soleil. (bottom right) One of the Toronto ferries.

The new century has brought renewed interest to Toronto's Harbourfront. Cranes dot the skyline as condominium buildings seemingly appear overnight. Pedestrian traffic increases as temperatures rise in spring and summer. Everyone wants to be overlooking, facing, or playing in Lake Ontario.

The lakefront is appealing for strolls, and myriad recreational and amusement options make it ideal for those craving fresh air and exercise or with kids in tow. Before the drastic decline of trucking due to the 1973 oil crisis reduced the Great Lakes trade, Toronto's waterfront was an important center for shipping and warehousing. It fell into commercial disuse and was neglected for a long time. The Gardiner Expressway, Lake Shore Boulevard, and a network of rusty rail yards stood as hideous barriers to the natural beauty of Lake Ontario; the area overflowed with grain silos, warehouses, and malodorous towers of malt, used by local breweries. In the 1980s the city began to develop the waterfront for people-friendly purposes, and the trend continues today.

BEST TIME TO GO

If it's sun and sand you're looking for, you'll want to aim for a visit in June, July, or August. The cool breeze coming off Lake Ontario can be the perfect antidote to one of Toronto's hot and humid summer days, but in the off-season it can make things a little chilly if you aren't packing an extra layer.

WAYS TO EXPLORE

BOAT

The best way to enjoy the waterfront is to get right onto Lake Ontario. There are many different boat tours—take your pick from the vendors lining the Harbourfront's lakeside boardwalk—but most offer the same deal: a pleasant, hour-long jaunt around the harbor for about C$25. More extravagant packages include dinner and dancing at sunset.

To soak up the sun and skyline views, use the public ferry to head for the **Toronto Islands.** The best beaches are those on the southeast tip of Ward's Island, Centre Island Beach, and Hanlan's Point Beach. This last one is the most secluded and natural beach on the islands, backed by a small dunes area, a portion of which is clothing-optional. Most families with kids head for Centre Island Beach.

BIKE AND STROLL

To get away from busy downtown and stretch your legs, the Toronto Islands are the perfect destination. This car-free open space has paved trails for biking, in-line skating, or strolling; miles and miles of green space to explore; and picture-perfect vistas of the surrounding lake and skyline.

Bicyclists, power-walkers, and Sunday strollers alike enjoy the **Martin Goodman Trail,** the Toronto portion of the 280-mile Lake Ontario Waterfront Trail. The string of beaches along the eastern waterfront (east of Coxwell Avenue) is connected by a continuous boardwalk that parallels the Martin Goodman Trail. At the western end of this walking and biking trail is **Sunnyside Park Beach,** once the site of a large amusement park, and now a favorite place for a swim in the "tank" (a huge heated pool) or a snack at the small restaurant inside the handsomely restored 1923 Sunnyside Bathing Pavilion. Between the eastern and western beaches is the downtown stretch of the trail that hugs the waterfront and passes by marinas, a waterfowl conservation area, a sugar refinery, the Harbourfront, and the Toronto Islands ferry terminal.

FESTIVALS AND EVENTS

The **Canadian National Exhibition** (CNE, or "the Ex") takes place the last two weeks of August and Labor Day weekend, attracting more than 1.6 million people each year. It began in 1879 primarily as an agricultural show and today is a collection of carnival workers pushing C$5 balloons, midway rides, bands, horticultural and technological exhibits, parades, dog swims, horse shows, and (sometimes) top-notch performances. Stick around for nightly fireworks at 10.

Throughout the year, **Harbourfront Centre** hosts a dizzying array of festivals, covering cultural celebrations such as Kuumba (February) and the Mexican Day of the Dead (November), foodie-friendly fetes like the Hot & Spicy Festival (August) and Vegetarian Food Fair (September), and literary events such as the International Festival of Authors (October).

Updated by
Rosemary
Counter

This is a big, beautiful, and efficient city, one that has emerged from relative obscurity over the past half-century to become the center of culture, commerce, and communications in Canada. With its colorful ethnic mix, rich history, and breathtaking architecture, Toronto is nonstop adventure, from the top of the CN Tower to as far as the eye can see.

More than half the 2.79 million residents who now live in Toronto were born and raised somewhere else, often very far away. Nearly 500,000 Italians give Greater Toronto one of the largest communities outside Italy, while South Asians, the biggest visible minority group inside Toronto, account for 12% of the population (more than 300,000 people). It's also the home of the largest Chinese community in Canada and the largest Portuguese community in North America. The city hosts close to 200,000 Jewish people, nearly as many Muslims and Germans, joined by Greeks, Hungarians, East Indians, West Indians, Vietnamese, Maltese, South Americans, and Ukrainians—more than 100 ethnic groups in all, speaking about the same number of different languages and dialects. Toronto is also the home of Canada's largest gay and lesbian community.

Although the assimilation of these various cultures into the overall fabric of the city is ongoing, several ethnic neighborhoods have become attractions for locals and visitors. These include Kensington Market (west of Spadina Avenue between College and Dundas), Chinatown (around the Spadina Avenue and Dundas Street intersection), Greektown (Danforth Avenue between Chester and Jones), Little Italy (College Street between Euclid and Shaw), Little Poland (Roncesvalles Avenue between Queen and Dundas), Little Portugal (Dundas Street West, west of Bathurst), Little India (Gerrard Street between Coxwell and Greenwood), and Koreatown (Bloor Street West between Bathurst and Christie).

What this immigration has meant to Toronto is the rather rapid creation of a vibrant mix of cultures that echoes turn-of-the-20th-century New York City—but without the slums, crowding, and tensions.

A BRIEF HISTORY OF TORONTO

The city officially became Toronto on March 6, 1834, but its roots are much older. In the early 1600s, a Frenchman named Étienne Brûlé was sent into the not-yet-Canadian wilderness by the famous explorer Samuel de Champlain to see what he could discover. He found the river and portage routes from the St. Lawrence to Lake Huron, possibly Lakes Superior and Michigan, and eventually Lake Ontario. The indigenous Huron peoples had known this area between the Humber and Don rivers for centuries—and had long called it "Toronto," believed to come from the Iroquois word *tkaronto,* which means "where there are trees in water."

A bustling village called Teiaiagon grew up here, which became the site of a French trading post. After the British won the Seven Years' War, the trading post was renamed York in 1793. More than 40 years later the city again took the name Toronto. Following the famous Sacking of York in 1813 by Americans, several devastating fires, and the rebellions in 1837, there was a slow but steady increase in the population of white Anglo-Saxon Protestants leading into the 20th century. Since World War II, Toronto has attracted residents from all over the world. Unlike the American "melting pot," Toronto is more of a "tossed salad" of diverse ethnic groups.

Torontonians embrace and take pride in their multicultural character, their tradition of keeping a relatively clean and safe city, and their shared belief in the value of everyone getting along and enjoying the basic rights of good health care, education, and a high standard of living.

Toronto is also filled with boutiques, restaurants, and cafés, and there are plenty of shops, both aboveground and on the PATH, Toronto's underground city—a 30-km-long (19-mile-long) subterranean walkway lined with eateries, shops, banks, and medical offices.

And then there are the oft-overlooked gems of Toronto, such as the beach-fringed Toronto Islands. These eight tree-lined islands—and nearly a dozen smaller islets—that sit in Lake Ontario just off the city's downtown have been attracting visitors since at least 1830, especially during summer, when their more than 825 acres of parklands, beaches, and quaint cottages are most irresistible. From any of the islands you have spectacular views of Toronto's skyline, especially as the setting sun turns the skyscrapers to gold, silver, and bronze.

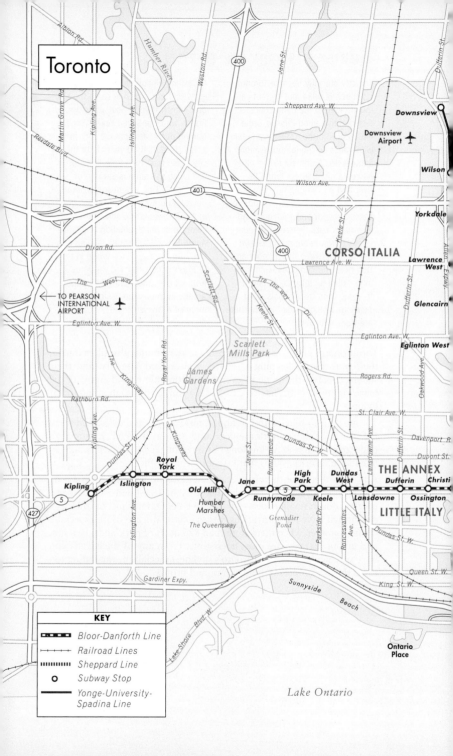

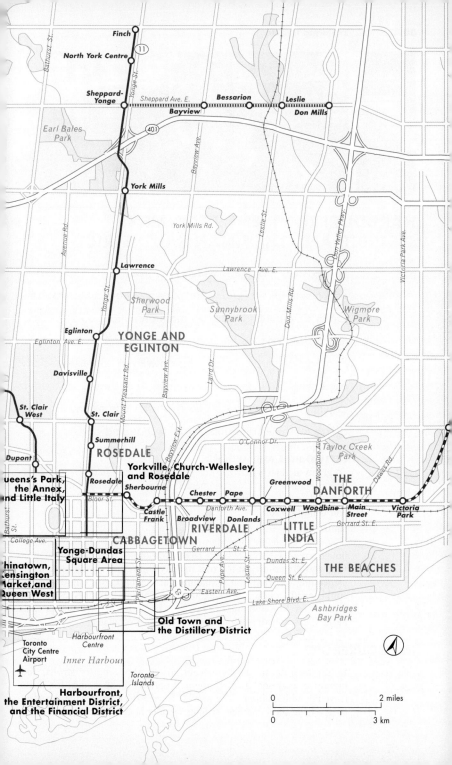

HARBOURFRONT, ENTERTAINMENT DISTRICT, AND THE FINANCIAL DISTRICT

Packed into this area, which runs from Bay Street east to Parliament Street and from Queen Street south to Lake Ontario, you'll find the city's main attractions and historical roots as well as the financial hub of the nation. As many of its attractions are outdoors, this downtown core is especially appealing during warm weather, but should a sudden downpour catch you off guard, shelter can be found in the area's museums and underground shopping city.

GETTING HERE AND AROUND

To get to the Harbourfront, take the 509 Queens Quay streetcar from Union Station. The Entertainment District is around St. Andrew and Osgoode subway stations. The Financial District is at Queen, King, and Union stations.

TIMING

If you have kids in tow, plan on spending a whole day in the Harbourfront area. If you're going to the Toronto Islands, add 45 minutes total traveling time just to cross the bay and return on the same ferry. Depending on what you're planning at the TIFF Bell Lightbox, you could spend an hour browsing an exhibit or several hours taking in a few movies. Museum buffs will want to linger for at least an hour each in the Hockey Hall of Fame and the Design Exchange.

HARBOURFRONT

In fair weather, the Harbourfront area is appealing for strolls, and myriad recreational and amusement options make it ideal for those traveling with children. The nearby Toronto Islands provide a perfect escape from the sometimes stifling summer heat of downtown.

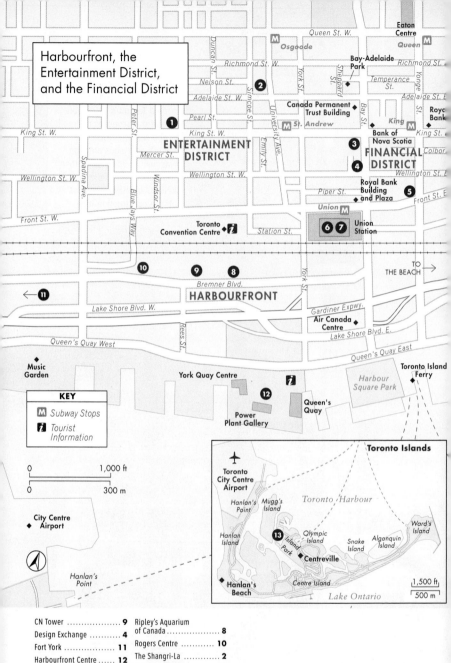

Harbourfront, the
Entertainment District,
and the Financial District

ENTERTAINMENT
DISTRICT

FINANCIAL
DISTRICT

HARBOURFRONT

Eaton Centre

Queen St. W.

Osgoode

Queen

Richmond St. W.

Bay-Adelaide
Park

Richmond St.

Nelson St.

Temperance
St.

Adelaide St. W.

Adelaide St.

Canada Permanent
Trust Building

Pearl St.

St. Andrew

Royal
Bank

King St. W.

King St. W.

King

Bank of
Nova Scotia

King St.

Mercer St.

Colbor.

Wellington St. W.

Wellington St. W.

Wellington St. E

Piper St.

Royal Bank
Building
and Plaza

Front St. E.

Union

Front St. W.

Toronto
Convention Centre

Station St.

Union
Station

TO
THE BEACH

Bremner Blvd.

Lake Shore Blvd. W.

Gardiner Expwy.

Air Canada
Centre

Lake Shore Blvd. E.

Queen's Quay West

Queen's Quay East

Music
Garden

Toronto Island
Ferry

York Quay Centre

Harbour
Square Park

KEY

Queen's
Quay

Power
Plant Gallery

M Subway Stops

Tourist
Information

Toronto Islands

Toronto
City Centre
Airport

Toronto Harbour

0   1,000 ft
0   300 m

Hanlan's
Point

Mugg's
Island

Ward's
Island

City Centre
Airport

Hanlan
Island

Olympic
Island

Snake
Island

Algonquin
Island

Island
Park

Centreville

Hanlan's
Point

Hanlan's
Beach

Centre Island

Lake Ontario

1,500 ft
500 m

TOP ATTRACTIONS

FAMILY

Fodor'sChoice

★

CN Tower. The tallest freestanding tower in the Western Hemisphere, this landmark stretches 1,815 feet and 5 inches high and marks Toronto with its distinctive silhouette. The CN Tower is tall for a reason: prior to the opening of this telecommunications tower in 1976, so many tall buildings had been built over the previous decades that lower radio and TV transmission towers had trouble broadcasting. It's worth a visit to the top if the weather is clear, despite the steep fee. Six glass-front elevators zoom up the outside of the tower at 20 feet per second, and the ride takes less than a minute. Each elevator has one floor-to-ceiling glass wall—three opaque walls make the trip easier on anyone prone to vertigo—and all have glass floor panels for the dizzying thrill of watching the earth disappear before your eyes.

There are four observation decks. The **Glass Floor Level,** which is exactly what it sounds like, is about 1,122 feet above the ground. This may be the most photographed indoor location in the city—lie on the transparent floor and have your picture taken from above like countless visitors before you. Don't worry—the glass floor can support more than 48,000 pounds. Above is the **LookOut Level,** at 1,136 feet; one floor more above, at 1,150 feet, is the excellent **360 Revolving Restaurant.** If you're here to dine, your elevator fee is waived. At an elevation of 1,465 feet, the **SkyPod** is the world's highest public observation gallery. All the levels provide spectacular panoramic views of Toronto, Lake Ontario, and the Toronto Islands. On really clear days you may see Lake Simcoe to the north and the mist rising from Niagara Falls to the south. Adrenaline junkies can try the **EdgeWalk** attraction, which allows harnessed tower-goers to roam "hands free" around a 5-foot ledge outside the tower's main pod. Reservations are required.

On the ground level, the Gift Shop at the Tower has 5,000 square feet of shopping space with quality Canadian travel items and souvenirs, along with a shop selling Inuit art. Displays and exhibits throughout the building feature the story of the construction and history of the Tower; how the Tower works today, including engineering components that make it such a unique attraction; and a dynamic weather display. Peak visiting hours are 11 to 4; you may wish to work around them, particularly on weekends. ✉ *301 Front St. W, at Bremner Blvd., Harbourfront* ☎ *416/868–6937, 416/362–5411 restaurant, 416/601–3833 EdgeWalk* ⊕ *www.cntower.ca* ➦ *First two observation levels C\$35, SkyPod C\$12, EdgeWalk C\$195* Ⓜ *Union.*

FAMILY

Harbourfront Centre. Stretching from just west of York Street to Spadina Avenue, this culture-and-recreation center is a match for San Francisco's Pier 39 and Baltimore's Inner Harbor. The original Harbourfront opened in 1974, rejuvenating more than a mile of city. Today Harbourfront Centre, a streamlined version of the original concept, draws more than 3 million visitors to the 10-acre site each year. **Queen's Quay Terminal** at Harbourfront Centre is a former Terminal Warehouse building, where goods shipped to Toronto were stored before being delivered to shops in the city. In 1983 it was transformed into a magnificent, eight-story building with specialty shops, eateries, the 450-seat Fleck Dance Theatre, and plenty of harbor views. Exhibits of contemporary painting, sculpture, architecture, video, photography, and design are mounted at the **Power Plant**, which can be spotted by its tall red smokestack; it was built in 1927 as a power station for the Terminal Warehouse's ice-making plant. Developed by renowned cellist Yo-Yo Ma and garden designer Julie Moir Messervy, the **Music Garden** on the south side of Queen's Quay is Yo-Yo Ma's interpretation of Johann Sebastian Bach's Cello Suite No. 1 (which consists of six movements—Prelude, Allemande, Courante, Sarabande, Minuet, and Gigue). Each movement is reflected in the park's elaborate design: undulating riverscape, a forest grove of wandering trails, a swirling path through a wildflower meadow, a conifer grove, a formal flower parterre, and giant grass steps. **York Quay Centre** hosts concerts, theater, readings, and even skilled artisans. The Craft Studio, for example, has professional craftspeople working in ceramics, glass, metal, and textiles from February to December, in full view of the public. A shallow pond outside is used for canoe lessons in warmer months and as the largest artificial ice-skating rink in North America in more wintry times. At the nearby Nautical Centre, many private firms rent boats and give lessons in sailing and canoeing. Among the seasonal events in Harbourfront Centre are the Ice Canoe Race in late January, Winterfest in February, a jazz festival in June, Canada Day celebrations and the Parade of Lights in July, the Authors' Festival and Harvest Festival in October, and the Swedish Christmas Fair in November. ✉ *235 Queen's Quay W, Harbourfront* ☎ *416/973–4000 event hotline, 416/973–4600 offices* ⊕ *www.harbourfrontcentre.com* Ⓜ *Union, then streetcar 509 or 510 west.*

QUICK BITES | There are plenty of places inside **Queen's Quay** for a quick sandwich, freshly squeezed juice, or ice-cream concoction. You can also check out one of the food trucks outside selling french fries.

FAMILY
Fodor'sChoice
★

Toronto Island Park. These eight narrow, tree-lined islands, plus more than a dozen smaller islets, just off the city's downtown in Lake Ontario, provide a gorgeous green retreat with endless outdoor activities. The more than 575 acres of parkland are hard to resist, especially in the summer, when they're usually a few degrees cooler than the city.

Sandy beaches fringe the islands; the best are on the southeast tip of Ward's Island, the southernmost edge of Centre Island, and the west side of Hanlan's Point. In 1999 a portion of Hanlan's Beach was officially declared "clothing-optional" by the Toronto City Council. The declaration regarding Ontario's only legal nude beach passed without protest—perhaps a testament to the city's live-and-let-live attitude. The section frequented by gays and lesbians is at the east end; the straight section is more westerly. In the summer, Centre Island has bike and row boat rentals. Bring picnic fixings or something to grill in one of the park's barbecue pits, or grab a quick (but expensive) bite at one of the snack bars. (Note that the consumption of alcohol in a public park is illegal in Toronto.) There are also supervised wading pools, baseball diamonds, volleyball nets, tennis courts, and even a disc-golf course. The winter can be bitterly cold on the islands, but snowshoeing and cross-country skiing with downtown Toronto over your shoulder are appealing activities.

All transportation is self-powered; no private cars are permitted. The boardwalk from Centre Island to Ward's Island is 2½ km (1½ miles) long. Bikes are allowed on all ferries, or you can rent one for an hour or so once you get there. Bike rentals can be found south of the Centre Island ferry docks on the Avenue of the Islands.

You may want to take one of the equally frequent ferries to Ward's Island or Hanlan's Point. Both islands have tennis courts and picnic and sunbathing spots. Late May through early September, the ferries run between the docks at the bottom of Bay Street and the Ward's Island dock between 6:35 am and 11:45 am; for Centre and Hanlan's islands, they begin at 8 am. Ward's Island Ferries run roughly at half-hour intervals most of the working day and at quarter-hour intervals during peak times such as summer evenings. In winter the ferries run only to Ward's Island on a limited schedule. ⊠ *Ferries at foot of Bay St. and Queen's Quay, Harbourfront* ☎ *416/392–8186 for island information, 416/392–8193 for ferry information* ⊕ *www.toronto.ca/parks/island* ⊠ *Ferry C$7.50 round-trip* Ⓜ *Union, then streetcar 509 or 510.*

WORTH NOTING

Fort York. The most historic site in Toronto is a must for anyone interested in the city's origins. Toronto was founded in 1793 when the British built Fort York to protect the entrance to the harbor during Anglo-American strife. Twenty years later the fort was the scene of the bloody Battle of York, in which explorer and general Zebulon Pike led U.S. forces against the fort's outnumbered British, Canadian, and First Nations defenders. The Americans won this battle—their first major victory in the War of 1812—and burned down the provincial buildings during a six-day occupation. A year later British forces retaliated when they captured Washington, D.C., and torched its public buildings, including the Executive Mansion. Exhibits include restored barracks, kitchens, and gunpowder magazines, plus changing museum displays. There are guided tours, marching drills, and cannon firings daily during the summer months. The visitor center features exhibits on the founding of York, the changing harbor, and the War of 1812, plus an area displaying rare and precious artifacts related to Toronto and Fort York's history. ⊠ *250 Fort York Blvd., between Bathurst St. and Strachan Ave., Harbourfront* ☎ *416/392–6907, 416/392–6907* ⊕ *www.fortyork. ca* ⊠ *C$9* Ⓜ *Bathurst, then streetcar 511 south.*

Ripley's Aquarium of Canada. North America's largest aquarium is sleek, angular, watery blue, and shaped like a shark. It contains more than 450 species of marine life spread out between 45 exhibit spaces. Maintaining their philosophy to "foster environmental education, conservation, and research," Ripley's also lives up to its reputation for providing a wow-inducing entertainment venue. One exhibit simulates a Caribbean scuba diving experience complete with bountiful tropical fish, coral reefs, and a bright blue sky above. Although the focus is on Canadian marine wildlife, sharks are a dominant theme: you can wind your way through tunnels that take you right into the almost 80,000-gallon shark tank, which houses three species of sharks and more than 5,000 other aquatic animals. The shark pattern on the roof is an unexpected treat for visitors peering down on the aquarium from the top of the CN

The TIFF Bell Lightbox is the focal point for the annual Toronto International Film Festival.

Tower. ✉ *288 Bremner Blvd., Harbourfront* ☎ *647/351–3474* ⊕ *www. ripleyaquariums.com/canada* 🎫 *C$30.*

FAMILY **Rogers Centre.** One of Toronto's most famous landmarks, Rogers Centre is home to baseball's Blue Jays and was the world's first stadium with a fully retractable roof. Rogers Communications, the owner of the Blue Jays, bought the stadium, formerly known as the SkyDome, in February 2005 for a mere C$25 million. One way to see the 52,000-seat stadium is to buy tickets for a Blue Jays game or one of the many other events that take place here. You might watch a cricket match, Wrestlemania, a monster-truck race, a family ice show, or a rock concert—even the large-scale opera *Aïda* has been performed here. You can also take a one-hour guided walking tour. Depending on several factors, you may find yourself in the middle of the field, in a press box, in the dressing rooms, or, if a roof tour is available, 36 stories above home plate on a catwalk. ✉ *1 Blue Jays Way, Harbourfront* ☎ *416/341–2770 for tours, 416/341–1000 for events and shows, 416/341–1234 for ticket information, 888/654–6529 for Blue Jays information* ⊕ *www.rogerscentre.com* 🎫 *Tour C$13.75* Ⓜ *Union.*

ENTERTAINMENT DISTRICT

The neighborhood originally got its name from the strip of nightclubs along Richmond Street West, but these days the neighborhood is so much more than that. The vibe is boisterous with pretheater crowds and movie buffs hitting the TIFF Bell Lightbox; a string of new hotels and restaurants has opened to field the crowds.

TOP ATTRACTIONS

The Shangri-La. In the Shangri-La Hotel's lobby lounge, a band performs, a fireplace soothes, and silk-clad waitresses seemingly float from sunken couch to sunken couch bringing light meals and cocktails to a mix of locals and hotel guests. You can take in the scene over Afternoon Tea, offered seven days a week. This experience starts at C$45 per person for a three-tier spread that includes a pot of one of the expertly blended teas—there's even a tea sommelier on staff to explain the 72 varieties of tea. Expect delicate pastries, buttery scones with homemade jam, and clever twists on finger sandwiches, such as brie, apple, and ham on marble rye on the menu. ⊠ *Shangri-La Hotel, 188 University Ave., Entertainment District* ☏ *647/788–8888* ⊕ *www.shangri-la.com/ toronto/shangrila.*

TIFF Bell Lightbox. A five-story architectural masterpiece in the city's center, this glass-paneled building houses the year-round headquarters of the internationally acclaimed, wildly popular Toronto International Film Festival. Throughout the year—except in September when TIFF fever paralyzes the city—visitors can attend film-related lectures, watch screenings, and enjoy smaller film festivals, including TIFF Kids International Film Festival, a celebration of children's films that takes place each April. A stellar educational program includes summer camps, ongoing workshops—how to produce a stop-motion movie, for example—and film-related gallery exhibitions that highlight big-shot filmmakers and artists such as Stanley Kubrick and Andy Warhol; faculty and university students get free admission to special "higher learning" TIFF offerings (check online for the full calendar). The TIFF Cinematheque, open to the public, plays world cinema classics and contemporary art house films all year. ⊠ *Reitman Square, 350 King St. W, at John St., Entertainment District* ☏ *416/599–8433, 888/599–8433* ⊕ *www.tiff.net.*

FINANCIAL DISTRICT

Toronto's Financial District pleases many tourists with its unique and wonderful architectural variety of skyscrapers. Most of the towers have bank branches, restaurants, and retail outlets on their ground floors and are connected to the PATH, an underground city of shops and tunnels.

TOP ATTRACTIONS

Design Exchange. A delightful example of streamlined modern design (a later and more austere version of art deco), this building is clad in polished pink granite and smooth buff limestone, with stainless-steel doors. Between 1937 and 1983, the DX (as it's now known) was home to the Toronto Stock Exchange. Don't miss the witty stone limestone carved above the doors—a banker in top hat marching behind a laborer and sneaking his hand into the worker's pocket. Only in Canada, where socialism has always been a strong force, would you find such a political statement on the side of a stock exchange. In the early 1990s, the building reopened as a nonprofit center devoted to promoting Canadian design. The permanent collection consists of more than 600 pieces that span six decades from 1945 to the present; it includes furniture, graphic design, housewares, lighting, and tableware. Check the website

for information about rotating exhibits. ⊠ *234 Bay St., at King St., Financial District* ☎ *416/363–6121* ⊕ *www.dx.org* 🎫 *Free* ⊘ *Closed Mon.* Ⓜ *King, St. Andrew.*

FAMILY **Hockey Hall of Fame and Museum.** Even if you're not a hockey fan, it's worth a trip here to see this shrine to Canada's favorite sport. Exhibits include the original 1893 Stanley Cup, as well as displays of goalie masks, skate and stick collections, great players' jerseys, video displays of big games, and a replica of the Montréal Canadiens' locker room. Grab a stick and test your speed and accuracy in the "shoot out" virtual experience, or strap on a goalie mask and field shots from big-name players like Wayne Gretzky and Mark Messier with the "shut out" computer simulation. It's also telling that this museum is housed in such a grand building, worthy of any fine art collection. A former Bank of Montréal branch designed by architects Darling & Curry in 1885, the building is covered with beautiful ornamental details. Note the richly carved Ohio stone and the Hermès figure supporting the chimney near the back. At the corner of Front and Yonge streets, the impressive statue—a 17-foot bronze entitled "Our Game"—is a good photo-op. ■TIP➔ **Entrance is through Brookfield Place on the lower level of the east side.** ⊠ *Brookfield Place, 30 Yonge St., at Front St., Financial District* ☎ *416/360–7765, 416/360–7765* ⊕ *www.hhof.com* 🎫 *C$18* Ⓜ *Union.*

Toronto-Dominion Centre. Ludwig Mies van der Rohe, a virtuoso of modern architecture, designed this five-building masterwork, though he died before its completion in 1992. As with his acclaimed Seagram Building in New York, Mies stripped the TD Centre's buildings to their skin and bones of bronze-color glass and black-metal I-beams. The tallest building, the Toronto Dominion Bank Tower, is 56 stories high. The only decoration consists of geometric repetition, and the only extravagance is the use of rich materials, such as marble counters and leather-covered furniture. In summer, the plazas and grass are full of office workers eating lunch and listening to one of many free outdoor concerts. Inside the low-rise square banking pavilion at King and Bay streets is a virtually intact Mies interior. ⊠ *55 King St. W, at Bay St., Financial District* Ⓜ *St. Andrew.*

WORTH NOTING

QUICK
BITES
Brookfield Place. A modern office and retail complex cleverly designed to incorporate the facades of the Bank of Montréal and other older buildings under a vaulted glass roof, Brookfield Place is one of the most impressive architectural spaces in Toronto. The atrium under the glass canopy makes a lovely place to sit and enjoy a cup of coffee and pastry from Marché, the bustling food market. ⊠ *181 Bay St., between Front St. W and Wellington St. W, Financial District* Ⓜ *Union.*

PATH. Though tunnels under the city date back to 1900, this subterranean universe expanded in the mid-1970s partly to replace the retail services in small buildings that were demolished to make way for the latest skyscrapers and partly to protect office workers from the harsh winter weather. As each major building went up, its developers agreed

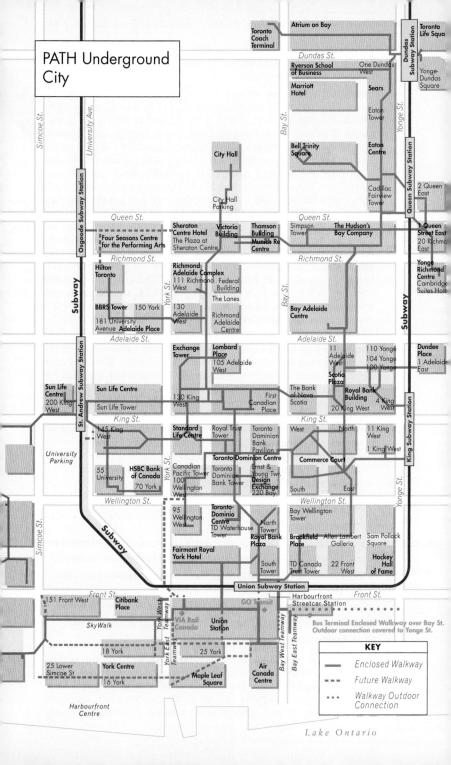

PATH Underground City

Toronto Coach Terminal

Atrium on Bay

Toronto Life Squa

Dundas Subway Station

Dundas St.

Ryerson School of Business

One Dundas West

Yonge-Dundas Square

Marriott Hotel

Sears

Eaton Tower

Bell Trinity Square

Eaton Centre

Cadillac Fairview Tower

Queen Subway Station

City Hall

City Hall Parking

Queen St.

Osgoode Subway Station

Simpson Tower

The Hudson's Bay Company

Queen St.

2 Queen East

1 Queen Street East

Four Seasons Centre for the Performing Arts

Sheraton Centre Hotel
The Plaza at Sheraton Centre

Victoria Building

Thomson Building

Munich Re Centre

20 Richmond East

Richmond St.

Hilton Toronto

Richmond Adelaide Complex
111 Richmond West

Federal Building

Richmond St.

Yonge Richmond Centre
Cambridge Suites Hote

SUBWAY

York St.

The Lanes

Bay St.

BBRS Tower   **150 York**

130 Adelaide West

Richmond Adelaide Centre

Bay Adelaide Centre

181 University Avenue **Adelaide Place**

Adelaide St.

Adelaide St.

Exchange Tower

Lombard Place
105 Adelaide West

11 Adelaide West

110 Yonge

104 Yonge

100 Yonge

Dundee Place
1 Adelaide East

Scotia Plaza

St. Andrew Subway Station

Sun Life Centre
200 King West

Sun Life Centre

Sun Life Tower

130 King West

The Bank of Nova Scotia

Royal Bank Building
20 King West

4 King West

King Subway Station

King St.

First Canadian Place

King St.

SUBWAY

145 King West

Standard Life Centre

Royal Trust Tower

Toronto Dominion Bank Pavilion

West

North

11 King West

1 King West

University Parking

55 University

HSBC Bank of Canada

70 York

Canadian Pacific Tower
100 Wellington West

Toronto Dominion Bank Tower

Ernst & Young Twr. **Design Exchange** 220 Bay

Commerce Court

Yonge St.

York St.

Wellington St.

South

East

Wellington St.

95 Wellington West

Toronto-Dominion Centre
TD Waterhouse Tower

North Tower

Bay Wellington Tower

Sun Life Centre

Toronto-Dominion Centre

Royal Bank Plaza

Brookfield Place

Allen Lambert Galleria

Sam Pollock Square

Fairmont Royal York Hotel

South Tower

TD Canada Trust Tower

22 Front West

Hockey Hall of Fame

Simcoe St.

Front St.

Union Subway Station

Front St.

151 Front West

Citibank Place

SUBWAY

GO Transit

Harbourfront Streetcar Station

SkyWalk

York West Teamway

VIA Rail Canada

Union Station

Bay West Teamway

Bay East Teamway

Bus Terminal Enclosed Walkway over Bay St.
Outdoor connection covered to Yonge St.

York East Teamway

18 York

25 York

25 Lower Simcoe St

York Centre

16 York

Maple Leaf Square

Air Canada Centre

Harbourfront Centre

KEY

———	*Enclosed Walkway*
- - -	*Future Walkway*
· · ·	*Walkway Outdoor Connection*

Lake Ontario

to build and connect their underground shopping areas with others
and with the subway system. You
can walk from beneath Union Station to the Fairmont Royal York
hotel, the Toronto-Dominion Centre, First Canadian Place, the Sheraton Centre, The Bay and Eaton
Centre, and City Hall without ever
seeing the light of day, encountering
everything from art exhibitions to
buskers (the best are the winners of citywide auditions, who are licensed
to perform throughout the subway system) and walkways, fountains,
and trees. There are underground passageways in other parts of the
city—one beneath Bloor Street and another under College Street (both
run from Yonge to Bay Street)—but this is the city's most extended
subterranean network. ⊠ *Financial District.*

> ### DOWN TOWN
>
> According to *Guinness World
> Records,* the PATH is the biggest
> underground shopping complex
> in the world. Maps to guide you
> through this labyrinth are avail-
> able in many downtown news and
> convenience stores.

Union Station. Historian Pierre Berton wrote that the planning of Union
Station recalled "the love lavished on medieval churches." Indeed, this
train depot can be regarded as a cathedral built to serve the god of
steam. Designed in 1907 and opened by the Prince of Wales in 1927,
it has a 40-foot-high Italian tile ceiling and 22 pillars weighing 70 tons
apiece. The main hall, with its lengthy concourse and light flooding in
from arched windows at each end, was designed to evoke the majesty
of the country that spread out by rail from this spot. The names of
the towns and cities across Canada that were served by the country's
two railway lines, Grand Trunk (incorporated into today's Canadian
National) and Canadian Pacific, are inscribed on a frieze along the
inside of the hall. As train travel declined, the building came very near to
being demolished in the 1970s, but public opposition eventually proved
strong enough to save it, and Union Station is now a vital transport hub.
Commuter, subway, and long-distance trains stop here. ⊠ *65 Front St.
W, between Bay and York Sts., Financial District* Ⓜ *Union.*

OLD TOWN AND THE DISTILLERY DISTRICT

Old Town is a mishmash of restored historic attractions and trendy new developments. Farther east, the historic Distillery District is one of Toronto's hottest entertainment destinations. It's filled with restored Victorian-era factories that house contemporary galleries, bustling pubs, and chic restaurants.

GETTING HERE AND AROUND

Located south of Front Street between Parliament and Cherry Streets, the Distillery District is accessible by car and public transit. The district is pedestrian only, but parking lots and street parking are available. On the TTC, take the Parliament bus from Castle Frank station, the Cherry Street bus from Union station, or the 405 King car to Parliament.

TIMING

Allow yourself at least two hours to wander the cobblestone streets and artisanal shops. Be sure to stop to see the modern art statues along Gristmill Lane and stop for a drink at Mill Street Brewery.

OLD TOWN

Old Town is where the city got its municipal start as the village of York in 1793. It now has a pleasing natural disorder with leafy streets that crisscross at odd angles, and a blend of old and new buildings that are home to residential and commercial space alike.

TOP ATTRACTIONS

Fodor's Choice ★ **St. Lawrence Market.** Both a landmark and an excellent place to sample Canadian bacon, this market was originally built in 1849 as the first true Toronto city hall. The building now has an exhibition hall upstairs—the Market Gallery—where the council chambers once stood. The food market, which began growing around the building's square in the early 1900s, is considered one of the world's best. Local and imported foods such as fresh shellfish, sausage, and cheeses are renowned. Stop and snack on Canadian bacon, also known as "peameal bacon," at the Market's Carousel Bakery. The brick building across Front Street, on the north side, is open

The outstanding St. Lawrence food market, one of the finest in the world, sells a huge variety of local and imported specialties.

on Saturday mornings for the 200-year-old farmers' market; it's a cornucopia of produce and homemade jams, relishes, and sauces from farms just north of Toronto. On Sunday the wares of more than 80 antiques dealers are on display in the same building. ⊠ *Front and Jarvis Sts., Old Town* ☎ *416/392–7219* ⊕ *www.stlawrencemarket.com* ⊘ *Closed Mon.* Ⓜ *Union.*

WORTH NOTING

Flatiron Building. One of several wedge-shape buildings scattered all over North America, Toronto's Flatiron occupies the triangular block between Wellington, Scott, and Front streets. It was erected in 1892 as the head office of the Gooderham and Worts distilling company. On the back of the building, a witty trompe l'oeil mural by Derek Besant is drawn around the windows, making it appear that part of the building has been tacked up on the wall and is peeling off. ⊠ *49 Wellington St. E, between Church and Scott Sts., Old Town* Ⓜ *King.*

St. James Cathedral. Even if bank towers dwarf it now, this Anglican church with noble Gothic spires has the tallest steeple in Canada. Its illuminated clock once guided ships into the harbor. This is the fourth St. James Cathedral on this site; the third burned down in the Great Fire of 1849. As part of the church's bicentennial in 1997, a peal of 12 bells was installed. Stand near the church most Sundays after the 9 am service ends (about 10:10 am) and be rewarded with a glorious concert of ringing bells. ⊠ *65 Church St., at King St., Old Town* ☎ *416/364–7865* ⊕ *www.stjamescathedral.on.ca* Ⓜ *King.*

St. Lawrence Hall. Erected on the site of the area's first public meeting space, St. Lawrence Hall, built in 1850–51, demonstrates Renaissance

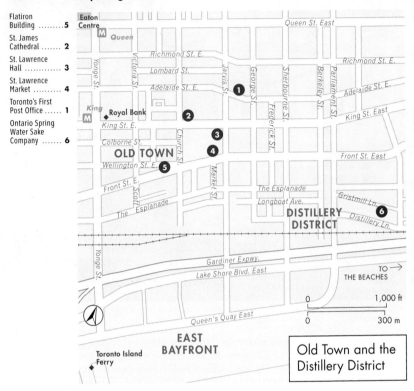

Old Town and the
Distillery District

Revival architecture at its finest. Erected for musical performances and balls, it is here that famed opera soprano Jenny Lind sang, where antislavery demonstrations were held, and where P. T. Barnum first presented the midget Tom Thumb. Take time to admire the exterior of this architectural gem, now used for everything from concerts to wedding receptions. If you find yourself taking part in one of the many walking tours of the area, you might be able to see the photos in the lounge on the third floor; the pictures feature notable figures who once performed, lectured, or were entertained here. ⊠ *157 King St. E, Old Town* 🕾 *416/392–7809* ⊕ *www.stlawrencemarket.com* Ⓜ *Union.*

FAMILY **Toronto's First Post Office.** This small working post office dates from 1833 and still uses quill pens, ink pots, and sealing wax—you can use the old-fashioned equipment to send a letter for C$2. Exhibits include reproductions of letters from the 1820s and 1830s. Distinctive cancellation stamps are used on all outgoing letters. ⊠ *260 Adelaide St. E, Old Town* 🕾 *416/865–1833* ⊕ *www.townofyork.com* 🖂 *Free* Ⓜ *King.*

DISTILLERY DISTRICT

This restored collection of Victorian industrial buildings, complete with cobblestone lanes, has become a hub of independent eateries, boutiques, and galleries. The carefully preserved former Gooderham and Worts

The cobblestoned historic Distillery District is now home to more than 100 upscale galleries, shops, and restaurants.

Distillery (founded in 1832) has been reborn as a cultural center. The 13-acre site includes 45 19th-century buildings and a pedestrian-only village that houses more than 100 tenants—including galleries, artist studios and workshops, boutiques, breweries, upscale restaurants, bars, and cafés. Other delicious detours include the SOMA Chocolatemaker, Mill Street Brewpub, and Brick Street Bakery. Live music, outdoor exhibitions, fairs, and special events take place year-round, but summer months are the best time to visit. Hour-long walking tours take place seven days a week, or you can join one of the 30-minute-long Go Tours lessons (C$39) at Segway of Ontario (⊕ *www.gotourscanada.com*). You can also combine a Go Tours lesson with a ghost tour for C$49.

TOP ATTRACTIONS

Ontario Spring Water Sake Company. Ontario's first sake distillery uses natural spring water from the nearby town of Huntsville for its softness and low mineral content, and highly polished rice from California to create its sake. The brewery features a small tasting bar and retail shop that offers products made with the sake *kasu* (the lees, or yeast, leftover from fermentation), such as soaps, salad dressings, and miso soup, as well as ceramics and sake glassware. You can also take tours (on weekends at 1 pm and 3:30 pm) to learn about Junmai (pure rice) and Namazake (unpasteurized sake), to find out how sake is made, and to enjoy a guided tasting of four sakes. ⊠ *51 Gristmill La., Bldg. 4, Distillery District* ☏ *416/365–7253* ⊕ *www.ontariosake.com* ☞ *Tours C$15.*

YONGE-DUNDAS SQUARE AREA

Yonge Street is the central vein of Toronto, starting at Lake Ontario and slicing the city in half as it travels through Dundas Square and north to the suburbs. Tourists gather below the enormous billboards and flashy lights in Dundas Square, especially in the summer, when the large public area comes alive with outdoor festivals and entertainment. The few sights in this neighborhood, namely the Eaton Centre and Nathan Phillips Square, get a lot of attention from both locals and visitors.

Tourists always end up here, whether they want to or not. Usually it's the enticement of nonstop shopping in the Eaton Centre, Toronto's biggest downtown shopping mall, or the shops lining Yonge Street nearby. Others see the allure of outdoor markets, ethnic food festivals, and street concerts in the bright and lively, larger-than-life Dundas Square.

To catch a glimpse of what locals are up to, grab lunch and dine alfresco at Nathan Phillips Square. Under the omnipresent gaze of City Hall—the two curving buildings were designed to resemble a watchful eye—nearby suits from the Financial District and spent shoppers populate the benches in all weather. During the winter, the water fountain at Nathan Phillips Square becomes an ice-skating rink that draws in gaggles of teenagers, young couples holding hands, and little ones testing out their skates for the first time.

There's also a selection of distinct museums. History buffs will enjoy the Mackenzie House, the former home of Toronto's first mayor; contemporary fashion and design are highlighted at the Textile Museum of Canada; and at the Toronto Police Museum, kids can learn about the exciting history of Toronto's police.

GETTING HERE AND AROUND

The subway stations Dundas and Queen, conveniently at either end of the Eaton Centre, are the main transportation hubs for this part of the city. There are also streetcar lines running along Dundas and Queen streets, linking this area to Chinatown and Kensington Market, and Queen West respectively.

TIMING

Depending on your patience and the contents of your wallet, you could spend anywhere from one to 10 hours in the colossal Eaton Centre, literally shopping until you drop. The Mackenzie House, Textile Museum of Canada, and Toronto Police Museum merit an hour each; and you could easily while away an afternoon people-watching in Yonge-Dundas or Nathan Phillips Square.

TOP ATTRACTIONS

Fodor's Choice ★   **Yonge-Dundas Square.** A public square surrounded by oversize billboards and explosive light displays, Toronto's answer to New York's Times Square is becoming one of the fastest-growing tourist destinations in the city. Visitors and locals converge on the tables and chairs that are scattered across the square when the weather is fine, and kids (and the young at heart) frolic in the 20 water fountains that shoot out of

the cement floor like miniature geysers. From May to October, there's something happening every weekend—it could be an artisan market, an open-air film viewing, a summertime festival, or a live musical performance. ⊠ *Yonge St., at Dundas St., Dundas Square Area* ⊕ *www. ydsquare.ca* Ⓜ *Dundas.*

Eaton Centre. The 1.7-million-square-foot CF Toronto Eaton Centre shopping mall has been both praised and vilified since it was built in the 1970s, but it remains incredibly popular. From the graceful glass roof, arching 127 feet above the lowest of the mall levels, to artist Michael Snow's exquisite flock of fiberglass Canada geese floating poetically in open space, there's plenty to appreciate.

Such a wide selection of shops and eateries can be confusing, so here's a simple guide: Galleria Level 1 contains the massive food court Urban Eatery; popularly priced fashions; photo, electronics, and music stores; and much "convenience" merchandise. Level 2 is directed to the middle-income shopper; Level 3, suitably, has the highest fashion and prices. Named for the store (Eaton's) that once anchored it, its biggest tenants are now Saks Fifth Avenue and H&M. The southern end of Level 3 has a skywalk that connects the Centre to the seven floors of the Bay (formerly Simpsons) department store, across Queen Street.

⊠ *220 Yonge St., Dundas Square Area* ☎ *416/598–8560* ⊕ *www.toron-toeatoncentre.com* Ⓜ *Dundas, Queen.*

Mackenzie House. Once home to journalist William Lyon Mackenzie, Toronto's first mayor (elected in 1834) and designer of the city's coat of arms, this Greek Revival row house is now a museum. Among the period furnishings and equipment preserved here is an 1845 printing press, which visitors may try. Mackenzie served only one year as mayor. In 1837, he gathered some 700 supporters and marched down Yonge Street to try to overthrow the government, but his rebels were roundly defeated, and he fled to the United States with a price on his head. When Mackenzie was pardoned by Queen Victoria years later, he returned to Canada and was promptly elected once again to the legislative assembly. By this time, though, he was so down on his luck that a group of friends bought his family this house. Mackenzie enjoyed the place for only a few years before his death in 1861. His grandson, William Lyon Mackenzie King, became the longest-serving prime minister in Canadian history. ⊠ *82 Bond St., at Dundas St. W, Dundas Square Area* ☎ *416/392–6915* ▣ *C$7* ⊘ *Closed Mon.* Ⓜ *Dundas.*

QUICK BITES

Trinity Square Café. This café at the Church of the Holy Trinity is a charming eatery serving sandwiches, soups, pastries, and tea. It's open for lunch weekdays 11:30 am to 2:30 pm. The church itself is fully operational and available for quiet contemplation in the midst of one of downtown Toronto's busiest sections. ⊠ *19 Trinity Sq., facing Bay St., Dundas Square Area* ☎ *416/598–2010* ⊕ *www.trinitysquarecafe.ca* Ⓜ *Dundas.*

WORTH NOTING

Textile Museum of Canada. With a 40-year history of exploring ideas and building cultural understanding through its collection of more than 13,000 artifacts from across the globe, this museum's exhibitions and programming connect contemporary art and design to international textile traditions. Wednesday evening (after 5) admission is Pay What You Can. ✉ *55 Centre Ave., at Dundas St. W, Dundas Square Area* ☎ *416/599–5321* ⊕ *www.textilemuseum.ca* ✆ *C$15* Ⓜ *St. Patrick.*

FAMILY **Toronto Police Museum and Discovery Centre.** A replica of a 19th-century police station, this collection is devoted exclusively to the Toronto police and also contains exhibits about infamous crimes. Interactive displays include law-and-order quizzes and a Harley-Davidson kids can jump on. They also enjoy climbing in and out of a car sliced in half and hearing a dispatcher squawk at them. ✉ *40 College St., at Bay St., Dundas Square Area* ☎ *416/808–7020* ⊕ *www.torontopolice.on.ca/museum* ✆ *C$3* ⊘ *Closed weekends* Ⓜ *College.*

2

CHINATOWN, KENSINGTON MARKET, AND QUEEN WEST

The areas along Dundas and Queen streets typify Toronto's ethnic makeup and vibrant youthfulness. To many locals, the Dundas and Spadina intersection means Chinatown and Kensington Market, while Queen West, which was the home of 1990s comedy troupe Kids in the Hall and pop-rockers Barenaked Ladies, has always been a haven for shoppers and trendsetters.

Chinatown and Kensington Market, often explored together, are popular destinations for tourists and locals alike. On a weekend morning, the sidewalks are jam-packed with pedestrians shopping for cheap produce and Chinese trinkets, lining up for a table at one of Chinatown's many restaurants, or heading to "the Market" for a little afternoon shopping. On the last Sunday of each month (May–October), Kensington Market goes car-free, and the streets explode with live entertainment, street performances, and vendors selling handicrafts and clothing.

Queen West is busy any time of the year, mostly with teenagers hanging out at the MuchMusic building and young fashionistas-in-training shopping up a storm.

GETTING HERE AND AROUND
The Osgoode subway station is ideal for getting to Queen West, as is the 501 streetcar. The 510 Spadina streetcar (which originates at the Spadina subway station) services Chinatown and Kensington Market.

TIMING
In Queen West, the Campbell House merits at least a half hour; the Art Gallery of Ontario an hour or more. Chinatown is at its busiest (and most fun) on Sunday, but be prepared for very crowded sidewalks and much jostling. Kensington is great anytime, although it can feel a bit sketchy at

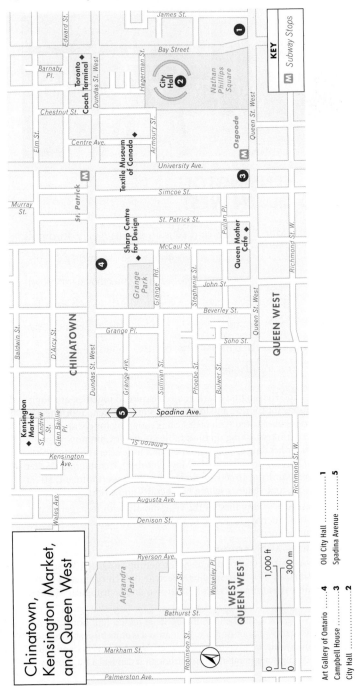

Chinatown, Kensington Market, and Queen West

KEY

Ⓜ Subway Stops

James St.
Bay Street
Nathan Phillips Square
City Hall ❷
Hagerman St.
Queen St. West
Osgoode Ⓜ
Edward St.
Barnaby Pl.
Toronto Coach Terminal ◆
Dundas St. West
Chestnut St.
Centre Ave.
Elm St.
Textile Museum of Canada ◆
Armoury St.
University Ave.
Murray St.
St. Patrick Ⓜ
Simcoe St.
❸
St. Patrick St.
Pullan Pl.
Queen Mother Cafe ◆
Sharp Centre for Design ◆
McCaul St.
❹
Grange Park
Grange Rd.
Stephanie St.
John St.
Beverley St.
QUEEN WEST
Queen St. West
Soho St.
Richmond St. W.
Grange Pl.
Baldwin St.
D'Arcy St.
CHINATOWN
Dundas St. West
Grange Ave.
Sullivan St.
Phoebe St.
Bulwer St.
Kensington Market ◆
St. Andrew St.
Glen Baillie Pl.
Kensington Ave.
❺ Spadina Ave.
Cameron St.
Wales Ave.
Richmond St. W.
Augusta Ave.
Denison St.
Ryerson Ave.
Alexandra Park
Wolseley Pl.
Carr St.
WEST QUEEN WEST
Markham St.
Robinson St.
Bathurst St.
Palmerston Ave.

1,000 ft
300 m

Art Gallery of Ontario **4**
Campbell House **3**
City Hall **2**
Old City Hall **1**
Spadina Avenue **5**

night, and it gets mobbed on weekend afternoons. Just strolling around any of these neighborhoods can gobble up an entire afternoon.

CHINATOWN

Compact and condensed, Toronto's Chinatown—which is actually the main or original Chinatown in the city, as five other areas with large Chinese commercial districts have sprung up elsewhere—covers much of the area of Spadina Avenue from Queen Street to College Street, running along Dundas Street nearly as far east as Bay Street. The population is more than 100,000, which is especially impressive when you consider that just over a century ago there was only a single Chinese resident, Sam Ching, who ran a hand laundry on Adelaide Street.

Especially jumbled at its epicenter, the Spadina–Dundas intersection, Chinatown's rickety storefronts selling (real and fake) jade trees, lovely sake sets, Chinese herbs, and fresh fish are packed every day of the week. On Sunday, Chinese music blasts from storefronts, cash registers ring, and bakeries, markets, herbalists, and restaurants do their best business of the week.

TOP ATTRACTIONS

Fodor's Choice
★

Art Gallery of Ontario. The AGO is hard to miss: the monumental glass and titanium facade designed by Toronto native son Frank Gehry hovering over the main building is a stunning beauty. Near the entrance, you'll find visitors of all ages climbing in and around Henry Moore's *Large Two Forms* sculpture, located in Grange Park, just south of the gallery. Inside, the collection, which had an extremely modest beginning in 1900, is now in the big leagues, especially in terms of its exhibitions of Canadian paintings from the 19th and 20th centuries. Be sure to take a pause in the light and airy Walker Court, to admire Gehry's spiraling Baroque Stair; climb the staircase and look straight up for the best view.

The Canadian Collection includes major works by such northern lights as Emily Carr, Cornelius Krieghoff, David Milne, and Homer Watson. The AGO also has a growing collection of works by such world-famous artists as Rembrandt, Warhol, Monet, Renoir, Rothko, Picasso, Rodin, Degas, Matisse, and many others. The bustling Weston Family Learning Centre offers art courses, camps, lectures, and interactive exhibitions for adults and children alike. Feature Tours (free with admission) run daily at 2 pm and on Wednesday evenings at 7 pm starting in Walker Court. Free AGO Highlight Tours run daily at 11 am, noon, 1 pm, 3 pm, and Wednesday evening at 7 pm (subject to volunteer availability). ⊠ *317 Dundas St. W, at McCaul St., Chinatown* ☎ *416/979–6648, 416/979–6648* ⊕ *www.ago.net* ➳ *C$19.50; permanent collection free on Wed. after 6 pm* ☾ *Closed Mon.* Ⓜ *St. Patrick.*

WORTH NOTING

Spadina Avenue. Pronounced "Spa-*dye*-nah," this avenue, running from the lakeshore north to Bloor Street (where it becomes Spadina Road), has never been chic. For decades it has housed a collection of inexpensive stores, factories that sell wholesale if you have connections, ethnic food stores, and eateries, including some first-class, if modest-looking,

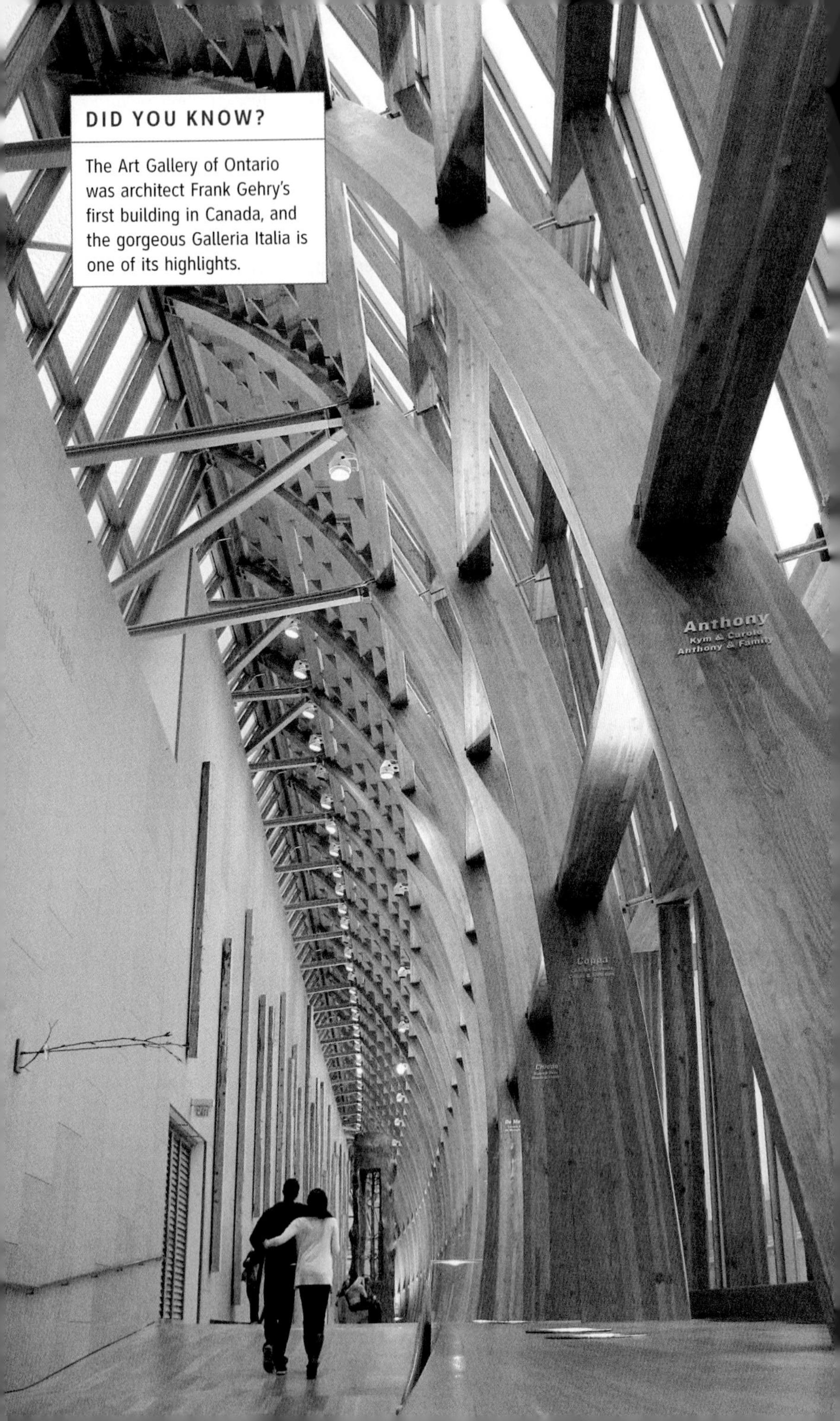
Anthony
Kym & Carole
Anthony & Family

DID YOU KNOW?

The Art Gallery of Ontario was architect Frank Gehry's first building in Canada, and the gorgeous Galleria Italia is one of its highlights.

Chinese restaurants. Each new wave of immigrants—Jewish, Chinese, Portuguese, East and West Indian, South American—has added its own flavor to the mix, but Spadina–Kensington's basic bill of fare is still bargains galore. Here you can find treasures at a fraction of Yorkville prices, yards of remnants piled high in bins, designer clothes minus the labels, and the occasional rock-and-roll nightspot and interesting greasy spoon. A streetcar line runs down the wide avenue to Front Street. ⊠ *Chinatown.*

KENSINGTON MARKET

This collection of colorful storefronts, crumbling brick houses, delightful green spaces, and funky street stalls titillates all the senses. On any given day you can find Russian rye breads, barrels of dill pickles, fresh fish, imported cheese, and ripe fruit. Kensington's collection of vintage-clothing stores is the best in the city.

The site sprang up in the early 1900s, when Russian, Polish, and Jewish inhabitants set up stalls in front of their houses. Since then the district, or "market"—named after the area's major street—has become a sort of United Nations of stores. Jewish and Eastern European shops sit side by side with Portuguese and Caribbean ones, as well as with a sprinkling of Vietnamese and Chinese establishments. ■ TIP→ Weekends are the best days to visit, preferably by public transit; parking is difficult. Also note that the neighborhood is pedestrianized from dawn to dusk on the last Sunday of every month.

QUICK BITES

King's Café. In a neighborhood where the bohemian vegetarian lifestyle is the norm, King's Café has become a mainstay for diners seeking healthy grub with an Asian accent. Artists, students, and young professionals flock to this serene and airy interior with wide windows overlooking bustling Augusta Avenue. Specialties include enoki mushrooms in seaweed and spinach and King's Special Mixed Vegetable Soup, a hearty broth with homemade veggie nuggets, taro, and fried tofu. ⊠ *192 Augusta Ave., Kensington Market* ☎ *416/591–1340* Ⓜ *St. Patrick, then streetcar 505 west.*

QUEEN WEST

Along Queen Street West, from University Avenue to Bathurst Street, is a shopper's dream. John Fluevog, Urban Outfitters, American Apparel, Zara, Lululemon—they all have outposts here. The area also attracts tourists for its iconic landmarks: the open-air Nathan Phillips Square at City Hall; the historic Campbell House; and the Horseshoe Tavern at 370 Queen Street West, which has been here since the 1940s and was a springboard for such performers as Bryan Adams and Stompin' Tom Connors.

TOP ATTRACTIONS

City Hall. Toronto's modern city hall resulted from a 1958 international competition to which some 520 architects from 42 countries submitted designs. The winning presentation by Finnish architect Viljo Revell was controversial—two curved towers of differing height—but logical: an

Toronto's network of streetcars provides an excellent method of transportation for getting around downtown.

aerial view of City Hall shows a circular council chamber sitting like an eye between the two tower "eyelids," which contain the offices of 44 municipal wards, with 44 city councillors. A remarkable mural within the main entrance, *Metropolis,* was constructed by sculptor David Partridge from 100,000 nails. Revell died before his masterwork was opened in 1965, but within months City Hall became a symbol of a thriving metropolis, with a silhouette as recognizable as the Eiffel Tower.

Annual events at City Hall include the the Cavalcade of Lights celebration, featuring fireworks and live music amidst the glow of more than 525,000 lights illuminated across both the new and old city halls.

In front of City Hall, the 9-acre **Nathan Phillips Square** (named after the mayor who initiated the City Hall project) has become a gathering place, whether for royal visits, protest rallies, picnic lunches, or concerts. The reflecting pool is a delight in summer, and even more so in winter, when office workers skate at lunch. The park also holds a Peace Garden for quiet meditation and Henry Moore's striking bronze sculpture *The Archer.* ✉ *100 Queen St. W, at Bay St., Queen West* ☎ *416/338–0338* ⊕ *www.toronto.ca* Ⓜ *Queen.*

QUICK BITES

Queen Mother Café. Queen Street West is lined with cafés and restaurants, and one solid choice is the Queen Mother Café, a neighborhood institution popular with art students and broadcast-media types. Serving Lao-Thai and Italian cuisine, the "Queen Mum" is open until 1 am (Sunday until 11 pm) for wholesome meals and rich desserts at reasonable prices. ✉ *208 Queen St. W, at St. Patrick St., Queen West* ☎ *416/598–4719* ⊕ *www.queen-mothercafe.ca* Ⓜ *Osgoode.*

WORTH NOTING

Campbell House. The Georgian mansion of Sir William Campbell, the sixth chief justice of Upper Canada, is now one of Toronto's best house museums. Built in 1822 in another part of town, the Campbell House was moved to this site in 1972. It has been restored with elegant early-19th-century furniture, and now guides detail the social life of the upper class. Note the model of the town of York as it was in the 1820s and the historic kitchen. ✉ *160 Queen St. W, Queen West* ☎ *416/597–0227* ⊕ *www.campbellhousemuseum.ca* 🖘 *C$6* ☾ *Closed Jan. and Mon.* Ⓜ *Osgoode.*

Old City Hall. Opened in 1899, and used until 1965 when "new" City Hall was built across the street, the old municipal building now operates solely as a courthouse. This imposing building was designed by E. J. Lennox, who was also the architect for Casa Loma and the King Edward Hotel. Note the huge stained-glass window as you enter. The fabulous gargoyles above the front steps were apparently the architect's witty way of mocking certain turn-of-the-20th-century politicians; he also carved his name under the eaves on all four faces of the building. The building has appeared in countless domestic and international TV shows and feature films. ✉ *60 Queen St. W, Queen West* ☾ *Closed weekends* Ⓜ *Queen.*

EAST AND WEST OF THE CITY CENTER

Toronto is sprawling, there's no doubt about it. However, the city's excellent public transportation system makes it a cinch to get outside the city center to explore the Toronto that locals know and cherish. And you should do just that: hit a trendy strip like Ossington to experience Toronto's burgeoning hipster culture; take in the vibe of a busy sidewalk café in Leslieville, teeming with young families; stroll the boardwalk and enjoy the lake breezes in The Beaches; or satisfy a hungry belly with Greek food along the Danforth or a spicy curry in Little India.

WEST QUEEN WEST, PARKDALE, AND OSSINGTON

Grunge meets chic along Queen Street west of Bathurst, dubbed "West Queen West" by locals. While it's still possible to find a run-down hardware store shouldering a high-end hipster bar, more of the latter are moving in these days. Almost completely devoid of the familiar chains that plague older sister Queen West, this area is instead filling with vegan spa resorts, trendy ethnic restaurants, and European kitchenware shops; much farther west a bustling art scene is blossoming.

The neighborhood's landmarks, the **Drake Hotel** and the **Gladstone Hotel**, enjoy much success for their creative, eclectic decor and their happening nightlife. Businesses like these, which revolutionized the once-shabby district and gave it its current über-cool image, helped pave the way for a second wave of émigrés. An eclectic smattering of restaurants and more than 300 art galleries vie for real estate with fair-trade coffee shops and boutiques featuring Canada's hottest new designers. Trinity Bellwoods Park punctuates the neighborhood at the center and provides a beautiful setting for a picnic or a bench break.

West Queen is home to an increasing number of trendy boutiques and cutting-edge galleries.

Farther west, after the overpass next to the Gladstone Hotel, is Parkdale, a once crime-infested and still fairly run-down neighborhood that's become home to North America's largest Tibetan community. Apartment buildings streaked with prayer flags and shops offering everything from beef *momos* (dumplings) to singing bowls have been a welcome improvement over the once derelict storefronts.

The previously shady strip along Ossington Street, north of Queen West, is Toronto's newest hotspot. Fashion designers, artists and musicians, and creative restaurateurs have flooded the street, and the area now attracts attention for its sudden and celebrated gentrification.

THE BEACHES

Queen Street West might represent the city's of-the-moment trends, but The Beaches neighborhood (15 minutes east of the Queen subway stop) has all the old-school bohemia. This pricey area is bounded by Victoria Park Avenue to the east and Woodbine Avenue to the west. The main strip, Queen Street East, has a funky flair and a small-town feel, and it's easy to spend an afternoon strolling the delightful yet crowded (in summer) boardwalk along the shore of Lake Ontario. Musicians often perform at the parks fronting the boardwalk, where you're also likely to see artists selling their wares. You could also do some window-shopping on Queen Street East, which is lined with antiques stores and specialty boutiques and shops. An annual jazz festival in July attracts more than 400 musicians and thousands of listeners to this laid-back community.

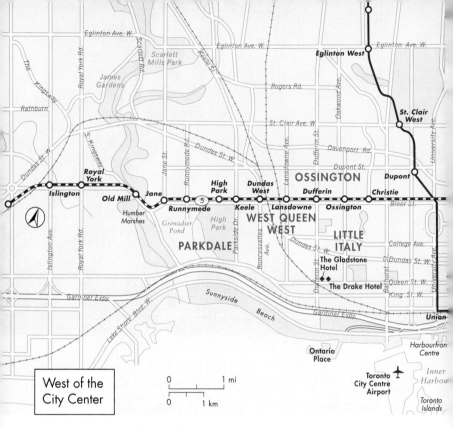

West of the
City Center

0   1 mi

0   1 km

This neighborhood's official name has been a source of controversy
since the 1980s. It boils down to whether you view the four separate beaches—Woodbine, Balmy, Kew, and Scarboro—as one collective entity or plural. When the area decided to welcome tourists with
fancy, emblematic street signs, the long-running debate surfaced. While
officially "The Beach" folks won, most Torontonians still call the neigh-
bourhood The Beaches.

THE DANFORTH

Once English-settled, this area along Danforth Avenue named after Asa
Danforth, an American contractor who cut a road into the area in 1799,
has a dynamic ethnic mix, although it's primarily a Greek community.

The western end, between Broadview and Chester subway stations, is
a health nut's haven. Juice bars, vegetarian food emporia, yoga studios,
and stores devoted to holistic healing, naturopathic medicine, and envi-
ronmentally friendly clothing and cleaning products abound.

East of Chester subway station is the area referred to as "Greektown."
Late-night taverns, all-night fruit markets, and some of the best Greek
food in North America keep this neighborhood busy at all hours. A
number of bakeries offer mouthwatering baklava, *tyropita* (cheese pie),

The Danforth neighborhood serves some of the best Greek food in North America.

and *touloumbes* (fried cinnamon-flavored cakes soaked in honey) if you prefer to snack and stroll. ■TIP➔ Summer is the best season to visit, as most eateries have patios open and are busy until the wee hours of morning.

Every August the Taste of the Danforth (⊕ *www.tasteofthedanforth. com*) pays tribute to the little nook of foodie paradise here. More than 1.65 million visitors come to sample the fare—mainly dolmades, souvlaki, and other Greek specialties—for C$1 to C$5 per taste.

But it's not just about food. Between bites, you might want to check out the independent, original boutiques in the neighborhood that offer everything from fair-trade gifts to funky kitchenware. For those who like to live on the edge, there's even a shop that sells nothing but hot sauce.

LITTLE INDIA

"Little India" and "Indian Village" both refer to Gerrard India Bazaar (⊕ *www.gerrardindiabazaar.com*), the largest collection of South Asian restaurants, sari stores, and Bollywood movie-rental shops in North America. Follow your nose through the sweets shops, food stalls, and curry restaurants, and allow your eyes to be dazzled by storefront displays of jewelry, Hindu deities, and swaths of sensuous fabrics ablaze with sequins.

Mornings are generally quiet. Afternoons see a trickle of visitors, but the area really comes alive in the evening, when those with hungry bellies stroll in search of a fiery madras, creamy korma, or hearty masala

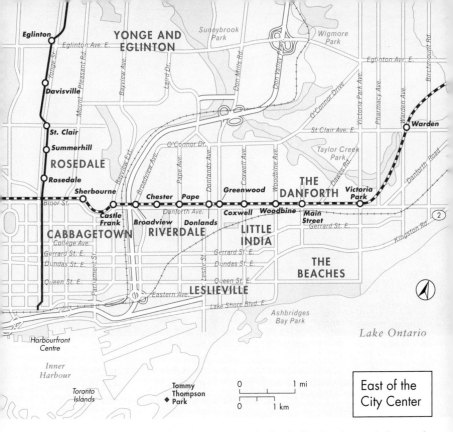

curry. Many of the restaurants offer buffet lunches and dinners for around C$12 per person, which draw huge crowds on the weekends. Sunday afternoons set the familiar scene of Indian families crowding the sidewalks, enjoying corn on the cob and *paan* (a mild Indian stimulant of spices, fruits, and sometimes sugar wrapped in leaves of the betel pepper), and window-shopping their way up and down Gerrard Street.

As this area represents such a diverse group of people, there are many festivals throughout the year. During the biggest event, the three-day Festival of South Asia in July (⊕ *www.festivalofsouthasia.com*), stages are set for colorful music and dance performances, and the streets fill with the tantalizing scents of snack stalls and the calls of vendors peddling everything from henna tattoos to spicy corn on the cob. In late autumn, the Hindu Festival of Lights (Diwali) is celebrated with a fun and fiery street fete.

LESLIEVILLE

Perhaps because of its location, far from much-hyped and highly publicized West Queen West and Ossington, Leslieville has been quietly gentrifying into a colorful and exciting strip of interior design shops, hip eateries, funky boutiques, and independent cafés that is often labeled by trend-spotters (much to the disdain of locals) as Toronto's Brooklyn.

Interior design shops stand out, but the vibe has more of a community feel due to a tight-knit collection of shop owners with regular customers. And like the nearby Beaches neighborhood, the sidewalks are often filled with baby strollers and dog walkers.

It's quaint at times, with dusty antiques shops, old-fashioned ice-cream parlors, and the occasional old-school appliance shop thrown into the mix, but the offerings lean more toward local designer boutiques, cute bakeries, organic butcher shops, cheese emporia, homey diners, chic eateries, and, in keeping with the chilled-out vibe of the area, an unusually large selection of independent coffee shops.

GETTING HERE AND AROUND

To explore Leslieville, take the 501 Queen streetcar east from downtown to Coxwell Avenue and walk west along Queen Street East.

TOP ATTRACTIONS

Tommy Thompson Park. This park comprises a peninsula that juts 5 km (3 miles) into Lake Ontario. It was created from bricks and rubble from construction sites around the city and sand dredged for a new port. It has quickly become one of the best areas in the city for cycling, jogging, walking, sailing, photography, and especially bird-watching. The strange, artificial peninsula is home (or a stopover) to the largest colony of double-crusted cormorants in North America, as well as dozens of species of terns, ducks, geese, and great egrets. At the end of the spit, you'll find a red-and-white lighthouse, in addition to amazing views of downtown and an awesome sense of isolation in nature. Bird-watching is best from May to mid-October. To get here, head east along Queen Street to Leslie Street, then south to the lake. No private vehicles are permitted in the park. ⊠ *Entrance at foot of Leslie St., south of Lakeshore Blvd. E, Leslieville* ☎ *416/661–6600* ⊕ *www.tommythompsonpark.ca* Ⓜ *Queen, then streetcar 501 east.*

QUEEN'S PARK, THE ANNEX, AND LITTLE ITALY

This vast area that encompasses a huge chunk of Toronto's downtown core holds several important attractions, but it couldn't feel further from a tourist trap if it tried, bringing together Toronto's upper crust, Ontario's provincial politicians, Canada's intellectual set, and a former Italian neighborhood turned entertainment district. Take a break in one of The Annex's many casual spots and you could be rubbing shoulders with a student cramming for an exam, a blocked author looking for inspiration, or a busy civil servant picking up a jolt of caffeine to go.

The large, oval Queen's Park circles the Ontario Provincial Legislature and is straddled by the sprawling, 160-acre downtown campus of the University of Toronto. Wandering this neighborhood will take you past century-old colleges, Gothic cathedrals, and plenty of quiet benches overlooking leafy courtyards and student-filled parks.

The University of Toronto's campus overflows west into The Annex, where students and scholarly types while away the hours after class. This frantic section of Bloor Street West abounds with ethnic restaurants and plenty of student-friendly cafés and bars, plus two of the city's must-see attractions: the Bata Shoe Museum and Casa Loma.

Similarly energetic is Little Italy, where music spills out of trendy eateries and patios are packed in the summertime. The myriad wine bars and boutique clubs in this neighborhood attract a young professional crowd.

GETTING HERE AND AROUND

Use the subway to reach the University of Toronto (St. George and Queen's Park stations), Casa Loma (Dupont station), The Annex (Spadina and Bathurst stations), and Queen's Park (Queen's Park station). Little Italy can be reached by streetcar 506 along College Street (since

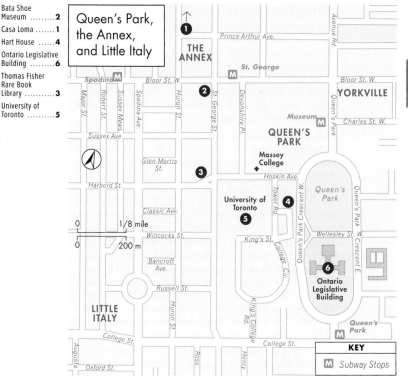

College Street turns into Carlton Street at Yonge, this streetcar's often called the "Carlton Car").

TIMING

The Queen's Park and Annex areas are nice places to take a stroll any time of year because many of the attractions bring you indoors. A visit to the legislature and one or two of the museums or libraries would make a nice half-day (or more) program. Give yourself at least a few hours for a full tour of Casa Loma and about an hour for the Bata Shoe Museum. Make an evening of dinner and drinks in the trendy Little Italy area.

QUEEN'S PARK

Many visitors consider this the intellectual hub of Toronto. Surrounding the large oval-shape patch of land are medical facilities to the south and the University of Toronto to the west and east. To most locals, Queen's Park is chiefly synonymous with politics, as the Ontario Legislative Building sits in its center.

TOP ATTRACTIONS

Hart House. A neo-Gothic student center built in 1911–19, Hart House represents the single largest gift to the University of Toronto. Vincent Massey, a student here at the turn of the 20th century, regretted the absence of a meeting place and gym for students and convinced his father to build one. It was named for Vincent's grandfather, Hart, the founder of Massey-Ferguson, once the world's leading supplier of farm equipment. Originally restricted to male students, Hart House has been open to women since 1972.

Keep your eyes peeled for artwork scattered throughout the building, including a revolving collection of works by famed Canadians like Emily Carr and evocative landscape paintings by the Group of Seven. As many as 200 works are on display throughout the building, most of which can be viewed by anyone willing to wander in and out of the rooms. Each year a new piece is added, carefully chosen by a committee made up of mainly students, and today the collection is reported to be worth several million dollars. Part of a federation with University of Toronto Art Centre, the **Justina M. Barnicke Gallery** comprises two rooms of mixed-media art showcasing homegrown talent. The stained-glass windows and vaulted ceiling in the Great Hall are impressive, but so is chef Suzanne Baby's cuisine at the resident **Gallery Grill**. Try one of the grilled fish dishes, a juicy steak, or a creative vegetarian torte while enjoying the elegant surroundings. ⊠ *U of T, 7 Hart House Circle, Queen's Park* ☎ *416/978–2452* ⊕ *www.harthouse.ca* Ⓜ *Museum.*

University of Toronto. Almost a city unto itself, U of T has a staff and student population of around 100,000. The institution dates to 1827, when King George IV signed a charter for a "King's College in the Town of York, Capital of Upper Canada." The Church of England had control then, but by 1850 the college was proclaimed nondenominational, renamed the University of Toronto, and put under the control of the province. Then, in a spirit of Christian competition, the Anglicans started Trinity College, the Methodists began Victoria, and the Roman Catholics began St. Michael's; by the time the Presbyterians founded Knox College, the University was changing at a great rate. Now the 12 schools and faculties are united, and they welcome anyone who can meet the admission standards and afford the tuition, which, thanks to government funding, is still somewhat reasonable. The architecture is interesting, if uneven, as one might expect on a campus that's been built in bits and pieces over 150 years. ⊠ *Visitors Centre, 25 King's College Circle, Queen's Park* ☎ *416/978–5000* ⊕ *www.utoronto.ca* Ⓜ *St. George, Queen's Park.*

WORTH NOTING

Ontario Legislative Building. Like City Hall, this home to the provincial parliament was the product of an international contest among architects, in this case won by a young Briton residing in Buffalo, New York. The 1893 Romanesque Revival building, made of pink Ontario sandstone, has a wealth of exterior detail; inside, the huge, lovely halls echo half a millennium of English architecture. The long hallways are hung with hundreds of oils by Canadian artists, most of which capture scenes of the province's natural beauty. Take one of the frequent,

30-minute-long tours from the lobby to see the chamber where the 107 MPPs (members of provincial parliament) meet. The many statues dotting the lawn in front of the building, facing College Street, include one of Queen Victoria and one of Canada's first prime ministers, Sir John A. Macdonald. The lawn is also the site of Canada Day celebrations and the occasional political protest. These buildings are often referred to simply as Queen's Park, after the park surrounding them. ⊠ *1 Queen's Park, Queen's Park* ☎ *416/325–7500* ⊜ *Free* ⊙ *No guided tours weekends in early Sept.–mid-May* Ⓜ *Queen's Park.*

Thomas Fisher Rare Book Library. Early writing artifacts such as a Babylonian cuneiform tablet, a 2,000-year-old Egyptian papyri, and books dating to the beginning of European printing in the 15th century are shown here in rotating exhibits, which change three times annually. Subjects of these shows might include William Shakespeare, Galileo Galilei, Italian opera, or contemporary typesetting. Registration is required to use the collections, so bring some form of identification with you, but there's no entrance fee to view the exhibition area. ⊠ *U of T, 120 St. George St., Queen's Park* ☎ *416/978–5285* ⊕ *fisher.library.utoronto.ca* ⊜ *Free* ⊙ *Closed weekends* Ⓜ *St. George.*

THE ANNEX

Born in 1887, when the burgeoning town of Toronto engulfed the area between Bathurst Street and Avenue Road north from Bloor Street to the Canadian Pacific Railway tracks at what is now Dupont Street, the countrified Annex soon became an enclave for the well-to-do; today it attracts an intellectual set. Timothy Eaton of department-store fame built a handsome structure at 182 Lowther Avenue (since demolished). The prominent Gooderham family, owners of a distillery, erected a lovely red castle at the corner of St. George Street and Bloor Street, now the home of the exclusive York Club.

As Queen Victoria gave way to King Edward, old money gave way to new money and ethnic groups came and went. Upon the arrival of developers, many Edwardian mansions were demolished to make room for bland 1960s-era apartment buildings.

Still, The Annex, with its hundreds of attractive old homes, can be cited as a prime example of Toronto's success in preserving lovely, safe streets within the downtown area. Examples of late-19th-century architecture can be spotted on Admiral Road, Lowther Avenue, and Bloor Street, west of Spadina Avenue. Round turrets, pyramid-shape roofs, and conical spires are among the pleasures shared by some 15,000 Torontonians who live in this vibrant community, including professors, students, writers, lawyers, and other professional and artsy types. Bloor Street between Spadina and Palmerston keeps them fed and entertained with its bohemian collection of used-record stores, whole-foods shops, juice bars, and restaurants from elegant Italian to aromatic Indian.

TOP ATTRACTIONS

Bata Shoe Museum. Created by Sonja Bata, wife of the founder of the Bata Shoe Company, this shoe museum holds a permanent collection of more than 30,000 varieties of foot coverings and, through the changing

fashions, highlights the craft and sociology of making shoes. Some items date back more than 4,000 years. Pressurized skydiving boots, iron-spiked shoes used for crushing chestnuts, and smugglers' clogs are among the items on display. Elton John's boots have proved wildly popular, but Marilyn Monroe's red leather pumps give them a run for their money. Other ongoing exhibits feature beautifully crafted kamiks from the Arctic and an area that showcases the development of fashion by the decade. Admission is Pay What You Can every Thursday from 5 to 8 pm. ⊠ *327 Bloor St. W, at St. George St., The Annex* ☎ *416/979–7799* ⊕ *www.batashoemuseum.ca* 🎫 *C$14* Ⓜ *St. George.*

FAMILY **Casa Loma.** A European-style castle, Casa Loma was commissioned by Sir Henry Pellatt, a soldier and financier. This grand display of extravagance has 98 rooms, two towers, creepy passageways, and lots of secret panels. Pellatt spent more than C$3.5 million to construct his dream (that's in 1913 dollars; it would cost about C$20 million today), only to lose his house to the tax man just over a decade later. Some impressive details are the giant pipe organ; the reproduction of Windsor Castle's Peacock Alley; the majestic, 60-foot-high ceiling of the Great Hall; the mahogany-and-marble stable, reached by a long, underground passage; and the extensive, 5-acre estate gardens. The rooms are copies of those in English, Spanish, Scottish, and Austrian castles. This has been the location for many a horror movie and period drama, an episode of the BBC's *Antiques Roadshow*, and several Hollywood blockbusters, including *Chicago* and *X-Men*. Included in the admission price are a self-guided audio tour (available in eight languages) and a docudrama about Pellatt's life. ■**TIP→ A tour of Casa Loma is a good 1½-km (1-mile) walk, so wear sensible shoes.** ⊠ *1 Austin Terr., The Annex* ☎ *416/923–1171* ⊕ *www.casaloma.org* 🎫 *C$25* ⊙ *Gardens closed Nov.–Apr.* Ⓜ *Dupont.*

LITTLE ITALY

Once a quiet strip of College Street with just a few unfrequented clothing shops and the odd, obstinate pizzeria, Little Italy has become one of the hippest haunts in Toronto. This is the southern edge of the city's Italian community, and though not much remains of this heritage—most Italians now live in the suburbs and throughout the city—the flavor lingers on many a table and in a few food markets.

Whether you're in the mood for old-school Italian trattorias (think checkered tablecloths) or polished martini bars, Little Italy won't disappoint. Pasta and pizza aren't the only things on the menus here—new ethnic restaurants open monthly, and every corner holds fashionable cafés and diners to match.

Surprisingly, this edge of downtown has a nightlife that rivals the clubs and bars of the Entertainment District (around Adelaide Street West). Bars and coffeehouses are busy into the night, and summer months bring out booming cruise-mobiles, patio revelers, and plenty of pedestrian animation.

YORKVILLE, CHURCH-WELLESLEY, AND ROSEDALE

Yorkville and Church-Wellesley may be stacked together, but their personalities are quite different. Yorkville whispers a tony elegance, where as Church-Wellesley is a casual, out-and-proud LGBTQ community. Farther northeast, Rosedale is a place to window-shop for fantasy Victorian houses.

YORKVILLE

Toronto's equivalent to Fifth Avenue or Rodeo Drive, Yorkville, and Bloor Street in particular, is a dazzling spread of high-price stores stocked with designer clothes, furs, and jewels, along with restaurants, galleries, and specialty boutiques. It's also where much of the excitement takes place in September during the annual Toronto International Film Festival, the world's largest and most people-friendly film festival, where the public actually gets to see premieres and hidden gems and attend industry seminars. Klieg lights shine over skyscrapers, bistros serve alcohol until 2 am, cafés teem with the well-heeled, and everyone practices air kisses. Yorkville is also home to a unique park on Cumberland Street, designed as a series of gardens along old property lines and reflecting both the history of the Village of Yorkville and the diversity of the Canadian landscape.

TOP ATTRACTIONS

FAMILY **Royal Ontario Museum.** Since its inception in 1914, the ROM, Canada's largest museum, has amassed more than 6 million items. What sets the ROM apart is that science, art, and archaeology exhibits are all appealingly presented in one gigantic complex, including the ultramodern **Michael Lee-Chin Crystal** gallery—a series of interlocking prismatic shapes spilling out onto Bloor Street.

Other highlights include the **Hyacinth Gloria Chen Crystal Court,** a four-story atrium with aircraft aluminum bridges connecting the old

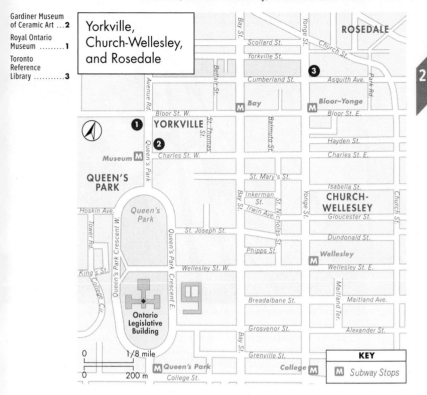

and new wings, and an angular pendant skylight through which light pours into the open space. A look through the windows reveals parts of the treasures inside, such as the frightful creatures from the **Age of Dinosaurs** exhibit standing guard. **The Patricia Harris Gallery of Textiles and Costume** angles out 80 feet over Bloor Street from its fourth-floor perch.

The **Daphne Cockwell Gallery of Canada** exhibits an impressive range of First Peoples historical objects and artifacts, from precontact time to the present. The **Chinese Sculpture Gallery** in the Matthews Family Court displays monumental Buddhist sculpture dating from the 6th through 17th centuries; and the **Gallery of Korea** is North America's largest permanent gallery devoted to Korean art and culture. The **Sir Christopher Ondaatje South Asian Gallery** houses the best objects of a 7,000-piece collection that spans 5,000 years, and includes items from Bangladesh, Bhutan, India, the Maldives, Nepal, Pakistan, Sri Lanka, and Tibet. ✉ *100 Queen's Park, Yorkville* ☎ *416/586–8000* ⊕ *www. rom.on.ca* 🎟 *C$17; C$10 Fri. 4:30–8:30* Ⓜ *Museum.*

WORTH NOTING

Gardiner Museum of Ceramic Art. This collection of rare ceramics includes 17th-century English delftware and 18th-century European porcelain; its pre-Columbian collection dates to Olmec and Maya times. Other

A striking modern addition showcases some of the 6 million items in the Royal Ontario Museum's collection.

galleries feature Japanese Kakiemon-style pottery and Chinese white-and-blue porcelain. If your visit coincides with lunchtime, hit the Gardiner Bistro for light dishes like West Coast salmon with local greens. Free guided tours take place at 2 pm daily; or you can join a drop-in session in the clay studio (Wednesday and Friday 6–8 pm; Sunday 1–3 pm; C$15). ■TIP➔ Admission is half price on Friday after 4 (and kids under 18 are always free). ⊠ *111 Queen's Park Crescent, Yorkville* ☎ *416/586–8080* ⊕ *www.gardinermuseum.on.ca* ✆ *C$12* Ⓜ *Museum.*

Toronto Reference Library. Designed by one of Canada's most admired architects, Raymond Moriyama, who also created the Ontario Science Centre, this five-story library is arranged around a large atrium, affording a wonderful sense of open space. One-third of the more than 5.5 million items—spread across 82 km (51 miles) of shelves—are open to the public. Audio carrels are available for listening to nearly 40,000 music and spoken-word recordings. The largest Performing Arts Centre in a public library in Canada is on the fifth floor; the **Arthur Conan Doyle Room**, which is of special interest to Baker Street fans, is on the fifth floor. It houses the world's finest public collection of Holmesiana, including records, films, photos, books, manuscripts, letters, and even cartoon books starring Sherlock Hemlock of *Sesame Street.* ⊠ *789 Yonge St., Yorkville* ☎ *416/395–5577* ⊕ *www.torontopubliclibrary.ca* ⊙ *Closed Sun. Oct.–May* Ⓜ *Bloor-Yonge.*

CHURCH-WELLESLEY

Colorful rainbow flags fly high and proud in this vibrant neighborhood, a little east of downtown. The area is energetic and boisterous any time of year, but absolutely frenetic during the annual Pride festival and parade in June. Given its long history, the area has evolved into a tight-knit, well-established community, with pharmacies, grocery stores, and dry cleaners rubbing shoulders with a mix of new and decades-old gay- and lesbian-centric nightspots.

ROSEDALE

This posh residential neighborhood northeast of Yorkville has tree-lined curving roads (it's one of the few neighborhoods to have escaped the city's grid pattern), many small parks, and a jumble of oversized late-19th-century and early-20th-century houses in Edwardian, Victorian, Georgian, and Tudor styles. An intricate ravine system weaves through this picturesque corner of downtown, its woodsy contours lined with old-money and old-world majesty. The neighborhood is bounded by Yonge Street, the Don Valley Parkway, St. Clair Avenue East, and the Rosedale Ravine.

GREATER TORONTO

Toronto's wealth of diverse neighborhoods and fascinating attractions caters to most tastes, but explore beyond downtown to find the ethnic enclaves, parks, museums, and attractions that make the Greater Toronto Area (GTA) even more intriguing. Most of these must-sees are accessible by public transportation, although a car would make the journey to some of the more far-flung destinations more convenient.

GETTING HERE AND AROUND

High Park is on the Bloor subway line. Buses run from various downtown subway stations to Edwards Gardens, the Ontario Science Centre, the Toronto Zoo, and Black Creek Pioneer Village. You'll need a car to visit the Kortright Centre for Conservation and the McMichael Canadian Art Collection. A special GO Transit bus serves Canada's Wonderland from May to October.

TIMING

You can explore each Greater Toronto sight independently or combine a couple of sights in one trip. The Ontario Science Centre and Edwards Gardens are very close together, for example, and would make a manageable day trip; and, if you're driving from the city, you could visit Black Creek Pioneer Village and the Kortright Centre for Conservation on the way to the McMichael Canadian Art Collection.

BLOOR WEST VILLAGE

TOP ATTRACTIONS

FAMILY
Fodor's Choice
★
High Park. One of North America's loveliest parks, High Park (at one time the privately owned countryside "farm" of John George Howard, Toronto's first city architect) is especially worth visiting in summer, when the many special events include professionally staged Shakespeare productions. Hundreds of Torontonians and guests arrive at dinnertime

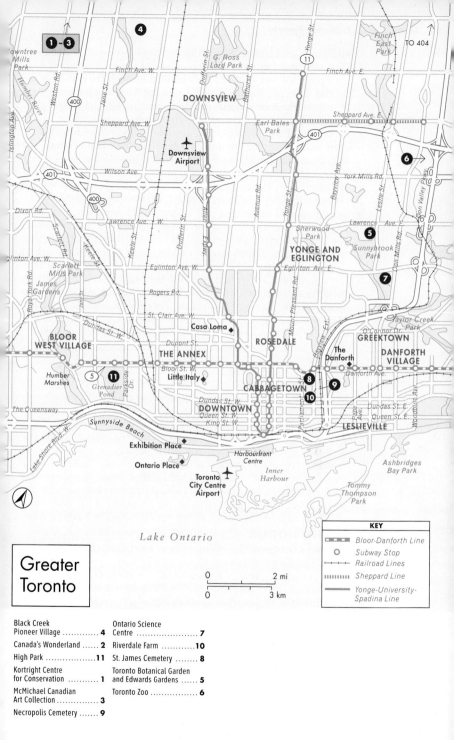

Greater Toronto

Lake Ontario

KEY

▄▄▄ ▄ *Bloor-Danforth Line*

○ *Subway Stop*

⊢⊣⊢⊣ *Railroad Lines*

▥▥▥ *Sheppard Line*

— *Yonge-University-
Spadina Line*

DOWNSVIEW

BLOOR
WEST VILLAGE

THE ANNEX

ROSEDALE

YONGE AND
EGLINGTON

GREEKTOWN

DANFORTH
VILLAGE

CABBAGETOWN

DOWNTOWN

LESLIEVILLE

TO 404

and picnic on blankets before the show. Admission is by donation. Grenadier Pond in the southwest corner of the park is named after the British soldiers who, it's said, crashed through the soft ice while rushing to defend the town against invading American forces in 1813. In summer there are concerts on Sunday afternoons, and there is skating in winter. At the south end of High Park, near Colborne Lodge, is the **High Park Zoo**, which is open daily from dawn to dusk. It's more modest than the Toronto Zoo but a lot closer to downtown and free. Even young children won't tire walking among the deer, Barbary sheep, emus, yaks, llamas, peacocks, and bison. **Colborne Lodge** was built more than 150 years ago by Howard on a hill overlooking Lake Ontario. This Regency-style "cottage" contains its original fireplace, bake oven, and kitchen, as well as many of Howard's drawings and paintings. Other highlights of the 399-acre park are a large swimming pool, tennis courts, fitness trails, and hillside gardens with roses and sculpted hedges. There's limited parking along Bloor Street north of the park, and along the side streets on the eastern side. ■TIP➔ June through August, on the first and third Sunday, free 1½-hour walking tours depart across the street from Grenadier Restaurant. ✉ *Bordered by Bloor St. W, Gardiner Expressway, Parkside Dr., and Ellis Park Rd. Main entrance off Bloor St. W at High Park Ave., Bloor West Village* ☎ *416/392–1748 nature center* ⊕ *www.highpark.org* Ⓜ *High Park.*

CABBAGETOWN

TOP ATTRACTIONS

Riverdale Farm. This spot once hosted the city's main zoo, but it's now home to a rural community representative of a late 19th-century farm. Permanent residents include horses, cows, sheep, goats, pigs, donkeys, ducks, geese, chickens, and a small assortment of other domestic animals. While it's not a petting zoo per se, kids get a real kick out of watching farmers go about their daily chores, which include feeding animals, cleaning the grounds, and bathing the animals. The playground adjacent to the farm has a wading pool. On Tuesday from mid-May to late October, there's a great farmers' market nearby in Riverdale Park. ✉ *201 Winchester St., Cabbagetown* ☎ *416/392–6794* 🎟 *Free.*

WORTH NOTING

Necropolis Cemetery. This nonsectarian burial ground, established in 1850, is the final resting place for many of Toronto's pioneers, including William Lyon Mackenzie, Toronto's first mayor. The cemetery's chapel, gate, and gatehouse date from 1872; the buildings constitute one of the most attractive groupings of small Victorian-era structures in Toronto. ✉ *200 Winchester St., Cabbagetown* ☎ *416/923–7911.*

St. James Cemetery. At the northeast corner of Parliament and Wellesley streets, this cemetery contains interesting burial monuments of many prominent politicians, business leaders, and families in Toronto. The small yellow-brick Gothic Chapel of St. James-the-Less has a handsome spire rising from the church nave and was built in 1861. Now a designated National Historical site, it's still considered one of the most beautiful church buildings in the country. ⊠ *635 Parliament St., Cab-bagetown* ⊕ *www.stjamescemetery.ca.*

NORTH TORONTO

TOP ATTRACTIONS

FAMILY **Ontario Science Centre.** It has been called a museum of the 21st century, but it's much more than that. Where else can you stand at the edge of a black hole or land on the moon? Even the building itself is extraordinary: three linked pavilions float gracefully down the side of a ravine and overflow with exhibits that make space, technology, and communications fascinating. The 25,000-square-foot Weston Family Innovation Centre, rife with hands-on activities, is all about experience and problem solving. Make a music soundtrack, take a lie-detector test, and measure fluctuations in your body chemistry as you flirt with a virtual celebrity. Younger visitors learn through play in KidSpark, a space specially designed for children eight and under to enjoy and explore. The Planetarium, Toronto's only public planetarium, uses state-of-the-art technology to take participants on a trip to the outer reaches of the universe. Demonstrations of papermaking, lasers, electricity, and more take place daily; check the schedule when you arrive. ⊠ *770 Don Mills Rd., at Eglinton Ave. E, North Toronto* ☎ *416/696–1000* ⊕ *www. ontariosciencecentre.ca* ➦ *C$22, parking C$10 (cash only)* Ⓜ *Eglinton, then No. 34 Eglinton East bus to Don Mills Rd. stop; then walk ½ block south.*

FAMILY **Toronto Botanical Garden and Edwards Gardens.** The beautiful 17 contemporary botanical garden areas and adjacent estate garden (once owned by industrialist Rupert Edwards) flow into one of the city's most visited ravines. Paths wind along colorful floral displays and exquisite rock gardens. Refreshments from the café are available, but no pets are allowed. There's also a signposted "teaching garden" for kids to touch and learn about nature. Free general tours between May and early September depart Tuesday at 10 am and Thursday at 6 pm. For a great ravine walk, start at the gardens' entrance and head south through Wilket Creek Park and the winding Don River valley. Pass beneath the Don Valley Parkway and continue along Massey Creek. After hours of walking (or biking or jogging) through almost uninterrupted park, you reach the southern tip of Taylor Creek Park on Victoria Park Avenue, just north of the Danforth. From here you can catch a subway back to your hotel. ⊠ *777 Lawrence Ave. E, entrance at southwest corner of Leslie St. and Lawrence Ave. E, North Toronto* ☎ *416/397–1340, 416/397–4145 tours* ⊕ *www.torontobotanicalgarden.ca* Ⓜ *Eglinton, then bus 54 or 54A.*

OUTLYING SUBURBS

TOP ATTRACTIONS

FAMILY **Canada's Wonderland.** Canada's first theme park, filled with more than 200 games, rides, restaurants, and shops, includes favorite attractions like KidZville, home of Snoopy, Charlie Brown, and the rest of the

The futuristic Ontario Science Centre engages visitors of all ages with hands-on exhibits and workshops.

Peanuts gang; Windseeker, which features 32 301-foot swings; and Sky-hawk, where riders take control of their own cockpit. The Whitewater Bay wave pool, the Black Hole waterslide, and a children's interactive water-play area are all a part of Splash Works, the 20-acre on-site water park. Look for strolling characters and the Fun Shoppe, arcade, and miniature golf. Other entertainment includes concerts, musicals, light shows, fireworks, and cliff divers. ■TIP➔ Order tickets online in advance for discount prices. ✉ 9580 Jane St., Vaughan ☎ 905/832–7000, 905/832–8131 Kingswood Theatre tickets ⊕ www.canadaswon-derland.com ☜ C$63 ⊙ Closed Nov.–late May and weekdays in Sept. and Oct.

McMichael Canadian Art Collection. On 100 acres of lovely woodland in Kleinburg, 30 km (19 miles) northwest of downtown, the McMichael is the only major gallery in the country with the mandate to collect Canadian art exclusively. The museum holds impressive works by Tom Thomson, Emily Carr, and the Group of Seven landscape painters, as well as their early-20th-century contemporaries. These artists were inspired by the wilderness and sought to capture it in bold, original styles. First Nations art and prints, drawings, and sculpture by Inuit artists are well represented. Strategically placed windows help you appreciate the scenery as you view art that took its inspiration from the vast outdoors. Inside, wood walls and a fireplace set a country mood. Free guided tours take place every Saturday and Sunday at 12:30 and 2. ✉ 10365 Islington Ave., west of Hwy. 400 and north of Major Mackenzie Dr., Kleinburg ☎ 888/213–1121, 905/893–1121 ⊕ www.mcmichael.com ☜ C$18, parking C$5.

FAMILY **Toronto Zoo.** With its varied terrain, from river valley to dense forest, the Rouge Valley was an inspired choice of site for this 710-acre zoo in which mammals, birds, reptiles, and fish are grouped according to their natural habitats. Enclosed, climate-controlled pavilions have botanical exhibits, such as the Africa pavilion's giant baobab tree. Daily activities might include chats with animal keepers and animal and bird demonstrations. An "Around the World Tour" takes approximately three hours and includes the Africa, Americas, Australasia, Indo-Malayan, and "Canadian Domain" pavilions. From late April through early September, the Zoomobile can take you through the outdoor exhibit area.

From 2013 until 2018, Er Shun and Da Mao, a pair of Chinese pandas, will call the Toronto Zoo their home. Panda cubs Jia Panpan and Jia Yueyue were born on October 13, 2015, and will stay with mom until they depart Toronto in 2018. In addition to viewing the couple up close, the Panda Interpretive Centre is also worth exploring.

The African Savanna is the country's finest walking safari, a dynamic reproduction that brings rare and beautiful animals and distinctive geological landscapes to the city's doorstep. You can also dine in the Savanna's Safari Lodge and camp overnight in the Serengeti Bush Camp (reservations required). ⊠ *Meadowvale Rd., Exit 389 off Hwy. 401, Scarborough* ☎ *416/392–5929, 416/392–5947 for Serengeti Bush Camp reservations* ⊕ *www.torontozoo.com* ✉ *C$28, parking C$10* ☽ *Closed Jan.–Apr.* Ⓜ *Kennedy, then bus 86A or Don Mills, then bus 85.*

WORTH NOTING

FAMILY **Black Creek Pioneer Village.** Less than a half-hour drive from downtown is a rural, mid-19th-century living-history-museum village that makes you feel as though you've gone through a time warp. Black Creek Pioneer Village is a collection of 40 buildings from the 19th century, including a town hall, a weaver's shop, a printing shop, a blacksmith's shop, and a one-room schoolhouse. The mill dates from the 1840s and has a 4-ton wooden waterwheel that can grind up to a hundred barrels of flour a day.

As men and women in period costumes go about the daily routine of mid-19th-century Ontario life, they explain what they're doing and answer questions. Visitors can see farm animals; take wagon rides, Victorian dance classes, and 19th-century baseball lessons; and explore a hands-on discovery center. There's a great brewery to try or you can book an afternoon tea (reservations required). ⊠ *1000 Murray Ross Pkwy., near intersection of Jane St. and Steeles Ave., North York* ☎ *416/736–1733* ⊕ *www.blackcreek.ca* ✉ *C$15, parking C$7* ☽ *Closed Jan.–Apr.* Ⓜ *Finch, then bus 60 west or Jane, then bus 35.*

Kortright Centre for Conservation. Only 15 minutes north of the city, this delightful conservation center has more than 16 km (10 miles) of hiking trails through forest, meadow, river, and marshland, as well as a renewable energy cottage that demonstrates what life would be like off the grid. In the magnificent woods there have been sightings of foxes, coyotes, rabbits, deer, wild turkeys, pheasants, chickadees, finches, and blue jays. Seasonal events include a spring maple-syrup festival, a Honey Harvest Festival, and a Magical Christmas Forest crafts fair. Nature day camps and day-long energy conservation workshops are offered throughout the year for an extra fee. To get here, drive 3 km (2 miles) north along Highway 400, exit west at Major Mackenzie Drive, and continue south 1 km (½ mile) on Pine Valley Drive to the gate. ✉ *9550 Pine Valley Dr., Woodbridge* ☎ *905/832–2289, 416/667–6295 for workshops and camps* ⊕ *www.kortright.org* 🎫 *C$6.50, special events C$10, parking C$4 (weekends only).*

WHERE TO EAT

Updated
by Natalia
Manzocco

Toronto's calling card—its ethnic diversity—offers up a potent mix of cuisines. But with that base, the city's chefs are now pushing into new territory. It's not enough to have consistently good food; kitchens are now pushed to be creative and embrace food trends from all over the world. Pop-up vendors such as Fidel Gastro's Lisa Marie and Seven Lives Tacos Y Mariscos drew cult followings big enough to open up brick-and-mortar locations, while those offering a more luxurious dining experience keep well-heeled diners on their toes with innovative tasting menus.

Top-notch tacos, tapas, ramen, and Korean fusion eats have all enjoyed trend status, with the best examples of each still packing 'em in night after night. Farm-to-table shows no sign of slowing down, with many menus citing the source of their meats and produce. While Toronto is still young as a foodie travel destination, it's drawing in the crowds, or at a minimum world-famous chefs such as Daniel Boulud and David Chang, who have landed in Toronto with Café Boulud and Momofuku. And as locals will tell you, first come the chefs, then come the savvy foodie travelers, always posting a tweet or photo to Instagram at the city's newest hot spots.

PLANNING

With new restaurants and shops opening up farther away from the downtown core, tourists have a lot more area to cover. We make it easy by sorting restaurants by price, cuisine, and neighborhood. Search our "Best Bets" chart for top recommendations.

DISCOUNTS

For 2½ weeks between January and February, more than 100 of the city's best restaurants offer the **Winterlicious** Program, where a fixed-price, three-course lunch is C$15 to C$25, and dinner is C$25 to C$40, and the regular menu is still served. Similarly, **Summerlicious** runs for around two weeks in July. For more details, see ⊕ *www.toronto.ca/special_events*.

DRESS

With the exception of high-end restaurants, the dining atmosphere in Toronto is generally cool and relaxed, with patrons donning trendy and polished attire. In the more elegant and upscale restaurants, or around the Financial District, men are likely to feel more comfortable wearing a jacket. We mention dress only when men are required to wear a jacket or a jacket and tie.

FESTIVALS

Taste of the Danforth Festival. The annual Taste of the Danforth Festival celebrates the mouthwatering diversity of the city as it welcomes millions to the Danforth strip each August. ⊠ *Toronto* ⊕ *www.tasteofthe-danforth.com*.

Taste of Little Italy. Taste of Little Italy takes place in June on College Street, where Italian-centric cuisine and live music are celebrated. ⊠ *Toronto* ⊕ *www.tasteoflittleitaly.ca*.

MEALTIMES

Lunch typically starts at 11:30 or noon, and dinner service begins around 5:30 or 6. Many restaurants close between lunch and dinner (roughly 2:30 to 5:30). On weekdays, kitchens usually close around 10:30 pm. Late-night dining has become easier to find in recent years, with spots along Queen West and King West and in Chinatown staying open until the wee hours. There are few all-night restaurants in the city. Unless otherwise noted, the restaurants listed in this guide are open daily for lunch and dinner.

RESERVATIONS

Reservations are always a good idea; we mention them only when they're essential or not accepted. Book as far ahead as you can. (Large parties should always call to check the reservations policy.) Many restaurants have lounges and sections for walk-ins only.

SMOKING

Toronto restaurants prohibit smoking, including areas outdoors under an awning or overhang. Some let diners get away with smoking in open-air outdoor dining areas.

TIPPING AND TAXES

There is no hard and fast rule when it comes to tipping; it is optional but customary, and some restaurants include gratuities on the bill for parties of six or more. It's common to leave 15%–20% for standard or good service and 20% or more for exceptional service. If you have brought your own wine or cake for a special occasion, it's proper etiquette to tip more for the extra service. The percentage of tips is generally calculated on the subtotal. Goods and Services Tax and Provincial Sales

Tax were combined into the Harmonized Sales Tax of 13%, meaning the tax on alcohol was lowered, and food and alcohol are no longer taxed separately.

WHAT IT COSTS

Credit cards are widely accepted in Toronto restaurants though some may accept only MasterCard and Visa. Most restaurants also accept debit cards, although smaller establishments, like cafés and takeout spots, might be cash-only.

WHAT IT COSTS IN CANADIAN DOLLARS				
	$	**$$**	**$$$**	**$$$$**
AT DINNER	under C$12	C$12–C$20	C$21–C$30	over C$30

Restaurant prices are the average cost of a main course at dinner or, if dinner is not served, at lunch.

RESTAURANT REVIEWS

Throughout the chapter, you'll see mapping symbols and coordinates (1:F2) after property names or reviews. To locate the property on a map, turn to the Toronto Dining maps within this chapter. The first number after the symbol indicates the map number. Following that are the property's coordinates on the map grid.

Listed alphabetically within neighborhoods.

HARBOURFRONT, ENTERTAINMENT DISTRICT, THE FINANCIAL DISTRICT

HARBOURFRONT

The vibe here is decidedly beachy; take a stroll along the lake, stopping for lunch on one of the breezy patios. If you brought your bathing suit, head to Sugar Beach—an urban oasis where locals sunbathe. Or work off that lunch by renting one of the city's public bikes and pedal around until you're ready for dinner.

$$
✕**Against the Grain Urban Tavern.** Making the most of its proximity to
CANADIAN Cherry Beach, Against the Grain is a sunbathing destination minutes from downtown, with a stellar patio in full sunny view of the lake. Sharable apps like nachos and wings, plus a great craft beer selection, capitalize on the laid-back vibe. Sink your teeth into comfort food mains like red ale mac 'n' cheese, flat-top burgers, or fried chicken sandwiches. $ *Average main: C$18* ⊠ *Corus Building, 25 Dockside Dr., Corus Bldg., Harbourfront* ☎ 647/344–1562 ⊕ *corusquay.atgurbantavern.ca* ⌂ *Reservations essential* Ⓜ *Union* ✚ *2:C6.*

$$$
✕**E11even.** By day, E11even presents steak-house fare for the downtown
AMERICAN business crowd; by night, Air Canada Centre concertgoers and sports fans (not the jerseys-and-face-paint crowd) slide into wooden booths for a refined meal or nightcap. The menu of North American classics

TORONTO DINING BEST BETS

Where can I find the best food the city has to offer? Fodor's writers and editors have selected their favorite restaurants by price, cuisine, and experience. The Fodor's Choice properties represent the "best of the best" across price categories.

CHILD-FRIENDLY

Christina's, $$
Pizza Banfi, $$
Terroni, $$

MOST ROMANTIC

Chabrol, $$$
The Fifth Grill, $$$
La Palette, $$$

Fodor's Choice ★

Alo, $$$$
Bar Raval, $$
Beast, $$
The Black Hoof, $$$
Boralia, $$$
Buca, $$$
Café Boulud, $$$$
Campagnolo, $$$
Canoe, $$$$
Chabrol, $$$
Edulis, $$$$
El Catrin, $$
Foxley, $$
Khao San Road, $$
La Palette, $$$
Lee Garden, $$
Luma, $$$
Mamakas, $$$
Mistura, $$$
Origin, $$$
Porchetta & Co., $
Rose and Sons, $$
Seven Lives Tacos y Mariscos, $
Sotto Sotto, $$$
Tabülè, $$

By Price

$
Burrito Boyz
Market 707
Porchetta & Co.
Salad King
Seven Lives Tacos y Mariscos

$$
Bar Raval
Foxley
Khao San Road
Kinka Izakaya
Live Organic Food Bar
Queen Margherita Pizza

$$$
Allen's
The Black Hoof
Buca
The Gabardine
Globe Bistro
Lamesa
La Palette
Mamakas

$$$$
Alo
Canoe
Edulis
Lai Wah Heen

By Cuisine

CHINESE
Lai Wah Heen, $$$$
Lee Garden, $$
Swatow, $$

FRENCH
Chabrol, $$$
The Fifth Grill, $$$
La Palette, $$$

ITALIAN
Buca, $$$
Mistura, $$$
Sotto Sotto, $$$
Terroni, $$
Zucca, $$$

MODERN CANADIAN
Boralia, $$$
Bymark, $$$$
Canoe, $$$$
Luma, $$$

By Experience

CELEB-SPOTTING
Alo, $$$$
Joso's, $$$$
One, $$$$
Sotto Sotto, $$$

includes savory-sweet maple-glazed bacon, salads flanked with seared tuna, steak frites, and casual fare like kosher beef dogs and lobster rolls. Most impressive is perhaps the 3,200-strong wine list, which diners can browse and choose from via iPad. $ *Average main: C$30* ⊠ *15 York St., Harbourfront* ☎ *416/815–1111* ⊕ *www.e11even.ca* ⊘ *Closed Sun. No lunch Sat.* Ⓜ *Union* ⊹ *1:G6.*

$$$$
STEAKHOUSE

✕ **Harbour Sixty Steakhouse.** Bucking the trend toward relaxed fine dining, Harbour Sixty goes for sheer opulence, the drama of which is apparent from the get-go as you walk up stone steps to the grand entrance of the restored Harbour Commission building. A baroque-inspired foyer leads to a sleek marble bar. On the lower level is the wall-to-wall wine storage, which houses bottles from their 36-page wine list. The kitchen rises to the occasion with starters like the zesty shrimp cocktail. Bone-in rib steak is a specialty, and the fluffy and luscious coconut cream pie is a must-eat dessert. $ *Average main: C$60* ⊠ *60 Harbour St., Harbourfront* ☎ *416/777–2111* ⊕ *www.harboursixty.com* ⊘ *No lunch weekends* Ⓜ *Union* ⊹ *1:G6.*

$$
AMERICAN

✕ **Real Sports Bar & Grill.** Packed with 200 television screens and more than 100 beer taps, Real Sports Bar is a big, bombastic shrine to the world of sports. No matter what game you want to catch—baseball, football, basketball, hockey, or tennis—you'll be able to pull up a seat near a television (the two-story HDTV that dominates the space, if you're lucky) and take in the action. While you're there, nosh on outside-the-box bar eats like actual popcorn chicken (fried chicken bites dusted with crushed buttery popcorn) or smoked ribs braised in soy sauce and lime juice. $ *Average main: C$19* ⊠ *15 York St., Harbourfront* ☎ *416/815–7325* ⊕ *www.realsports.ca* ⌔ *Reservations essential* Ⓜ *Union* ⊹ *1:G6.*

ENTERTAINMENT DISTRICT

This neighborhood seems quiet, but comes to life at night and on weekends when women put on their little black dresses and men don their best button-downs. A row of nightclubs and bars beckon post-dinner. Or, for a more refined evening, catch a show at the theater or head over to the TIFF Bell Lightbox to see what's playing.

$$
INTERNATIONAL
Fodor's Choice
★

✕ **Beast.** In a quiet dining room tucked into the first floor of a house just off King West, this carnivore's mecca serves up dishes such as succulent pork hocks with kimchi and roasted peanuts or duck breast with sheep's milk feta cheese. Pescatarians are well-served, too, with mains like grilled squid tostadas and smoked trout. Brunch fans can dig into maple-bacon doughnuts or the restaurant's signature beastwich: fried chicken, pork sausage gravy, egg, and cheese on a biscuit. $ *Average main: C$14* ⊠ *96 Tecumseth St., King West* ☎ *647/352–6000* ⊕ *www. thebeastrestaurant.com* ⊘ *Closed Sun. and Mon. No lunch Tues.–Thurs.* Ⓜ *St. Andrew* ⊹ *1:C6.*

$$$
ITALIAN
Fodor's Choice
★

✕ **Buca.** With its refreshing roster of stylish Italian classics, Buca may have just spearheaded a boom in trendy dining on this strip of King. Tucked into an alley just off the main drag, the repurposed boiler room has exposed brick walls, metal columns, and wooden tables that reflect the natural philosophy behind the menu. Start with a selection of cured meats including fennel salami, wild boar sausage and duck breast, or

3

nodini, warm bread knots seasoned with rosemary and sea salt. For a simple pasta, order the *lorghittas* , with olives, capers, anchovies, cherries, tomato sauce, and *cacio di fossa* cheese. Wines are meticulously procured from Italy by the sommelier to complement the dishes. Ⓢ *Average main: C$24* ⊠ *604 King St. W, Entertainment District* ☎ *416/865–1600* ⊕ *www.buca.ca* ☾ No lunch Ⓜ Osgoode ✛ 1:C6.

$
MEXICAN

✕**Burrito Boyz.** One of the best places to stuff yourself silly, Burrito Boyz answers the call for rice-filled tortillas stuffed with succulent halibut or hearty steak at all hours. And vegetarians also have options, like soy or sweet potato. Pick your base and pile it on with some of the 17 toppings. The casual eatery is always busy, but it's the most alive in the wee hours of the morning with the post-clubbing crowd looking to refuel and sleep soundly on a full stomach. Ⓢ *Average main: C$8* ⊠ *224 Adelaide St. W, Entertainment District* ☎ 647/439–4065 ⊕ *www. burritoboyz.ca* Ⓜ *St. Andrew* ✛ 1:E6.

$$$$
EUROPEAN
Fodor'sChoice
★

✕**Edulis.** European bistro meets local forager is the theme at Edulis, a restaurant devoted to classic rustic dishes. Bentwood chairs, rough-hewn wood walls, and burlap breadbaskets evoke a farmhouselike feel, and the soft lighting adds to the intimacy. Five- and seven-course tasting menus change daily, with a focus on intricate, often seafood-oriented dishes like fresh scallops with strawberry puree or wild salmon seasoned with spruce. You'll also find all manner of mushrooms, with special menus spotlighting black and white truffles when the rare fungi are in season. Reservations are highly encouraged. Ⓢ *Average main: C$75* ⊠ *169 Niagara St., King West* ☎ *416/703–4222* ⊕ *www.edulisrestaurant.com* ☾ *Closed Mon. and Tues. No lunch Wed.–Sat.* ⌂ *Reservations essential* Ⓜ *St. Andrew* ✛ 1:B6.

$$$
FRENCH

✕**The Fifth Grill.** Enter through the Fifth Social Club, a main-floor dance club, and take a freight elevator to this semiprivate dining club and loft space with the right balance of formality and flirtation. The mood is industrial-strength romance. In winter, sit on a sofa in front of a huge fireplace; in summer, dine on the gazebo terrace. Entrées include a wide variety of steaks, lobster risotto, and rack of lamb with potato gratin. Ask about the daily special bowl of house-made pasta. Ⓢ *Average main: C$30* ⊠ *225 Richmond St. W, Entertainment District* ☎ *416/979–3005* ⊕ *www.thefifthgrill.com* ☾ *Closed Sun.–Wed. No lunch* ⌂ *Reservations essential* Ⓜ *Osgoode* ✛ 1:E5.

$$
THAI
Fodor'sChoice
★

✕**Khao San Road.** Named for a street in Bangkok bursting with nightlife and excellent street eats, Khao San Road lives up to its moniker. The garlic tofu might just be the vegetarian equivalent of chicken nuggets with a sweet-and-sour tamarind dip. For heartier dishes, opt for the *khao soi,* a dish of egg noodles in a rich coconut milk sauce, or try the warming *massaman,* a tamarind-infused curry with peanuts, potatoes, and deep-fried shallots. Ingredients are sourced directly from Thailand wherever possible. Ⓢ *Average main: C$14* ⊠ *11 Charlotte St., Entertainment District* ☎ *647/352–5773* ⊕ *www.khaosanroad.ca* ☾ *No lunch Sun.* ⌂ *Reservations not accepted* Ⓜ *St. Andrew* ✛ 1:E6.

$$$
ASIAN

✕**Lee.** Everyone looks beautiful here, on pink barstools or under the glow of fuchsia Lucite tables surrounded by abacus-like copper screens hung around the dining room. Famed Toronto chef Susur Lee's creations mix Asian and European sensibilities and are appropriately served on handmade plates from mainland China and Hong Kong. Small, perfect dishes like spicy jerk pork ribs that fill your nose with heady aromas, black-pepper-charred tuna sashimi and spicy tartare, and Peking and *char siu* duck with steamed pancake and foie gras all tickle your senses. ⑤ *Average main: C$26* ⊠ *601 King St. W, Entertainment District* ☎ *416/504–7867* ⊕ *www.susur.com/lee* ⊗ *No lunch* ⬧ *Reservations essential* Ⓜ *St. Andrew* ⊕ *1:D6.*

$$$
CANADIAN
Fodor's Choice
★

✕ **Luma.** Duck out of a double-feature at the TIFF Bell Lightbox to grab a meal at Luma. Within the bustling glass-paneled film festival and film education venue, the restaurant is a mini oasis on the second floor complete with a patio overlooking the lively Entertainment District and the CN Tower. But the star attraction is the menu, built on locally sourced ingredients. Start with gochujang-laced octopus, feast on grilled quail or steak with truffle-parm fries, and finish things off with a lemon tart topped with sour cream ice cream. ⑤ *Average main: C$30* ⊠ *330 King St. W, Entertainment District* ☎ *647/288–4715* ⊗ *No lunch Sat. Closed Sun.* Ⓜ *St. Andrew* ⊕ *1:E6.*

$$$
SEAFOOD

✕ **Rodney's Oyster House.** A den of oceanic delicacies, this playful basement raw bar is frequented by solo diners and showbiz types. Among the options are soft-shell steamer clams, a variety of smoked fish, and "Oyster Slapjack Chowder," plus Merigomish oysters from Nova Scotia or perfect Malpeques from owner Rodney Clark's own oyster beds on Prince Edward Island. A zap of Rodney's in-house line of condiments or a splash of vodka and freshly grated horseradish are eye-openers. ■TIP➜ Shared meals and half orders are okay. Be sure to ask about the daily "Grace's soup" and "white-plate" specials. ⑤ *Average main: C$26* ⊠ *469 King St. W, Entertainment District* ☎ *416/363–8105* ⊕ *www.rodneysoysterhouse.com* ⊗ *Closed Sun.* Ⓜ *St. Andrew* ⊕ *1:D6.*

$$$$
CANADIAN

✕ **Toca.** The swanky Ritz Carlton dining experience comes to Toronto in the form of Toca, where diners partake in dishes like caprese with Canadian lobster, lemon risotto with fried sweetbreads, and purple potato gnocchi with smoked Ontario trout. The dining room, a tasteful blend of wood and warm metals, has a curvaceous wood-beamed ceiling and a glass cheese cave. High rollers can sit at the chef's table, inside a private dining nook in the kitchen. The restaurant also caters to business diners with a 30-minute "express" lunch option on weekdays. ■TIP➜ Splurge on the Sunday Market Brunch, which includes a cold seafood station of oysters, shrimp, and lobster, as well as made-to-order omelets and all-you-can-drink mimosas and bellinis. ⑤ *Average main: C$44* ⊠ *181*

TORONTO'S POUTINE

A Québécois classic (traditionally made from french fries, cheese curds, and gravy) is getting dressed up and refined here in Toronto. Modern takes might include pulled pork and other meats, as well as different sauces and ethnic spices. Poutini's House of Poutine (⊕ www.poutini.com), Poutineville (⊕ www.poutineville.com), and Smoke's Poutinerie (⊕ www.smokespoutinerie.com) are restaurants dedicated to it. Caplansky's (⊕ www.caplanskys.com) makes the gravy with their famous smoked meat.

3

Wellington St. W, Entertainment District ☎ *416/572–8008* ⊕ *www. tocarestaurant.ca* ⊗ *No lunch Sat.* Ⓜ *St. Andrew* ⟡ *1:F6.*

$ ✕ **WVRST.** You don't need to wait around until Oktoberfest to drink
GERMAN   great German beer and indulge in delicious bratwurst; just walk into WVRST, a modern beer hall on King West. Choose from a selection of sausages, from the traditional pork to vegetarian, or get a little wild with selections such as pheasant, duck, or bison. And since you're already indulging, be sure to order a pint of one of the 24 craft beers and ciders on tap as well as a side of double-fried duck fat fries. Ⓢ *Average main: C$8* ⊠ *609 King St. W, King West* ☎ *416/703–7775* ⊕ *www. wvrst.com* Ⓜ *St. Andrew* ⟡ *1:D6.*

$$ ✕ **Young Wandee Thailand.** Chef Wandee Young impressed Toronto's taste buds
THAI   when she launched Canada's first Thai restaurant in 1980, and her dishes have stood the test of time. Chicken satay with peanut sauce, Thai-spiced calamari with sweet chili, and refreshing salad rolls are a nice start. Move on to zingy lemon chicken soup and shared mains like green mango salad, red-curry duck breast, spicy basil chicken, and Thai-style eggplant. Ⓢ *Average main: C$12* ⊠ *936 King St. W, King West* ☎ *416/366–8424* ⊕ *www.youngthailand.com* ⊗ *No lunch Sun.* Ⓜ *St. Andrew* ⟡ *1:A6.*

THE FINANCIAL DISTRICT

As one of the city's major employment hubs and the center for business, the Financial District has no shortage of places to eat. Venues cater to all the worker bees, from the assistant out on an espresso run to the executives with large expense accounts. Luckily, these restaurants are also good bets for visitors, too.

$$ ✕ **Beer Bistro.** A culinary tribute to beer, the creative menu here incor-
EUROPEAN   porates its star ingredient in every dish, but in subtle and clever ways without causing a malted-flavor overload. Start the hoppy journey with a taster flight of three draft beers, chosen from almost 20 options, arranged from mild to bold. Follow that with a beer-bread pizza made with oatmeal stout; a mussel bowl, available in five different broths; pulled pork *Primanti* (sandwich); house-smoked pork, or Dragon Stout and Skor ice cream. The warm, modern interior includes an open kitchen, allowing for a peek into the heart of the restaurant. The patio is a joy in summer. Ⓢ *Average main: C$19* ⊠ *18 King St. E, Financial District* ☎ *416/861–9872* ⊕ *www.beerbistro.com* Ⓜ *King* ⟡ *1:G6.*

$$$$ ✕ **Bymark.** Wood, glass, and water create drama in a space anchored
CANADIAN   by a 5,000-bottle wine "cellar" inside a two-story glass column. *Top Chef* Canada judge Mark McEwan has created a refined modern menu showcasing sophisticated seafood dishes, like Newfoundland cod with beluga lentils, and simply prepared meats, like the signature 8-ounce burger with molten Brie de Meaux and grilled porcini mushrooms. The glass-encased bar upstairs oozes extreme comfort and has a good view of the Toronto Dominion Centre Plaza. Ⓢ *Average main: C$40* ⊠ *66 Wellington St. W, Concourse Level, Financial District* ☎ *416/777–1144* ⊕ *www.bymark.mcewangroup.ca* ⊗ *Closed Sun. No lunch Sat.* Ⓜ *St. Andrew* ⟡ *1:G6.*

CLOSE UP

Local Chains Worth a Taste

For those times when all you want is a quick bite, consider these local chains where you're assured of fresh, tasty food and good value.

Burger's Priest: Junk-food faithful flock to this local chain for old-school burgers, fries, and shakes. Their not-so-secret secret menu (find it on their website) features awe-inspiring items like the Four Horsemen of the Apocalypse, a double cheeseburger with two extra veggie patties (fried and cheese-stuffed mushroom caps). ⊕ www.theburgerspriest.com.

Freshii: This is a healthier choice where baseball-capped salad artists get through the lunch rush like a championship team. The interior is all steely white and blond wood, and designer greens and custom-made sandwiches clearly appeal to the masses. The Cobb is a standout. ⊕ www.freshii.com.

Harvey's: Harvey's says it makes a hamburger a beautiful thing, and we agree—whether it's a beef, salmon, or veggie burger. Made-to-order toppings will please even the most discerning kids. The fries are a hit, too. ⊕ www. harveys.ca.

Milestones: Duck into the cool comfort of this very happening

spot for Cajun popcorn shrimp or stone-oven pizza. Spit-roasted half chicken with curly fries and gloriously spicy corn-bread muffins may be the kitchen's best. ⊕ www.milestonesrestaurants.com.

Second Cup: You'll find coffees plain and fancy, as well as flavored hot chocolates, a variety of teas, Italian soft drinks, and nibbles that include muffins, bagels, and raspberry–white chocolate scones. ⊕ www.secondcup.com.

Spring Rolls: Appealing soups and spiced salads, savory noodle dishes, and spring rolls all satiate lunchtime hunger pangs here. ⊕ www.springrolls.ca.

Swiss Chalet Rotisserie and Grill: Children are welcome at this Canadian institution known for its rotisserie chicken and barbecued ribs, in portions that suit every family member. ■ TIP➔ Ask for extra sauce for your french fries. ⊕ www. swisschalet.ca.

Tim Horton's: It never closes, and coffee is made fresh every 20 minutes. Check out the variety of fresh doughnuts, muffins, bagels, and soup-and-sandwich combos. The Canadian Maple doughnut is an obvious front-runner. ⊕ www.timhortons.com.

$$$ ✕ **Cactus Club Cafe.** The Toronto flagship of a Vancouver-based casual
STEAKHOUSE fine dining chain, this massive, modern Financial District spot is all about buzzy luxury. Sprawling over 15,000 feet and decked out with real Basquiat and Warhol paintings, Cactus Club has become the business district's trendiest dining destination. Stellar dishes include extraordinarily rich ravioli topped with sage and truffle butter, and a beef tenderloin duo flanked with pave potatoes. The rooftop deck is outfitted with a retractable roof for a year-round patio experience. $ *Average main: C$22* ⊠ *First Canadian Place, 77 Adelaide St. W, Financial District* ☎ *647/748–2025* ⊕ *www.cactusclubcafe.com* Ⓜ *King* ✛ *1:G6.*

$$$$
CANADIAN
Fodor's Choice
★

✕ **Canoe.** Huge dining-room windows frame breathtaking views of the Toronto Islands and the lake at this restaurant, thanks to a location on the 54th floor of the Toronto Dominion Bank Tower. Begin with dishes like venison tartare with bannock bread and pink peppercorns. Entrées like gin-cured duck with mushrooms and foie gras dumplings nod to both tradition and trend. Classic Canadian desserts such as raisin butter tart round out the exceptional meal. ■ TIP➔ **Book a table at the chef's rail for a close-range prespective on the kitchen's artistry.** ⑤ *Average main: C$44* ✉ *Toronto-Dominion Centre, 66 Wellington St. W, 54th fl., Financial District* ☎ *416/364–0054,* ⊕ *www.canoerestaurant.com* ☾ *Closed weekends* ⚐ *Reservations essential* Ⓜ *King* ✛ *1:G6.*

$$$$
SEAFOOD

✕ **The Chase.** Located on the fifth floor of the historic Dineen Building and overlooking the Financial District, the Chase offers an excellent fine-dining balance of casual and refined. In good weather you can choose to sit on the rooftop patio, but those seated in the elegant Park Avenue–style dining room won't miss out; the marvelous Chambord-style lighting fixtures and the floor-to-ceiling windows provide an equally glamorous setting. The menu, composed of dishes meant for sharing, has a selection of fish flown in fresh daily, available pan-roasted, poached, or in opulent platters layered with shrimp, oysters, and king crab. ⑤ *Average main: C$35* ✉ *10 Temperance St., 5th fl., Financial District* ☎ *647/348–7000* ⊕ *www.thechasetoronto.com* ☾ *Closed Sun. No lunch Sat.* ⚐ *Reservations essential* Ⓜ *King* ✛ *1:G5.*

$$$
INTERNATIONAL

✕ **Drake One Fifty.** While Queen West's Drake Hotel has become synonymous with Toronto's art and nightlife scene, its sister restaurant in the Financial District provides a cool yet clubby luxury dining experience. In a striking space decked out with pop art–inspired murals and understated retro fixtures, chef Ted Corrado presents a wide range of crowd-pleasing fare, including charcuterie, oysters, flavorful pork and shrimp dumplings, steaks and short-rib burgers, and a handful of pizzas. Cocktails are creative and tasty—try the brown butter maple old-fashioned. ⑤ *Average main: C$25* ✉ *150 York St., Financial District* ☎ *416/363–6150* ⊕ *www.drakeonefifty.ca* Ⓜ *Osgoode* ✛ *1:F6.*

$$$
BRITISH

✕ **The Gabardine.** Cozy and unpretentious, this gastro-pub stands out from the other restaurants in the area that cater mostly to those with a corporate AmEx. An airy room of white walls, ceilings, and counters is the backdrop for classics like Cobb and Caesar salads, chicken pot pie, and deviled eggs, plus international flourishes like skirt steak topped with piri piri. Their rich mac and cheese topped with buttery herbed bread crumbs is great comfort food, as is the house-ground sirloin bacon cheeseburger with Thousand Island dressing. ⑤ *Average main: C$22* ✉ *372 Bay St., Financial District* ☎ *647/352–3211* ⊕ *www. thegabardine.com* ☾ *Closed weekends* Ⓜ *Queen* ✛ *1:G5.*

$$$
SEAFOOD

✕ **Pearl Diver.** A laid-back and rustic-chic haunt for seafood lovers steps from the Financial District, Pearl Diver specializes in a global array of oysters. Whether its France, PEI, New Zealand, or Maine, they're all displayed on ice behind the handsome bar (when in season, of course). Big groups can do some damage during the bar's Tuesday night seafood tower specials, or their famed 100 oysters for $100 deal every Thursday. If that's not enough, their excellent trout and the dry-aged beef burger will make you fall for the Pearl Diver hook, line, and sinker. Ⓢ *Average main: C$25* ✉ *100 Adelaide St. E, Financial District* ☎ *416/366–7827* ⊕ *www.pearldiver.to* ⊗ *No lunch Mon.* ▬ *No credit cards* Ⓜ *King* ✢ *1:H6.*

$$ ✕ **Terroni.** Open shelving lined with Italian provisions decorates this cool
ITALIAN pizza joint, but it's the thin-crust pies, bubbled and blistered to perfec-
FAMILY tion, that keep diners coming. The menu suits all pizza lovers—from the simple Margherita to the bombastic Polentona of tomato, mozzarella, fontina, speck (smoked prosciutto), and pine nuts. Daily specials can be hit-or-miss, but desserts—like a warm, oozing round of flourless chocolate cake—are universally delicious. The secluded back patio is lovely in good weather. Ⓢ *Average main: C$19* ✉ *57 Adelaide St. E, Financial District* ☎ *416/504–1992* ⊕ *www.terroni.ca* ⊗ *No lunch Sun.* Ⓜ *Queen* ✢ *1:H6.*

OLD TOWN AND THE DISTILLERY DISTRICT

OLD TOWN

One of the most historic neighborhoods in Toronto, Old Town is home to major landmarks such as the St. James Cathedral and the St. Lawrence Market Building, formerly the home of the province's food terminal where restaurateurs would awaken at the wee hours of the morning to get their hands on the best produce. Today, it is still one of the go-to places to find the season's freshest ingredients.

$$ ✕ **Irish Embassy Pub & Grill.** Popular both with the after-work crowd and
IRISH late-night revelers, this handsome pub is the place for hearty home-made food and a proper pint. The soaring ceilings and columns of mahogany wood make an authentic backdrop for the approachable lineup of imported beers, such as Guinness, Smithwick's, Harp, and Kilkenny, and a good variety of whiskeys and scotches. As for the pub food, the chicken curry is sure to satisfy, as will the lineup of traditional eats like cottage pie and bangers and mash. Ⓢ *Average main: C$19* ✉ *49 Yonge St., Old Town* ☎ *416/866–8282* ⊕ *www.irishembassypub.com* Ⓜ *King* ✢ *1:G6.*

$$$ ✕ **Origin.** A sleek, industrial space of exposed brick, spun-wire lamps,
ASIAN FUSION and charcoal-color upholstery gives a suitably chic backdrop to this
Fodor'sChoice global food bar. Throughout the menu, ingredients are allowed to shine
★ without being overworked, as in the Japanese-style tuna salad with Asian pear, avocado, and spicy ponzu dressing; the fried calamari with pineapple slaw and caramelized peanut sauce; and the showstopping 32-ounce rib eye with chimichurri. Wash it down with clever cocktails like the Jake Gin-enhaal with jasmine-infused gin and a house-made grape syrup. Ⓢ *Average main: C$22* ✉ *107 King St. E, Old Town* ☎ *416/603–8009* ⊕ *www.origintoronto.com* Ⓜ *King* ✢ *1:H6.*

$$ ✕ **PJ O'Brien.** This traditional pub will make you feel like you're in
IRISH Dublin the second you set foot on its wooden floors. And unlike the legions of cookie-cutter imitation Irish pubs, with token Irish beers, phony Irish names, and shamrocks galore, this is the real deal. Tuck into an authentic meal of Irish Kilkenny Ale–battered fish-and-chips, beef and Guinness stew, or corned beef and cabbage, ending with

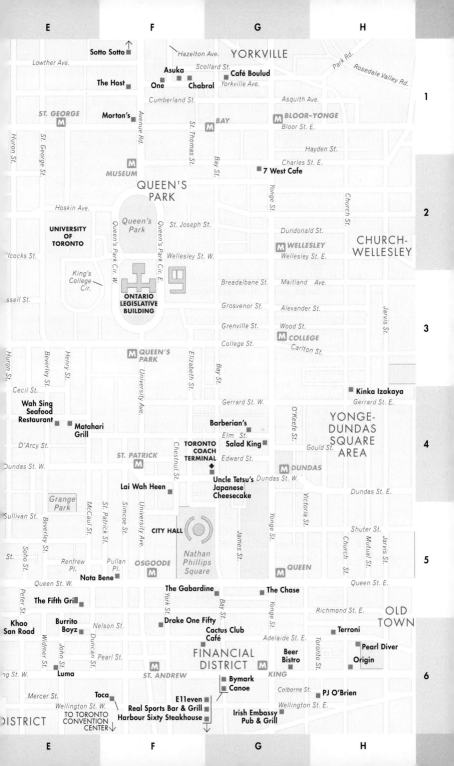

E

Sotto Sotto ■
Lowther Ave.

The Host ■

ST. GEORGE Ⓜ   Morton's ■

Hoskin Ave.

UNIVERSITY
OF
TORONTO

Icocks St.

ssell St.

Huron St.   Beverley St.   Henry St.

Cecil St.

Wah Sing
Seafood
Restaurant ■   ■ Matahari
Grill

D'Arcy St.

Dundas St. W.   ST. PATRICK Ⓜ

Beverley St.   McCaul St.

Grange
Park

Sullivan St.

Soho St.

St.   Renfrew   Pullan
Pl.   Pl.
Queen St. W.   ■ Nota Bene

Peter St.   ■ The Fifth Grill

Khao   Burrito
San Road   Boyz

Widmer St.   John St.   Duncan St.   Nelson St.

Pearl St.

g St. W.   ■ Luma

Mercer St.   ■ Toca

DISTRICT   Wellington St. W.
TO TORONTO
CONVENTION
CENTER ↓

E

F

↑
■ ← Hazelton Ave.
Asuka ■   Scollard St.
■   ■
One   Chabrol
Cumberland St.

Avenue Rd.

St. Thomas St.

MUSEUM Ⓜ

QUEEN'S
PARK

Queen's
Park

Queen's Park Cir. W.   Queen's Park Cir. E.

King's
College
Cir.

ONTARIO
LEGISLATIVE
BUILDING

Ⓜ QUEEN'S
PARK

University Ave.

Elizabeth St.

Chestnut St.

Barberian's ■
Elm   St.
TORONTO   Salad King ■
COACH
TERMINAL
◆   Edward St.

Lai Wah Heen ■

Simcoe St.

St. Patrick St.

CITY HALL

Nathan
Phillips
Square

OSGOODE Ⓜ

The Gabardine ■

York St.

Drake One Fifty ■
Cactus Club
Café ■

FINANCIAL
DISTRICT Ⓜ

ST. ANDREW Ⓜ

Bymark ■
Canoe ■

E11even ■
Real Sports Bar & Grill ■
Harbour Sixty Steakhouse ■

F

G

Hazelton Ave.   YORKVILLE

Café Boulud ■
Yorkville Ave.

BAY Ⓜ

St. Joseph St.

Wellesley St. W.

Breadalbane St.

Grosvenor St.

Grenville St.

College St.

Gerrard St. W.

Bay St.

Yonge St.

Uncle Tetsu's
Japanese
Cheesecake

Dundas St. W.

James St.

The Chase ■

Yonge St.

Cactus Club
Café

Adelaide St. E.

Beer
Bistro ■

Victoria St.

Colborne St.

Irish Embassy
Pub & Grill ■

G

H

Park Rd.   Rosedale Valley Rd.

Asquith Ave.

Ⓜ BLOOR-YONGE
Bloor St. E.

Hayden St.

Charles St. E.
■ 7 West Cafe

Church St.

CHURCH-
WELLESLEY

Dundonald St.

Ⓜ WELLESLEY
Wellesley St. E.

Maitland   Ave.

Alexander St.

Wood St.

Jarvis St.

Ⓜ COLLEGE
Carlton St.

■ Kinka Izakaya
Gerrard St. E.

YONGE-
DUNDAS
SQUARE
AREA

O'Keefe St.

Gould St.

Ⓜ DUNDAS

Dundas St. E.

Shuter St.

Church St.

Mutual St.

Jarvis St.

Ⓜ QUEEN   Queen St. E.

Richmond St. E.   OLD
TOWN

■ Terroni

Toronto St.

■ Pearl Diver

Origin ■

KING Ⓜ

■ PJ O'Brien
Wellington St. E.

H

1

2

3

4

5

6

bread pudding steeped in whiskey and custard, just like Gran made. The bar upstairs is even cozier than the one on the main floor. ⑤ *Average main: C$15* ⊠ *39 Colborne St., Old Town* ☎ *416/815–7562* ⊕ *www.pjobrien.com* ⊘ *Closed Sun.* Ⓜ *King* ✛ *1:H6.*

DISTILLERY DISTRICT

Just a short distance away from Old Town, the Distillery District is a pedestrian-only shopping and dining oasis paved in cobblestone. Here you'll find one-of-a-kind vendors and great alfresco dining options.

$
BAKERY
✕ **Brick Street Bakery.** If the smell of fresh bread and buttery croissants doesn't draw you into this charming bakery, the decadent sweets on display—like the sticky ginger cake loaves, maple-walnut butter tarts, or French macarons—certainly will. For heartier items, opt for a pulled pork sandwich or steak-and-stout pie. ⑤ *Average main: C$4* ⊠ *55 Mill St., Bldg. 45A, Distillery District* ☎ *416/214–4949* ⊕ *www.brickstreet-bakery.ca* Ⓜ *Union* ✛ *2:C5.*

$$
MEXICAN
Fodor's Choice
★
✕ **El Catrin.** With a 5,000-square-foot patio and stunning and vibrant floor-to-ceiling murals by artist Oscar Flores, El Catrin is the hottest place to be in the Distillery District. Delight in the traditional tacos *al pastor* with shaved pork and pineapple salsa, a selection of ceviches, mains like 24-hour braised short rib in mole sauce, or bowls of guacamole (adventurous diners can opt to add flash-fried crickets). Tequila lovers have a long list of options to choose from—served straight up or in a refreshing margarita. Finish the evening on a sugar high with churros rolled in sugar served with a trio of chocolate, strawberry, and dulce de leche dipping sauces. ⑤ *Average main: C$16* ⊠ *18 Tank House La., Distillery District* ☎ *416/203–2121* ⊕ *www.elcatrin.ca* ⚑ *Reservations essential* Ⓜ *Union* ✛ *2:C5.*

$$
INTERNATIONAL
✕ **Mill Street Beer Hall.** One of the best spots to try bier schnapps (a traditional German-style spirit akin to tequila), this modern gastropub features classics with a twist such as beer-brined blackened chicken, duck confit wings, or elk burgers. Fondue is served up with a hot pot of Oka, raclette, Emmental, and Gruyère alongside roasted beets, house-made bratwurst, apples, mini-potatoes, and fresh pretzels. Be sure to grab a spot on the stunning side patio in good weather. ⑤ *Average main: C$20* ⊠ *21 Tank House La., Distillery District* ☎ *416/681–0338* ⊕ *toronto. millstreetbrewpub.ca* Ⓜ *Union* ✛ *2:C5.*

ST. LAWRENCE MARKET

For a great place to nibble and sample a variety of yummy eats, head to the historic **St. Lawrence Market** building, a place where food connoisseurs go to acquire seasonal produce, fancy cuts of meat, and fresh seafood. Those who don't have time to cook can choose from a selection of baked goods like croissants or butter tarts; head to Carousel Bakery to try the iconic peameal bacon sandwich or Buster's Sea Cove for a scrumptious lobster roll.

YONGE-DUNDAS SQUARE AREA

Hailed as Toronto's Times Square, Dundas Square has bright neon screens beaming down the newest fashions and trends. It's also home to one of the city's largest shopping centers, and an array of events on the square ranging from food to film.

$$$$ ✕ **Barberian's.** A Toronto landmark where wheeling, dealing, and lots of
STEAKHOUSE eating have gone on since 1959, Barberian's also has a romantic history: Elizabeth Taylor and Richard Burton got engaged here (for the first time). It's one of the oldest steak houses in the city, and the menu is full of classic dishes like tomato and onion salad and jumbo shrimp cocktail. Mains are all about the meat, be it a perfectly timed porterhouse, New York strip loin, or rib steak. Fresh fish of the day and grilled free-range capon also hold their charms. Barberian's offers a selection of 2,500 labels in its underground two-story wine cellar. Ⓢ *Average main: C$45* ✉ *7 Elm St., Dundas Square Area* ☎ *416/597–0335* ⊕ *www.barberians. com* ⊙ *No lunch weekends* ⌔ *Reservations essential* Ⓜ *Dundas* ✛ *1:G4.*

$$ ✕ **Kinka Izakaya.** When Kinka opened in 2009, it quickly defined the
JAPANESE Japanese izakaya-style dining experience (drinks and small plates) in the minds of Torontonians. It's noisy, rowdy, and ultrafriendly, complete with an open space and communal tables. The salmon *natto yukke* (a mixture of chopped salmon, *natto*, wonton chips, garlic chips, and egg yolk wrapped in crunchy seaweed) makes the introduction to natto (fermented soybeans) a pleasant experience and offers amazing textural differences among its elements. Kinoko cheese *bibimbap* (rice and garlic sautéed mushrooms with seaweed sauce and cheese in a hot stone bowl) take this humble dish to new heights. Choose from an array of sake cocktails to sip. Ⓢ *Average main: C$16* ✉ *398 Church St., Dundas Square Area* ☎ *416/977–0999* ⊕ *www.kinkaizakaya.com* Ⓜ *College* ✛ *1:H4.*

$$$$ ✕ **Lai Wah Heen.** The service is formal in Lai Wah Heen's elegant dining
CHINESE room, topped with a sculpted ceiling and surrounded with etched-glass turntables and silver serving dishes. Here mahogany-color Peking duck is wheeled in on a trolley with fanfare and cut into paper-thin slices. The 100-dish inventory features excellent dishes like wok-fried shredded beef tenderloin with sundried chili peppers alongside delicacies dotted with truffle and foie gras. Dim sum is divine for lunch; translucent dumplings burst with juicy fillings like shrimp, pork, lobster, and seared crab claw. Ⓢ *Average main: C$40* ✉ *Metropolitan Hotel, 108 Chestnut St., 2nd fl., Dundas Square Area* ☎ *416/977–9899* ⊕ *www.laiwahheen. com* ⌔ *Reservations essential* Ⓜ *St. Patrick* ✛ *1:F4.*

$ ✕ **Salad King.** A long-running favorite for local students and shoppers in
THAI need of a pad Thai break, Salad King occupies a gleaming cafeteria-style dining room high above Yonge Street. Mains hover at the $10 mark, including a variety of curries and hefty stir-fries; the house special is a secret menu item, the Islamic noodles, which layers coconut penang curry sauce over a massive platter of noodles and veggies. Test your palate with the spice rating system, which rates the spiciness of a dish on a scale from one to 20 (20 being "may cause stomach upset"). Ⓢ *Average main: C$10* ✉ *340 Yonge St., 2nd fl., Dundas Square Area* ☎ *416/593–0333* ⊕ *www. saladking.com* ▭ *No credit cards* Ⓜ *Dundas* ✛ *1:G4.*

$ ✕**Uncle Tetsu's Japanese Cheesecake.** After this Japanese franchise came to
JAPANESE Canada, people lined up for months to try a bite of these cakes, which
are a little eggier, firmer, and less sweet than your usual New York
variety cheesecakes. It's an acquired taste to some, but still absolutely
worth a sample. The company was so successful, they launched two
sister locations steps from the original café to produce additional specialty treats (and handle the overflow of hungry guests). Next door is the
Matcha Café, home to green tea–flavored cheesecake, fresh-baked mad-
eleines, and soft-serve ice cream. Down the street is the Japanese Angel
Café, a sit-down spot where you can try several cheesecake flavors and
perhaps catch a musical number performed by the maid-uniformed
waitresses. ⑤ *Average main: C$8* ✉ *191 Dundas St. W, Dundas Square
Area* ☎ *591/591–0555* ▭ *No credit cards* Ⓜ *Dundas* ✛ *1:G4.*

CHINATOWN, KENSINGTON MARKET, AND QUEEN WEST

CHINATOWN

While urban sprawl has led to the creation of many mini-Chinatowns in
the city, this is the historic original. University students and chefs alike
gather here for cheap eats and late-night bites. Experience various regional
Chinese cuisines from spicy Szechuan to exotic Cantonese. Or skip brunch
and opt for dim sum—it's a great way to sample Chinese staples.

$$ ✕**Lee Garden.** This Cantonese eatery has print-outs of recommended
CHINESE dishes taped up on its green walls, but no matter what you order, it's
Fodor'sChoice hard to go wrong. Lobster with garlic, ginger, and green onions is
★ a house favorite; the grandfather chicken smoked over oolong tea
leaves is aromatic and moist; and the flash-fried garlic pepper shrimp
is addictive. The place is often packed, so try to go during off-hours
and be prepared for slow-ish service. ⑤ *Average main: C$16* ✉ *331
Spadina Ave., Chinatown* ☎ *416/593–9524* ⊕ *www.leegardenspadina.
ca* ◎ *Closed Mon. No lunch* Ⓜ *St. Patrick* ✛ *1:D4.*

$$ ✕**Matahari Grill.** It's hard to pass up any of the southeast Asian dishes
MALAYSIAN here, so you might use size as a decision-making tool. If you have a taste
for adventure, order the platter for two: a sampling of satays, spring
rolls, deep-fried wontons, shrimp crackers, and *achar achar* (pickled
vegetables in a spicy marinade). Then get into more exotic flavors with
the *sambal udang*—grilled tamarind-scented prawns in sweet, sour, and
spicy tamarind-shallot sauce. In summer there's a tiny outdoor patio,
but most people prefer the sophisticated green-and-white decor inside.
⑤ *Average main: C$16* ✉ *39 Baldwin St., Chinatown* ☎ *416/596–2832*
⊕ *www.mataharigrill.com* ◎ *Closed Sun. No lunch Sat.* ◬ *Reservations
essential* Ⓜ *St. Patrick* ✛ *1:E4.*

$ ✕**Pho Pasteur.** Open 24/7, this is the place to hit when you're having a
VIETNAMESE pho craving. Slurp up a bowl of rice noodles with your choice of beef
cuts (flank, tendon, or tripe); bowls come in three sizes, but a small
should be more than enough for most appetites. For a lighter dish on a
summer day, the shrimp summer rolls with citrus dipping sauce make
a refreshing snack. Or swing by for a soursop milkshake or a cup of
slow-drip Vietnamese coffee; the dark roast sweetened with condensed
milk beats Starbucks every time. ⑤ *Average main: C$10* ✉ *525 Dundas*

St. W, Chinatown ☎ *416/351–7188* 🚫 *No credit cards* Ⓜ *St. Patrick* ✢ *1:D4.*

$$ ✕ **Swatow.** If there is an equivalent to a fast-paced, casual Hong Kong–

CHINESE style diner in Chinatown, this would be it; here you'll find cheap, honest, and authentic food. In bright and clean surrounds, communal diners enjoy heaping bowls of congee and customized noodle soups, including the best fish balls and shrimp dumpling bowls in town. Rice dishes are also a filling specialty, the best of which, *fuk-kin ,* tosses fried rice together with shrimp, crab, scallops, chicken, and egg. The beef fried rice noodles and lo mein are also must-eats. Ⓢ *Average main: C$12* ✉ *309 Spadina Ave., Chinatown* ☎ *416/977–0601* 🚫 *No credit cards* Ⓜ *St. Patrick* ✢ *1:D4.*

$$ ✕ **Wah Sing Seafood Restaurant.** Just one of a jumble of Asian eateries

CHINESE clustered on a tiny street opposite Kensington Market, this meticulously clean and spacious restaurant is beloved for its two-for-one lobster deals. The lobsters are scrumptious and tender, with black-bean sauce or ginger and green onion. You can also choose giant shrimp Szechuan-style or one of the lively queen crabs from the tank. Chicken, beef, and vegetarian dishes are great, too. Ⓢ *Average main: C$17* ✉ *47 Baldwin St., Chinatown* ☎ *416/599–8822* ⊕ *www.wahsing.ca* Ⓜ *St. Patrick* ✢ *1:E4.*

KENSINGTON MARKET

An eclectic mishmash of restaurants and shops makes Kensington Market a popular destination for tourists and locals alike. In true Toronto fashion, it's a melting pot of cuisines from Mexican to French. Locals come to grab a quick bite, but it's also excellent for a leisurely meal.

$ ✕ **Market 707.** The stretch of Dundas Street west of Kensington Market

INTERNATIONAL is a bit on the gritty side, but it's worth venturing through to check out one of the city's most unique sources of cheap eats. Just east of Bathurst is Market 707, a strip of food stalls built out of repurposed shipping containers. Highlights include authentic Montréal poutine and fresh crepes served with a smile at Nom Nom Nom Crepes; Colombian snacks and desserts (including cricket empanadas) at Cookie Martinez; soul-warming Filipino at Kanto by Tita Flips; or enormous skewers of Japanese fried chicken at Gushi. Ⓢ *Average main: C$9* ✉ *707 Dundas St. W, Kensington Market* ✢ *East of Bathurst St.* ☎ *416/392–0335* ⊕ *www.scaddingcourt.org/market_707* ⊗ *Closed Mon.* 🚫 *No credit cards* Ⓜ *St. Patrick* ✢ *1:C4.*

$ ✕ **Otto's Berlin Doner.** A more recent addition to the time-worn mom-

GERMAN and-pop shops of Kensington, Otto's brings a nightlife-worthy spin to street snacks. The owners are former club promoters who fell in love with Berlin's most popular street eats and set about bringing them to Toronto. You can sample shaved meat-stuffed pita wraps, kebabs, and currywurst (sausages sliced and smothered in a ketchuplike curry sauce). Ⓢ *Average main: C$10* ✉ *256 Augusta Ave., Kensington Market* ☎ *647/347–7713* ⊕ *www.ottosdoner.com* Ⓜ *Queen's Park* ✢ *1:D3.*

$ ✕ **Seven Lives Tacos y Mariscos.** Pop-up vendor turned city sensation, this

MEXICAN small taco joint in Kensington Market brings in the crowds. With only

Fodor's Choice 10 seats, Seven Lives doesn't have much space, but most are willing to

★ take the food to go. Bringing the best of SoCal and Tijuana seafood together, the menu features baja fish tacos, *gobernador* tacos (smoked marlin and shrimp), and *camarones a la diabla* tacos (spicy shrimp and cheese). The tacos are made with 100% corn tortillas. Juices include refreshing, unexpected options like cucumber-lime. Ⓢ *Average main: C$9* ⊠ *69 Kensington Ave., Kensington Market* ☎ *416/803–1086* ⊕ *www.sevenlives.ca* ▤ *No credit cards* ⚞ *Reservations not accepted* Ⓜ *St. Patrick* ✛ *1:D4.*

QUEEN WEST

Queen West is a boisterous neighborhood of cafés, organic food shops, galleries, funky clothing stores, and lots of good restaurants at manageable price points. Urban, young, and laid-back bistros line the street, adding to the inviting atmosphere of the area.

\$\$\$\$
FRENCH FUSION
Fodor'sChoice
★

✕**Alo.** The five-course dinners here have breathed new life into the concept of the tasting menu for many Torontonians, thanks to a chef who channels refined French cooking techniques into beautifully composed plates. Past courses from the ever-changing offerings include striped bass with chanterelles and baby artichokes, Nova Scotia lobster tail paired with romesco and shishito peppers, and rack of pork offset with bing cherries, Swiss chard, and a dusting of pistachios. But even something as simple as the bread (*pain au lait* topped with *fleur de sel*) and butter here is memorable. Reservations book up several weeks in advance, but you might get lucky with a seat at the bar, where you can choose from the excellent à la carte menu. Ⓢ *Average main: C$60* ⊠ *163 Spadina Ave., 3rd fl., Queen West* ☎ *416/260–2222* ⊕ *www.alorestaurant.com* ☾ *Closed Sun. and Mon. No lunch* Ⓜ *Osgoode* ✛ *1:D5.*

\$
ASIAN FUSION

✕**Banh Mi Boys.** Brothers David, Philip, and Peter Chau have banh mi in their blood—their parents opened one of the original Vietnamese sandwich shops in Chinatown—but they've taken the classic and decked it out with fillers such as melt-in-your-mouth pork belly, duck confit, and kalbi beef. Other offerings include Asian-inspired tacos and steamed buns. Make the meal complete with a side of kimchi fries—dare we call it Asian poutine? There's a second location at 399 Yonge Street north of Dundas Square. Ⓢ *Average main: C$9* ⊠ *392 Queen St. W, Queen West* ☎ *416/363–0588* ⊕ *www.banhmiboys.com* Ⓜ *Osgoode* ✛ *1:D5.*

\$\$\$
FRENCH
Fodor'sChoice
★

✕**La Palette.** Formerly in Kensington Market, this bright spot moved to the hip and trendy Queen West area, and continues to stake its claim as one of Toronto's truly authentic bistros. The new location goes for simple decor of exposed brick interior and wooden floors and chairs. Game meats are the signature dishes here (horse and venison tenderloin are menu staples), but other favorites include steak frites, duck confit with roasted pearl onions, and many nice wines, including a long list of European choices. A three-course prix fixe is available; it's a great spot for brunch, too. Ⓢ *Average main: C$28* ⊠ *492 Queen St. W, Queen West* ☎ *416/929–4900* ⊕ *www.lapalette.ca* Ⓜ *Osgoode* ✛ *1:D5.*

\$\$\$
PHILIPPINE

✕**Lamesa.** Filipino ex-pats represent one of the biggest ethnic groups in Toronto, and Lamesa showcases the country's flavorful cuisine with style on Queen West. Chef Daniel Cancino gives a modern twist and colorful presentation to classic dishes like *kinilaw* (tuna served ceviche-style with coconut milk) or chicken adobo stewed in soy sauce and vinegar (reimagined here as seared chicken thigh with a soy-vinegar jus and confit garlic). On Sunday evening, Lamesa offers traditional *kamayan* dinners, where diners eat meals served on banana leaves with their hands. $ *Average main: C$22* ✉ *669 Queen St. W, Queen West* ☎ *647/346–2377* ⊕ *www.lamesafilipinokitchen.com* ⊘ *Closed Mon. No lunch weekdays* ⊟ *No credit cards* Ⓜ *Osgoode* ✛ *1:C5.*

$$ ✕ **Lisa Marie.** Beloved food truck Fidel Gastro's brought creative street
INTERNATIONAL food to Queen West, combining Asian street vendor dishes with classic Italian cuisine until the food found a permanent, nonmobile home here at Lisa Marie. The still tasty as ever menu begins with a selection of small plates: zesty nachos topped with white tuna ceviche, veggie-friendly selections like eggplant-goat cheese meatballs, or smoked cauliflower with grilled lemon. The Alabama tailgaters (beef wrapped in smoked bacon and stuffed with cheddar and kimchi) are a must-try. The signature Elvis dessert—layers of peanut butter whipped cream, booze-soaked brioche French toast, and caramelized bacon in an oversized coupe glass—would make even the King of Rock 'n' Roll swoon. $ *Average main: C$20* ✉ *638 Queen St. W, Queen West* ☎ *416/999–6822* ⊕ *www.fidelgastros.com/lisa-marie-main.html* ⊘ *Closed Mon. No lunch Tues.–Fri. No dinner Sun.* Ⓜ *Osgoode* ✛ *1:C5.*

$$$ ✕ **Nota Bene.** Once the first name in Toronto fine dining, Nota Bene
CANADIAN has loosened up ever so slightly over the years, becoming a refined yet approachable spot just as perfect for a cocktail and a snack as for a memorable full meal. The pretheater prix-fixe menu, with options like heirloom beet salad, sea bass, or pappardelle with Bolognese sauce, is available from 5 to 6:30 pm, while luxe bar snacks like porcini mushroom arancini and a slider topped with Ontario beef are just $4 between 4 and 7 pm. $ *Average main: C$29* ✉ *180 Queen St. W, Queen West* ☎ *416/977–6400* ⊕ *www.notabenerestaurant.com* ⊘ *Closed Sun. No lunch Sat.* Ⓜ *Osgoode* ✛ *1:F5.*

$$ ✕ **Oyster Boy.** Whether you get them baked (à la Rockefeller, Rustico, or
SEAFOOD Royale), fried, or raw, oysters are the thing at this casual neighborhood spot. A chalkboard spells out what's fresh and available, along with sizing and prices for each. There's a pleasing array of house condiments with which to slurp up your choices. Other treats include beer-battered fish-and-chips, lobster mac and cheese, and excellent onion rings. A nice selection of wines and beers, as well as cool, friendly servers, makes for a fun night out. $ *Average main: C$20* ✉ *872 Queen St. W, Queen West* ☎ *416/534–3432* ⊕ *www.oysterboy.ca* ⊘ *No lunch* Ⓜ *Osgoode* ✛ *1:A5.*

$$ ✕ **To-ne Sushi.** There's nothing splashy about this sushi spot, but if you're
JAPANESE looking for great sashimi at a reasonable price, you're in the right place. A wide range of apps, noodle dishes, meat entrées, and sushi rolls are also available, including some fun locally themed rolls (like the Sky Dome Roll, a nod to the Rogers Centre's former moniker, which pairs shrimp tempura with Japanese squash). Sashimi boat combos are beautifully presented. $ *Average main: C$15* ✉ *414 Queen St. W* ☎ *416/866–8200* ⊕ *www.tonesushi.com* ⊘ *No lunch Sun.* Ⓜ *Osgoode* ✛ *1:D5.*

EAST AND WEST OF THE CITY CENTER

OSSINGTON

All along this narrow strip you'll find the city's best restaurants in a range of cuisines from classic French to Asian fusion and all manner of other options. It is also a vibrant spot for local bars and watering holes west of the city.

$$$
CANADIAN
Fodor's Choice
★

✕**Boralia.** If you're wondering what exactly Canadian cuisine is, this romantic spot on Ossington offers a unique interpretation, serving a menu derived from recipes left behind by early Canadian settlers. The resulting menu features buttery whelks served in the shell, or pigeon pie stuffed with squab breast. But on the plate, the cooking is profoundly modern; just take a look at the absolutely jaw-dropping bowl of mussels served under a dome of billowing pine needle–scented smoke. ⑤ *Average main: C$30* ⊠ *59 Ossington Ave., Ossington* ☎ *647/351–5100* ⊕ *www.boraliato.com* ☉ *Closed Mon. and Tues. No lunch* Ⓜ *Osgoode* ✛ *2:A5.*

$$
ASIAN FUSION
Fodor's Choice
★

✕**Foxley.** Like the appealingly bare-bones aesthetic of its space (exposed brick, hardwoods, candlelight), this creative bistro offers unadorned dishes that are jammed with flavor. After traveling for a year, chef-owner Tom Thai returned to Toronto with newfound inspiration from places like Asia, Latin America, and the Mediterranean. There are daily ceviches like sea bream or Arctic char, as well as a couple dozen other tapas-style offerings, including spicy blue crab and avocado salad, lamb and duck prosciutto dumplings, and grilled side ribs with sticky shallot glaze. All can be paired with an impressive list of red, white, and sparkling wine, sake and soju, from dry Hungarian Tokaji to a bold Barolo—most modestly priced. ■TIP➜ **The restaurant doesn't take reservations, and it does get busy. Plan accordingly and go early or late.** ⑤ *Average main: C$20* ⊠ *207 Ossington St., Ossington* ☎ *416/534–8520* ☉ *No lunch. Closed Sun.* ⚖ *Reservations not accepted* Ⓜ *St. Patrick* ✛ *2:A5.*

$$$
GREEK
Fodor's Choice
★

✕**Mamakas.** The Danforth might be the epicenter of Greek food in Toronto, but across town on trendy Ossington, Mamakas is doing some of the city's best Greek cooking. In a bright interior meant to subtly recall an Athenian market, snack on classics like rich, creamy tzatziki and roasted eggplant before diving into more creative dishes like goat tartare with mint and chili or braised rabbit with tomato and olive. The seafood is particularly worth ordering, like the grilled octopus or the market-price catch of the day. ⑤ *Average main: C$28* ⊠ *80 Ossington Ave., Ossington* ☎ *647/346–2377* ⊕ *www.mamakas.ca* ☉ *No lunch* 🗐 *No credit cards* Ⓜ *Osgoode* ✛ *2:A5.*

$$
PIZZA

✕**Pizzeria Libretto.** Authentic thin-crust pizzas are fired in an imported wood-burning oven at this pizza joint on the Ossington strip, where the chef adheres to the rules set by Naples's pizza authority. Go classic with the pizza Margherita D.O.P. with San Marzano tomatoes, fresh basil, and local *fior di latte* mozzarella, or branch out with versions topped with *nduja* (spicy salami) or duck confit. ⑤ *Average main: C$16* ⊠ *221 Ossington Ave., Ossington* ☎ *416/532–8000* ⊕ *www.pizzerialibretto. com* ⚖ *Reservations not accepted* Ⓜ *St. Patrick* ✛ *2:A5.*

THE DANFORTH

Historically known as Greektown, The Danforth has gotten an infusion of non-Greek restaurants, which makes for more varied dining options. But you'll still find those classic Greek spots along with local watering holes and busy patios.

$$$ ✕ **Allen's.** Slide into a well-worn wood booth or sit at a blue-and-white-
IRISH checkered table at this New York–style saloon, complete with oak bar and pressed-tin ceiling. If the traditional interior isn't your style, perhaps the famous willow-shaded patio is. Their whiskey selection, at 380 varieties, is one of the best in town; the beer list lags slightly, at 140 options in bottles and 16 or so on draft. The Guinness-braised lamb shanks and the liver and onions get rave reviews, but the hamburgers, ground in-house from a single steer so you can get them as rare as you like, just might be Allen's secret weapon. Desserts come in small portions to offset their extraordinary richness. $ *Average main: C$25* ✉ *143 Danforth Ave., Danforth* ☎ *416/463–3086* ⊕ *www.allens. to* ✍ *Reservations essential* Ⓜ *Broadview* ⊹ *2:C5.*

$$ ✕ **Christina's.** Who doesn't have a foodie love affair with Greek dips?
GREEK Here they're served individually or as a large platter combination that
FAMILY comes with a warm pita. Order a bottle of Greek wine and specials like *saganaki* (an iron plate of Kefalograviera cheese flamed in brandy), and you'll be shouting "*Opa*" with the waiters. The atmosphere is cheery, with the colors of the Aegean Sea and sun on the walls; Greek musicians and belly dancers perform on Friday and Saturday evenings. $ *Average main: C$20* ✉ *492 Danforth Ave., Danforth* ☎ *416/463–4418* ⊕ *www. christinas.ca* Ⓜ *Chester* ⊹ *2:D4.*

$$$ ✕ **Globe Bistro.** The motto here is "Think global. Eat local," and Globe
CANADIAN does justice to this by letting the locally raised main ingredients shine in Canadian-inspired dishes like elk loin with spruce jam and kohlrabi puree. The interior is classy, if a tad dated; weather permitting, you may want to try the swanky rooftop patio. Their weekend brunch menu is particularly noteworthy; meat lovers will spring for the Swine & Dine option featuring pork done seven ways, while those with a sweet tooth will love the French toast stuffed with citrus cream cheese. $ *Average main: C$27* ✉ *124 Danforth Ave., Danforth* ☎ *416/466–2000* ⊕ *www. globebistro.com* ☉ *Closed Mon. No lunch Tues.–Thurs.* Ⓜ *Broadview* ⊹ *2:C4.*

LESLIEVILLE

Just a little east of the city, Leslieville is a quaint neighborhood of great local eateries, pastry shops, and coffee bars. Take a break from bustling downtown and spend an afternoon hopping from boutique stores to bakeries where you can indulge in *pain au chocolat* or cupcakes.

$ ✕ **Leslieville Pumps.** This is the ultimate place to fuel up, and we're not
AMERICAN just talking about the gas tank. Leslieville Pumps is a 24/7, kitschy gas station and general store with a look straight out of a John Wayne western. But—surprise!—it serves some of the best barbecue in town. Slow and low is their cooking philosophy, which they show off in tender pulled pork and brisket sandwiches. Country sides such as BBQ corn salad and Southern coleslaw make the meal complete. $ *Average main:*

C$9 ⊠ 929 *Queen St. E, Leslieville* ☎ 416/465–1313 ⊕ *www.leslievil-lepumps.com* Ⓜ *Pape* ✛ *2:D5.*

$$ ✕ **Queen Margherita Pizza.** One of the best pizza places east of town,
PIZZA Queen Margherita is all about authenticity. Inside this industrial-chic space with dark wooden floors and tables, the Neapolitan pizza oven pumps out selections like the classic Margherita, topped with tomato sauce, mozzarella, and basil; or the Dominator, which features rapini, fennel sausage, smoked mozzarella, and chili oil. Each pizza is cooked quickly at an ultrahigh heat to give it that beautifully blistering crust. Ⓢ *Average main: C$18* ⊠ *1402 Queen St. E, Unit 8, Leslieville* ☎ 416/466–6555 Ⓜ *Pape* ✛ *2:D5.*

$ ✕ **Rashers.** For all things bacon, Rashers has no equal. The full bacon
CANADIAN experience is represented, from the sizzling strips of American to the iconic Canadian peameal. The showstopper is definitely the Hogtown, the ultimate breakfast sandwich made from peameal bacon topped with an egg on a white butter-brushed bun with crunchy ale mustard. Those looking for a bit of English flair can opt for the Bacon Butty, featuring rashers (Irish/British style bacon) with tangy house-made HP-style sauce. Or you can go for a bit of a French flair with the grilled brie and caramelized onion sandwich (plus smoked bacon, naturally). Ⓢ *Average main: C$9* ⊠ *948 Queen St. E, Leslieville* ☎ 416/710–8220 ⊕ *www.rashers.ca* Ⓜ *Pape* ✛ *2:D5.*

$$ ✕ **Tabülè.** Bold Middle Eastern flavors and spices are showcased at
MIDDLE EASTERN Tabülè. Get hands-on as you dip warm flatbread into *babaganüj*
Fodor's Choice (roasted eggplant puree) or hummus. The falafels are fried to a deep
★ golden brown and served with a tahini sauce that's thick and rich. Lamb chops are a must-try, grilled to a perfect medium-rare atop a bed of fragrant and savory rice with vegetables. And if you're feeling a little tired, order a cup of Lebanese coffee—the small cup packs quite the punch. Head to the charming back patio in nice weather, decked out with bench seats and bold pops of orange. Ⓢ *Average main: C$19* ⊠ *810 Queen St. E, Leslieville* ☎ 416/465–2500 ⊕ *www.tabule.ca* Ⓜ *Broadview* ✛ *2:C5.*

QUEEN'S PARK, THE ANNEX, AND LITTLE ITALY

QUEEN'S PARK

Steps away from the busy shopping hub that is Bloor/Yorkville, Queen's Park is also home to the provincial parliament. Pair your lunch with a public tour and learn about the province's political makeup or visit the Royal Ontario Museum.

$$ ✕ **7 West Cafe.** No late-night craving goes unsatisfied at this 24-hour
ECLECTIC haven for the hip and hungry. Snacks, pastas, sandwiches, soups, and drinks are all served in this eclectic, three-story, dimly lit café. Everything is homemade and comes with a green salad. Soups like Moroccan or vegetarian chili are comforting and filling, and dinner-size sandwiches like the grilled herbed chicken breast with honey mustard are huge. The menu of basic foods sets the tone for simple wine, beer, and cocktail choices. Ⓢ *Average main: C$15* ⊠ *7 Charles St. W, Queen's Park* ☎ 416/928–9041 ⊕ *www.7westcafe.com* Ⓜ *Bloor-Yonge* ✛ *1:G2.*

THE ANNEX

The Annex caters to a winning mix of students, professors, historic homes, and treed spaces, a kind of bookish kaffeeklatsch amid the hubbub of the city. Come here for everything from authentic fish-and-chips to a thriving new restaurant row along Harbord Street.

$ ✕ **Future Bakery & Café.** Aside from European-style baked goods, this
CAFÉ   spot also serves old-world recipes like borscht, buckwheat cabbage rolls, and potato-cheese pierogi slathered with thick sour cream. It's a place beloved by the pastry-and-coffee crowd, students wanting great value, and people-watchers, from early morning until late at night. Health-conscious foodies looking for fruit salad with homemade yogurt and honey get their sweet fix, while those who like to indulge can order a slice from the dozen or so cakes on display in the pastry case. $ *Average main: C$10* ⊠ *483 Bloor St. W, The Annex* ☎ *416/922–5875* ⌲ *Reservations not accepted* Ⓜ *Spadina* ✛ *1:C1.*

$$ ✕ **Live Organic Food Bar.** The sunny decor will charm you, but the real
VEGETARIAN   appeal here lies with the imaginative (and enthusiastic) owners, and the amazing raw foods they create. A manicotti of cashew-dill ricotta, cherry tomatoes, cashew Parmesan, and zucchini noodles is a crowd favorite. Satisfy Mexican food cravings with refried bean enchiladas with almond mole and faux sour cream, or go for a stir-fry with sweet potato noodles, tofu, and a host of veggies. A long list of freshly squeezed juices is also served. $ *Average main: C$16* ⊠ *264 Dupont St., The Annex* ☎ *416/515–2002* ⊕ *www.livefoodbar.com* Ⓜ *Spadina* ✛ *1:C1.*

$$ ✕ **Rose and Sons.** Located inside a gently restored greasy spoon on
DINER   Dupont Street, Rose & Sons strives to satisfy your comfort food
FAMILY   cravings with reimagined diner fare like Caesar salad (here, griddled
Fodor's Choice   romaine with toscano cheese and asparagus) and patty melts, with Chi-
★   nese fried rice, grilled cornbread, and an impressive 10-piece bucket of buttermilk chicken thrown in. Out back is Big Crow, a BBQ restaurant that serves camping-inspired dishes on an all-weather patio. $ *Average main: C$18* ⊠ *176 Dupont St., The Annex* ☎ *647/748–3287* ⊕ *www. roseandsons.ca* Ⓜ *Dupont* ✛ *1:D1.*

LITTLE ITALY

Some of the city's best pastas and pizzas are served up in Little Italy, a place where chefs still strive to reproduce the taste of Nonna's cooking. Specialties like charcuterie and ceviche have local followings, as do the quaint patios and neighborhood bakeries.

$$ ✕ **Bar Raval.** Inside a breathtaking room swathed in undulating waves
SPANISH   of wood, you'll find Bar Raval, a tapas restaurant known for some
Fodor's Choice   marvelous food and drink. Stop in for breakfast and pick a *pintxo*
★   (a single-serving Spanish snack, often served on a skewer) or two off the bar, feast on house-smoked tins of seafood and miniature blood sausage–egg toasts for a full meal, or stop in late for a nightcap. The all-weather patio helps alleviate the crush in the standing-only dining room considerably. $ *Average main: C$20* ⊠ *505 College St., Little Italy* ⊕ *www.thisisbarraval.com* Ⓜ *Queen's Park* ✛ *1:C3.*

$$$ ✕ **BENT.** With its gleaming white floor tiles and bench seating, BENT
SEAFOOD feels like a school cafeteria abuzz with twentysomethings looking to
catch up on the latest gossip. Vintage Pachinko machines line the walls
alongside a great selection of sakes, and childhood figurines are dis-
played like a meticulous collector's show-and-tell. Feast on the day's
selections from the raw bar, whether its sashimi, oysters, or tuna-water-
melon ceviche, or indulge in one of the fusion creations, like lump crab
tacos or sundried tomato-crusted scallops with yuzu-dressed butter-
nut squash. ⑤ *Average main: C$25* ✉ *777 Dundas St. W, Little Italy*
☎ *647/352–0092* ⊕ *www.bentrestaurant.com* ☾ *Closed Sun. No lunch.*
⌲ *Reservations essential* Ⓜ *St. Patrick* ✛ *1:C4.*

$$$ ✕ **The Black Hoof.** A typical evening in this narrow nose-to-tail cuisine
CANADIAN hot spot features exotic meats, creative cocktails, and the ability to
Fodor's Choice see the cooks hard at work at the tiny stove to the left of the bar. The
★ house-made charcuterie plates can feature anything from venison *bresaola* (air-dried, salted meat) and duck prosciutto to seal salami. Other
house specialties include tongue on brioche, smoked sweatbreads, and
horse tartare, a first for many in Toronto and not available in the United
States. Even if you don't order wine, the list is worth perusing for the
quirky bottle descriptions. ⑤ *Average main: C$25* ✉ *928 Dundas St.
W, Little Italy* ☎ *416/551–8854* ⊕ *www.theblackhoof.com* ▬ *No credit
cards* ☾ *Closed Tues. and Wed. No lunch* ⌲ *Reservations not accepted*
Ⓜ *St. Patrick* ✛ *1:B4.*

$$$ ✕ **Campagnolo.** Serving its Italian grandmother–inspired cooking in a
ITALIAN cozy space of wooden tables and gold-leaf striped walls, Campagnolo
Fodor's Choice is one of the most praised restaurants in Toronto. Start with fresh
★ burrata cheese and roasted grapes on crusty bread—the perfect play
of sweet and savory. Lovers of curious cuts can opt for the roasted
bone marrow with oxtail marmalade and plums, but traditional pasta
dishes also satisfy. ⑤ *Average main: C$25* ✉ *832 Dundas St. W, Little
Italy* ☎ *416/364–4785* ⊕ *www.campagnolotoronto.com* ☾ *No lunch*
⌲ *Reservations essential* Ⓜ *St. Patrick* ✛ *1:B4.*

$$$$ ✕ **Chiado.** It's all relaxed elegance here, beginning with the fine selection
PORTUGUESE of appetizers at Senhor Antonio Tapas and Wine Bar, and continu-
ing through the French doors to the polished wood floors and plum
velvet armchairs of the dining room. The exquisite fish, which form
the menu's base, are flown in from the Azores and Madeira. Grilled
octopus, grouper, and salted cod are standard, while market price spe-
cials may include monkfish or *peixe espada* (scabbard fish). Traditional
Portuguese dishes include *assorda,* in which seafood is folded into a
thick, custardlike soup made with bread and eggs. But there's much for
meat eaters, too—like a roasted rack of lamb that sparkles with Douro
wine sauce. ⑤ *Average main: C$45* ✉ *864 College St. W, Little Italy*
☎ *416/538–1910* ⊕ *www.chiadorestaurant.com* ☾ *No lunch weekends*
⌲ *Reservations essential* Ⓜ *Ossington, Queen's Park* ✛ *2:A5.*

$ ✕ **Porchetta & Co.** Specializing in, you guessed it, porchetta, this spot
ITALIAN perfects what is considered by many a labor of love for Italian cooks.
Fodor's Choice First, pork shoulder is marinated for 24 hours, then it's wrapped in
★ slices of prosciutto and bacon, then slow-roasted in an oven to get a
crispy crackling skin. Eat it piled on a bun with rapini, truffle mayo,

and Parmesan, or you can even skip the bun entirely. There isn't much sitting room (it's more of a lunch counter), so call ahead and grab your meal to go. Ⓢ *Average main: C$8* ✉ *825 Dundas St. W, Little Italy* ☎ *647/352–6611* ⊕ *www.porchettaco.com* ▭ *No credit cards* ⊘ *Closed Sun. and Mon.* Ⓜ *St. Patrick* ✛ *1:C4.*

YORKVILLE AND CHURCH-WELLESLEY

YORKVILLE

3

Home to the rich and fabulous, Yorkville is the prime spot for celebrity sightings, especially during the Toronto International Film Festival. Posh bars and lively patios all provide a chance to do a little people-watching, and sample some of the city's best high-end cuisine.

$$
SUSHI
✕ **Asuka.** Among expensive and often pretentious establishments, this sunken space stands out for its simplicity and coziness, and proves that celebrity spotting and fine Asian cuisine are not exclusive to upscale restaurants. You won't find any avant-garde dishes here, but you will find well-crafted and fresh sushi and sashimi at a reasonable price. Ⓢ *Average main: C$20* ✉ *108 Yorkville Ave., Yorkville* ☎ *416/975–9084* Ⓜ *Bay* ✛ *1:F1.*

$$$$
FRENCH
Fodor's Choice
★
✕ **Café Boulud.** Spearheaded by world-renowned restaurateur Daniel Boulud, Café Boulud occupies the coveted dining room of the Four Seasons Toronto and presents itself as a serene, airy French brasserie decked out with sage-green banquettes and gilded accents. Boulud does simple French fare, executed perfectly, like steak tartare tossed tableside with gaufrette chips, duck confit, and mouthwatering rotisserie chicken on a bed of crisp-skinned potatoes. The celebrated chef still has a little fun with international touches like a Middle Eastern-spiced grilled kale salad and a grapefruit-and-halva frozen dessert. Ⓢ *Average main: C$34* ✉ *60 Yorkville Ave., Yorkville* ☎ *416/963–6000* ⊕ *www.cafeboulud.com/toronto/* Ⓜ *Bay* ✛ *1:G1.*

$$$
FRENCH
Fodor's Choice
★
✕ **Chabrol.** Sequestered down a pedestrian walkway in the heart of Yorkville, this jewel box–like spot oozes romance. In the minuscule, wide-open kitchen, diners can crane their necks as the chef turns out gratins, bouillabaisse, and parchment-wrapped whitefish that's brought to your table with choreographed grace. The apple tart, baked to order and smothered in apple-brandy cream, is a must. Ⓢ *Average main: C$30* ✉ *90 Yorkville Ave., Yorkville* ☎ *416/428–6641* ⊕ *www.chabrolrestaurant.com* Ⓜ *Bay* ✛ *1:F1.*

$$
INDIAN
✕ **The Host.** Dine in the garden room among flowering plants or in the handsome dining room at this well-established curry spot while waiters rush around carrying baskets of hot naan. The menu of tandoor-cooked entrées, spanning from lobster and shrimp to mustard-marinated whitefish and chicken coated in green chili paste, is particularly noteworthy. End your meal with classic Indian desserts like *golabjabun*, little round cakes soaking in rosewater-scented honey. Ⓢ *Average main: C$17* ✉ *14 Prince Arthur Ave., Yorkville* ☎ *416/962–4678* ⊕ *www.welcometohost.com* ⊘ *No lunch Mon.* ⬧ *Reservations essential* Ⓜ *Bay* ✛ *1:F1.*

$$$$
SEAFOOD
✕ **Joso's.** Artistic *objets*, sensuous paintings of nudes and the sea, and signed celebrity photos line the walls at this two-story seafood

institution that might catch you off-guard with its eccentricity. The kitchen prepares dishes from the Dalmatian side of the Adriatic Sea, and members of the international artistic community who frequent the place adore the unusual and healthy array of seafood and fish. The black risotto with squid, served in a sharable portion size, is a must, as are the grilled prawns lashed with lemon garlic butter. $ *Average main: C$36 ⊠ 202 Davenport Rd., Yorkville* 🕾 *416/925–1903* ⊕ *www.josos. com* ☙ *Closed Sun. No lunch Sat.* Ⓜ *Dupont* ✛ *2:B4.*

$$$
ITALIAN
Fodor's Choice
★

✕ **Mistura.** The combination of comfort and casual luxury here has made Mistura a Yorkville staple. The menu features a modern Italian flair with dishes like beef carpaccio flanked by truffled peaches, while lamb ribs are glazed with balsamic vinegar and served with mint-flecked yogurt. Daily whole fish is a carefully thought-out triumph. Vegetarians are given their due with signature dishes like beet risotto. $ *Average main: C$30 ⊠ 265 Davenport Rd., Yorkville* 🕾 *416/515–0009* ⊕ *www. mistura.ca* ☙ *Closed Sun. No lunch* Ⓜ *Dupont* ✛ *2:B4.*

$$$$
STEAKHOUSE

✕ **Morton's.** This international chain, which calls the Park Hyatt its home in Toronto, is all about classic steakhouse fare in a handsomely clubby atmosphere. Rib eyes, porterhouse, and filet mignon are all there, plus peppercorn and Cajun-spiced variations. All beef is aged for 23 to 28 days and shipped in chilled, not frozen. Round things out with oysters Rockefeller, baked escargot, or ultrarich au gratin potatoes. On weeknights, check out their menu of affordable bar snacks, like mini-filet mignon sandwiches and short-rib steak tacos. $ *Average main: C$50 ⊠ 4 Avenue Rd., Yorkville* 🕾 *416/925–0648* ⊕ *www.mortons.com/ toronto* ☙ *No lunch* Ⓜ *Bay* ✛ *1:F1.*

$$$$
INTERNATIONAL

✕ **One.** In the buzzing Hazelton Hotel, One has become a celeb-spotting free-for-all during September's Film Festival, and has of the hippest patio scenes any time of year. The modern and elegant dining room— rich woods, smoked glass, cowhide, and onyx—is the brainchild of designer Yabu Puschelberg, and thankfully the food lives up to all the razzle-dazzle. Korean-spiced chicken tacos and miso-glazed black cod share menu space with Moroccan chicken and branzino with salsa verde and olive tapenade. But the exceptional house-aged beef tenderloin is all from Prince Edward Island, and the all-Canadian cheese lineup also does the home country proud. $ *Average main: C$40 ⊠ The Hazelton Hotel Toronto, 118 Yorkville Ave., Yorkville* 🕾 *416/961–9600* ⊕ *www. one.mcewangroup.ca* ⌲ *Reservations essential* Ⓜ *Bay* ✛ *1:F1.*

$$$
ITALIAN
Fodor's Choice
★

✕ **Sotto Sotto.** This Southern Italian hideaway has been a magnet for visiting celebrities and well-heeled Yorkville locals alike since the early '90s, and these days if hip-hop megastar Drake is in town, you'll likely find him holding court in a private dining room. The dozen or so pasta options, including freshly made gnocchi, are reliably excellent, but the menu of grilled seafood, spanning Dover sole to scallops to calamari, is also a standout. $ *Average main: C$30 ⊠ 120 Avenue Rd., Yorkville* 🕾 *416/962–0011, 416/962–0011* ⊕ *www.sottosotto.ca* ☙ *No lunch Sun.* Ⓜ *Bay* ✛ *1:F1.*

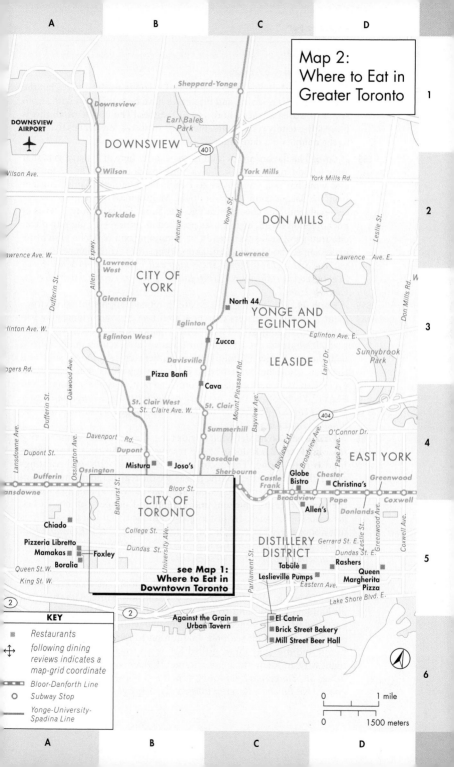

A   B   C   D

1

DOWNSVIEW
AIRPORT
✈

Downsview

Downsview

Earl Bales
Park

DOWNSVIEW

401

Wilson Ave.

Wilson

York Mills

York Mills Rd.

2

awrence Ave. W.

Yorkdale

Lawrence
West

Avenue Rd.

Yonge St.

DON MILLS

Leslie St.

Lawrence   Ave. E.

Don Mills Rd.

W

Allen Expwy.

CITY OF
YORK

Glencairn

Lawrence

North 44

YONGE AND
EGLINTON

Eglinton Ave. E.

LEASIDE

Laird Dr.

Sunnybrook
Park

3

linton Ave. W.

Dufferin St.

Eglinton West

Eglinton

Zucca

Davisville

Pizza Banfi

Cava

Mount Pleasant Rd.

gers Rd.

Oakwood Ave.

Dufferin St.

St. Clair West
St. Claire Ave. W.

St. Clair

Summerhill

Bayview Ave.

404

Bayview Ext.

Broadview Ave.

O'Connor Dr.

Pape Ave.

EAST YORK

4

Lansdowne Ave.

Ossington Ave.

Davenport   Rd.

Dupont St.

Dupont

Rosedale

Sherbourne

Mistura   Joso's

Dufferin

Ossington

Bathurst St.

Bloor St.

CITY OF
TORONTO

University Ave.

Castle
Frank

Globe
Bistro

Broadview

Chester

Pape

Christina's

Allen's

Donlands

Greenwood

Leslie St.

Greenwood Ave.

Coxwell

Coxwell Ave.

ansdowne

2

College St.

Dundas   St.

see Map 1:
Where to Eat
in Downtown
Toronto

Parliament St.

DISTILLERY
DISTRICT

Gerrard St. E.

Dundas St. E.

Tabülè

Leslieville Pumps

Eastern Ave.

Rashers

Queen
Margherita
Pizza

Lake Shore Blvd. E.

5

Chiado

Pizzeria Libretto
Mamakas
Boralia

Foxley

Queen St. W.

King St. W.

Against the Grain
Urban Tavern

El Catrin

Brick Street Bakery

Mill Street Beer Hall

0   1 mile

0   1500 meters

6

GREATER TORONTO

YONGE AND EGLINTON

This neighborhood used to be a haven for young professionals, but the demographic is evolving and briefcases have been replaced with strollers, as the area attracts more young families. The upside of all this is more kid-friendly restaurants. But there are also a few venues that cater to the couple on a date night.

$$$
SPANISH
✕ **Cava.** The flavors are as loud as the chatter here at Cava, a gem that truly is hidden, as it's tucked away on a plaza terrace. This restaurant and wine bar is a great place to experience regional Spanish cuisines from the Basque country to Catalonia. Make a meal out of pintxo skewers—valdeon blue cheese with figs, the Super Gilda with two types of anchovies on bread, or foie gras poached in gamay— or dig into duck-chestnut stew, veal sweetbreads, or a stunning pan of paella with little-neck clams, chorizo, chicken, and shrimp from Argentina. ⑤ *Average main: C$22* ✉ *1560 Yonge St., Yonge and Eglinton* ☎ *416/979–9918* ⊕ *www.cavarestaurant.ca* ⊘ *No lunch* ⚄ *Reservations essential* Ⓜ *St. Clair* ✛ *2:B4.*

$$$$
CANADIAN
✕ **North 44.** The lighting here creates a refined, sophisticated environment, and the appetizers match: seared foie gras with blueberry brioche and shaved hearts of palm with asparagus tips awaken your taste buds. It's hard to choose from the creative and exciting main courses, including five-spice buffalo tenderloin, herb-crusted Dover sole, and roasted Cornish hen with morels. The sprawling global wine list ensures every dish has a perfect glass to complement it. ⑤ *Average main: C$40* ✉ *2537 Yonge St., 4½ blocks north of Eglinton Ave., Yonge and Eglinton* ☎ *416/487–4897* ⊕ *north44.mcewangroup.ca* ⊘ *Closed Sun. No lunch* Ⓜ *Eglinton* ✛ *2:C3.*

$$
ITALIAN
FAMILY
✕ **Pizza Banfi.** No matter what day or time, there's usually a line for two reasons: Pizza Banfi doesn't take reservations, and the classic Italian food is really good. The decor is slightly cliché, with wall paintings over light-color bricks, but the pizzas are the real attraction here. Thin-crust pies are tossed in full view, then baked with aplomb, especially the popular pesto, chicken, and roasted red pepper combo. Pastas, generously portioned, are just as good, and the stellar Caesar salad tops just about every table. ⑤ *Average main: C$15* ✉ *333B Lonsdale Rd., Yonge and Eglinton* ☎ *416/322–5231* ⊘ *Closed Sun.* ⚄ *Reservations not accepted* Ⓜ *Eglinton West* ✛ *2:B3.*

$$$
ITALIAN
✕ **Zucca.** This classic Italian joint delivers the purest made-from-scratch Italian food in a modern, sleek, and friendly room. The wine list of more than 150 labels, all Italian varieties, is beautifully paired with the pasta, all handmade and hand-rolled. Options include semolina pasta with basil and fresh peperoncino, ricotta gnocchi with crispy prosciutto, and squid-ink pasta with seafood. In addition to meat dishes like braised rabbit and muscovy duck, grilled fish is a specialty here. Finish your night with an Amaretto crème caramel. ⑤ *Average main: C$24* ✉ *2150 Yonge St., Yonge and Eglinton* ☎ *416/488–5774* ⊕ *www.zuccatrattoria.com* ⊘ *No lunch* ⚄ *Reservations essential* Ⓜ *Eglinton* ✛ *2:C3.*

WHERE TO STAY

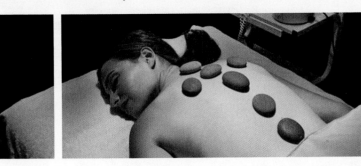

Updated
by Natalia
Manzocco

Given that more than 100 languages and dialects are spoken in the Greater Toronto area, it's not surprising that much of the downtown hotel market is international-business-traveler-savvy. But these same ore hotels are close to tourist attractions—Harbourfront and the Toronto Islands, the cavernous Rogers Centre, the Air Canada Centre, the Four Seasons Centre for the Performing Arts, and the Royal Ontario Museum.

Not wanting to miss out on potential customers, hotels like the Chelsea have instituted perks for the younger set, such as complimentary milk and cookies, kid-size bathrobes, and children's day camp. Another key trend in Toronto's downtown lodgings is the emergence of small, upscale boutique hotels, such as the Hotel Le Germain, the Pantages and Cosmopolitan hotels, and the swank SoHo Metropolitan. An explosion of ultraluxe chains has struck Toronto in recent years, and the city now boasts outposts of Shangri-La, Ritz-Carlton, Trump International, and the Four Seasons.

City-center accommodations are usually within a few minutes' walk of Yonge Street and the glittering lights of the Entertainment District, the soaring office towers of the Financial District, the shops of the Dundas Square Area, and the bars and art galleries of Queen West. Within a 15-minute drive west of downtown are the forested High Park and the meandering Humber River, an area where there are few major hotels but an ample array of B&Bs and the lovely Old Mill Inn. The buzzy West Queen West area has some unique places to stay, such as the restored Gladstone and Drake hotels, as well as funky restaurants and galleries. Lester B. Pearson International Airport is 29 km (18 miles) northwest of downtown; airport hotels are airport hotels, but staying in this area also means quick connections to areas beyond, such as Niagara Falls.

PLANNING

Where should you stay? With hundreds of Toronto hotels, it may seem like a daunting question. But fret not—our expert writers and editors have done most of the legwork. The 50-plus selections here represent the best the city has to offer—from the best budget motels to the sleekest boutique hotels.

RESERVATIONS

Hotel reservations are a necessity—rooms fill up quickly, so book as far in advance as possible. The city's rising profile as a tourist destination has caused hotel rates in the city core to jump dramatically in recent years. If a major event is taking place downtown, it's not uncommon for hotel rates (especially downtown) to take a huge leap, reaching into the mid-three figures per night. Summer is the busiest time, and if you plan on visiting during the Pride Festival (late June), Caribbean Carnival Toronto (late July), or Toronto International Film Festival (September), note that hordes of visitors will be joining you in search of a room, especially anywhere in the downtown area. At these times it doesn't hurt to search farther afield, but look for places along the subway lines to the north, west, or east, unless you have a car.

FACILITIES

Unless otherwise noted in individual descriptions, all the hotels listed have private baths, central heating, and private phones. Almost all hotels have Wi-Fi and phones with voice mail. Most large hotels have video or high-speed checkout capability, and many can arrange babysitting.

Driving a car in Toronto can be a headache unless your hotel provides free parking (which is extremely rare outside of airport hotels). Downtown hotel parking can cost up to $50 per day, and street-side parking isn't available in most neighborhoods, but many city-owned parking lots have favorable rates on weekends and holidays.

WITH KIDS

Many of the downtown chain hotels offer free stays for kids under 12, but it would be best to check in advance when making reservations. Bed-and-breakfasts won't impose any rules against bringing children, but they will be considerably less accommodating. In recent years, boutique hotels have begun to embrace the "family-friendly" philosophy, and many now offer welcoming gifts for little ones such as cookies or teddy bears. *In the listings, look for the "Family" tag, which indicates a property that we recommend for when you're traveling with children.*

DISCOUNTS AND DEALS

When booking, remember first to ask about discounts and packages. Even the most expensive properties regularly reduce their rates during low-season lulls and on weekends. If you're a member of a group (senior citizen, student, auto club, or the military), you may also get a deal. Downtown hotels regularly have specials that include theater tickets, meals, or museum passes. It never hurts to ask for these kinds of perks up front.

WHERE SHOULD I STAY?

	Neighborhood Vibe	Pros	Cons
Harbourfront and the Financial District	This tourist hub includes the towering skyscrapers of the Financial District, and the many activities of Harbourfront.	Good eats in the historic Distillery District, close to island escapes in Lake Ontario, and surrounded by the city's top attractions.	Quiet at night and a bit removed from the action of Toronto's livelier neighborhoods.
Old Town	Toronto's first buildings crowd this leafy area, which extends to the historic Distillery District.	The St. Lawrence Market is here, and for a bustling night scene, you can hit the Esplanade.	Some streets can be sketchy or attract a noisy party crowd.
Dundas Square Area	Dundas Square, Toronto's hottest new events center, faces the mammoth Eaton Centre shopping mall.	These areas have a festival-like atmosphere, and patios teem at sunset.	Things can get slightly sketchy late at night, and there aren't many noteworthy restaurants in the immediate vicinity.
Yorkville	Upscale Yorkville houses the priciest boutiques and is a short walk from Canada's largest gay community on Church Street.	Always busy and lively, and teeming with locals.	Yorkville can be painfully expensive.
Queen West	Funky boutiques, cutting-edge design shops, and experimental restaurants and hotels.	This area sets the trends in Toronto, the restaurants and bars attract diverse clientele, and the Queen Street streetcar is frequent and runs 24 hours.	The area's bar scene can make things noisy late at night, parking options are few, and the trend factor can make it tough to get a room.

PRICES

The lodgings we list are the best in each price category. Properties are assigned price categories based on the price of a standard double room during Toronto's busy summer season. When pricing accommodations, always ask what's included and what costs extra.

Many hotels that cater to business travelers cut rates for weekends, and these hotels typically have special packages for couples and families. Toronto hotels usually slash rates a full 50% in January and February. Smaller hotels and apartment-style accommodations downtown are also moderately priced (and, therefore, popular in summer).

WHAT IT COSTS IN CANADIAN DOLLARS			
$	$$	$$$	$$$$
For two people under C$150	C$150–C$250	C$251–C$350	over C$350

Prices are for two people in a standard double room in high season, excluding service and 13% hotel tax.

HOTEL REVIEWS

Listed alphabetically within neighborhoods.

Throughout the chapter, you'll see mapping symbols and coordinates (F2) after property names or reviews. To locate the property on a map, turn to the Where to Stay Toronto map within this chapter. The numbers after the symbol indicate its coordinate on the map grid.

Hotel reviews have been shortened. For full information, visit Fodors.com.

HARBOURFRONT, ENTERTAINMENT DISTRICT, AND FINANCIAL DISTRICT

HARBOURFRONT

Situating yourself here is a good idea for exploring the greatest concentration of Toronto's must-see attractions—especially the kid-friendly ones—like the Rogers Centre, Ontario Place, and the CN Tower.

$$$ **Delta Hotel Toronto.** Just steps from the Rogers Centre, CN Tower,
HOTEL and Ripley's Aquarium (as well as the waterfront), the Delta Toronto offers rooms with some great views. **Pros:** connected to the PATH, convention center, and Union Station; modern decor and clean, spacious rooms; attentive staff. **Cons:** Internet for streaming video or heavy data use requires extra charge; parking is expensive and can fill up quickly. ⑤ *Rooms from: C$309* ✉ *75 Lower Simcoe St., Harbourfront* ☎ *416/849–1200, 888/890–3222* ⊕ *www.deltatoronto.com* ⌖ *541 rooms* ⧩ *Breakfast* ⊟ *No credit cards* Ⓜ *Union* ✣ *E6.*

$$$ **Le Germain Hotel Maple Leaf Square.** Inside the Maple Leaf Square complex, this ultrastylish hotel is perfectly poised to receive traffic from the
HOTEL Air Canada Centre across the street and the Rogers Centre just minutes away. **Pros:** great service; attached to PATH network; near Billy Bishop Toronto City Airport. **Cons:** area is boisterous when events are happening at nearby Air Canada Centre. ⑤ *Rooms from: C$296* ✉ *75 Bremner Blvd., Harbourfront* ☎ *416/649–7575, 888/940–7575* ⊕ *www.germainmapleleafsquare.com* ⌖ *167 rooms* ⧩ *Breakfast* Ⓜ *Union* ✣ *E6.*

$$$ **Radisson Hotel Admiral Toronto–Harbourfront.** You can't get much closer
HOTEL to Toronto's waterfront than at this hotel, where unobstructed Lake
FAMILY Ontario and verdant Toronto Islands vistas come standard. **Pros:** easy access to local attractions; excellent views. **Cons:** quiet and seems out of the way in winter and spring; prices getting higher and higher. ⑤ *Rooms from: C$309* ✉ *249 Queen's Quay W, at York St., Harbourfront* ☎ *416/203–3333, 800/395–7046* ⊕ *www.radisson.com* ⌖ *157 rooms* ⧩ *No meals* Ⓜ *Union* ✣ *E6.*

$$$ **Westin Harbour Castle.** On a clear day you can see the skyline of Roch-
HOTEL ester, New York, across the sparkling blue Lake Ontario from most
FAMILY rooms at this mid-range, kid-friendly hotel. **Pros:** very comfortable beds; great kids' programs; pet-friendly. **Cons:** not right in downtown; hotel can feel overwhelmingly large; decor is dated. ⑤ *Rooms from: C$349* ✉ *1 Harbour Sq., at Bay St., Harbourfront* ☎ *416/869–1600, 866/716–8101* ⊕ *www.westinharbourcastletoronto.com* ⌖ *977 rooms* ⧩ *No meals* Ⓜ *Union* ✣ *F6.*

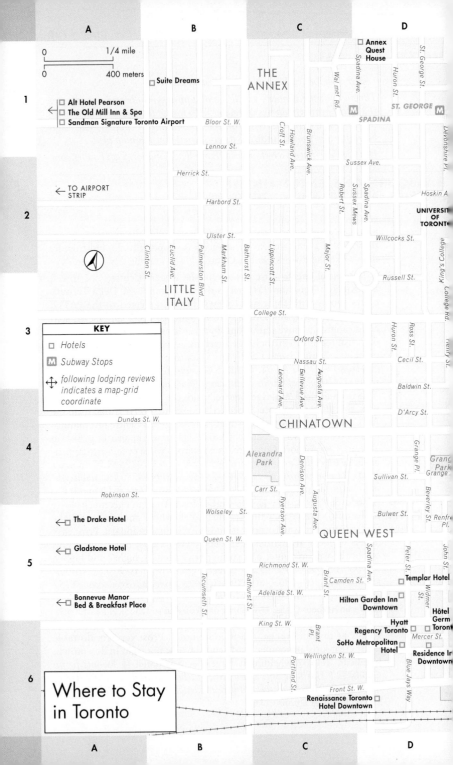

Where to Stay in Toronto

A

0 _____ 1/4 mile
0 _____ 400 meters

□ Alt Hotel Pearson
← □ The Old Mill Inn & Spa
□ Sandman Signature Toronto Airport

← TO AIRPORT STRIP

KEY

□ Hotels

Ⓜ Subway Stops

⬦ following lodging reviews indicates a map-grid coordinate

Robinson St.

← □ The Drake Hotel

← □ Gladstone Hotel

← □ Bonnevue Manor Bed & Breakfast Place

Clinton St.
Euclid Ave.
Palmerston Blvd.
Markham St.

LITTLE ITALY

B

□ Suite Dreams

Bloor St. W.

Lennox St.

Herrick St.

Harbord St.

Ulster St.

College St.

Dundas St. W.

Wolseley St.

Queen St. W.

Tecumseth St.

Bathurst St.

Richmond St. W.

Adelaide St. W.

King St. W.

Portland St.

Wellington St. W.

Front St. W.

C

THE ANNEX

Wal mer Rd.
Croft St.
Howland Ave.
Brunswick Ave.

Sussex Ave.

Robert St.
Sussex Mews

Lippincott St.

Major St.

College St.

Oxford St.

Nassau St.

Leonard Ave.
Bellevue Ave.
Augusta Ave.

CHINATOWN

Alexandra Park

Carr St.

Denison Ave.

Ryerson Ave.

Augusta Ave.

QUEEN WEST

Spadina Ave.
Brant St.
Camden St.

Brant St.
Brant Pl.

Hilton Garden Inn Downtown

Hyatt Regency Toronto □

SoHo Metropolitan Hotel □

Renaissance Toronto □ Hotel Downtown

D

□ Annex Quest House

Spadina Ave.
Huron St.
St. George St.

Ⓜ ST. GEORGE Ⓜ

SPADINA

Devonshire Pl.

Hoskin A

UNIVERSIT OF TORONT

Willcocks St.

Russell St.

King's College Rd.
College Rd.
Henry St.

Huron St.
Ross St.
Cecil St.

Baldwin St.

D'Arcy St.

Grange Pl.

Gran Park Grange

Sullivan St.

Beverley St.

Bulwer St.

Renfre Pl.

Peter St.
John St.

□ Templar Hotel

Widmer St.

Hôtel Germ Toront □

Mercer St.

Residence In Downtown □

Blue Jays Way

THE ENTERTAINMENT DISTRICT

It's hard to imagine the quiet, empty-looking warehouses in the Entertainment District spontaneously exploding with activity, but when the sun goes down this neighborhood is party central. The bustle and excitement generated by Toronto's clubbers, theatergoers, and night owls keep the action alive until 3 am most nights.

$$$
HOTEL
Hilton Garden Inn Downtown. Like the downtown entertainment hub that surrounds it, this hotel pulses with activity around the clock. **Pros:** central downtown location; excellent service. **Cons:** some rooms can get noisy due to nearby nightclub; pool and gym on the smaller side. $ *Rooms from: C$329* ⊠ *92 Peter St., Entertainment District* 📞 *416/593–9200* ⊕ *hiltongardeninn.hilton.com* ⮑ *224 rooms* ❖│*No meals* Ⓜ *Osgoode, St. Andrew* ✛ *D5.*

$$$
HOTEL
Hilton Toronto. With everything that you'd expect from a Hilton, this central outpost near the Entertainment and Financial Districts is decorated in golds and browns in the lobby with wooden floors and subtle earth tones. **Pros:** across the street from the Four Seasons Centre for the Performing Arts; popular on-site Ruth's Chris Steak House; connected to PATH. **Cons:** rooms can be small; service lags at times; Wi-Fi complimentary only in executive rooms. $ *Rooms from: C$289* ⊠ *145 Richmond St. W, at University Ave., Entertainment District* 📞 *416/869–3456, 800/267–2281* ⊕ *www.hilton.com* ⮑ *648 rooms* ❖│*No meals* Ⓜ *Osgoode* ✛ *E5.*

$$$$
HOTEL
Fodor'sChoice
★
Hôtel Le Germain Toronto. The retro, redbrick exterior of this chic hotel—conveniently located near the TIFF Bell Lightbox, site of the Toronto International Film Festival—blends seamlessly with the historic architecture of the surrounding theater district. **Pros:** complimentary continental breakfast; attentive staff; putting green and outdoor terrace on 11th floor. **Cons:** rooms fill up fast; things can get noisy on weekends. $ *Rooms from: C$375* ⊠ *30 Mercer St., at John St., Entertainment District* 📞 *416/345–9500, 866/345–9501* ⊕ *www.germaintoronto.com* ⮑ *122 rooms* ❖│*Breakfast* Ⓜ *St. Andrew* ✛ *D6.*

$$$
HOTEL
Hyatt Regency Toronto. Request views of the CN Tower at this luxury hotel smack in the middle of the pulsating Entertainment District. **Pros:** closest large hotel to King Street West theaters; dozens of excellent restaurants and cinemas nearby. **Cons:** rooms can be small; guest rooms on lower floors facing King Street may be noisy. $ *Rooms from: C$269* ⊠ *370 King St. W, Entertainment District* 📞 *416/343–1234, 800/633–7313 in U.S.* ⊕ *www.torontoregency.hyatt.com* ⮑ *426 rooms* ❖│*No meals* Ⓜ *St. Andrew* ✛ *D6.*

$$$
HOTEL
InterContinental Toronto Centre. Attached to the Metro Toronto Convention Centre, this large but unassuming hotel is a good bet for visiting businesspeople, but leisure travelers can also find deals on weekends or during slow periods. **Pros:** atypical convention hotel; bright and airy lobby restaurant; pet-friendly. **Cons:** no shopping nearby; expensive parking. $ *Rooms from: C$280* ⊠ *225 Front St. W, west of University Ave., Entertainment District* 📞 *416/597–1400, 877/660–8550* ⊕ *www.torontocentre.intercontinental.com* ⮑ *576 rooms* ❖│*No meals* Ⓜ *Union* ✛ *E6.*

$$ 🏨 **Renaissance Toronto Hotel Downtown.** This is the world's only hotel
HOTEL completely integrated into the Rogers Centre, a massive sports and
FAMILY entertainment dome that serves as the home of the Toronto Blue Jays.
Pros: likable staff; parking charges not as steep as some other area
hotels; guest rooms best place to watch Blue Jays baseball games. **Cons:**
little natural light in guest rooms overlooking field; rooms and common
spaces can feel dated. ⓢ *Rooms from: C$229* ⊠ *1 Blue Jays Way, at
Front St. W, Entertainment District* 🕾 *416/341–7100, 800/237–1512*
⊕ *www.renaissancetoronto.com* ⟿ *348 rooms* ⦿ *No meals* Ⓜ *Union*
✛ *D6.*

$$$$ 🏨 **Residence Inn Downtown.** A big hit with families and long-term visi-
HOTEL tors to Toronto, the modern suites at the Residence Inn come with
FAMILY full kitchens, spacious living and dining rooms, and comfortable bed-
Fodor'sChoice rooms. **Pros:** close to Toronto's major attractions; a smart choice for
★ large families; no minimum stay. **Cons:** valet parking only; breakfast
buffet gets extremely crowded during peak season. ⓢ *Rooms from:
C$359* ⊠ *255 Wellington St. W, at Windsor St., Entertainment Dis-
trict* 🕾 *416/581–1800* ⊕ *www.residenceinn.marriott.com* ⟿ *256 suites*
⦿ *Breakfast* Ⓜ *Union* ✛ *D6.*

$$$$ 🏨 **Shangri-La Toronto.** This hotel embodies the attention to service for
HOTEL which the Shangri-La brand is known while putting an art-focused
Fodor'sChoice twist on its traditional East-meets-West aesthetic. **Pros:** stellar service
★ and ambience; noted art collection; luxurious amenities and excellent
dining on-site. **Cons:** pricey. ⓢ *Rooms from: C$455* ⊠ *188 University
Ave., Entertainment District* 🕾 *647/788–8888* ⊕ *www.shangri-la.com/
toronto/shangrila* ⟿ *202 rooms* ⦿ *No meals* Ⓜ *Osgoode, St. Andrew*
✛ *E5.*

$$$ 🏨 **Sheraton Centre.** Views from this hotel in the city center are marvel-
HOTEL ous—to the south are the CN Tower and the Rogers Centre; to the
north, both new and old city halls. **Pros:** underground access to PATH
network; pool open late; walk to Four Seasons Centre for Performing
Arts, shopping, and restaurants. **Cons:** expensive parking and Internet;
hotel is overwhelmingly large. ⓢ *Rooms from: C$309* ⊠ *123 Queen St.
W, at Bay St., Entertainment District* 🕾 *416/361–1000, 866/716–8101*
⊕ *www.sheratontoronto.com* ⟿ *1,377 rooms* ⦿ *No meals* Ⓜ *Osgoode*
✛ *E5.*

$$$$ 🏨 **SoHo Metropolitan Hotel.** Saturated in pampering detail, the SoHo
HOTEL Met conjures luxury with Frette linens, down duvets, walk-in closets,
marble bathrooms with heated floors, and Molton Brown bath products. **Pros:** no detail left to chance, including electric do-not-disturb
signs and curtains; stylish but not showy. **Cons:** lap pool only 3-feet
deep; located slightly away from main streets. ⓢ *Rooms from: C$435*
⊠ *318 Wellington St. W, east of Spadina Ave., Entertainment District*
🕾 *416/599–8800, 866/764–6638* ⊕ *www.soho.metropolitan.com* ⟿ *91
rooms* ⦿ *No meals* Ⓜ *St. Andrew* ✛ *D6.*

$$ 🏨 **Templar Hotel.** A small boutique hotel nestled into the Entertainment
HOTEL District, Templar offers compact and sleekly designed rooms outfitted
with floor-to-ceiling windows, platform beds, and open-concept bath-
rooms with rain showerheads. **Pros:** award-winning decor; unique din-
ing experience. **Cons:** minimalist rooms may seem uninviting to some;

service occasionally hit-or-miss. ⑤ *Rooms from: C$249* ⊠ *348 Adelaide St. W, Entertainment District* ☎ *416/479–0847* ⊕ *www.templarhotel. com* ⤺ *27 rooms* ❚◎❙ *No meals* ▬ *No credit cards* Ⓜ *St. Andrew* ✥ *D5.*

FINANCIAL DISTRICT

While the sidewalks are brimming with suits and cell phones during the day, this area really quiets down after the sun sets. On the weekend, it can feel almost eerie. Still, there are a few notable attractions here that appeal to diverse palettes, such as the Hockey Hall of Fame and the Design Exchange.

$$$ ⌸ **Cambridge Suites.** With just 12 suites per floor, this self-dubbed bou-
HOTEL tique hotel focuses on service: rooms are cleaned twice daily, and there's same-day dry cleaning and laundry, a rooftop gym with a view (and a whirlpool), and complimentary Wi-Fi. **Pros:** central location; social hour with discounted drinks at on-site bar; late checkout. **Cons:** four-guest-per-room maximum is strictly enforced by the hotel. ⑤ *Rooms from: C$297* ⊠ *15 Richmond St. E, at Victoria St., Financial District* ☎ *416/368–1990, 800/463–1990* ⊕ *www.cambridgesuitestoronto.com* ⤺ *229 suites* ❚◎❙ *No meals* Ⓜ *Queen* ✥ *F5.*

$$ ⌸ **Cosmopolitan Toronto Hotel.** Tucked away on a side street in the heart of
HOTEL Toronto, this überboutique, all-suite hotel seamlessly blends a modern Eastern aesthetic with apartment-style amenities. **Pros:** central location; hipness factor; friendly staff. **Cons:** side streets dark at night; recent construction has blocked out lake views. ⑤ *Rooms from: C$234* ⊠ *8 Colborne St., at Yonge St., Financial District* ☎ *416/350-2000, 888/388–3932* ⊕ *www.cosmotoronto.com* ⤺ *95 suites* ❚◎❙ *No meals* Ⓜ *King* ✥ *F6.*

$$$$ ⌸ **Fairmont Royal York.** Like a proud grandmother, the Royal York stands
HOTEL serenely on Front Street in downtown Toronto, surrounded by gleaming skyscrapers and the nearby CN Tower. **Pros:** lots of history; excellent health club (lap pool, whirlpool, saunas, well-appointed gym, and more); steps from Union Station. **Cons:** rooms can be small; charge for in-room Internet access; expensive parking. ⑤ *Rooms from: C$499* ⊠ *100 Front St. W, at York St., Financial District* ☎ *416/368–2511, 866/540–4489* ⊕ *www.fairmont.com/royalyork* ⤺ *898 rooms* ❚◎❙ *No meals* Ⓜ *Union* ✥ *E6.*

$$$ ⌸ **Hotel Victoria.** A local landmark built in 1909, "the Vic" is Toronto's
HOTEL second-oldest hotel, with a long-standing reputation for excellent service. **Pros:** 24/7 gym privileges at nearby health club; stylish rooms; upgraded rooms feature extras like complimentary newspapers and Apple TV/Netflix. **Cons:** inconvenient, off-site parking; second-floor rooms noisy from street. ⑤ *Rooms from: C$259* ⊠ *56 Yonge St., at Wellington St., Financial District* ☎ *416/363–1666, 800/363–8228* ⊕ *www. hotelvictoria-toronto.com* ⤺ *56 rooms* ❚◎❙ *No meals* Ⓜ *King* ✥ *F6.*

$$$ ⌸ **One King West Hotel & Residence.** Made up entirely of suites, this 51-story
HOTEL tower is attached to the old Dominion Bank of Canada (circa 1912) in the city's downtown business and shopping core. **Pros:** great views from upper floors; central location; excellent service. **Cons:** charge for Wi-Fi; parking is expensive and valet-only. ⑤ *Rooms from: C$309* ⊠ *1 King St. W, at Yonge St., Financial District* ☎ *416/548–8100, 866/470–5464* ⊕ *www.onekingwest.com* ⤺ *340 suites* ❚◎❙ *No meals* Ⓜ *King* ✥ *F6.*

$$$$ 🏨 **Ritz-Carlton, Toronto.** This Ritz has a great location—across from
HOTEL Roy Thompson Hall and smack-dab in the center of the Financial District—and a solid elegance, embellished with a Canadian motif of brass maple leaves and local woods. **Pros:** reliable Ritz service; top-of-the-line amenities; large rooms. **Cons:** five-star prices; expensive valet parking. ⑤ *Rooms from: C$469* ✉ *181 Wellington St. W, Financial District* ☎ *416/585–2500* ⊕ *www.ritzcarlton.com/toronto* ⌁ *319 rooms* ⑪ *No meals* Ⓜ *St. Andrew, Union* ✛ *E6.*

$$$$ 🏨 **Trump International Hotel & Tower Toronto.** Though the Trump's status
HOTEL as a hot spot for the local glitterati has cooled somewhat since its 2012 opening, the 65-story hotel/condo tower is still a popular draw for visitors looking to soak up a little luxury. **Pros:** luxurious, tastefully decorated rooms; attentive service; little extras abound, like electric fireplaces and heated bathroom floors. **Cons:** area gets quiet at night; business-oriented; valet-only parking. ⑤ *Rooms from: C$565* ✉ *325 Bay St., Financial District* ☎ *416/306–5800, 855/878–6700 reservations* ⊕ *www.trumphotelcollection.com/toronto* ⌁ *261 rooms* ⑪ *No meals* Ⓜ *St. Andrew, Osgoode* ✛ *F5.*

OLD TOWN

A pleasant mix of Toronto's oldest buildings, modern coffee shops and restaurants hiding behind historic redbrick facades, and newish condo developments, staying in this evolving neighborhood puts you near some of the city's oldest landmarks, such as the St. Lawrence Market, the historic Distillery District, and St. James Cathedral.

$$$ 🏨 **Grand Hotel and Suites.** A gorgeous 30-foot facade leads into a lobby
HOTEL of gleaming marble and granite pillars peppered with plush furnishings. **Pros:** great proximity to Eaton Centre and Yonge St.; friendly staff; striking pool facilities. **Cons:** area is a bit sketchy, especially at night; some fixtures are a little worn. ⑤ *Rooms from: C$349* ✉ *225 Jarvis St., Old Town* ☎ *416/863–9000, 877/324–7263* ⊕ *www.grandhotel-toronto.com* ⌁ *177 suites* ⑪ *Breakfast* Ⓜ *Dundas* ✛ *G4.*

$$ 🏨 **Novotel Toronto Centre.** A good-value, few-frills, modern hotel, the
HOTEL Novotel is in the heart of the animated, bar-lined Esplanade area, near the St. Lawrence Market, the Air Canada Centre, Union Station, and the Entertainment District. **Pros:** excellent location; solid value; great breakfast buffet. **Cons:** small in-hotel parking spaces; spotty service and housekeeping; neighborhood can get noisy. ⑤ *Rooms from: C$199* ✉ *45 The Esplanade, at Church St., Old Town* ☎ *416/367–8900* ⊕ *www.novotel.com* ⌁ *262 rooms* ⑪ *No meals* Ⓜ *Union* ✛ *F6.*

$$$ 🏨 **The Omni King Edward Hotel.** Toronto's landmark "King Eddy" Hotel,
HOTEL which has hosted the well-heeled for over a century, continues to be a favorite choice for special occasions and a nod to grand hotels of the past. **Pros:** great location; mix of historic charm with modern luxury; friendly service. **Cons:** parking is expensive and valet-only; high daily Internet fee. ⑤ *Rooms from: C$309* ✉ *37 King St. E, east of Yonge St., Old Town* ☎ *416/863–9700, 888/444–6664* ⊕ *www.thekingedward-hotel.com* ⌁ *301 rooms* ⑪ *No meals* Ⓜ *King* ✛ *G6.*

Toronto Lodging Alternatives and Resources

APARTMENT RENTALS
If you want a home base that's roomy enough for a family and comes with cooking facilities, consider a furnished rental.

Airbnb. Most of Toronto's bed-and-breakfasts or long-term stay apartments use this site for booking. If you're on a budget, you'll also find average Torontonians renting out their spare rooms or temporarily empty apartments. ⊕ www.airbnb.com.

BED-AND-BREAKFASTS
Au Petit Paris. A great alternative to big chain hotels in this area, this B&B (which sadly no longer offers breakfast) is southeast of Yorkville, west of the Church Wellesley district, and north of the Dundas Square neighborhood. ✉ 3 Selby St., Church–Wellesley ☎ 416/928–1348 ⊕ www.aupetitparis.ca ⟿ 2 rooms ⦿ No meals Ⓜ Sherbourne.

By the Park B&B. This B&B is the brainchild of a couple who happen to be alumni of the Ontario College of Art and Design; their attention to design is evident. ✉ 92 and 89 Indian Grove, at Bloor St. W, Greater Toronto ☎ 416/520–6102 ⊕ www.bythepark.ca ⟿ 17 rooms.

The Downtown Toronto Association of Bed & Breakfast Guest Houses. This organization represents privately owned B&Bs. ☎ 647/654–2959 ⊕ www.bnbinfo.com.

Islington Bed & Breakfast House. At this good-value B&B, paintings and tapestries reflect the local landscape. ✉ 1411 Islington Ave., Greater Toronto ☎ 416/236–2707 ⊕ www.islington-house.com ⟿ 1 room.

Les Amis. The charming Parisian host Paul-Antoine fills Les Amis with beautiful photos of his travels through South America and Africa and the tantalizing aromas of his legendary fruit crepes and Belgian-style waffles. ✉ 31 Granby St., at Yonge St., Dundas Square Area ☎ 416/928–1348 ⊕ www.bbtoronto.com ⟿ 5 rooms.

DUNDAS SQUARE AREA

This tourist-centric area feels like the heart of Toronto with the ginormous Eaton Centre as its anchor. The sprawling Dundas Square bustles every day with an open-air market, an impromptu concert, a mini festival, or, on those rare days when no events are scheduled, kids leaping around water fountains.

$$$
HOTEL
FAMILY
Chelsea Hotel. Canada's largest hotel has long been popular with families and tour groups, so be prepared for a flurry of activity. **Pros:** all-inclusive atmosphere; good service; extremely family-friendly. **Cons:** busy and noisy lobby at times; can be long lines for check-in/checkout; slow elevators. ⑤ Rooms from: C$255 ✉ 33 Gerrard St., at Yonge St., Dundas Square Area ☎ 416/595–1975, 800/243–5732 ⊕ chelsea.eaton-hotels.com ⟿ 1,635 rooms ⦿ No meals Ⓜ College or Dundas ✛ F3.

$$
HOTEL
DoubleTree by Hilton Downtown. A modern look carries through from the 26-story facade to the neutral color schemes and square-edged furnishings in guest rooms. **Pros:** excellent restaurants; reasonable price for the location; convenient to Eaton Centre shopping. **Cons:** some

furnishings show wear and tear; parking lot can fill up quickly. $ *Rooms from: $229* ✉ *108 Chestnut St., Dundas Square Area* ☎ *416/977–5000, 800/668–6600* ⊕ *www.doubletree.hilton.com* ↝ *422 rooms* ⦿ *No meals* Ⓜ *St. Patrick* ✛ *E4.*

$$ ⛨ **Pantages Hotel.** Clean lines, gleaming hardwood flooring, and brushed-
HOTEL steel accents exude contemporary cool at this hotel. **Pros:** central location close to Eaton Centre and St. Lawrence Market; excellent spa; great for long stays. **Cons:** some rooms in need of upgrading; lobby and lower floors can be noisy; dark hallways. $ *Rooms from: C$212* ✉ *200 Victoria St., at Shuter St., Dundas Square Area* ☎ *416/362–1777, 855/852–1777* ⊕ *www. pantageshotel.com* ↝ *95 suites* ⦿ *No meals* Ⓜ *Queen* ✛ *F4.*

$$ ⛨ **Saint James Hotel.** This hidden-gem might be low on extras, but is
HOTEL high on clean-cut charm, with modern rooms outfitted with contemporary furniture, comfy beds, hardwood floors, 42-inch televisions, and rain showers. **Pros:** good value for the area; reasonably priced parking available next door. **Cons:** some rooms can be dark. $ *Rooms from: C$239* ✉ *26 Gerrard St. E, Dundas Square Area* ☎ *416/645–2200, 844/645–2200* ⊕ *www.thesaintjameshotel.com* ↝ *36 rooms* ⦿ *Breakfast* ▭ *No credit cards* Ⓜ *Dundas* ✛ *F3.*

$$$ ⛨ **Toronto Downtown Marriott Eaton Centre.** Guest rooms at the Marriott's
HOTEL flagship hotel in Canada are connected to Eaton Centre through an aboveground walkway. **Pros:** knowledgeable employees; good value; large guest rooms. **Cons:** may be noisy; parking area fills up quickly; charge for Wi-Fi. $ *Rooms from: C$319* ✉ *525 Bay St., at Dundas St. W, Dundas Square Area* ☎ *416/597–9200, 800/905–0667* ⊕ *www. marriotteatoncentre.com* ↝ *459 rooms* ⦿ *No meals* Ⓜ *Dundas* ✛ *F4.*

QUEEN WEST

In this trendsetting neighborhood, along Queen Street West beyond Bathurst Street, the hotels get more experimental and cutting-edge the farther west you go. Many highlight local art and music, and have noteworthy restaurants that practice sustainability.

$ ⛨ **Bonnevue Manor Bed & Breakfast Place.** True craftsmen created this
B&B/INN 5,000-square-foot house, and it shows in every enchanting nook and cranny, in the high plastered ceilings, and in the richly aged hardwood floors. **Pros:** safe and comfortable neighborhood; excellent breakfasts; free Wi-Fi. **Cons:** not downtown; petite rooms; not all rooms have private bathrooms. $ *Rooms from: C$149* ✉ *33 Beaty Ave., south of Queen St. W, Queen West* ☎ *416/536–1455* ⊕ *www.bonnevuemanor.com* ↝ *4 rooms* ⦿ *Breakfast* Ⓜ *Osgoode, then streetcar 501 west* ✛ *A5.*

$$$ ⛨ **The Drake Hotel.** Once a notorious flophouse, this 19th-century build-
HOTEL ing is now an ultrahip hotel that spawned several restaurants, gift
Fodor'sChoice shops, and the Drake Devonshire Inn, a satellite location two hours
★ outside the city. **Pros:** attracts Toronto's hippest crowd; excellent food; complimentary access to off-site gym. **Cons:** can be noisy at night; not great for children; hard to get a room. $ *Rooms from: C$309* ✉ *1150 Queen St. W, at Beaconsfield Ave., Queen West* ☎ *416/531–5042, 866/372–5386* ⊕ *www.thedrakehotel.ca* ↝ *19 rooms, 1 suite* ⦿ *No meals* Ⓜ *Osgoode, then streetcar 501 west* ✛ *A5.*

$$$
HOTEL
Fodor's Choice
★

Gladstone Hotel. An intimate size and focus on local art and products helped this hotel earn raves as the "antichain-hotel Toronto experience"—really, it's a sort of community event space, with artist-designed guest rooms and an emphasis on everything that is one-of-a-kind. **Pros:** local flavor; intimate service and setting; every guest room has a different playful design. **Cons:** rooms are on the smaller side; long walk or transit ride to downtown core. $ *Rooms from: C$269* ⊠ *1214 Queen St. W, at Gladstone Ave., Queen West* ☏ *416/531–4635, 416/531–4635* ⊕ *www.gladstonehotel. com* ⌨ *37 rooms* ❑| *No meals* Ⓜ *Osgoode, then streetcar 501 west* ✛ *A5.*

THE ANNEX

The Annex may bustle along Bloor Street West, but the long residential streets running north hide quiet B&Bs that lend a small-town feel to the middle of the city.

$
B&B/INN

Annex Quest House. Ecologically friendly and following the eastern design rules of *Vastu* (a sort of Hindu feng shui), the 18 rooms at this Victorian house are decked out in colorful Asian textiles, wooden sculptures and furniture, and splashes of sequined silk. **Pros:** good value; excellent location; helpful, friendly hosts. **Cons:** Vastu decor not for everyone; no breakfast; old house means creaky floors and narrow stairways. $ *Rooms from: C$95* ⊠ *83 Spadina Rd., The Annex* ☏ *416/922–1934* ⊕ *www. annexquesthouse.com* ⌨ *18 rooms* ❑| *No meals* Ⓜ *Spadina* ✛ *D1.*

$$
B&B/INN
Fodor's Choice
★

Suite Dreams. At the western end of the Annex, almost bordering the lively Koreatown area, this elegant B&B has four lovely suites that remain in high demand. **Pros:** interesting location; owner is wealth of tourist information. **Cons:** only four rooms means you need to reserve well in advance. $ *Rooms from: C$189* ⊠ *390 Clinton St., at Bloor St. W, The Annex* ☏ *416/898–8461* ⊕ *www.suitedreamstoronto.com* ⌨ *4 rooms, 3 with bath* ❑| *Breakfast* Ⓜ *Christie* ✛ *B1.*

YORKVILLE

In keeping with its lofty image as Toronto's most upscale neighborhood, Yorkville boasts a handful of glamorous, ultradecadent hotels. This is a great destination for shopaholics and style gurus who want to take in designer boutiques, visit see-and-be-seen cafés and restaurants, and stargaze during the Toronto International Film Festival.

$$$$
HOTEL
Fodor's Choice
★

Four Seasons Toronto. This gleaming, 55-story tower in the leafy Yorkville neighborhood is the long-awaited Toronto home for the luxury brand, with interiors by noted hospitality design firm Yabu Pushelberg. **Pros:** on-site dining hot spots; excellent spa and gym; central location; on-point service. **Cons:** free Wi-Fi runs slowly; hefty price tag. $ *Rooms from: C$585* ⊠ *60 Yorkville Ave., at Bloor St. W, Yorkville* ☏ *416/964–0411, 800/819–8053* ⊕ *www.fourseasons.com/toronto* ⌨ *259 rooms* ❑| *No meals* Ⓜ *Bay* ✛ *F1.*

$$$$
HOTEL
Fodor's Choice
★

Hazelton Hotel. Stepping through a discreet check-in area, guests are personally ushered through plush hallways to palatial guest rooms with sumptuous furnishings and floor-to-ceiling windows. **Pros:** excellent service; Toronto's Hollywood hangout; on-site spa. **Cons:** high quality

CLOSE UP

Toronto's Best Spas

The spa scene in Toronto is both established and ever evolving, with a wrap, massage, and facial to match every mood and personality type. The problem with spa-hopping in Toronto isn't about finding a good spa but more a matter of choosing one.

All of the city's best boutique hotels offer high-end spa treatments, often with added perks like an infrared sauna or saltwater pool. The **Hyatt's Stillwater Spa** has been touted as the city's best by Toronto's choosiest spa connoisseurs, although a dip in the Bissaza mosaic-tile lap pool after a Copper Relaxation Body Scrub at the **Hazelton** or a scrub in the Moroccan temple–inspired hammam at the **Shangri-La** are experiences you won't soon forget. For the royal treatment, book at the **Ritz-Carlton** spa; its aromatherapy massages, purifying facials, and attentive service live up to the luxury brand's reputation.

Elmwood. Since 1982, the Elmwood, hidden inside a historic redbrick building, has been offering classic spa packages including hot stone massages, anti-aging facials, microdermabrasion treatments, and invigorating body scrubs. ✉ *18 Elm St., Dundas Square Area* ☎ *416/977–6751* ⊕ *www.elmwoodspa.com* Ⓜ *Dundas.*

Hammam Spa. At Hammam Spa devoted Entertainment District clients come to soak up eucalyptus-scented steam in a 500-square-foot marble-tile Turkish bath following a massage or detoxifying algae wrap. ✉ *602 King St. W, at Portland, Entertainment District* ☎ *416/366–4772* ⊕ *www.hammam-spa.ca* Ⓜ *Spadina or St. Andrew.*

Novo Spa. A perennial favorite among Toronto's day-spa enthusiasts, this Yorkville hideaway offers massages (couples, prenatal), facials, manicures, pedicures, and various waxing treatments. The calming staff members always have soothing refreshments on hand. ✉ *66 Avenue Rd., Yorkville* ☎ *416/926–9303* ⊕ *www.novospa.ca* Ⓜ *Bay.*

Ten Spot. With 16 locations around Toronto, this chain of beauty bars specializes in waxing, manicures, and facials and carries a selection of beauty products from independent and luxury brands. ✉ *749 Queen St. W, Queen West* ☎ *416/915–1010* ⊕ *www.the10spot.com.*

with prices to reflect it; next to impossible to get a reservation during the Toronto International Film Festival. $ *Rooms from: C$525* ✉ *118 Yorkville Ave., at Avenue Rd., Yorkville* ☎ *416/963–6300, 800/745–8883* ⊕ *www.thehazeltonhotel.com* ↪ *77 rooms* ⦿ *No meals* Ⓜ *Bay* ⊹ *E1.*

$$$
HOTEL
🏨 **InterContinental Toronto Yorkville.** Handsome and intimate, this outpost of the respected InterContinental chain is a two-minute walk from the Yorkville shopping area and directly across from the Royal Ontario Museum's stunning Crystal addition. **Pros:** close to the Royal Ontario and Gardiner museums; good value for the area; ultracool lobby bar. **Cons:** decor a bit dated; expensive Internet. $ *Rooms from: C$256* ✉ *220 Bloor St. W, west of Avenue Rd., Yorkville* ☎ *416/960–5200, 877/660–8550* ⊕ *www.toronto.intercontinental.com* ↪ *208 rooms* ⦿ *No meals* Ⓜ *Museum* ⊹ *E1.*

$$$$ 🏨 **Park Hyatt Toronto.** The experience here is *très* New York Park Avenue,
HOTEL with elegant, 400-square-foot guest rooms overlooking Queen's Park and
Lake Ontario. **Pros:** large marble baths and fancy toiletries; impeccable
amenities; must-visit rooftop bar. **Cons:** breakfast is pricey; lower rooms
can be loud; room decor is a bit dated. $ *Rooms from: C$359* ⊠ *4 Avenue
Rd., at Bloor St. W, Yorkville* ☎ *416/925–1234, 800/233–1234* ⊕ *www.
parktoronto.hyatt.com* 📵 *336 rooms* ⍨ *No meals* Ⓜ *Museum* ✛ *E1.*

$$$$ 🏨 **Windsor Arms.** With a guest-to-staff ratio of 5:1 and 24-hour butler
HOTEL on duty, the Windsor Arms places high importance on personalized
service. **Pros:** high repeat business due to privacy and personalized
service; ultracomfortable beds; complimentary continental breakfast.
Cons: high service standards mean high prices; some fourth-floor rooms
noisy due to downstairs functions. $ *Rooms from: C$356* ⊠ *18 St.
Thomas St., at Bloor St. W, Yorkville* ☎ *416/971–9666, 877/999–2767*
⊕ *www.windsorarmshotel.com* 📵 *28 rooms* ⍨ *Breakfast* Ⓜ *Bay* ✛ *E1.*

GREATER TORONTO

A breath of fresh air, the Old Mill Inn is closer to natural beauty but
still well situated on the subway line.

$$ 🏨 **The Old Mill Inn & Spa.** Tucked into the Humber River Valley, the Old
B&B/INN Mill is the only country inn within the city limits of Toronto. **Pros:**
whirlpool tubs; parking is free and transit is close by; live jazz Friday
and Saturday. **Cons:** residential neighborhood is too quiet for some;
you must reserve by telephone; gets busy with weddings. $ *Rooms
from: C$229* ⊠ *21 Old Mill Rd., at Bloor St. W, Greater Toronto*
☎ *416/236–2641, 866/653–6455* ⊕ *www.oldmilltoronto.com* 📵 *57
rooms* ⍨ *Breakfast* Ⓜ *Old Mill* ✛ *A1.*

NEAR PEARSON INTERNATIONAL AIRPORT

If you have an early-morning departure or late-night arrival at Pearson
International Airport, staying nearby might be the best option, consider-
ing the drive from downtown Toronto can take up to two hours when
traffic is at its worst.

$$ 🏨 **Alt Hotel Pearson.** Not your average airport hotel, this hip boutique
HOTEL hotel offers a convenient location adjacent to long-term parking and a
LINK station, as well as plush digs at affordable prices. **Pros:** great value;
convenient location; interesting decor. **Cons:** some noise from hallways
and highway; no full-service restaurant. $ *Rooms from: C$169* ⊠ *6080
Viscount Rd., Mississauga* ☎ *905/362–4337, 855/855–6080* ⊕ *www.
althotels.com/en/torontoairport* 📵 *153 rooms* ⍨ *No meals* ✛ *A1.*

$$ 🏨 **Sandman Signature Toronto Airport.** Reasonable prices, great parking
HOTEL deals, and quiet, modern rooms are the advantages of this Sandman
FAMILY property just down the road from Pearson International Airport. **Pros:**
good value; excellent service; free Internet. **Cons:** on-site restaurant
gets extremely busy. $ *Rooms from: C$164* ⊠ *55 Reading Ct., Mis-
sissauga* ☎ *416/798–8840* ⊕ *www.sandmanhotels.com* 📵 *256 rooms*
⍨ *No meals* ✛ *A1.*

5

NIGHTLIFE

Updated by Natalia Manzocco

The nightlife scene in Toronto is as varied as its many neighborhoods. Downtown—in the Entertainment and Financial districts and Old Town—bars cater to theatergoers and weekday worker bees. They can be dead on weekends after dark, however (especially in the Entertainment District) until 11 pm rolls around and the big loft-style dance clubs get going. To hang with locals at their neighborhood joints, head to Little Italy or the Annex, where university students mix with residents of the surrounding Victorian-lined streets.

Gay nightlife centers on Church and Wellesley streets northeast of the downtown core. Everyone under 40 ends up on Queen West at some point, patronizing the once-bohemian, now-established arty bars and cafés. Ladies who lunch meet for midday martinis in swanky Yorkville and later clink glasses at the tony lounges. Throughout the city are dedicated music venues, bars, and supper clubs that specialize in jazz, Latin, blues, rock, hip-hop, and everything in between.

Most recently Toronto has emerged as a food-obsessed city with late-night restaurants (from holes in the wall to the crème de la crème in fine dining), offering sips and nibbles to those who wish to feast past the usual dinner hour. Other emerging trends include a flourish of local brewpubs and luxury hotels offering unique evening programs that have locals and tourists swarming.

PLANNING

BARS
Establishments in Toronto that serve alcohol must also serve some kind of food. This might account for the fact that many bars in the city are also restaurants. Getting just drinks is within your rights at any hour, but at these resto-bars you may be asked to sit at the bar rather than at a table before 10 or 11 pm. This is not to say that all bars serve

proper meals; some get around the law with meager offerings like chips and microwavable cups of Mr. Noodles, or by striking a deal with a neighboring pizza joint.

Several bars are also music venues that either have a separate space (with cover only for that space) or charge a cover for the bar (maybe C$5–C$10) on performance nights.

It's not unusual for smaller bars to be cash-only.

DANCE CLUBS

The majority of Toronto's big dance clubs are in the Entertainment District, specifically along Richmond and Adelaide between University and Spadina. But you can find more intimate spaces on Ossington, Queen West, and in the Church-Wellesley area (the "Gay Village"). Always call ahead or check websites to get on the guest list to avoid a wait at the door. Doors at clubs usually open at 10 but don't get busy until after 11 or midnight. Cover charges of C$10–C$20 are standard. Most clubs are open until 2 or 3 am. Dress codes are usually in effect but aren't over the top; avoid sneakers, shorts, and casual jeans and you should be fine. Some of the classier lounges in the theater and business districts cater to suit- and stiletto-clad clientele.

The club scene can be fickle, with new venues opening and closing all the time. Our choices have been going strong for years, but for the flavor of the month, special events, and DJ bookings, check weekly papers.

MUSIC VENUES

Toronto is a regular stop for top musical performers from around the world. Most venues have covers that range from C$5 to C$15. Tickets are often available on **Ticketmaster** (⊕ *www.ticketmaster.ca*). Record shops **Rotate This!** (*801 Queen St. W 416/504–8447 ⊕ www.rotate.com*) and **Soundscapes** (*572 College St. 416/537–1620 ⊕ www.soundscapes-music.com*) also sell tickets.

Toronto's major arena venues are the Air Canada Centre (home of the Maple Leafs and Raptors), the Rogers Centre (home of the Blue Jays; formerly the SkyDome), and the outdoor summer-only Molson Canadian Amphitheatre on the waterfront with city skyline views. ⇨ *For large-venue shows see Major Venues in Performing Arts.*

GAY AND LESBIAN NIGHTLIFE

Much of Toronto's gay and lesbian nightlife is centered on Church and Wellesley streets. You can easily cruise up Church from Alexander to a couple of blocks north of Wellesley and pop into whichever bar is most happening that night.

There are plenty of LGBT-friendly places outside the Church Street strip. Queen Street West, for example, is sometimes called Queer West, due to the number of not-exclusively-gay-but-gay-friendly bars and restaurants like the Beaver, the Drake, and the Gladstone. Bloor West also has an increasing queer presence, with bars like the Steady and Holy Oak hosting LGBTQ-oriented dance nights.

Check out *X-Tra* (⊕ *www.xtra.ca*), an online publication aimed at Toronto's LGBTQ community, for information on nightlife, community issues, and events.

FESTIVALS

North by Northeast (*NXNE*). Each June, Toronto hosts North by Northeast, an annual festival that brings hundreds of musicians to the indoor and outdoor venues around the city. Affiliated with the similar South by Southwest festival in Austin, Texas, NXNE also presents a digital interactive media conference as part of the week-long festivities. There are performances on a massive open stage in the waterfront Port Lands, as well as live sets in Dundas Square and club shows around downtown. Tickets and passes are available on the website and go on sale as early as mid-January. ☒ *Toronto* ☎ *416/863–6963* ⊕ *www.nxne.com.*

Nightlife listings are organized by neighborhood.

HARBOURFRONT, ENTERTAINMENT DISTRICT, AND THE FINANCIAL DISTRICT

The historic brick buildings of Toronto's oldest district mingle with office towers in this downtown neighborhood, popular for weeknight drinks with coworkers and midday power-broker lunches. Many of the city's hotels are concentrated here.

HARBOURFRONT

In general, this area is quiet after dark, but a nightlife scene is slowly emerging as more condos are erected and the waterfront is developed. Waterfront concerts take place here in summer, while dinner cruises leave from the Harbourfront.

BARS

Real Sports Bar & Grill. No hole-in-the-wall sports bar, this sleek 25,000-square-foot space adjacent to the Air Canada Centre lights up with 199 high-definition flat-screen TVs and amazing sightlines from every club-style booth, table, or stool at one of the three bars. Head to the second floor to watch a game on the 200th TV, an HDTV screen two stories high. For popular sporting events, or any day or night the Leafs or Raptors play, it's best to get a reservation (accepted up to three weeks in advance), though the bar does reserve a third of its seats for walk-in traffic an hour before face-off. ☒ *15 York St., at Bremner Blvd., Harbourfront* ☎ *416/815–7325* ⊕ *www.realsports.ca* Ⓜ *Union.*

BREWERIES

Amsterdam BrewHouse. This brewpub features two massive bars with more than 10 brews on tap, an open-concept kitchen with an imported Italian wood-burning pizza oven, and a sprawling patio with stunning views of the Toronto Islands. The building, a former 1930s boathouse, also houses a brewery; tours and beer tastings are available daily. ☒ *245 Queens Quay W., Harbourfront* ☎ *416/504–1020* ⊕ *www.amsterdambrewhouse.com* Ⓜ *Union.*

THE ENTERTAINMENT DISTRICT

Traditionally this was Toronto's center for dance clubs cranking out house music. A few of the more popular clubs are still going strong (especially along Richmond), but this area is transitioning as condos are erected and professionals in their thirties and forties move in. It's also home to three of the big Broadway-style theaters and tourist-oriented preshow restaurants with bars. The King West neighborhood has experienced a surge of swanky lounges, bars, and restaurants ever since the Toronto International Film Festival moved its headquarters to the area from Yorkville.

BARS

Lobby Lounge at Shangri-La. The Shangri-La Hotel has become wildly popular with refined younger crowds keen for live music, top-notch cocktails, and bar bites. The hotel's spacious Lobby Lounge serves up trendy cocktails and selections from an 800-label wine list, while musical talent performs live piano in the afternoon, jazz in the evenings, and a four-piece combo late into the night. ■ **TIP→ The Fazioli piano sitting in the lounge is signed by Canadian-born Joni Mitchell.** ✉ *188 University Ave., Entertainment District* ☎ *647/788–8888* ⊕ *www.shangri-la. com* Ⓜ *Osgoode.*

Momofuku Nikai. Located across the street from the Four Seasons Centre for the Performing Arts, those looking for a cocktail before or after the ballet and opera will find comfort in this bar and lounge of celebrity chef David Chang's fourplex of Momofuku restaurants. Pull up a living room–style leather couch and enjoy playful cocktails and dishes pulled from the menus of the adjoining Daisho and Noodle Bar, and ponder Zhang Huan's sculpture entitled "Rising," which features a flock of birds flying across the Nikai window. ✉ *190 University Ave., 2nd fl., Entertainment District* ☎ *647/325–6226* ⊕ *momofuku.com* ☯ *Closed Sundays* Ⓜ *Osgoode.*

Wayne Gretzky's Toronto. The pregame Jays and Leafs fans and the postcomedy-club crowd from Second City next door flock to this sports bar. When he's in town, the eponymous hockey icon and owner can often be seen in the crowd. The sports bar downstairs has Gretzky memorabilia, 40 flat-screen TVs (broadcasting all sports, not just hockey) and pub-style grub. On the cabana-chic rooftop patio (open from May through September), considered one of the best in town, strings of white lights twinkle and partygoers order buckets of mini-Coronas while mingling over the blasting music. ✉ *99 Blue Jays Way, at Mercer St., Entertainment District* ☎ *416/979–7825* ⊕ *www.gretzkys.com* Ⓜ *St. Andrew.*

COMEDY CLUBS

Fodor'sChoice
★ **The Second City.** Since it opened in 1973, Toronto's Second City—the younger sibling of the Second City in Chicago—has been providing some of the best comedy in Canada. Regular features are sketch comedy, improv, and revues. Seating is cabaret-style with table service and is assigned on a first-come, first-served basis. ■ **TIP→ Arrive 30 minutes prior to showtime.** Weekend shows tend to sell out. Tickets usually run between C$14 and C$30. ✉ *51 Mercer St., 1 block south of King, Entertainment District* ☎ *416/343–0011* ⊕ *www.secondcity.com* Ⓜ *St. Andrew.*

Yuk Yuk's. Part of a Canadian comedy franchise, this venue headlines stand-up comedians on the rise (Jim Carrey and Russell Peters performed here on their way up), with covers usually between C$11 and C$25. Admission is C$4 on Tuesday for amateur night. The small space is often packed; getting cozy with your neighbors and sitting within spitting distance of the comedians is part of the appeal. Booking a dinner-and-show package guarantees better seats. ⊠ *224 Richmond St. W, 1½ blocks west of University Ave., Entertainment District* ☎ *416/967–6431* ⊕ *www.yukyuks.com* Ⓜ *Osgoode.*

THE FINANCIAL DISTRICT

After happy hour, this business- and high-rise-dense part of town quiets down. Bars and restaurants here are tony affairs, equally suited to schmoozing clients and blowing off steam after a long day at the office.

BARS

Bymark. Located in the heart of the Financial District, this culinary oasis is popular with the business suits that work in the area. Don't let that keep you away though, because this downtown hot spot offers a sun-filled patio that's hidden from the hustle and bustle of Wellington Street. Bartenders whip up phenomenal cocktails and servers pour selections from the massive wine cellar, while the kitchen creates harmonious textures and flavors on your plate. ⊠ *66 Wellington St. W, Financial District* ☎ *416/777–1144* ⊕ *www.bymark.mcewangroup.ca/* Ⓜ *King.*

Fodor's Choice ★ **Canoe.** Though it's primarily a restaurant, Canoe, on the 54th floor of the Toronto-Dominion Bank tower, is worth a trip just for a drink at the bar and a panoramic view of the lake. It has what might be the city's best Niagara wine selection and an extensive list of international bottles, as well as cocktails and beer. It's popular with finance types from the neighboring towers, who suit the swank surroundings. Go just before sunset to make the most of the view. ⊠ *66 Wellington St. W, between York and Bay Sts., Financial District* ☎ *416/364–0054* ⊕ *www.canoerestaurant.com* ⊘ *Closed Sat. and Sun.* Ⓜ *King.*

C'est What. Located in a cozy underground setting that's part beer cellar, part library, and part pool hall, C'est What offers 40 rotating taps of Canadian beer, plus a menu of globally inspired pub grub. The main room is home to a couple of pool tables and a comfy fireplace area lined with couches, while an adjoining room hosts live folk, rock, and roots acts a few times a week. ⊠ *67 Front St. E, Financial District* ☎ *416/867–9499* ⊕ *www.cestwhat.com* Ⓜ *Union.*

OLD TOWN AND THE DISTILLERY DISTRICT

OLD TOWN

On weeknights, an after-work crowd frequents the easygoing bars and restaurants in Toronto's historic district. Weekends see a fair number of suburbanites living it up.

BARS

Bier Markt. With more than 150 beers from 30 countries, including 50 on tap, this enormous restaurant/bar has a corner on the international beer market, but the best thing about it is the oversized sidewalk patio on the Esplanade, ideal for an afternoon brew. ■ TIP→ The lines are ridiculous on weekends—do as the locals do and go midweek instead. ⊠ *58 The Esplanade, just west of Church St., Old Town* ☎ *416/862–7575* ⊕ *www.thebiermarkt.com* Ⓜ *Union, King.*

Pravda Vodka Bar. A deliberately faded elegance, like a Communist-era club gone rough around the edges, permeates Pravda. Huge paintings of Mao Tse-tung adorn the brick walls, and crystal chandeliers run the length of the two-story room with exposed ductwork. Weekday happy-hour specials draw after-work clientele to lounge on well-worn leather sofas, around low wooden tables, or in a red-velvet-curtained VIP bottle-service area upstairs. Some 75 to 100 vodkas from around the globe are always on the menu, as are vodka flights, martinis, and Czech and Russian beers, along with caviar, smoked fish, and pierogi. ✉ *44 Wellington St. E, between Church and Yonge Sts., Old Town* ☎ *416/366–0303* ⊕ *www.pravdavodkabar.com* Ⓜ *King.*

The Sultan's Tent and Cafe Moroc. Not far from the historic St. Lawrence Market, the Sultan's Tent and its front bar, Cafe Moroc, re-create a traditional Moroccan banquet atmosphere, complete with belly dancers, plush divans, beautiful lantern lit tents, and classic North African dishes—be sure to sample the addictive *maftoul*, a hand-rolled pastry stuffed with spiced beef, cashews, and raisins. There's live music and belly dancers every evening. If you're keen to extend your evening after the show, head downstairs to Berber for an intimate North African bar vibe. ■ **TIP➔ This is a unique spot for brunch, lunch, and dinner as well as a cocktail.** ✉ *49 Front St. E, Old Town* ☎ *416/961–0601* ⊕ *www. thesultanstent.com* Ⓜ *King.*

BREWERIES

Steam Whistle Brewery. The Steam Whistle Brewery brews an authentically crafted pilsner and offers tours (C$10) of its historic premises daily. It has tastings and hosts other special events, like the not-to-be-missed Oktoberfest and the Roundhouse Craft Beer Festival in winter and summer. It's also a great place to stop before or after a Blue Jays Game. ✉ *The Roundhouse, 255 Bremner Blvd., Old Town* ☎ *416/362–2337* ⊕ *www.steamwhistle.ca* Ⓜ *Union.*

DISTILLERY DISTRICT

A visit to Toronto isn't complete without a stroll along the cobblestone streets of the city's iconic Distillery District. Originally the heart of Toronto's spirit production in the late 1800s—the Gooderham and Worts Distillery produced whiskey here—stunning heritage buildings now house art galleries, bars, restaurants, and cafés.

BARS

Mill Street Brew Pub & Beer Hall. Home to some of Toronto's most widely enjoyed craft brews, Mill Street Brewery runs a pair of adjoining brew pubs in the Distillery District. Enter off Tank House Lane to find the Brew Pub, home of dressed-up bar eats like lager-spiked shepherd's pie, or veer down a side alley to feast on an Oktoberfest-inspired menu in the modern setting of the Beer Hall. A bottle shop attached to the Brew Pub offers a selection of Mill Street offerings to go. Both bars offer 14 beer taps, with choices ranging from Mill Street staples like Organic Lager and Dark Tankhouse Ale to seasonal and one-off beers.

YONGE-DUNDAS SQUARE AREA

With more neon lights than anywhere else in the city, and a big central square used for outdoor concerts and films, Yonge–Dundas Square is decidedly commercial. But remnants of its past remain in Victorian houses on side streets, and there are some worthwhile bars ideal for a drink before or after a show at Massey Hall and the Canon and Elgin theaters.

BARS

Jazz Bistro. Finding a quiet place to relax and listen to great music is a rarity in busy Dundas Square (the Times Square of Toronto). Luckily, there's the Jazz Bistro. In the busiest part of the city, it's the perfect spot to sit back and relax while sipping on a glass of red wine or snacking on crab cakes or carpaccio. It features a state-of-the-art sound system and a beautiful Steinway piano that's affectionately referred to by regulars as the Red Pops. Blues, jazz, Latin, and world music acts perform almost every night. ⊠ *251 Victoria St., Dundas Square Area* ☎ *416/363–5299* ⊕ *www.jazzbistro.ca* Ⓜ *Dundas.*

The Queen and Beaver Public House. Toronto's British heritage thrives at this classy bar with a full restaurant, where the black-and-white photos on the walls reveal its true passion: soccer. A Manchester United game is never missed, though NHL and other sporting events are also shown in the library-like sports bar. On weekend mornings when an early game is on, they'll open sometimes as early as 7 am. The wine list is admirable for a pub while the beer selection is surprisingly small and focused on Ontario microbrews. Dressed-up British staples—available in the bar or ground-floor dining room—range from Scotch eggs to a killer hand-chopped-beef burger. ⊠ *35 Elm St., between Yonge and Bay Sts., Dundas Square Area* ☎ *647/347–2712* ⊕ *www.queenandbeaver-pub.ca* Ⓜ *Dundas.*

CHINATOWN, KENSINGTON MARKET, AND QUEEN WEST

CHINATOWN AND KENSINGTON MARKET

Chinatown bustles along Spadina Avenue, offering lots of late night cheap and cheerful Hong Kong–style restaurants, while the bohemian Kensington Market bustles during the day as locals pick up groceries and hipsters shop vintage. The zone is slowly picking up speed at night and worth strolling through after dark.

BARS

Cold Tea. This hidden bar in the heart of Kensington Market isn't exactly a closely guarded secret, but the tucked-away entrance and intimate setting still add an underground thrill to a night out. Head through the corridor of an indoor minimall and past the dim sum cart (where a vendor sells hefty BBQ pork buns), and you'll find a cozy room where rotating DJs play eclectic sets that encompass hip-hop, funk, electro, and garage rock. On Sunday afternoons, up-and-coming local chefs take turns manning the BBQ for pop-up lunches. ■TIP➜ **There is no phone number, website, or sign so be sure to ask locals if you're having a hard**

time finding the place. ✉ *60 Kensington Ave., Chinatown* 🚇 Ⓜ *Queen's Park*.

MUSIC CLUBS

The Silver Dollar Room. This time-worn music venue has a long history in the world of blues, but thanks to the efforts of local bookers, it's become a hub for Toronto's thriving garage rock scene. The room is dark, drafty, and low on aesthetic charm, but show up on the right night, and you might see a blues legend or an indie legend in the making. The venue's outdoor backyard area is a popular hangout in the summer. ✉ *486 Spadina Ave., at College St., Chinatown* 🕾 *416/975–0909* ⊕ *www.silverdollarroom.com* Ⓜ *505 Spadina or 506 College streetcar*.

QUEEN WEST

To an outsider, Queen West, with its mix of young owner-operated clothing boutiques, decades-old appliance and antiques stores, dive bars, and hipper-than-thou establishments, might seem to be a neighborhood undergoing a metamorphosis. But it has arrived, firmly grounded in bohemian chic.

BARS

BarChef. The dark interior at BarChef features dimly lit chandeliers and tabletop candles, which set the stage for the wild and wonderful concoctions that force patrons to reimagine classic cocktails. The bartender's bag of tricks includes liquid nitrogen, so cocktails foam over like a foggy mist onto the table or turn into ice shards for a sensory experience that looks as good as it tastes. Fans of whiskey should order the signature Vanilla and Hickory Smoked Manhattan, served in a smoke-filled jar (but be warned, it clocks in at a hefty C$45). ✉ *472 Queen St. W., Queen West* 🕾 *416/868–4800* ⊕ *www.barcheftoronto.com* Ⓜ *501 Queen Streetcar*.

Bar Hop. One of the city's most interesting destinations for beer, Bar Hop features an ever-changing lineup of 40 rare and one-off beers on tap. The location on Queen West features an aging room for beers, a large and sunlit rooftop patio overlooking the main drag, and a menu of refined beer-laced eats like Scotch olives with pimento beer cheese, beer-laced mussels with sourdough, and bone marrow poutine. ✉ *137 Peter St., Queen West* 🕾 *647/348–1137* ⊕ *www.barhoptoronto.com* Ⓜ *Osgoode*.

MUSIC VENUES

Fodor'sChoice ★ **Horseshoe Tavern.** This legendary, low-ceilinged club on Queen West has earned a reputation as the place to play for local acts and touring bands alike. Opened in 1947 as a country music venue, the Shoe (as it's often called) hosted greats like Loretta Lynn, Willie Nelson, Hank Williams, and the Carter Family. The venue's scope widened to include the burgeoning folk, rock, and punk scenes in the '60s and '70s, giving way to early appearances by the Police, Tom Waits, and the Talking Heads. The Rolling Stones even played a now-legendary surprise set here in 1997. Today, the venue books rock, indie, and punk acts from at home and abroad. ✉ *370 Queen St. W, at Spadina Ave., Queen West* 🕾 *416/598–4226* ⊕ *www.horseshoetavern.com* Ⓜ *Osgoode*.

JAZZ FESTIVALS

Toronto Jazz Festival. Late June and early July bring music lovers to Toronto for the Toronto Jazz Festival. Past bills have included Sarah McLachlan, Chick Corea, and Sharon Jones and the Dap-Kings, with performances at various venues around town. Concerts are priced individually, but you can buy a three- or five-show pass for a 10% or 15% discount on Mainstage shows. ✉ Toronto ☏ 416/928–2033 ⊕ www.torontojazz.com.

The Beaches International Jazz Festival. Held in late July, the 10-day Beaches International Jazz Festival in the east Toronto Beach neighborhood showcases jazz, Latin, R&B, funk, soul, and world-music performers at its Woodbine Park and Kew Gardens stages. Musicians and food vendors also line Queen Street East, which is closed to traffic for the event. All performances are free. ✉ Toronto ☏ 416/698–2152 ⊕ www.beachesjazz.com Ⓜ 501 Queen streetcar to Woodbine.

The Rex Hotel Jazz & Blues Bar. Legendary on the Toronto jazz circuit since it opened in the 1980s, the Rex has two live shows every night, three acts on Friday nights, and afternoon shows on weekends. Shows range from free (bring some cash for when the band passes the tip jar) to C$10. The kitchen serves diner fare, and there are affordable hotel rooms available on-site. ✉ 194 Queen St. W, at St. Patrick St., Queen West ☏ 416/598–2475 ⊕ www.therex.ca Ⓜ Osgoode.

Rivoli. One of Queen West's oldest venues, the Rivoli showcases intriguing independent music, theater, and comedy. Arcade Fire, Adele, and Tori Amos all graced the intimate back room's stage early in their careers, and for a cover charge (usually under C$12), you can catch what might be Toronto's next big thing. The low-lit front dining room offers a cozy atmosphere for noshing on pad Thai or sweet potato fries. Head upstairs to shoot some pool at one of 11 pay-by-the-hour tables. ✉ 332 Queen St. W, at Spadina Ave., Queen West ☏ 416/596–1501 ⊕ www.rivoli.ca Ⓜ Osgoode.

EAST AND WEST OF CITY CENTER

WEST QUEEN WEST AND OSSINGTON

Originally a residential area for Portuguese immigrants and a home to Vietnamese karaoke bars and restaurants, Ossington and West Queen West are now *the* place for bohemian artists to set up shop, young chefs to take risks, and hipsters to party until the sun comes up.

BARS

The Drake. Locals know the Drake as a hub for art, culture, food, and perhaps above all—nightlife, with multiple spaces hosting parties, shows, and events on any given night. The basement is home to the Drake Underground, a venue best known for its free weekly Elvis Mondays indie music showcase. Head to the main floor restaurant for seasonally driven lunches, dinners, and brunches, to the adjoining Drake Lounge for a tipple and some low-key live music, or up to the rooftop

Sky Yard patio for drinks surrounded by eye-popping art installations. ✉ *1150 Queen St. W, 2 blocks east of Gladstone Ave., West Queen West* ☎ *416/531–5042* ⊕ *www.thedrakehotel.ca* Ⓜ *501 Queen streetcar.*

Gladstone Hotel. In a restored Victorian hotel, the Gladstone draws a young, stylish Toronto crowd who appreciate a multitude of creative events like karaoke, music performances, spoken word, burlesque, queer nights, art shows, and more. The Ballroom is the main event space—and frequent wedding venue—with tall ceilings, exposed brick walls, and a long, dark-wood bar. The Melody Bar hosts bands and serves cocktails and sharable eats until late. The tiny Art Bar has exhibitions, performances, and private events; there are also art galleries on the second, third, and fourth floors as well as rotating exhibits throughout the hotel's public spaces. ✉ *1214 Queen St. W, at Dufferin, Queen West* ☎ *647/793–7024* ⊕ *www.gladstonehotel.com* Ⓜ *501 Queen streetcar to Dufferin St.*

Fodor's Choice **The Lockhart.** Don't go in expecting wizarding robes and animatronic
★ owls at this Harry Potter–themed bar; think of the laid-back, neon-lit little watering hole as the cocktail bar J.K. Rowling's Diagon Alley never had. Grab a seat next to the wall of Potions and Elixirs and spot the references hidden around the bar while sipping fantastical cocktails like boozy Butterbeer or a Befuddlement Draft served on fire in a glass cauldron. ✉ *1479 Dundas St. W., Little Portugal* ✛ *At Dufferin* ☎ *647/748–4434* ⊕ *www.thelockhart.ca* ☞ *Closed Mon.* Ⓜ *505 Dundas streetcar.*

Reposado Bar. The Toronto bar buzz is largely centered on Ossington Avenue, where watering holes, shops, and galleries have sprung up like wildflowers over the past few years. One of the first (in 2007) and still going strong is this classy tequila bar. The dark wood, large windows, big back patio, and live jazz (cover is Pay What You Can) set the tone for a serious list of tequilas meant to be sipped, not slammed, and Mexican nibbles like tequila-cured salmon with crostini. ✉ *136 Ossington Ave., between Queen and Dundas Sts., Ossington* ☎ *416/532–6474* ⊕ *www.reposadobar.com* Ⓜ *501 Queen streetcar, or Ossington subway/bus.*

BREWERIES

Bellwoods Brewery. This restaurant, bar, and on-site brewery has been a smash hit since it opened in 2012. If the sun is shining, expect a line for the spacious patio, a great spot to sample the always evolving craft beer selection. If it's available, be sure to sip the White Picket Fence Belgian Wit, which pairs perfectly with a plate of fresh oysters. The cheese and charcuterie board is perfect for sharing with a group. ✉ *126 Ossington Ave., Ossington* ☎ *416/535–4586* ⊕ *bellwoodsbrewery.com* Ⓜ *501 Queen streetcar.*

DANCE CLUBS

Lula Lounge. Latin-music lovers of all ages dress up to get down to live Afro-Cuban, Brazilian, and salsa music at this Little Portugal hot spot. Pop and rock musicians also perform occasionally. Dinner-and-a-show tickets are available on weekends and include a salsa lesson on Saturday. Lula is also an arts center, with dance and drumming lessons and a multitude of festivals and cultural events. ⊠ *1585 Dundas St. W, 1½ blocks west of Dufferin St., West Queen West* ☎ *416/588–0307* ⊕ *www. lula.ca* Ⓜ *505 Dundas streetcar.*

LESLIEVILLE AND THE DANFORTH

This area of Queen Street was up-and-coming for years, and is now a bonafide reason to cross the DVP (Don Valley Parkway), thanks to a flurry of small but excellent restaurants, artisanal food shops, niche design stores, and relaxed labor-of-love bars catering to a discerning and artistic local community. Farther north is the Danforth, otherwise known as Greektown; it's a little sleepier at night, but home to one of the city's buzziest concert venues as well as some great local pubs.

BARS

The Céilí Cottage. Owned and operated by an oyster-loving Irishman, locals rave about the cottage's authentic pub vibe, large sun-filled front patio, and inventive Emerald Isle–inspired food. The Whiskey Wall has won numerous awards and features more than 100 whiskeys—you'll find Irish, Scotch, American, and Canadian. A traditional Irish band performs live on Tuesday. ■TIP➜ End your night (or meal) with the Sticky Toffee Pudding. ⊠ *1301 Queen St. E, Leslieville* ☎ *416/406–1301* ⊕ *www.ceilicottage.com* Ⓜ *501 Queen streetcar.*

Skin and Bones. The name is a coy indicator of the playful atmosphere offered up at this east end wine bar and restaurant—Skin refers to grape skins and the owners' passion for wine, and Bones refers to the menu's focus on meat and seafood. The bar keeps about 75 bottles on the wine list at any given time, with a rotating selection available by the glass. ⊠ *980 Queen St. E, Leslieville* ☎ *416/524–5209* ⊕ *skinandbonesto.com* ↻ *Closed Mon.* Ⓜ *501 Queen streetcar.*

MUSIC VENUES

Fodor's Choice
★

Danforth Music Hall. Originally a cinema built in 1919, this stately theater is now a live music venue that attracts popular touring acts stopping in Toronto. The Danforth hosts punk, rock, rap, folk, and electro acts, and even stand-up comedy. Notable performers who have graced its stage include Rihanna, Blue Rodeo, St. Vincent, and Dave Chappelle. ⊠ *147 Danforth Ave., Danforth* ☎ *416/778–8163* ⊕ *www.thedanforth. com* Ⓜ *Broadview.*

Opera House. This late 19th-century vaudeville theater retains some of its original charm, most notably in its proscenium arch over the stage. The 850-capacity venue hosts internationally touring acts of all genres. Throughout the years, it's hosted such diverse acts as Nirvana, Lucinda Williams, Kings of Leon, LCD Soundsystem, M.I.A., the Black Keys, and more. ⊠ *735 Queen St. E, 1 block east of Broadview, Leslieville* ☎ *416/466–0313* ⊕ *www.theoperahousetoronto.com* Ⓜ *501 Queen streetcar.*

THE ANNEX

Along Bloor between Spadina and Bathurst, the Annex is an established neighborhood of leafy side streets with large Victorian houses that attracts university students and young professionals to its mix of true-blue pubs and well-loved lounges.

BARS

Bar Begonia. Chef/restaurateur Anthony Rose is king of the Dupont strip (he's got five restaurants within a few short blocks in the north of the Annex), and he funnels tons of low-lit Parisian charm into this striking date spot. In the glow of red-lacquered walls, sip on cocktails spiked with fernet and absinthe (try the Benediction, with Canadian rye, brown butter calvados, and orange bitters), savor a glass of Canadian or French wine, or share snacks like the excellent steak tartare. ✉ *252 Dupont St., The Annex* ☎ *647/352–3337* ⊕ *www.barbegonia. com* Ⓜ *Dupont.*

Kinka Izakaya Bloor. Wowing local audiences with its rowdy Izakaya atmosphere—every guest is greeted with a cheerful hello in Japanese by both kitchen and serving staff when you walk through the door—Kinka has gained quite a cultlike following. A few shots of sake are a must-try, but don't miss the imported plum wine or Japanese vodka-infused cocktails. The food is delicious and perfect for sharing ✉ *559 Bloor St. W, The Annex* ☎ *647/343–1101* ⊕ *www.kinkaizakaya.com* Ⓜ *Bathurst.*

Playa Cabana Hacienda. The sister property of one of the city's favorite *tequilerias* (Playa Cabana), the Hacienda, as it's fondly known, offers a small second floor patio that overlooks Dupont, as well as a massive outdoor patio behind the restaurant—it may be the largest outdoor space to sip a margarita north of Bloor. The interior wows with a wild and wonderful assortment of glowing bar signs, hanging pulleys, industrial lamps, leather horse saddles, and endless bottles of booze—not to mention great tacos. ✉ *14 Dupont St., The Annex* ☎ *647/352–6030* ⊕ *www.playacabana.ca/hacienda* Ⓜ *Dupont.*

MUSIC VENUES

Lee's Palace. Some of the most exciting young bands in rock, indie, and punk, from Toronto and elsewhere, play at this midsize club with a psychedelic graffiti facade on the edge of the University of Toronto campus. Grab a burrito from Big Fat Burrito's on-site service window between sets. Upstairs is the Dance Cave, a no-fills dance club popular with students. ✉ *529 Bloor St. W, 1½ blocks east of Bathurst St., The Annex* ☎ *416/532–1598* ⊕ *www.leespalace.com* Ⓜ *Bathurst.*

LITTLE ITALY

College Street between Bathurst and Ossington isn't so much an old-school Italian neighborhood these days as it is a prime destination for bars and restaurants of all cuisines. Student-friendly pubs and rowdy clubs mix with candlelit martini bars. The party often spills out onto the streets on weekends.

BARS

Café Diplomatico. Holding court over a central Little Italy corner since 1968, Diplomatico is popular for one reason: its big sidewalk patio with umbrella-shaded tables, one of the best in the city for people-watching. "The Dip," as it's locally known, serves up middle-of-the-road Italian fare and affordable beer and wine. It's really all about the outdoor space, which is open from 8 am daily and has one of the few neighborhood kitchens serving after midnight. ⊠ *594 College St., at Clinton St., Little Italy* ☎ *416/534–4637* ⊕ *www.cafediplomatico.ca* Ⓜ *506 College streetcar.*

La Carnita. Originally started as a pop-up taco stand, La Carnita became a permanent fixture when lines started forming well into the late evening. The tacos, hand-crafted cocktails, and sweet churros are well worth the wait. The space is filled with funky graffiti and the sounds of vintage beats, hip-hop, and DJ mixes. There's also a soft-serve counter, Sweet Jesus, home to the city's most outlandishly Instagrammable ice-cream cones. ⊠ *501 College St., at Palmerston Ave., Little Italy* ☎ *416/964–1555* ⊕ *www.lacarnita.com* Ⓜ *506 College Streetcar.*

MUSIC VENUES

Free Times Cafe. This casual restaurant specializes in Jewish, Middle Eastern, and Canadian food, with many vegetarian and organic options. There's live acoustic and folk music every night of the week on its backroom stage, plus a highly popular traditional Jewish brunch buffet called "Bella! Did Ya Eat?" complete with live klezmer and Yiddish music every Sunday. ⊠ *320 College St., at Major St., Queen's Park* ☎ *416/967–1078* ⊕ *www.freetimescafe.com* Ⓜ *Queen's Park.*

Mod Club Theatre. This sexy black-on-black midsize space has great sight lines and killer acoustics and lighting. Past shows have included Lana Del Rey and Digitalism, but upstart Canadian indie rockers are frequent guests. The Mod Club is also a popular venue for DJs and dance nights, and it's not uncommon for the venue to host an early live show, then clear the venue out for the dance crowd. ⊠ *722 College St., at Crawford St., Little Italy* ☎ *416/588–4663* ⊕ *www.themodclub.com* Ⓜ *506 College streetcar.*

YORKVILLE AND CHURCH-WELLESLEY

YORKVILLE

The trendy bars of Yorkville tend to draw a well-heeled clientele for excellent drinks, food, and views.

BARS

dBar. This high-end lounge, located in the flagship Four Seasons Toronto, is modern and subdued. The bartender serves up some top cocktails, including the rose-and-elderflower-infused Yorkville Affair and a suitably Canadian maple margarita. The food is spearheaded by French chef Daniel Boulud, so the menu goes far above and beyond simple bar bites—charcuterie is house-made, and larger options include lamb confit ribs and a merguez sausage hot dog. ⊠ *21 Avenue Rd., Yorkville* ☎ *416/964–0411* ⊕ *www.fourseasons.com* Ⓜ *Bay.*

Hemingways. One of the few Toronto pubs that isn't overtaken by rowdy sports fans or students, Hemingways is a homey bastion in a sea of Yorkville swank. The three-story complex, with indoor and outdoor spaces (including a heated rooftop patio), is a mish-mash of booths, tables, several bars, mirrors, artsy posters, and books. The pub grub menu, which covers everything from brunch to late night, is a big draw, too. About three-quarters of the over-30 professionals who frequent this place are regulars. ✉ *142 Cumberland St., just east of Avenue Rd., Yorkville* ☎ *416/968–2828* ⊕ *www.hemingways.to* Ⓜ *Bay.*

Fodor'sChoice ★ **The Roof Lounge.** Such Canadian literary luminaries as Margaret Atwood and Mordecai Richler have used the 18th-floor Roof Lounge as a setting in their writings. The tiny bar is chic and refined without stuffiness or pretension and has dark wood and leather accents. Martinis and cosmopolitans are the specialties, though the menu also includes a nice selection of single malts, tequilas, and small plates. The adjoining patio affords lovely views of the downtown skyline and lake. ✉ *Park Hyatt Hotel, top fl., 4 Avenue Rd., Yorkville* ☎ *416/925–1234* ⊕ *www.parktoronto.hyatt.com* Ⓜ *Bay or St. George.*

La Société. This French-inspired space features a chic dining room that boasts a 20-by-30-foot illuminated stained-glass ceiling, a Parisian-style bar top, and the best patio Yorkville has to offer. Guests can sip on a variety of French wines, Champagne, and carefully crafted cocktails while people-watching on one of two European-style terraces that overlook Bloor Street glamour. Nights are filled with always-changing DJs who offer up French house music to well-heeled fashion fans. ✉ *131 Bloor St. W, Yorkville* ☎ *416/551–9929* ⊕ *www.lasociete.ca* Ⓜ *Bay.*

CHURCH-WELLESLEY

The "Gay Village," the "gayborhood," or just plain old "Church and Wellesley"—whatever you call it, this strip of bars, restaurants, shops, and clubs is a fun, always-hopping hangout for the LGBTQ crowd or anyone with an open mind.

BARS

Fodor'sChoice ★ **Bar Volo.** Widely known as one of the city's top destinations for beer lovers, Bar Volo specializes in rare and one-off brews. The family-run spot, located in a sprawling former mansion on Church Street, carefully curates its tap list with oddball selections from around Ontario, plus plenty of top-notch brews imported from Québec. On certain

---

TORONTO COMEDIANS

Since the Second City opened, Toronto has been a comedic hub. Gilda Radner, John Candy, Dan Aykroyd, Dave Thomas, Martin Short, Eugene Levy, Catherine O'Hara, and Rick Moranis all cut their teeth here or on SCTV, a TV offshoot of the theater and precursor to *Saturday Night Live.* Toronto native Lorne Michaels cast Aykroyd and Radner in the first season of *SNL.* Mike Myers, Dave Foley, Bruce McCulloch, and Mark McKinney started at the Bad Dog Theatre. Jim Carrey and Howie Mandel debuted at Yuk Yuk's, and Samantha Bee frequented the Rivoli before joining *The Daily Show.*

weekends, they'll host brewery takeovers, dedicating every tap in the place to a single brewer. To quell the inevitable munchies that come from sampling, indulge in all-Ontario charcuterie and cheese boards, or southern Italian favorites like pizzas and panini. ⊠ *582 Church St., Church–Wellesley* ☎ *416/928–0008* ⊕ *www.barvolo.com* Ⓜ *Wellesley.*

Woody's. A predominantly upscale, professional male crowd (twenties to forties) frequents this cavernous pub where DJs mix every night. Check out weekly events like the Best Chest and Best Butt contests, which are hosted by some of the city's most beloved drag queens. The exterior of Woody's was used on the television show *Queer as Folk.* ⊠ *467 Church St., at Maitland St., Church–Wellesley* ☎ *416/972–0887* ⊕ *www.woodystoronto.com* Ⓜ *Wellesley.*

DANCE CLUBS

CHURCH on Church. This queer bar and lounge is a popular spot for 20- to 40-year-olds with a penchant for well-crafted cocktails and a rowdy dance floor. The space is best described as a refined boutique club where DJs spin and well-dressed professional gays come to mix and mingle late at night. ⊠ *504 Church St., Church–Wellesley* ☎ *647/352–5223* ⊕ *www.churchonchurch.com* Ⓜ *Wellesley.*

Crews & Tangos. Downstairs is Crews, a gay and lesbian bar with a stage for karaoke or drag shows (depending on the night), a dance floor in back with a DJ spinning house beats, and a sizable back patio. Tangos, upstairs, has a bar and a small dance floor that gets packed with twenty- to thirtysomething guys and gals kicking it to old-school hip-hop and '80s beats. The male–female ratio is surprisingly balanced and the drag shows lots of fun. There's usually a C$5 cover on weekends. ⊠ *508 Church St., Church–Wellesley* ☎ *416/972–1662* ⊕ *crewsandtangos. com* Ⓜ *Wellesley.*

Fly. Some of the biggest and best DJs from around the world have spun records at the original "Babylon" from television's *Queer as Folk.* An impressive sound system, light show, and 10,000 square feet over several floors have won this queer-positive club several Best Dance Club in Toronto awards. The hot—and generally young—clientele doesn't hurt, either. Cover ranges from C$10 to C$20. ⊠ *8 Gloucester St., just east of Yonge St., Church–Wellesley* ☎ *416/410–5426* ⊕ *www.flynightclub. com* Ⓜ *Wellesley.*

6

PERFORMING ARTS

TORONTO'S FILM SCENE

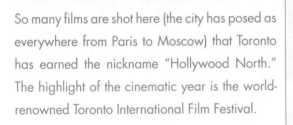

So many films are shot here (the city has posed as everywhere from Paris to Moscow) that Toronto has earned the nickname "Hollywood North." The highlight of the cinematic year is the world-renowned Toronto International Film Festival.

North America's third-largest film production center after L.A. and New York, Toronto keeps cameras rolling with its excellent local crews and production facilities and plenty of filmmaker tax credits. It helps, too, that Toronto's chameleonic streets easily impersonate other cities and time periods. Credits include: Yonge Street as Harlem (*The Incredible Hulk*), the Distillery District as Prohibition-era Chicago (*Chicago*), Casa Loma as the school for young mutants in *X-Men*, and the U of T campus as Harvard (*Good Will Hunting*). Spotting Toronto "tells" in films is fun, but locals get even more jazzed when the city represents itself for a change, as in 2010's *Scott Pilgrim vs. the World*.

MORE FESTIVALS

Hot Docs. Taking place every April, this is North America's largest documentary film festival. ⊠ *Toronto* ⊕ *www.hotdocs.ca.*

Inside Out Toronto LGBT Film Festival. Held at the TIFF Lightbox in late May, this major event features films made by and about lesbian, gay, bi, and transgender people. ⊠ *Toronto* ⊕ *www.insideout.ca/ torontofestival.*

TIFF Kids International Film Festival. TIFF Kids features new and classic films aimed at the 3- to 13-year-old crowd every April. ⊠ *Toronto* ⊕ *www. tiff.net/kids.*

Toronto After Dark. This festival that takes place in late October is dedicated to horror, sci-fi, and thriller films. ⊠ *Toronto* ⊕ *www. torontoafterdark.com.*

Toronto International Film Festival. Widely considered the most important film festival in the world after Cannes and Sundance, TIFF is open to the public with even star-studded galas accessible to the average joe. More than 300 of the latest works of great international directors and lesser-known independent-film directors from around the world are shown. Movies that premiere at TIFF have gone on to win Academy Awards and launch the careers of emerging actors and directors. In recent years, TIFF audiences have been among the first in the world to see *The King's Speech* , *Slumdog Millionaire,* and *Juno,* to mention just a few. The red carpet is rolled out, and paparazzi get ready for big-budget, star-studded premieres ("galas"), for which actors and directors may be on hand afterward for Q&As. Along with the serious documentaries, foreign films, and Oscar contenders, TIFF has fun with its Midnight Madness program, screening campy horror films, comedies, and action movies into the wee hours. ✉ *TIFF Bell Lightbox, 350 King St. West, at John St., Harbourfront* ☎ *416/599–8433, 888/599–8433* ⊕ *www.tiff.net.*

WHERE TO WATCH

Oddball series and theme nights: Revue

Documentaries: Bloor Cinema

Pure cinephelia: TIFF Bell Lightbox

IMAX: Ontario Science Centre OmniMax Theatre (Toronto's only 70mm celluloid IMAX); Cineplex Cinemas Yonge-Dundas; Scotiabank Theatre

3-D: Scotiabank Theatre; TIFF Bell Lightbox; Varsity and Varsity VIP; Cineplex Cinemas Yonge-Dundas

Summer films alfresco: Harbourfront Centre (Wed., free); Polson Pier Drive-In (Fri. and Sat., C$15/person; Sun., C$25 per car load) 176 Cherry St.; TIFF in the Park (Wed., free); City Cinema (Tues., free). Most screenings start at sunset (usually 8:30 to 9 pm) and run through July and August.

DOING THE FESTIVAL

When: The 11-day festival begins in early September.

Where: Screenings are at movie theaters and concert halls throughout the city, as are ticket booths, but the festival HQ is the TIFF Bell Lightbox building, at *350 King St. W (at John St.).*

Tickets: If you plan to see 10 or more films, consider a festival ticket package, which go on sale in July; you can choose screenings on the website. Individual tickets go on sale four days before the start of the festival. You may not get your first choice, but discovering something new is part of the fun. Ticket prices start at C$25 per film and C$49 for premium screenings. If you have your heart set on a particular film and you don't get a ticket, keep checking each morning at 7—TIFF releases extra tickets each day of the festival. Tickets are almost always available for something, even at the last minute, and even sold-out shows have a rush line.

Tips

■ Book a hotel as early as possible: some hotels near the theaters are booked by May.

■ Read ticket-buying instructions carefully; you'll need to call TIFF to fix anything, but luckily there's no fee to exchange tickets.

■ Pick up your order at least an hour before your screening to ensure you don't get stuck in a long line and miss the best seats.

■ Arrive at least two hours early if you're trying to get a rush ticket. They're released 10 minutes before the start of a film.

Updated by
Rosemary
Counter

In terms of culture, Toronto truly is Canada's New York—the city to which artists flock to make a name for themselves. And the rest of us reap the rewards. With all the options available, these days the biggest obstacle to arts and culture in Toronto is deciding what to experience while you're here. The capital of the performing arts in English-speaking Canada, Toronto has world-class resident symphony, opera, and ballet companies.

But the arts scene wasn't always this lively. Before 1950, Toronto had no opera company, no ballet, and very little theater worthy of the title "professional." Then came the Massey Report on the Arts, and money began to pour in from government grants. The Canada Council, the Canadian Opera Company, CBC television, and the National Ballet of Canada were born. A number of small theaters began to pop up as well, culminating in an artistic explosion throughout the 1970s in every aspect of the arts. (This was also when the Toronto International Film Festival was born.) Adding fuel to the fire was a massive spike in immigration, a recognition that if Canadians did not develop their own arts the Americans would do it for them, and a severing of the political apron strings tying Canada to England, resulting in a desire to cement Canada's independence and to encourage homegrown talent.

Now Toronto is growing, with new performance venues opening and old ones being refurbished. The current flurry of artistic activity shows no signs of abating. The city has more than 50 dance companies; film festivals and retrospectives overtake screens year-round; and the numerous theatrical troupes and big-budget musicals staged here have earned it the nickname "Broadway North." Theater is where it really shines, from spit-and-chewing-gum new works to Broadway-style, no-expenses-spared extravaganzas. In fact, Toronto is the largest center for English-speaking theater in the world after New York and London—not bad for a city that's only the fourth largest in North America by population.

PLANNING

WHAT'S ON NOW?

Check free alternative newsweekly *NOW* (⊕ *www.nowtoronto.com*) and monthly magazine *Toronto Life* (⊕ *www.torontolife.com*) for reviews, concerts, movie times, and events.

The WholeNote (⊕ *www.thewholenote.com*) publishes classical, jazz, opera, and world music concert dates and news online and in its free print publication.

LATE-NIGHT TRANSPORTATION

Subway and streetcar service ends at 1:30 am, so for late-night outings, hailing a cab is your best bet. Some streetcars and buses along major streets (including Queen, Bloor, and Yonge) run 24 hours but pick up only every half hour.

TICKETS

StubHub. Check ticket reseller StubHub for sold-out events or last-minute deals. ⊠ *Toronto* ☎ *866/788–2482* ⊕ *www.stubhub.com.*

Ticketmaster. Tickets for almost any event can be obtained through Ticketmaster. ⊠ *Toronto* ☎ *855/985–5000* ⊕ *www.ticketmaster.ca.*

FESTIVALS

Luminato. Every June, Luminato packs in several events spanning the arts from plays and tango lessons to puppetry and poetry. The festival attracts some big names such as Joni Mitchell, the National Theatre of Scotland, and Marina Abramović. ⊠ *Toronto* ☎ *416/368–3100* ⊕ *www. luminatofestival.com.*

FREE CONCERTS

Free Concert Series. The Canadian Opera Company's Free Concert Series takes place September through June with music and dance performances most Tuesdays and Thursdays (and the occasional Wednesday evening) at noon in the Four Seasons Centre's Richard Bradshaw Amphitheatre. Check the calendar on the COC website to see what's on. ⊠ *145 Queen St. W., Queen West* ☎ *416/363–8231* ⊕ *www.coc. ca* Ⓜ *Osgoode Station.*

CLASSICAL MUSIC AND OPERA

CLASSICAL MUSIC

Fodor's Choice **Koerner Hall.** Artists and audiences quickly fell in love with this hand-
★ some 1,135-seat concert hall with rich acoustics and undulating wood "strings" floating overhead when it opened in 2009. Performers have included such greats as Yo-Yo Ma, Chick Corea, Ravi Shankar, Midori, Taj Mahal, and Savion Glover. The hall is part of the Royal Conservatory's arts-education facility, the TELUS Centre for Performance and Learning. ⊠ *273 Bloor St. W, at Avenue Rd., Yorkville* ☎ *416/408–0208* ⊕ *www.performance.rcmusic.ca* Ⓜ *St. George (Bedford exit).*

Tafelmusik. Internationally renowned as one of the world's finest period ensembles, Tafelmusik presents baroque and classical music on original

With its circular shape and striking glass canopy, Roy Thomson Hall is a classic of Toronto architecture.

instruments. Most performances are in the recently revitalized Trinity–St. Paul's Centre in Jeanne Lamon Hall; the pews have been replaced by seats, and the acoustics are much improved. Tafelmusik's Sing-Along *Messiah* at Massey Hall is a rollicking Christmas season highlight where the audience is invited to join in; tickets start at C$30 and it usually sells out. ⊠ *Trinity–St. Paul's Centre, Jeanne Lamon Hall, 427 Bloor St. W, The Annex* ☎ 416/964–6337 ⊕ *www.tafelmusik.org* Ⓜ *Spadina.*

Toronto Mendelssohn Choir. This group of more than 120 choristers was formed in 1894 and performs major classical choral works at various venues, including the Royal Conservatory's lovely Koerner Hall and Yorkminster Park Baptist Church at Yonge and St. Clair. The choir often performs with the Toronto Symphony Orchestra, including its annual Christmas performance of Handel's *Messiah.* ⊠ *Yorkminster Park Baptist Church, 1585 Yonge St., north of St. Clair, Rosedale* ☎ 416/598–0422 ⊕ *www.tmchoir.org* Ⓜ *Spadina.*

Toronto Symphony Orchestra. Since 1922 this orchestra has achieved world acclaim with music directors such as Sir Ernest MacMillan, Seiji Ozawa, and Sir Andrew Davis. Canadian-born Peter Oundjian reinvigorated the ensemble and significantly strengthened its presence in the world when he took over as musical director in 2004. Guest performers have included pianist Lang Lang, violinist Itzhak Perlman, and singer-songwriter Rufus Wainwright. Each season the orchestra screens a classic film, such as *Casablanca* or *West Side Story* , and plays the score as it runs. The TSO also presents about three concerts weekly at Roy Thomson Hall from September through June. ⊠ *Roy Thomson Hall, 60 Simcoe St., Entertainment*

District ☎ *416/593–1285 TSO information and tickets, 416/593–4828 Roy Thomson Hall ticket line ⊕ www.tso.ca* Ⓜ *St. Andrew.*

University of Toronto. Performances by professors and students of the University of Toronto Faculty of Music and visiting artists, ranging from symphony to jazz to full-scale operas, take place September through May, at little or no cost, in two spaces: the 815-seat MacMillan Theatre and the 490-seat **Walter Hall.** ✉ *University of Toronto Faculty of Music, Edward Johnson Bldg., 80 Queen's Park Crescent, Queen's Park* ☎ *416/408–0208* ⊕ *www.music.utoronto.ca* Ⓜ *Museum.*

CONTEMPORARY AND EXPERIMENTAL MUSIC

Fodor'sChoice
★
The Music Gallery. Toronto's go-to spot for experimental music, the self-titled "Toronto's Center for Creative Music" presents an eclectic selection of avant-garde and experimental music from world and classical to jazz and avant-pop in a relaxed environment. ✉ *St. George the Martyr Church, 197 John St., 2 blocks north of Queen St. at Stephanie St., Queen West* ☎ *416/204–1080* ⊕ *www.musicgallery.org* Ⓜ *Osgoode.*

OPERA

Canadian Opera Company. Founded in 1950, the COC has grown into the largest producer of opera in Canada, and has proven innovative and often daring with presentations that range from popular operas to more modern or rarely performed works. The COC maintains its international reputation for artistic excellence and creative leadership by presenting new productions from a diverse repertoire, collaborating with leading opera companies and festivals, and attracting the world's foremost Canadian and international artists. It often hosts world-renowned performers, and it pioneered the use of scrolling "surtitles," which allow the audience to follow the libretto in English in a capsulized translation that appears above the stage. Tickets sell out quickly. Tours (C$20 for adults, C$15 for seniors/students) of the COC's opera house, the magnificent **Four Seasons Centre for the Performing Arts**, are given when the performance schedule allows (usually on Sunday); check the website for times and dates. ✉ *Four Seasons Centre for the Performing Arts, 145 Queen St. W, at University Ave., Queen West* ☎ *416/363–8231, 800/250–4653* ⊕ *www.coc.ca* Ⓜ *Osgoode.*

Opera Atelier. Since its opening in 1985, Opera Atelier has been dedicated to staging 17th- and 18th-century baroque operas, with extravagant sets and costumes and original instruments. The two annual productions are staged at the Elgin Theatre each fall and spring. ✉ *Elgin Theatre, 189 Yonge St., just north of Queen St.* ☎ *416/703–3767* ⊕ *www.oper-aatelier.com.*

MAJOR VENUES

It's not uncommon for a concert hall to present modern dance one week, a rock- or classical-music concert another week, and a theatrical performance the next. Arenas double as sports stadiums and venues for the biggest names in music and the occasional monster-truck rally or other spectacle.

Air Canada Centre. Most arena shows are held here rather than at the larger Rogers Centre due to superior acoustics. Past performances at the nearly 20,000-capacity arena have included Beyoncé, Rod Stewart, American Idol Live!, and Nine Inch Nails. ⊠ *40 Bay St., at Gardiner Expressway, Harbourfront* ☎ *416/815–5500* ⊕ *www.theaircanadacentre.com* Ⓜ *Union.*

Fodor's Choice
★
Elgin and Winter Garden Theatre Centre. This jewel in the crown of the Toronto arts scene consists of two former vaudeville halls, built in 1913, one on top of the other. It is the last operating double-decker theater complex in the world and a Canadian National Historic Site. Until 1928, the theaters hosted silent-film and vaudeville legends like George Burns, Gracie Allen, and Edgar Bergen with Charlie McCarthy. Today's performances are still surrounded by magnificent settings: Elgin's dramatic gold-leaf-and-cherub-adorned interior and the Winter Garden's *A Midsummer Night's Dream*–inspired decor, complete with tree branches overhead. These stages host Broadway-caliber musicals , comedians, jazz concerts, operas, and Toronto International Film Festival screenings. The Elgin, downstairs, has more than 1,500 seats; the 992-seat Winter Garden is upstairs. Guided tours (C$12) are given Thursday at 5 pm and Saturday at 11 am (subject to change; check the website first). ⊠ *189 Yonge St., at Queen St., Dundas Square Area* ☎ *855/622–2787 tickets, 416/314–2871 tours* ⊕ *www.heritagetrust.on.ca/ewg* Ⓜ *Queen.*

Harbourfront Centre. When looking for cultural events in Toronto, always check the schedule at the Harbourfront Centre. A cultural playground, it has an art gallery (the Power Plant), two dance spaces, a music garden co-designed by Yo-Yo Ma, and chockablock festivals and cultural events, some especially for kids and many of them free. ⊠ *235 Queen's Quay W, at Lower Simcoe St., Harbourfront* ☎ *416/973–4000* ⊕ *www.harbourfrontcentre.com* Ⓜ *Union, then 510 streetcar.*

Fodor's Choice
★
Massey Hall. Near-perfect acoustics and handsome, U-shape tiers have made Massey Hall a great place to enjoy music since 1894, when it opened with a performance of Handel's *Messiah*. It's always been a venerable place to catch big-time solo acts like Neil Young and Gilberto Gil, comedians, indie bands, and occasional dance troupes. However, this grand old venue is showing its age, and there are finally plans under way to expand the size, increase the amenities, improve accessibility, and scrub up the facade. Check the website for the latest on scheduled performances. ⊠ *178 Victoria St., at Shuter St., Dundas Square Area* ☎ *416/872–4255* ⊕ *www.masseyhall.com* Ⓜ *Queen.*

Rogers Centre. Toronto's largest performance venue, with seating for up to 52,000, is the spot for the biggest shows in town—Rolling Stones, Bruce Springsteen, Justin Bieber—though the acoustically superior Air Canada Centre is the more widely used arena venue. ⊠ *1 Blue Jays Way, at Spadina Ave., Harbourfront* ☎ *855/985–5000 concert and event tickets* ⊕ *www.rogerscentre.com* Ⓜ *Union.*

In addition to producing numerous works by Canadian artists, the Toronto Dance Theatre collaborates with choreographers from throughout the United States and Europe.

Fodor's Choice **Roy Thomson Hall.** Toronto's premier concert hall, home of the Toronto
★ Symphony Orchestra (TSO), also hosts visiting orchestras, popular
entertainers, and Toronto International Film Festival red-carpet screen-
ings. The 2,630-seat auditorium opened in 1982 and is named after Roy
Thomson, who was born in Toronto and founded the publishing empire
Thomson Corporation (now Thomson Reuters). ⊠ *60 Simcoe St., at
King St., Entertainment District* ☎ *416/872–4255 tickets, 416/593–
4822 tours* ⊕ *www.roythomson.com* Ⓜ *St. Andrew.*

Sony Centre for the Performing Arts. This iconic 3,191-seat hall boasts an
international program of diverse yet mostly mainstream artists such
as Paul Simon, the Just for Laughs Comedy Festival, the Alvin Ailey
American Dance Theater, and numerous other cultural and language-
specific acts that cater to the diversity of Toronto. When this theater
opened in 1960 as the O'Keefe Centre, it showcased the world premiere
of *Camelot,* starring Julie Andrews, Richard Burton, and Robert Gou-
let. Recent renovations restored original elements of the design and
made technological improvements. ⊠ *1 Front St. E, at Yonge St., Old
Town* ☎ *855/872–7669 tickets, 416/368–6161* ⊕ *www.sonycentre.ca*
Ⓜ *Union, King.*

St. Lawrence Centre for the Arts. This center has been the site of great
theater, music, dance, opera, and film since 1970. The two main halls
are the luxuriously appointed **Bluma Appel Theatre** and the **Jane
Mallett Theatre,** both venues for recitals and performances by companies like the Canadian Stage Company, the Toronto Operetta, and
Music Toronto. ⊠ *27 Front St. E, 1 block east of Yonge St., Old Town*
☎ *416/366–7723* ⊕ *www.stlc.com* Ⓜ *King, Union.*

DANCE

Toronto's rich dance scene includes pretty interpretations of classical ballet and edgy, emotionally charged modern-dance performances.

The National Ballet of Canada. Canada's internationally recognized classical-ballet company was founded in 1951 and is made up of more than 70 dancers and its own orchestra. It's the only company in Canada to perform a full range of traditional full-length ballet classics, including frequent stagings of *Swan Lake* and *The Nutcracker*. The company also performs contemporary works and is dedicated to the development of Canadian choreography. The season runs fall through spring at the Four Seasons Centre for the Performing Arts, Canada's first purpose-built ballet opera house, which the ballet shares with the Canadian Opera Company. ⊠ *Four Seasons Centre for the Performing Arts, 145 Queen St. W, Queen West* ☎ *416/345–9595, 866/345–9595 outside Toronto* ⊕ *national.ballet.ca* Ⓜ *Osgoode.*

Harbourfront Centre. This venue has two theaters for dance and two renowned dance series: Next Steps, which runs from September through the spring, and World Stage, which also includes theater and begins in January. The **Fleck Dance Theatre** was built specifically for modern dance in 1983. The proscenium stage hosts some of the best local and Canadian modern and contemporary companies, in addition to some international acts. The **Enwave Theatre** welcomes these same types of dance performances as well as plays and concerts. Both theaters are small (446 and 422 seats, respectively) so you're never far from the stage. ⊠ *Harbourfront Centre, 207 Queen's Quay W, at Lower Simcoe St., Harbourfront* ☎ *416/973–4000* ⊕ *www.harbourfrontcentre.com* Ⓜ *Union.*

Fodor's Choice ★ **Toronto Dance Theatre.** The oldest contemporary dance company in the city, TDT has created more than 100 original works since its beginnings in the 1960s, often using original scores by Canadian composers. Two or three pieces are performed each year in its home theater in Cabbagetown, and one major production is performed at the Harbourfront Centre's Fleck Dance Theatre. ⊠ *80 Winchester St., 1 block east of Parliament St., Greater Toronto* ☎ *416/967–1365* ⊕ *www.tdt.org* Ⓜ *Castle Frank.*

FILM

Toronto has a devoted film audience. The result is a feast of riches—commercial first- and second-run showings, independent films and documentaries, cult classics, myriad festivals, and lecture series for every taste. For movie times, contact the theaters directly, or check CinemaClock (⊕ *www.cinemaclock.com*) or *NOW* (⊕ *www.nowtoronto.com*), online or free on newsstands. Advance tickets are sold through the larger theaters' websites.

FIRST-RUN AND MAINSTREAM MOVIES

Cineplex Cinemas Yonge-Dundas. This 23-screen stadium-seated multiplex shows first-run blockbusters, as well as 3-D and Canada's only 4-DX movie experience. Once you have your ticket, it's five escalators up to the screens themselves. If you want to catch the trailers, take the elevator. ⊠ *Suite 402, 10 Dundas St. E, at Yonge St., Dundas Square Area* 🕾 *416/977–9262* ⊕ *www.cineplex.com* Ⓜ *Dundas.*

MORE LISTINGS TO PERUSE

Toronto has many more theaters, festivals, and film events than we're able to fit within these pages. A great source for what's new and interesting in alternative cinema and festivals is the online magazine *Toronto Film Scene* (⊕ *thetfs.ca*).

Cineplex Varsity and Varsity VIP. The 12 screens here show new releases. The smaller, licensed VIP screening rooms (ages 19 and up, C$20) have seat-side waitstaff ready to take your beverage and concession-stand orders. There's a licensed lounge for prescreening drinks as well. Regular movie tickets start at C$13. ⊠ *Manulife Centre, 3rd fl., 55 Bloor St. W, at Bay St., Yorkville* 🕾 *416/961–6304* ⊕ *www.cineplex.com* Ⓜ *Bay or Bloor.*

Polson Pier Drive-in Theatre. For an old-fashioned treat, park your car at this downtown drive-in that locals still refer to by its former name, the Docks. Open Victoria Day weekend in May to Labour Day in September (except for major electrical storms), it shows first-run double features on Friday, Saturday, and Sunday evenings. The gates open at 8:30 pm, and films start at sundown, usually around 9:30. Purchase tickets on-site (C$15); on Sunday, admission is C$25 per carload. ⊠ *176 Cherry St., south of Lake Shore Blvd., Harbourfront* 🕾 *416/465–4653* ⊕ *www.thedocks.com.*

Scotiabank Theatre Toronto. In the heart of the Entertainment District, this megaplex with 14 screens shows all the latest blockbusters and is the place to see films with impressive special effects. Tickets are C$13; a few dollars more for 3-D and three-screen panoramic viewing. ⊠ *259 Richmond St. W, at John St., Entertainment District* 🕾 *416/368–5600* ⊕ *www.cineplex.com* Ⓜ *Osgoode.*

INDEPENDENT, FOREIGN, AND REVIVAL FILMS

Harbourfront Centre. In July and August, free movies are screened outdoors as part of the Free Flicks program. Documentaries, frequently accompanying summer festivals, cultural events, and retrospectives, are presented ad hoc throughout the year. ⊠ *235 Queen's Quay W, at Lower Simcoe St., Harbourfront* 🕾 *416/973–4000* ⊕ *www.harbourfrontcentre.com* Ⓜ *Union.*

Hot Docs Ted Rogers Cinema. If you like your films factual, informative, and inspiring, then the Hot Docs Cinema is for you. Come here for documentaries on political movements, such as *Under the Sun* , or perhaps something more esoteric like *Mussels in Love*. The only documentary-focused cinema in North America, the Hot Docs Cinema (formerly the

Bloor) is the permanent home of the annual Hot Docs festival; numerous other festivals, including TIFF, have screenings here, too. There are occasional showings of classics and rep-cinema favorites, such as *Fitzcarraldo* or *The Rocky Horror Picture Show*. Tickets are C$12. Festival screenings and some special presentations are pricier. ✉ *506 Bloor St. W, at Bathurst St., The Annex* ☎ *416/637–3123* ⊕ *www.hotdocscinema.ca* Ⓜ *Bathurst.*

The Revue. This beloved neighborhood movie house (the oldest in Toronto) is operated by the nonprofit Revue Film Society. Onscreen are second-run Hollywood films, documentaries, classics (cult and non-), silent films accompanied by live piano, and the occasional live music performance. Admission is C$12. ✉ *400 Roncesvalles Ave., at Howard Park Ave., Greater Toronto* ☎ *416/531–9950* ⊕ *www.revuecinema.ca* Ⓜ *Dundas West, then 504 streetcar to Howard Park Ave.*

The Royal. This fully restored 1939 single-screen theater shows indie documentaries, features, and art films on a state-of-the-art digital projector. ✉ *608 College St., at Clinton St., Little Italy* ☎ *416/466–4400* ⊕ *www.theroyal.to* Ⓜ *506 streetcar across College St.*

TIFF Bell Lightbox. Operated by the Toronto International Film Festival (TIFF) organization, this state-of-the-art five-screen, five-story complex shows classic and avant-garde films, director retrospectives, actor tributes, national cinema spotlights, exclusive limited runs, and new documentaries and artistic films. Tickets are C$14. ✉ *350 King St., at John St., Entertainment District* ☎ *416/599–8433* ⊕ *www.tiff.net/ tiffbelllightbox* Ⓜ *St. Andrew.*

THEATER

Toronto has the third-largest theater scene in the world, following London and New York. Here you can see Broadway shows as well as a range of smaller Canadian and international productions from reproduced "straight" plays to experimental performances.

For reviews, news, and schedules, check ⊕ *www.stage-door.com* (a wealth of information—this is where industry types browse), the *Globe and Mail* Arts section (⊕ *www.theglobeandmail.com/arts*), and the free newsweekly *Now* (⊕ *www.nowtoronto/stage*).

COMMERCIAL THEATERS

Ed Mirvish Theatre. This 1920 vaudeville theater has had a checkered history—it was chopped up into six cinemas in the '70s—and has had numerous names over the years, including the Pantages, the Imperial, and most recently the Canon. Now named in honor of local businessman and theater impresario Ed Mirvish, the theater is one of the most architecturally and acoustically exciting live theaters in Toronto. Today it hosts big-budget musicals, such as *Wicked, Matilda ,* and *Beautiful*, and occasionally plays and dance shows. The theater itself is considered one of the most beautiful in the world and was refurbished in 1989 in preparation for the Canadian debut of the 10-year engagement of

SUMMER THEATER

Summer is the off-season for noncommercial theaters, but—lucky for us—there's no rest for the weary thespians. To avoid getting stuck with a stinker, read reviews for individual festival plays in local newspapers.

Shakespeare in High Park. Every summer, Shakespeare's most popular plays are performed under the stars at this outdoor amphitheater. Productions are usually knockouts and run from July through August, weather permitting. Performances are Pay What You Can, with a suggested C$20 donation, and regular seating is on a first-come, first-served basis. To ensure you get a spot, reserve a cushion in the Premium Zone online for C$25. Performances are Tuesday through Sunday at 8; gates open at 6 pm. It gets cold in this leafy park, so bring layers and a blanket to sit on; picnicking is encouraged. ✉ *High Park, High Park Ave., main entrance off Bloor St. W., Greater Toronto* ☎ *416/368–3110* ⊕ *www.canadianstage.com* Ⓜ *High Park.*

SummerWorks Performance Festival. More than 50 plays, performances, concerts, and happenings deemed sufficiently forward-thinking and provocative are staged at various venues around Queen West for the 11-day SummerWorks Performance Festival in August. Tickets are about C$15 per show. ✉ *Queen West* ☎ *416/628–8216* ⊕ *www. summerworks.ca.*

Toronto Fringe Festival. The city's largest theater festival, with more than 140 shows taking place in over 30 unique venues (previous spots include a laundromat, storage space, and a back alley), takes place over 12 days in late June and early July. Raw and untested works by emerging (and sometimes established) artists are the norm. Tickets are C$12 or less per show. The most popular shows are given extended runs in the Best of the Fringe Festival. ✉ *Toronto* ☎ *416/966–1062* ⊕ *www.fringetoronto.com.*

The Phantom of the Opera , Canada's longest-running stage musical. Designed by world-renowned theater architect Thomas Lamb, it has columns, a grand staircase, gold-leaf detailing, and crystal chandeliers. ✉ *244 Victoria St., 1 block south of Dundas St. E, Dundas Square Area* ☎ *416/364–4100 theater, 416/872–1212 tickets, 800/461–3333 tickets* ⊕ *www.mirvish.com* Ⓜ *Dundas.*

Princess of Wales. State-of-the-art facilities and wonderful murals by American artist Frank Stella grace this 2,000-seat theater, built by father-and-son producer team Ed and David Mirvish in 1993 to accommodate the technically demanding musical *Miss Saigon*. Big-budget musicals like *Lion King* and *The Book of Mormon* and plays such as *War Horse* are showcased. ✉ *300 King St. W, at John St., Entertainment District* ☎ *416/351–9011 theater, 416/872–1212 tickets, 800/461–3333 tickets* ⊕ *www.mirvish.com* Ⓜ *St. Andrew.*

Royal Alexandra. The most historic of the Mirvish theaters, the "Royal Alex" has been the place to be seen in Toronto since 1907 and is the oldest continuously operating legitimate theater in North America. The restored and reconfigured theater features 1,244 plush red seats, gold plasterwork, and baroque swirls and flourishes that make theatergoing a refined experience. Charleston Heston made his debut here and Lawrence Olivier, Edith Piaf, Mary Pickford, Alan Bates, and John Gielgud have also graced the stage. Programs are a mix of blockbuster musicals and dramatic productions, some touring before or after Broadway appearances. ✉ *260 King St. W, Entertainment District* ☎ *416/593–4216 theater, 416/872–1212 tickets, 800/461–3333 tickets* ⊕ *www.mirvish.com* Ⓜ *St. Andrew.*

SMALL THEATERS AND COMPANIES

Seasons at most of these smaller theaters are September or October through May or June, though some special performances might be scheduled in summer. Soulpepper is open year-round.

Buddies in Bad Times Theatre. Canada's largest queer theater company presents edgy plays and festivals, as well as specialty after-hours events like burlesque and stand-up. Most tickets for Sunday shows are Pay What You Can. ✉ *12 Alexander St., just east of Yonge St., Church–Wellesley* ☎ *416/975–8555* ⊕ *www.buddiesinbadtimes.com* Ⓜ *Wellesley.*

Canadian Stage. Canadian- and European-inspired plays that incorporate dance, photography, video, and other media are at the heart of this company's mission, but it is known also for its excellent Shakespeare in High Park productions. The **Bluma Appel Theatre** at the St. Lawrence Centre for the Arts seats 868, while the more intimate **Berkeley Street Theatre** has a capacity of 244. ✉ *Bluma Appel Theatre, 27 Front St. E, Old Town* ☎ *416/368–3110 box office, 877/399–2651 toll-free* ⊕ *www.canadianstage.com* Ⓜ *King.*

Factory Theatre. This is the country's largest producer of exclusively Canadian plays. Many of the company's shows are world premieres that have gone on to tour Canada and win prestigious awards. ✉ *125 Bathurst St., at Adelaide St., Entertainment District* ☎ *416/504–9971* ⊕ *www.factorytheatre.ca* Ⓜ *511 Bathurst, 501 Queen or 504 King streetcars to Bathurst St.*

Hart House Theatre. The main theater space of U of T since 1919, Hart House mounts four emerging-artist and student productions per season (September through March). At least one musical and one Shakespeare play are always part of the program. The theater is also home to many student-produced works and professional performing arts groups. Tickets can be bought on-site or through the website. ✉ *7 Hart House Circle, off Wellesley St. university entrance, Queen's Park* ☎ *416/978–8849* ⊕ *www.harthousetheatre.ca* Ⓜ *Museum, St. George, Queen's Park.*

Fodor'sChoice
★
Soulpepper Theatre Company. Established in 1997 by 12 of Canada's leading theater artists, this repertory theater company produces classic plays and shows year-round, reimagining the works of Henrik Ibsen, Anton Chekhov, and Samuel Beckett while commissioning new adaptations by Canadian talent . The company makes its home in the Young Centre for the Performing Arts in the historic Distillery District. ✉ *50 Tank House*

Lane, Distillery District ☎ *416/866–8666* ⊕ *www.soulpepper.ca* Ⓜ *504 King streetcar to Parliament St.*

Tarragon Theatre. The natural habitat for contemporary Canadian theater is in this old warehouse in the railroad district. The main stage is 205 seats and presents plays by new and established Canadian playwrights. Maverick companies often rent the smaller of the Tarragon's theaters (100 seats) or one of the studio spaces upstairs for interesting experimental works. ✉ *30 Bridgman Ave., 1 block north of Dupont St., The Annex* ☎ *416/531–1827* ⊕ *www.tarragontheatre.com* Ⓜ *Dupont.*

Théâtre Français de Toronto. High-quality French-language drama—with English subtitles—is performed at this theater, whose French and French-Canadian repertoire ranges from classical to contemporary. A children's play and a teen show are part of the season, which features about a half dozen plays. ✉ *Berkeley Street Theatre, 26 Berkeley St., 2nd fl., at Front St. E, Old Town* ☎ *416/534–6604* ⊕ *www.theatre-francais.com* Ⓜ *King then 504 King streetcar eastbound to Ontario.*

Theatre Passe Muraille. Toronto's oldest alternative theater company, established in 1968, has long been the home of fine Canadian collaborative theater and has launched the careers of many Canadian actors and playwrights. ✉ *16 Ryerson Ave., near Queen and Bathurst Sts., Queen West* ☎ *416/504–7529* ⊕ *www.passemuraille.ca* Ⓜ *Osgoode, 501 Queen streetcar west to Bathurst; or Bathurst, then 511 streetcar to Queen.*

FAMILY **Young People's Theatre.** Plays are contemporary, relevant and kid-focused at YPT, whether a heavily interactive romp, such as *Where the Wild Things Are*, which is based on Maurice Sendak's classic book, or a dramatic thought-provoker, *Hana's Suitcase*, the story of a young girl living during the Holocaust. Productions aren't condescending nor do they compromise on dramatic integrity. They are as entertaining for adults as for kids. ✉ *165 Front St. E, between Jarvis and Sherbourne Sts., Old Town* ☎ *416/862–2222* ⊕ *www.youngpeoplestheatre.ca* Ⓜ *King or Union.*

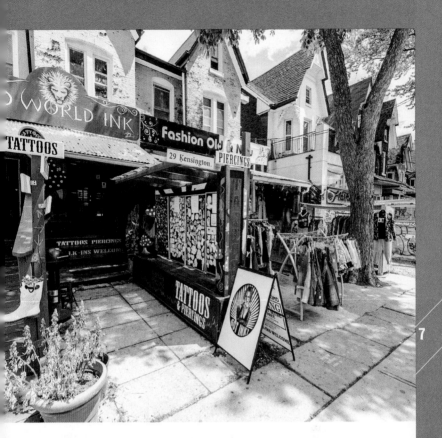

SHOPPING

Updated
by Natalia
Manzocco

Toronto prides itself on having some of the finest shopping in North America. Indeed, many of the world's most famous boutiques have branches here, especially in the Yorkville area, where you can find such luxury labels as Chanel, Prada, and Cartier. For those a little leaner of wallet, you can join in one of Torontonians' favorite pastimes: bargain hunting. Locals wear discount threads like badges of honor and stretch their dollar at Winners—where overstocked and liquidated designer pieces and last-season fashions are slashed to a fraction of their original retail prices.

Toronto has a large arts-and-crafts community, with numerous art galleries, custom jewelers, clothing designers, and artisans. Sophisticated glass sculpture and Inuit art are ideal as gifts or for your own home. A few record stores are still going strong despite the dominance of digital music. The survivors' trump card has been focused inventory and knowledgeable staff—head to Rotate This for alternative and indie music or Atelier Grigorian for classical and jazz. Bookstores such as Indigo have lounge areas where you can sip a coffee from the in-store café while perusing books by Canadian authors such as Alice Munro, Ann-Marie MacDonald, and Rohinton Mistry; don't miss popular independent bookstore, Type Books.

When it comes to department stores, all roads lead to Holt Renfrew on Bloor Street West, the epicenter of Toronto's designer shopping. A mere block east is the more mid-price department store Hudson's Bay. A second Hudson's Bay can be found across from Eaton Centre, a sprawling shopping complex with multilevel parking in the heart of the city.

PLANNING

HOURS

Most shops open by 10 am Monday to Saturday and close at 6 or 7 pm Monday to Thursday, 8 or 9 pm Friday, and as early as 6 pm Saturday. On Sunday, most downtown shops open noon to 5 pm. There are, however, exceptions. Large chain stores downtown often stay open weeknights until 9 or 10 pm.

SALES

The biggest sale day of the year is Boxing Day, the first business day after Christmas, when nearly everything in the city is marked down significantly. In fact, clothing prices tend to drop even further as winter fades. Summer sales start in late June and continue through August.

SHIPPING

Nearly all stores that sell larger items like sculpture and furniture will ship to anywhere in the United States or Canada.

TAXES

A hefty rate of 13% Harmonized Sales Tax is levied on most goods and services.

Shopping listings are organized by neighborhood.

HARBOURFRONT, ENTERTAINMENT DISTRICT, AND THE FINANCIAL DISTRICT

7

HARBOURFRONT

Shopping in the Harbourfront area is somewhat limited, but the Harbourfront Centre complex is worth a look for crafts and design items.

SPECIALTY GIFTS

The Centre Shop. You'll find plenty of locally made crafts and clever design objects here, including textiles, jewelry, ceramics, wood carvings, and glass pieces blown in Harbourfront's own studios. The shop also carries quirky design items from outside Toronto, including Alvar Aalto vases and gadgets for the kitchen or office by Kikkerland. ⊠ *Harbourfront Centre, 235 Queens Quay W, Harbourfront* ☎ *416/973–4993* ⊕ *www.harbourfrontcentre.com* Ⓜ *Union.*

THE ENTERTAINMENT DISTRICT

While there aren't a ton of shops between the theaters and restaurants of King Street West between Bay and Spadina, those that are there are some of the city's best.

ANTIQUES

Fodor'sChoice **Toronto Antiques on King.** The 7,000 square feet of this shop provide
★ ample opportunity for browsing pre- or postshow (the Princess of Wales theater is next door) among the cabinets, shelves, and bins overflowing with porcelain, silver tea sets, majolica pottery, Lalique vases,

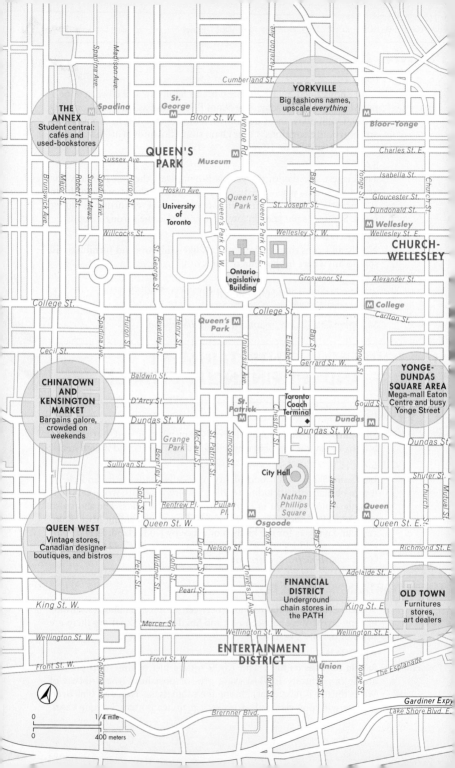

THE ANNEX
Student central: cafés and used-bookstores

YORKVILLE
Big fashions names, upscale *everything*

CHINATOWN AND KENSINGTON MARKET
Bargains galore, crowded on weekends

YONGE-DUNDAS SQUARE AREA
Mega-mall Eaton Centre and busy Yonge Street

QUEEN WEST
Vintage stores, Canadian designer boutiques, and bistros

FINANCIAL DISTRICT
Underground chain stores in the PATH

OLD TOWN
Furnitures stores, art dealers

QUEEN'S PARK

CHURCH-WELLESLEY

University of Toronto

Ontario Legislative Building

Queen's Park

Museum

City Hall

Nathan Phillips Square

Toronto Coach Terminal

Grange Park

ENTERTAINMENT DISTRICT

Bloor-Yonge

Spadina

St. George

Museum

Wellesley

College

St. Patrick

Dundas

Queen

Osgoode

Union

Cumberland St.

Bloor St. W.

Charles St. E.

Isabella St.

Sussex Ave.

Hoskin Ave.

St. Joseph St.

Gloucester St.

Dundonald St.

Wellesley St. W.

Wellesley St. E.

Willcocks St.

Grosvenor St.

Alexander St.

College St.

College St.

Carlton St.

Cecil St.

Gerrard St. W.

Baldwin St.

D'Arcy St.

Dundas St. W.

Dundas St. W.

Dundas St.

Sullivan St.

Shuter St.

Renfrew Pl.

Pullan Pl.

Queen St. W.

Queen St. E.

Nelson St.

Richmond St. E

Adelaide St. E.

Pearl St.

King St. W.

King St. E

Mercer St.

Wellington St. W.

Wellington St. W.

Wellington St. E.

Front St. W.

Front St. W.

The Esplanade

Brenner Blvd.

Gardiner Expy.

Lake Shore Blvd. W.

Spadina Ave.

Madison Ave.

Brunswick Ave.

Major St.

Robert St.

Sussex Mews

Spadina Ave.

Huron St.

St. George St.

Beverley St.

Henry St.

McCaul St.

St. Patrick St.

Simcoe St.

Soho St.

Peter St.

John St.

Widmer St.

Duncan St.

University Ave.

York St.

Chestnut St.

Elizabeth St.

Bay St.

Bay St.

Yonge St.

Yonge St.

Church St.

Mutual St.

James St.

Bay St.

Avenue Rd.

Hazelton Ave.

Queen's Park Cir. W.

Queen's Park Cir. E.

0   1/4 mile
0   400 meters

collectibles, and antique maps. It's also Toronto's leading purveyor of vintage and estate jewelry, making it a popular stop for those seeking out engagement rings. ✉ *284 King St. W (2nd fl.), at John St., Entertainment District* ☎ *416/260–9057* ⊕ *www.cynthiafindlay.com* ⊙ *Closed Mon.* Ⓜ *St. Andrew.*

OUTDOOR EQUIPMENT AND CLOTHING

Fodor's Choice ★ **Mountain Equipment Co-op.** MEC (rhymes with "check"), the much-beloved Toronto spot for anyone remotely interested in camping, sells wares for minor and major expeditions. It's also a go-to spot for cycling gear. A baffling assortment of backpacks allows you to choose anything from a schoolbag to a globe-trotting sack. For $5, you get lifetime membership to the co-op. ✉ *400 King St. W, at Charlotte St., Entertainment District* ☎ *416/340–2667* ⊕ *www.mec.ca* Ⓜ *St. Andrew.*

SPECIALTY GIFTS

Fodor's Choice ★ **TIFF Shop.** This sleek little gift shop, located at the cinematic HQ of the Toronto International Film Festival, the TIFF Bell Lightbox, stocks an ever-changing selection of cinematic paraphernalia linked to TIFF's current program (James Bond, Chinese cinema, etc.) The exhaustive inventory of film books includes many difficult-to-find titles, biographies of just about every director you can think of, and studies of even the most obscure film movements. There's also unusual gift items and cute items for children. ✉ *TIFF Bell Lightbox, 350 King St. W, at John St., Entertainment District* ☎ *416/934–7959* ⊕ *tiff.net/tiffshop* Ⓜ *St. Andrew.*

THE FINANCIAL DISTRICT

Toronto's Financial District has a vast underground maze of shopping warrens that burrow between and underneath its office towers. The tenants of this Underground City are mostly the usual assortment of chain stores, with an occasional surprise. Marked PATH, the walkways (the underground street system) help visitors navigate the subterranean mall, though it can be confusing for novices. The network runs roughly from the Fairmont Royal York hotel near Union Station north to the Atrium at Bay and Dundas.

CLOTHING

Moores Clothing For Men. Browse through thousands of discounted Canadian-made dress pants, sport coats, and suits, including many famous labels. Sizes run from extra short to extra tall and from regular to oversize; the quality is solid and the service is good. ✉ *100 Yonge St., at King St., Financial District* ☎ *416/363–5442* ⊕ *www.mooresclothing.com* Ⓜ *King.*

SPORTING GOODS

Running Room. The knowledgeable staff at this chain can guide you to the perfect pair of running shoes. Running Rooms have spawned a running community, and shops have sprouted up all over the city; group runs commence every Wednesday evening and Sunday morning. ✉ *53 Yonge St., at Wellington, Financial District* ☎ *416/867–7575* ⊕ *www.runningroom.com* Ⓜ *King.*

OLD TOWN AND THE DISTILLERY DISTRICT

OLD TOWN

Regal, historic buildings housing upscale businesses dominate this area, but if you're into furniture, design, high-end antiques, or discerning galleries, walking King Street east of Yonge will be an afternoon well spent. ■ TIP→ Satiate your appetite at the enormous St. Lawrence Market.

ART AND CRAFTS GALLERIES

Feheley Fine Arts. Browse contemporary and even avant-garde Canadian Inuit art—a far cry from the traditional whale carvings and stone-cut prints you may expect—at this family-owned gallery founded in 1964. ⊠ *65 George St., at King St. E,, Old Town* ☎ *416/323–1373* ⊕ *www. feheleyfinearts.com* Ⓜ *King, then 504 streetcar east.*

HOME DECOR

UpCountry. This 44,000-square-foot store holds a unique mix of furniture collections that reflect leading-edge design principles. Well-made and reasonably priced, many of the upholstered sofas and chairs are built in small runs by Canadian manufacturers; there are European designers, too. ⊠ *310 King St. E, at Parliament St., Old Town* ☎ *416/366–7477* ⊕ *www.upcountry.com* Ⓜ *King, then 504 streetcar east.*

MARKETS

Fodor'sChoice ★ **St. Lawrence Market.** Nearly 70 vendors occupy the historic permanent indoor market and sell items such as fish, meats, produce, caviar, and crafts. The building, on the south side of Front Street, was once Toronto's first city hall. ⊠ *92–95 Front St. E , at Jarvis St., Old Town* ☎ *416/392–7219* ⊕ *www.stlawrencemarket.com* Ⓜ *Union or King.*

DISTILLERY DISTRICT

The Distillery District's pedestrianized brick alleyways and Victorian industrial buildings boast some of the city's best shopping. Come here for one-of-a-kind crafts, artisanal food, stylish urban threads, and art to hang on your walls. Restaurants and cafés abound—as do tourists—and there's a brewpub to quench your thirst. A once neglected pocket, the Distillery District sits on its own east of downtown. Take a streetcar along King or a bus down Parliament, and then walk south from where the two roads intersect.

ART GALLERIES

Corkin Gallery. With work by contemporary artists such as Iain Baxter& and David Urban, this gallery is one of the most fascinating in town. See hand-painted photos, documentary photos, fashion photography, and mixed-media art. ⊠ *7 Tank House La., Distillery District* ☎ *416/979–1980* ⊕ *www.corkingallery.com* Ⓜ *King, then 504 streetcar east to Parliament; or Castle Frank, then 65 Parliament bus to King.*

CLOTHING

Fodor'sChoice ★ **Gotstyle.** This Torontonian start-up has hit the nail on the head, providing stylish men clothes—Tiger of Sweden, Ted Baker, and John Varvatos—to the residents of the city's downtown condos. This huge airy branch carries ladies' clothing as well, including Montréal's Mackage outerwear and Malene Birger dresses. Head up to the lush purple-carpeted mezzanine level for business and eveningwear and a round on the purple pool table. ⊠ *21 Trinity St., Distillery District* ☎ *416/260–9696* ⊕ *www.gotstyle.com* Ⓜ *King, then 504 streetcar east to Parliament; or Castle Frank, then 65 Parliament bus to King.*

JEWELRY AND ACCESSORIES

Corktown Designs. Most of the reasonably priced jewelry at this Distillery District shop is Canadian-designed, and all of it is unique and handmade. Pieces range from inexpensive glass-and-silver pendants to Swiss-made stainless steel rings and pricier pieces set with pearls and other semiprecious stones. ⊠ *5 Trinity St., Distillery District* ☎ *416/861–3020* ⊕ *www.corktowndesigns.com* Ⓜ *King, then 504 streetcar east to Parliament; or Castle Frank, then 65 Parliament bus to King.*

SHOES, HANDBAGS, AND LEATHER GOODS

Fodor's Choice ★ **John Fluevog.** Fluevog's funky shoes look their best in this barely converted high-ceilinged industrial space. The building was once the distillery boiler house, which would explain the three-story brick oven that accounts for a third of the floor-space, and the safety ladder leading to an overhead catwalk. Take a seat on the stunning embossed leather couch when trying on the fun, cutting-edge merchandise—some shoes can be custom-colored right in the shop. ⊠ *4 Trinity St., Distillery District* ☎ *416/583–1970* ⊕ *www.fluevog.com* Ⓜ *King, then 504 streetcar east to Parliament; or Castle Frank, then 65 Parliament bus to King.*

WINE AND SPECIALTY FOOD

Soma Chocolatemaker. Satisfy your sweet tooth just by inhaling the delicate wafts of chocolate, dried fruits, and roasted nuts in this gourmet chocolate shop that specializes in microbatch, fair-trade chocolate. Big sellers include crystallized Australian ginger tumbled in dark Peruvian chocolate, spiced chai tea truffles, and gelato. For something different, try the Bicarin, a thick mixture of melted chocolate, espresso, and whipped cream. ⊠ *32 Tank House La., Distillery District* ☎ *416/815–7662* ⊕ *www.somachocolate.com* Ⓜ *King, then 504 streetcar east to Parliament; or Castle Frank, then 65 Parliament bus to King.*

YONGE-DUNDAS SQUARE AREA

Dundas Square is the go-to place for chain stores like Gap, Zara, Roots, and Aritzia, electronics giant Best Buy, and cheap souvenir shops, which line Yonge Street to the north (though their numbers are beginning to dwindle). The mammoth Eaton Centre shopping mall, which opens up into the square, has more than 230 stores (Coach, Banana Republic, and the Apple Store, to name a few) and is anchored by Hudson's Bay and Nordstrom at either end.

CLOTHING

Urban Outfitters. The young and trendy scan the racks here for the latest "it" piece. Prices are comparatively high considering the clothes' often low quality. Don't miss the quirky, modern housewares and oddball coffee-table books. There is another location in Queen West at 481 Queen Street West, and one in the Yonge Eglinton Centre at 2300 Yonge Street. ⊠ *235 Yonge St. W, north of Queen St., Dundas Square Area* ☎ *416/214–1466* ⊕ *www.urbanoutfitters.com* Ⓜ *Dundas, Queen.*

DEPARTMENT STORES AND SHOPPING CENTERS

Eaton Centre. This two-block-long complex with exposed industrial-style ceilings is anchored at its northern end (Dundas Street) by Nordstrom, Uniqlo, and H&M. Across the street from the southern end is the flagship of Canadian department store Hudson's Bay, which shares a home with luxury department store Saks Fifth Avenue. ■ TIP➔ **Prices at Eaton Centre increase with altitude—Level 1 offers popularly priced merchandise, Level 2 is directed to the middle-income shopper, and Level 3 sells more expensive fashion and luxury goods.** The complex is bordered by Yonge Street on the east, and James Street and Trinity Square on the west. ⊠ *220 Yonge St., Dundas Square Area* ☎ *416/598–8560* ⊕ *www. torontoeatoncentre.com* Ⓜ *Dundas, Queen.*

CHINATOWN, KENSINGTON MARKET, AND QUEEN WEST

CHINATOWN

While Chinese-Canadians have made Spadina Avenue their own from Queen Street north to College Street, Spadina's basic bill of fare is still "bargains galore." Its collection of inexpensive Chinese clothing stores, Chinese restaurants, ethnic food and fruit shops, and eateries (not only Chinese, but also Vietnamese, Japanese, and Thai) give you your money's worth. A cluster of galleries surrounds the Art Gallery of Ontario (AGO) just east of the area. Take the (north–south) Spadina streetcar or the (east–west) College or Dundas streetcars to Spadina Avenue, or walk from St. Patrick.

ART GALLERIES

Bau-Xi Gallery. Paul Wong, an artist and dealer from Vancouver, started this gallery, which is directly across the street from the Art Gallery of Ontario. The paintings and sculpture are a window into contemporary Canadian art, with both emerging and established artists featured. Just a few steps down at 324 Dundas West is Bau-Xi Photo, which shows Canadian and international fine art photography. ⊠ *340 Dundas St. W, at McCaul St., Chinatown* ☎ *416/977–0600* ⊕ *www.bau-xi.com* Ⓜ *St. Patrick.*

TORONTO'S GALLERIES

Toronto is Canada's cosmopolitan art center, with a few hundred commercial art galleries carrying items as varied as glass sculpture, Inuit designs, and multimedia pieces. Queen West has long been the arts hub of Toronto, but as rents rise, few galleries remain. Most have moved north and west to Dundas West around Ossington, or as far north as the industrial stretches of Dupont. ■TIP➔ If you're really dedicated, it's worth heading up Ossington to Dundas West, and then farther west to Morrow to the fixtures of Olga Korper and Christopher Cutts. The galleries in Yorkville and the historic Distillery District tend to show well-established artists. Head to 401 Richmond for a smattering of cutting-edge galleries under one

roof. Naturally, the area around the Art Gallery of Ontario is saturated with contemporary art galleries, too, most of which offer affordable pieces by Canadian artists.

To find out about special art exhibits, check *NOW*, a free weekly local newspaper on culture distributed on Thursday—or *Toronto Life* magazine. You can pick up a copy of *Slate* (⊕ www.slateartguide.com) at most galleries; the listings are very comprehensive. The website of *Canadian Art* magazine (⊕ www. canadianart.ca) is also a good source of information on gallery happenings. ■TIP➔ Most galleries are open Tuesday through Saturday from 10 to 5 or 6, but call to confirm.

HOME DECOR

Tap Phong Trading Co. Inc. The mops, brooms, and multicolor bins and buckets stacked outside make this kitchenware and restaurant equipment store appear much like all the other Chinese knickknack shops along Spadina. However, once you're inside you'll find endless aisles stacked to the rafters with rice bowls and bamboo steamers, and restaurateurs piling up their shopping trollies with glasses and servingware to feed the masses. ■TIP➔ A gap halfway along the north wall leads to the industrial-scale equipment. ⊠ *360 Spadina Ave., south of Baldwin St., Chinatown* ☎ *416/977–6364* ⊕ *www.tapphong.com* Ⓜ *Spadina, then streetcar 510.*

MUSEUM STORES

shopAGO. The store attached to the Art Gallery of Ontario has an overwhelming selection of curiosities, from books on maximal architecture to pop art–inspired toys to prints of celebrated paintings. Adults and kids can shop side by side among the books and fun educational items. ⊠ *317 Dundas St. W, at McCaul St., Chinatown* ☎ *416/979–6610* ⊕ *www.ago.net/shop* Ⓜ *St. Patrick.*

Fodor's Choice ★ **Textile Museum Shop.** Tucked away on the second floor of the already hidden Textile Museum, this shop is one of the city's best-kept secrets and an absolute treasure trove. It overflows with textile-based art from Canadian artisans, as well as works by craftspeople from around the world keeping traditional, and often disappearing, skills alive. There are loads of books, scarves galore, unusual bags and hats, and crafty stuff for kids too; many items are accessibly priced. ■TIP➔ Check out the changing exhibition on the second and third floors while you're here (admission charge) to develop a taste for the shop's featured items; past exhibits have included Finnish designer Marimekko and Afghan war rugs. ✉ *55 Centre Ave., at Dundas St. W and University Ave., Chinatown* ☎ *416/599–5321* ⊕ *www.textilemuseum.ca* Ⓜ *St. Patrick.*

KENSINGTON MARKET

Tucked behind Spadina west to Bathurst Street, between Dundas and College streets to the south and north, is this hippie-meets-hipster collection of inexpensive vintage-clothing stores, cheap ethnic eateries, coffee shops, head shops, and specialty food shops specializing in cheeses, baked goods, fish, dry goods, health food, and more. ■TIP➔ Be warned—this area can be extraordinarily crowded on weekends; do not drive. Take the College streetcar to Spadina or Augusta, or the Spadina streetcar to College or Nassau.

CLOTHING

Bungalow. Teak tables, chairs, and cabinets give this vintage shop the feel of a strangely cavernous 1970s bungalow. Organized racks are filled with Hawaiian and second-hand T-shirts, vintage 1970s dresses, and comfortably worn jeans, but you'll also find new styles, too. ✉ *273 Augusta Ave., Kensington Market* ☎ *416/598–0204* ⊕ *www.bungalow. to* Ⓜ *Spadina, then streetcar 510 to College or Baldwin.*

Fodor's Choice ★ **Courage My Love.** The best and longest-running vintage store in Kensington Market is crammed with the coolest retro stuff, from sunglasses to sundresses, plus an ample supply of cowboy boots for guys and gals, all at low prices. Not everything is secondhand here: there's a wall of sparkly Indian-inspired clothing, lots of costume jewelry, and a selection of unique buttons. ✉ *14 Kensington Ave., at Dundas St. W, Kensington Market* ☎ *416/979–1992* Ⓜ *St. Patrick, then streetcar 504 west.*

Tom's Place. Find bargains aplenty on brand-name suits and shirts from brands like Calvin Klein, Armani, and DKNY. Tom Mihalik, the store's owner, keeps his prices low (and will often go lower, if you ask politely). The sales staff can quickly navigate the selection and help you put together a complete and well-accessorized look. ✉ *190 Baldwin St., at Augusta Ave., Kensington Market* ☎ *416/596–0297* ⊕ *www.toms-place.com* Ⓜ *St. Patrick, then streetcar 505 west.*

SPECIALTY GIFTS

Fodor's Choice ★ **Kid Icarus.** At this old-school printing company, you'll find a range of very cool retro designs including band posters, mock-retro tourism posters, and other one-of-a-kind creations. You'll also find screen-printed Greetings from Toronto postcards, art supplies, and contemporary indie crafts in the gift shop. ✉ *205 Augusta Ave., Kensington Market* ☎ *416/977–7236* ⊕ *www.kidicarus.ca* Ⓜ *Spadina, then streetcar 510 to Baldwin or Dundas.*

QUEEN WEST

In the 1980s, the strip of Queen from University to Spadina was synonymous with all things hip—it was a vibrant area filled with students. After years of gentrification, the area is now dominated by chains, but it's still busy, buzzy, and a great place to shop. West of Spadina, a few gems are mixed in with textile shops clinging to earlier days and a couple of incongruous newcomers.

ANTIQUES

Abraham's Trading Inc. Indicative of a Queen West long gone, the most remarkable thing about Abraham's is that somehow it survives. Handwritten signs snarl "don't even think about it" amid a jumble of haphazardly piled rusty props and dusty "antiques" from doctor's bags and deer trophies to worn church doors, creepy clown shoes, and a sparkling collection of 1950s microphones. Purchasing anything will take some guts—few prices are marked, although everything, they say, is for sale. ⊠ *635 Queen St. W, at Bathurst St., Queen West* ☎ *416/504–6210* Ⓜ *Osgoode, then 501 Queen streetcar west; Bathurst, then 511 streetcar.*

ART GALLERIES

Fodor's Choice
★

401 Richmond. Packed with galleries, a couple of interesting shops, and two cafés, this beautifully refurbished industrial building is an essential component of an exploration of Toronto's contemporary art scene. Check out **YYZ Artists' Outlet,** which holds consistently engaging shows in its two rooms, or **Gallery 44** for contemporary photography. There's also the respected artist collective **Red Head Gallery.** Pick up a Ukranian zither or South African kora at temple-to-world-music **Musideum;** concerts are also held in the space. Make sure you don't miss well-stocked **Swipe** for books on all things design and **Spacing** for stylish Toronto-themed T-shirts, prints, and knickknacks that make perfect souvenirs. ⊠ *401 Richmond Ave., at Spadina, Queen West* ☎ *416/595–5900* ⊕ *www.401richmond.net* ☾ *Closed Sun.* Ⓜ *Spadina, then 510 streetcar; or Osgoode, then 501 streetcar west.*

BOOKS

Fodor's Choice
★

Swipe Design Books & Objects. Books on advertising, art, and architecture pack the shelves of this aesthetically pleasing store, fittingly located in the arty 401 Richmond heritage building. Part of the store is devoted to modern gifts, including elegant writing tools, modern jewelry, and Pantone-themed everything. ⊠ *Suite 121, 401 Richmond St. W, at Spadina Ave., Queen West* ☎ *416/363–1332, 800/567–9473* ⊕ *www.swipe.com* Ⓜ *Osgoode then 501 streetcar west; or Spadina, then 510 streetcar.*

CLOTHING

Black Market. Determined vintage buffs hunt through the racks of band T-shirts, faded jeans, worn shoes, and biker jackets in this cavernous basement. There are more cheap sunglasses than you could ever imagine, along with adjoining stalls hosting a barbershop and a record store. ⊠ *256A Queen St. W, at John St., Queen West* ☎ *416/599–5858* ⊕ *www.blackmarkettoronto.com* Ⓜ *Osgoode, then streetcar 501 west.*

7

Durumi. Feminine, Korean-inspired styles such as slip dresses, wide-leg trousers, blousy tops, and delicate jewelry are sold at Durumi. ✉ *416 Queen St. W, west of Spadina, Queen West* ☎ *647/727–2591* ⊕ *facebook.com/durumiapparel* Ⓜ *Osgoode, then streetcar 501 west; Spadina, then streetcar 510.*

lululemon athletica. While there are several locations across Toronto for this Canadian yoga brand, their massive concept store on Queen West is a must-visit for yoga lovers. Along with plenty of staple athletic and loungewear for men and women, there's a juice bar, a 1,000 square foot yoga and dance studio, and displays by local artists. ✉ *318 Queen W, at Spadina Ave., Queen West* ☎ *416/703–1399* ⊕ *www.lululemon.com* Ⓜ *Osgoode, then streetcar 501 west.*

Original. A blaze of rainbow colors, Original is glamorous, life-affirming and more than a little outrageous. If you're heading to a gala or you're after a crinoline dress (in fuchsia), you *need* to come here. The endless selection of platforms, pumps, and wedges is outdone only by the dress section, found up a multicolor flight of stairs. ✉ *515 Queen St. W, at Augusta Ave., Queen West* ☎ *416/603–9400* ⊕ *www.originaltoronto.com* Ⓜ *Osgoode, then 501 streetcar west.*

Tribal Rhythm. A few vintage gems and pretty silk scarves may be found among the army jackets, cub scout uniforms, and '70s polyester shirts and cowgirl attire, but most of the inventory is simply fun, kitschy, and kooky. Imported Thai and Indian trinkets, rows of body jewelry, tiaras, and wigs are part of the charming and eclectic mix. ✉ *248 Queen St. W, below street level, at John St., Queen West* ☎ *416/595–5817* Ⓜ *Osgoode; 501 Queen streetcar.*

JEWELRY AND ACCESSORIES

eko. Jewelry boutique eko's award-winning minimalist design pulls you in. Its whiter-than-white walls hide panels of glass that compel the eye to gaze at each display separately. It's an effective, if slightly intimidating, way to get the shopper to consider the international one-of-a-kind jewelry designs carefully. ✉ *288 Queen St. W, at Peter St., Queen West* ☎ *416/593–0776* ⊕ *www.ekojewellery.com* Ⓜ *Osgoode.*

Goorin Bros. Look no further than this suitably traditional hat shop for wide-brim fedoras, panamas, and pork pies. The Goorin Bros. have been making hats in the States for four generations, and many of the hats on display were handmade in Pittsburgh; this is their first foray into Canada. For the ladies, you'll find 1920s felt cloches, fascinators, and sunhats. ✉ *320 Queen St. W, east of Spadina, Queen West* ☎ *416/408–4287* ⊕ *www.goorin.com* Ⓜ *Osgoode.*

New Era Cap Co. Here's your chance to officially "wear your allegiance." Mounted with reverence, the caps that cover New Era's walls represent every MLB team, all teams in the NFL and Canadian Football League, as well as numerous NBA and NHL teams. Caps come in every team color combo you can imagine, and some are emblazoned with beloved old logos. And, if your own cap is looking a little past its prime, you can bring it in to have it steamed and reshaped. ✉ *202A Queen St. W, at St Patrick St., Queen West* ☎ *416/597–2277* ⊕ *www.neweracap.com* Ⓜ *Osgoode.*

MUSIC

Sonic Boom. More than 1,500 daily arrivals fill the rows of this bright and cavernous store with a dizzying array of both used and new CDs, vinyl records, and DVDs. They carry many albums of local musicians—if the timing is right, you might catch one of those bands giving a live performance inside the store. ⊠ *215 Spadina Ave., at Sullivan, Queen West* ☎ *416/532–0334* ⊕ *www.sonicboommusic.com* Ⓜ *Spadina, then 510 to Queen; Osgoode, then 501 to Spadina.*

SHOES, HANDBAGS, AND LEATHER GOODS

Getoutside. There are styles for men and women, including Hunter wellies, Frye boots, Birkenstock sandals, Sperry top-siders, and a great selection of Laurentian Chief and Minnetonka street moccasins and mukluks. There are loads of Converse and Vans sneakers, too. ⊠ *437 Queen St. W, at Spadina Ave., Queen West* ☎ *416/593–5598* ⊕ *www.getoutsideshoes.com* Ⓜ *Osgoode, then streetcar 501 west; or Spadina, then streetcar 510.*

SPECIALTY GIFTS

Malabar Ltd. If you're in the market for fake blood or eyelashes, a '50s wig, or a prosthetic nose, than look no further than Malabar. However, the real treasures are found in the costume rental department. Whether you're after a bishop's cassock, caveman's hides, a dirndl, or Edwardian frock and parasol, the costume maker upstairs has pieced one together, which you can check out on the racks groaning under decades' worth of designs. Dancewear for adults and children can be found as well, from pointe ballet shoes and tutus to leotards and leg warmers. ⊠ *14 McCaul St., Queen West* ☎ *416/598–2581* ⊕ *www.malabar.net* Ⓜ *Osgoode.*

QUEEN'S PARK, THE ANNEX, AND LITTLE ITALY

THE ANNEX

In a neighborhood near the University of Toronto campus populated by academics, students, and '60s hippies, a mix of restored and run-down Victorians and brick low-rises house cafés and bistros, used-book and music stores, and the occasional fashion boutique.

BOOKS

Bakka Phoenix. Canada's oldest science fiction and fantasy bookstore, opened in 1972, Bakka Phoenix has several thousand new and used titles for adults, young adults, and children, as well as some graphic novels. Knowledgeable staff is always on hand to give advice. ⊠ *84 Harbord St., at Spadina Ave., The Annex* ☎ *416/963–9993* ⊕ *www.bakkaphoenixbooks.com* Ⓜ *Spadina; 510 Spadina streetcar.*

BMV. An impressive selection of new and used books is shelved side by side over two floors at BMV (which stands for "Books Magazines Video"). The staff is knowledgeable and helpful. ⊠ *471 Bloor St. W, at Brunswick Ave., The Annex* ☎ *416/967–5757* ⊕ *www.bmvbooks.com* Ⓜ *Spadina.*

CLOTHING

Risqué. Trendy dresses, blouses, jumpers, and jeans from independent brands, including plenty of Canadian designers, fill this boutique. The colorful, of-the-moment selections change weekly. ✉ *404 Bloor St. W, at Brunswick Ave., The Annex* ☎ *416/960–3325* Ⓜ *St. George.*

Secrets From Your Sister. The art of the brassiere is taken seriously at this bra-fitting boutique. Knowledgeable (but pretension-free) staff are on hand for advice. A fitting session can be booked online or in-person, and usually lasts from 30 minutes to an hour. Or you can simply peruse the massive selection of prêt-à-porter undergarments, including sports, fashion, strapless, seamless, and nursing bras in wide-ranging sizes and fits. ✉ *560 Bloor St. W, at Bathurst St., The Annex* ☎ *416/538–1234* ⊕ *www.secretsfromyoursister.com.*

HOME DECOR

Nella Cucina. Shop alongside Toronto chefs for quality kitchen novelties and supplies: cheese knives, seafood shears, cast-iron cookware, espresso machines and parts, or unique showpieces like locally made salvaged-wood platters. A teaching kitchen upstairs hosts classes, from Italian cooking to knife skills. ✉ *876 Bathurst St., at London St., The Annex* ☎ *416/922–9055* ⊕ *nellacucina.ca* Ⓜ *Bathurst.*

LITTLE ITALY

Despite the waning Italian influence, Little Italy is a likeable neighborhood and you'll find a few genuine cafés and gelato shops among the restaurants and bars. You'll also find a mix of small boutiques, book and record shops, and trendy lifestyle and housewares stores.

BOOKS

Balfour Books. This hushed but cozy secondhand bookshop has a tempting selection of coffee table–sized art and photography books. There's also more "luggage-friendly" fiction, too. ✉ *468 College St., west of Bathurst St., Little Italy* ☎ *416/531–9911* ⊕ *balfourbooks.squarespace.com* Ⓜ *Bathurst, then streetcar 511 to College.*

JEWELRY AND ACCESSORIES

Lilliput Hats. Wide-brimmed hats decorated with silk orchids in vibrant shades, fascinators, close-fitting cloches, a practical straw hat that packs flat, outrageous or tailored hats—all can be found in handmade, custom-fit head coverings. For the men there are trilbies, wide-brimmed fedoras, and pork pies. Karyn Gingras, who has a huge following, works away with her team of milliners in the back half of the shop. Brides-to-be and their moms will have a field day. ✉ *462 College St., at Bathurst St., Little Italy* ☎ *416/536–5933* ⊕ *www.lilliputhats.com* Ⓜ *Bathurst, then streetcar 511 to College; or Queen's Park, then 506 streetcar west.*

MUSIC

Fodor's Choice ★ **Soundscapes.** Crammed with pop, rock, jazz, blues, folk, ambient, psychedelic, garage, avant-garde, and electronic titles, this shop satisfies hipsters as well as fans of early Americana. Selections and organization reflect a love of music and its ever-expanding history. It's also a great place to pick up tickets for local concerts. ✉ *572 College St., at Manning Ave., Little Italy* ☎ *416/537–1620* ⊕ *www.soundscapesmusic. com* Ⓜ *Bathurst, then 511 streetcar; or College or Queen's Park, then streetcar 506 west.*

YORKVILLE AND ROSEDALE

YORKVILLE

In the 1960s, Yorkville was Canada's hippie headquarters. Today it's a well-heeled shopping and dining destination: the place to find high-end everything. North of Bloor, west of Bay, is the heart of Yorkville—pedestrian-friendly streets with tony cafés and designer stores that are fun to browse even if you're not buying. From Yonge Street to Avenue Road, Bloor Street is a virtual runway for fashionistas, with world-renowned designer shops like Bulgari, Prada, Chanel, and quality chains.

Stanley Wagman Antiques. Stanley Wagman carries a large selection of art deco pieces and lighting, Louis XVI furniture and accessories, and French and Italian pieces from the '40s and '50s. This is the place to find exquisite marble fireplaces and Murano glass lamps. It also ships worldwide. ✉ *224 Davenport Rd., at Avenue Rd., Yorkville* ☎ *416/964–1047* Ⓜ *Dupont, St George.*

ART GALLERIES

Loch Gallery. This intimate gallery in an old Victorian house almost exclusively exhibits representational historic and contemporary Canadian painting and sculpture, and specializes in 19th- and 20th-century Canadian artists. ✉ *16 Hazelton Ave., at Yorkville Ave., Yorkville* ☎ *416/964–9050* ⊕ *www.lochgallery.com* Ⓜ *Bay.*

CHILDREN'S CLOTHING

FAMILY **Jacadi.** The city's prettiest and priciest children's clothes are stocked here, in vibrant colors and fine fabrics from Paris, designed by stylish French women. ✉ *87 Avenue Rd., in Yorkville Village, Yorkville* ☎ *416/923–1717* ⊕ *www.jacadi.com* Ⓜ *Bay.*

CLOTHING

Chanel. Coco herself would have loved this boutique, one of the company's largest in North America. The lush surroundings showcase most of Chanel's latest offerings, including classic and seasonal bags and accessories. The staff is welcoming, knowledgeable and helpful, just what you'd expect from a store of this caliber. ✉ *100 Yorkville Ave., at Hazelton, Yorkville* ☎ *416/925–2577* ⊕ *www.chanel.com* Ⓜ *Bay.*

Escada. The spacious store carries the luxurious, modern creations of Italian fashion house Escada, including clothing, accessories, and fragrances. ✉ *131 Bloor St. W, at Avenue Rd., Yorkville* ☎ *416/964–2265* ⊕ *www.escada.com* Ⓜ *Bay.*

Free People. Yorkville is not generally the stomping ground of hippie fashion, but if you've dropped down at Bay, head here for beaded jewelry, jean cutoffs, caftans, floppy hats, maxi dresses, and all things faded, layered, and '70s. ⊠ *79 Yorkville Ave., Yorkville* 🕾 *416/515–1555* ⊕ *www.freepeople.com* Ⓜ *Bay.*

Fodor's Choice **George C.** If you're put off by the anonymous uniformity of the big
★ designers along Bloor, but you have some money to spend and want
a touch of originality, head to this three-story Victorian refurb. Inside
you'll find an inspired selection of sophisticated shoes, bags, and clothes
for men and women from French, Italian, American, and Australian
designers that you won't find anywhere else; think quirky pastel-hued
loafers from AGL, graphic pieces from Fausto Puglisi, and dramatic
looks from Altuzarra and Philosophy. ⊠ *21 Hazelton Ave., Yorkville*
🕾 *416/962–1991* ⊕ *georgec.ca* Ⓜ *Bay.*

Fodor's Choice **Harry Rosen.** This miniature department store is dedicated to the fin-
★ est men's fashions, stocked to the gills with suits, shirts, outerwear,
shoes, and accessories from designers such as Hugo Boss, Armani, and
Zegna. Meanwhile, there's a casual section that stocks preppy classics
for a more relaxed look. ⊠ *82 Bloor St. W, at Bellair St., Yorkville*
🕾 *416/972–0556* ⊕ *www.harryrosen.com* Ⓜ *Bloor-Yonge.*

Hermès. The Parisian design house caters to the upscale horse- and
hound-loving set, selling its classic sportswear, handbags, and accessories. ⊠ *130 Bloor St. W, at Avenue Rd., Yorkville* 🕾 *416/968–8626*
⊕ *www.hermes.com* Ⓜ *Bay.*

Hugo Nicholson. This boutique's selection of evening wear by Oscar
de la Renta, Christian Dior, Carolina Herrera, Alexander McQueen,
and more is vast and exclusive. The service offered by the owners,
the Rosenstein sisters, is old-school, with exacting alterations, a selection of accessories, and home delivery. ⊠ *43 Hazelton Ave., Yorkville*
🕾 *416/927–7714* ⊕ *www.hugonicholson.com* Ⓜ *Bay.*

James Perse. This California-based company specializes in comfy yet
luxe clothing in muted tones. There are T-shirts of course, but you'll
also find fatigues, fleeces, and button-down shirts as well as breezy jeans
and cashmere or velvet tops. The collection is spread over two floors
of a Victorian house; there's a Ping-Pong table on the second floor if
you're up for a game. ⊠ *18 Hazelton Ave., Yorkville* 🕾 *416/513–0926*
⊕ *www.jamesperse.com* Ⓜ *Bay.*

Fodor's Choice **Kate Spade.** Bright, optimistic, and youthful, Spade's sophisticated, fun
★ designs really "pop" in this white-washed, rehabbed property at the
corner of Old York Lane. Step through the turquoise door and feast
your eyes on party dresses, sparkling pumps, and sweet bags to match.
⊠ *138 Cumberland Ave., Yorkville* 🕾 *416/927–8282* ⊕ *www.katespade.com* Ⓜ *Bay.*

Motion. This Toronto-based boutique features unique, comfortable
clothing in cottons, linens, and wools. Many pieces are designed and
made in-house, but outside designers such as Issey Miyake and Oska
are also featured. Bold, chunky accessories complement the earthy,
arty look perfectly. ⊠ *106 Cumberland St., Yorkville* 🕾 *416/968–0090*
⊕ *www.motionclothing.com* Ⓜ *Bay.*

m0851. If you're looking for a good leather jacket, or perhaps a coat
that's weather-proof, head to this industrial-scale shop. Full-grain,

City Chains

Below are some of the city's most interesting national and international chains.

Anthropologie. Clothing, housewares, and accessories attract fashionistas looking for mass-produced pieces with one-of-a-kind appearance. ⊠ *80 Yorkville Ave., west of Bay St., Yorkville* ☎ *416/964–9700* ⊕ *www.anthropologie.com* Ⓜ *Bay.*

Aritzia. Young urban women come here for modern funky pieces by lines such as TNA, Wilfred, and the house line Talula. There are other locations throughout the city. ⊠ *280 Queen St. W, at Beverley St., Queen West* ☎ *416/977–9919* ⊕ *www. aritzia.ca* Ⓜ *Osgoode, then streetcar 501 to Beverly.*

Club Monaco. The bright and airy flagship store of this successful chain, now owned by Ralph Lauren, has homegrown design basics, sleek mid-price sportswear, and career clothes. ⊠ *157 Bloor St. W, at Avenue Rd., Yorkville* ☎ *416/591–8837* ⊕ *www. clubmonaco.com* Ⓜ *Museum or Bay.*

DavidsTea. When you step into DavidsTea, you're faced with a wall of up to 150 stainless steel canisters, categorized and color-coded (blue for oolong, purple for maté, black for black), with bold-printed names of blends like jumpy monkey, pumpkin chai, blueberry jam, and birthday cake. Sleek tea accessories are also available for purchase. ⊠ *10 Dundas St. E, Dundas Square Area* ⊕ *At Yonge* ☎ *416/546–9555* ⊕ *www.davidstea. com* Ⓜ *Dundas.*

Indigo. A huge selection of books, magazines, and gift items is stocked at this store, which has a Starbucks and occasional live entertainment. ⊠ *55 Bloor St. W, Yorkville* ☎ *416/925–3536* ⊕ *www.chapters. indigo.ca* Ⓜ *Bay.*

Winners. Toronto's best bargain outlet has designer lines at rock-bottom prices. The Yonge and College branch is enormous, but there are a dozen branches scattered all over the city. ⊠ *College Park, 444 Yonge St., Dundas Square Area* ☎ *416/598–8800* ⊕ *www.winners.ca* Ⓜ *College.*

Zara. The Spanish chain consistently attracts crowds craving gorgeous knockoffs of the hottest runway trends. ⊠ *50 Bloor St. W, at Yonge St., Yorkville* ☎ *416/916–2401* ⊕ *www. zara.com* Ⓜ *Bloor.*

---

durable leather coats and bags—made in neighboring Québec—follow utilitarian designs. Gorgeous leather bags and accessories, such as wallets and toiletry bags, also line the shelves, along with weather-proof jackets in polyurethane-coated cotton twill. ⊠ *38 Avenue Rd., across from Yorkville Ave., Yorkville* ☎ *416/920–4001* ⊕ *www.m0851.com* Ⓜ *Bay or St George.*

Over the Rainbow. This denim center carries every variety of cut and flare: the trendy, the classic, and the questionable from lines like Fidelity and Naked & Famous fill the shelves. ⊠ *101 Yorkville Ave., at Hazelton Ave., Yorkville* ☎ *416/967–7448* ⊕ *www.rainbowjeans.com* Ⓜ *Bay.*

119 Corbò. Some of the most tasteful designers—Miu Miu, Givenchy, Jimmy Choo, and Alexander McQueen, to name a few—are gathered here under one roof, along with some of the finest footwear in town.

✉ *119 Yorkville Ave., at Hazelton Ave., Yorkville* ☎ *416/928–0954* ⊕ *www.119corbo.com* Ⓜ *Bay.*

Fodor's Choice **Pink Tartan.** Ontario-born designer Kimberly Newport-Mimran opened
★ this, her flagship store, in 2011 after selling her sophisticated sportswear
in high-end shops around the globe. Expect tailored Oxford shirts,
classic little black dresses, and crisp, snug-fitting trousers in expensive
fabrics, as well as objets d'art, shoes, and accessories hand-picked by
the designer. ✉ *77 Yorkville Ave., (entrance on Bellair St.), Yorkville*
☎ *416/967–7700* ⊕ *www.pinktartan.com* Ⓜ *Bay.*

Prada. The avant-garde designs of this luxury Italian fashion house are
overshadowed only by the gleaming interior of the store and the traffic-
stopping window displays. ✉ *131 Bloor St. W, Unit 5, at Bellair St.,*
Yorkville ☎ *416/975–4300* ⊕ *www.prada.com* Ⓜ *Bay.*

Fodor's Choice **Roots.** Canadians' favorite leather jackets, varsity jackets, bags, and
★ basics are crafted from tumbled leather and stamped with the country's
national icon (the beaver) at Roots. The homegrown company's impressive flagship store showcases the more modern styling possibilities of
their laid-back offerings. ✉ *80 Bloor St. W, at Bellair St., Yorkville*
☎ *416/323–3289* ⊕ *www.roots.com* Ⓜ *Bay.*

Second Time Around. If you're after a designer handbag but can't bear to
pay retail, head to this dark, little consignment shop. The selection is
extensive without being overwhelming, and you might find that perfect,
lightly used Fendi, Dior, or Dooney & Bourke at an accessible price.
High-fashion preowned clothes, including Chanel, Gucci, Vuitton, and
Vivienne Westwood, and loads of shoes are here, too. ✉ *70 Yorkville*
Ave., Unit 9, Yorkville ☎ *416/916–7669* ⊕ *www.facebook.com/Second-*
TimeAroundToronto Ⓜ *Bay.*

Shan. Montréal designer Chantal Levesque founded this label in 1985,
and now stocks locations in more than 25 countries with her creative
couture swimwear, swimwear accessories, and wraps. There's a separate collection for men. ✉ *38 Avenue Rd., at Yorkville Ave., Yorkville*
☎ *416/961–7426* ⊕ *www.shan.ca* Ⓜ *Bay or St. George (Bedford exit).*

Uncle Otis. Cool, casual, and ever so slightly street (UO was once the
preferred shop of skaters), this purveyor of with-it menswear carries
the wearable-when-you're-over-30 styles of Fred Perry, Oliver Spen-
cer, Canada Goose, and Wings + Horns. There are Filson bags, too,
along with sneakers, sunglasses, and watches. ✉ *26 Bellair St., Yorkville*
☎ *416/920–2281* ⊕ *www.uncleotis.com* Ⓜ *Bay.*

DEPARTMENT STORES AND SHOPPING CENTERS

Hudson's Bay. The modern descendant of the Hudson's Bay Company,
which was chartered in 1670 to explore and trade in furs, the Bay (as
it's known among Canadians) carries mid-price clothing, furnishings,
housewares, and cosmetics, including designer names as well as in-house
lines. Another Bay, which shares its sprawling space with a Saks Fifth
Avenue location, is located on Yonge Street, connected to Eaton Centre
by a covered skywalk over Queen Street. ✉ *44 Bloor St. E, at Yonge St.,*
Yorkville ☎ *416/972–3333* ⊕ *www.thebay.com* Ⓜ *Bloor-Yonge.*

Fodor's Choice   **Holt Renfrew.** This multilevel national retail specialty store is the style
★   leader in Canada. On the ground floor, there are handbags, watches,
cosmetics, and fragrances from London, New York, Paris, and Rome.
Head to the upper floors for footwear and clothing from boldface
designers (including Fendi, Burberry, and Gucci) as well as items from
contemporary designers. Gents can head a few steps west for a wider
men's selection at the two-floor Holt Renfrew Men. ■**TIP**➜ **Con-
cierge service and personal shoppers are available, but just browsing
makes for a rich experience.** ⊠ *50 Bloor St. W, at Bay St., Yorkville*
☎ *416/922–2333* ⊕ *www.holtrenfrew.com* Ⓜ *Bay.*

Yorkville Village. Formerly Hazelton Lanes, this upscale shopping mall
got a much-needed facelift in 2016. Stores include fashion-forward
TNT Woman and Man (TNT is short for The Next Trend); structured
womenswear by Judith & Charles; Jacadi's Parisian kidswear; and
downtown Toronto's only Whole Foods Market. ⊠ *55 Avenue Rd.,
at Yorkville Ave., Yorkville* ☎ *416/968–8600* ⊕ *www.yorkvillevillage.
com* Ⓜ *Bay.*

FOOD AND TREATS

Pusateri's. From humble beginnings as a Little Italy produce stand,
Pusateri's has grown into Toronto's favorite high-end supermarket,
with in-house prepared foods, local and imported delicacies, and desserts and breads from the city's best bakers, among many other treats.
⊠ *57 Yorkville Ave., at Bay St., Yorkville* ☎ *416/785–9100* ⊕ *www.
pusateris.com* Ⓜ *Bay.*

Whole Foods. This vast, health-conscious high-end grocery store and café
in the Yorkville Village shopping center has mid- and high-priced items.
Although imported delicacies and the Yorkville address make it a haven
for the well-off, students and young professionals come for the organic
produce and specialty vegetarian fare, including salad and pasta bars,
freshly baked goods, and an impressive selection of prepared foods.
⊠ *55 Avenue Rd., in Yorkville Village, Yorkville* ☎ *416/944–0500*
⊕ *wholefoodsmarket.com* Ⓜ *Bay.*

HOME DECOR

William Ashley. Ashley's has an extensive collection of china patterns
that range from Wedgwood to Kate Spade and can often secure those
it doesn't already carry. Crystal and china are beautifully displayed.
Prices are decent—and sales are frequent—on expensive names such
as Waterford. The store is happy to pack and ship all over the world.
⊠ *55 Bloor St. W, at Bay St., Yorkville* ☎ *416/964–2900* ⊕ *www.wil-
liamashley.com* Ⓜ *Bay.*

JEWELRY AND ACCESSORIES

Cartier. The Toronto location of this internationally renowned luxury
jeweler caters to the city's elite. The glass cases feature a good selection
of the jewelry designer's classic creations, including the triple-gold-band
Trinity Ring, the striking nail-shaped Juste Un Clou collection, and the
diamond-studded Tortue Watch. ⊠ *131 Bloor St. W, at Avenue Rd.,
Yorkville* ☎ *416/413–4929* ⊕ *www.cartier.com* Ⓜ *Bay.*

Royal De Versailles. Don't let the front-door security scare you away from
some of the most striking and elegant jewelry designs in town. Royal De

Versailles has a reputation as one of Toronto's most luxurious jewelers, in large part due to their huge collection of high-end watches (they have one of the largest Rolex selections in Canada). ⊠ *101 Bloor St. W, at St. Thomas St., Yorkville* ☎ *416/967–7201* ⊕ *www.royaldeversailles. com* Ⓜ *Bay.*

Tiffany & Co. Good things come in little blue boxes, and this two-floor Tiffany location is filled with them—namely, rows and rows of classic, wearable fine jewelry designs. The sales staff here has a reputation for being patient, helpful, and friendly. ⊠ *150 Bloor St. W, at Avenue Rd., Yorkville* ☎ *416/921–3900, 800/265–1251* ⊕ *www.tiffany.ca* Ⓜ *Bay.*

MUSIC

L'Atelier Grigorian. Since 1980, L'Atelier Grigorian has been specializing in classical, opera, jazz, and world music, making it Toronto's must-visit destination for music lovers from around the globe. More than 50,000 selections are in stock on CD, DVD, Blu-ray, and vinyl. Collectors and audiophiles will find rare recordings and high-end audio formats. ⊠ *70 Yorkville Ave., Yorkville* ☎ *416/922–6477* ⊕ *www.grigorian.com* Ⓜ *Bay.*

SHOES, HANDBAGS, AND LEATHER GOODS

Davids. The collection at this high-ceilinged, two-floor shoe shop includes pairs for men and women and runs the gamut from the classical to the whimsical. Designers usually include Marc Jacobs, Kate Spade, Christian Louboutin, Manolo Blahnik, Jimmy Choo, and Chloe. Hung high along one wall is a selection of handbags from brands like Ferragamo and Tory Burch. ⊠ *66 Bloor St. W, at Bay St., Yorkville* ☎ *416/920–1000* ⊕ *www.davidsfootwear.com* Ⓜ *Bay.*

Specchio. This is the place for fine shoes and boots on the cutting edge of style for every season, from designers like Dries Van Noten, Giuseppe Zanotti, Marni, and more. It might be tiny, but it has a surprisingly large selection. ⊠ *1240 Bay St., at Cumberland St., Yorkville* ☎ *416/961–7989* Ⓜ *Bay.*

SPECIALTY GIFTS

redLetter. Pretty tea sets and tiered pastry stands lure romantics into this gift shop, but push past the china and you'll find cool desk sets, quirky novelties, and plenty of stationery. Designs are fun, funky, and colorful, from Cath Kidston's rural-retro home wares to modern Pantone color-block mugs. Pick up some locally made Sloane teas in pretty tins as souvenirs. ⊠ *128 Cumberland St., Yorkville* ☎ *647/340–7294* ⊕ *www. redletterstore.ca* Ⓜ *Bay.*

ROSEDALE

One of Toronto's most exclusive neighborhoods, Rosedale has a strip of upscale antiques and interiors shops. If the thought of freight charges dissuades you from serious spending, you can take home packable gourmet food from Pusateri's or accessories from Putti.

ANTIQUES

Absolutely Inc. Curios, from porcupine quills to vertebrae walking sticks, are sold at this fascinating interiors shop; its sister branch is just a few blocks north. You'll also find an array of vintage jewelry; antique boxes made of materials ranging from horn to shagreen (ray or shark skin); English campaign furniture; and French architects' drafting tables. When you're done, head to Absolutely North at 1236 Yonge Street in Rosedale. ✉ *1132 Yonge St., at MacPherson Ave., Rosedale* ☎ *416/324–8351* ⊕ *www.absolutelyinc.com* Ⓜ *Rosedale.*

Putti. This home decor shop is very romantic, and very turn-of-the-century. Everywhere you look, you'll see antiques, reproduction furniture, and home accessories piled so high that they scrape the chandeliers, with a few metallic and geometric touches to keep things modern. There's an impressive array of French toiletries, as well as frilly frocks and fairy wings for children's flights of fancy. ✉ *1104 Yonge St., at Roxborough St., Rosedale* ☎ *416/972–7652* ⊕ *www.putti.ca* Ⓜ *Rosedale.*

HOME DECOR

Hollace Cluny. Though it's off the main shopping drag, Hollace Cluny is a must-visit for modern design aficionados looking for that special piece. Along with classics from brands like Knoll, they carry a huge array of pieces from contemporary designers, with everything from ceramics to eye-popping statement lighting fixtures. ✉ *160 Pears Ave., at Bedford, Greater Toronto* ☎ *416/968–7894* ⊕ *www.hollacecluny.ca* Ⓜ *Rosedale, then walk west; Bay, then take the 6 bus to Bedford.*

SHOES, HANDBAGS, AND LEATHER GOODS

Mephisto. These walking shoes have been around since the 1960s and are made entirely from natural materials. Passionate walkers swear by them and claim they never, ever wear out—even on cross-Europe treks. Their styles, which include options for men and women, run the gamut from smart ankle boots to minimalist slides. ✉ *1177 Yonge St., at Summerhill Ave., Rosedale* ☎ *416/968–7026* ⊕ *www.mephisto-toronto. com* Ⓜ *Summerhill.*

EAST AND WEST OF THE CENTER

BEACHES

Relaxed and upper-middle-class, this strip of Queen East is just a few blocks from the boardwalk and Lake Ontario's sandy shore. It's packed with casual-clothing stores, gift and antiques shops, and bars and restaurants. It's a long ride to Woodbine on the Queen streetcar, but you'll pass through Riverside and Leslieville on the way.

FOOD AND TREATS

Nutty Chocolatier. A Beaches institution, the Nutty Chocolatier serves up hand-scooped ice cream and handmade molded chocolates and truffles from Port Perry, just northeast of Toronto. Even more popular is the old-school candy—Charleston Chew and Tootsie Rolls—and British imports like Irn Bru, Walker's Crisps, Flakies, and Yorkshire

Tea. ✉ *2179 Queen St. E, at Lee Ave., The Beach* ☎ *416/698–5548* ⊕ *thenuttychocolatier.com* Ⓜ *Queen 501 streetcar; or Woodbine station, then bus 92.*

HOME DECOR

Nesters. French-country wares in creamy tones dominate this white-floored homewares and furnishings shop, and 1920s-inspired chandeliers clink above refurbished fireplace surrounds, garden statuary, and Provincial dressers. You'll also find beautiful bed linens, lavender sachets, and French soaps and toiletries. ✉ *2207 Queen St. E, east of Lee Ave., The Beach* ☎ *416/698–2207* ⊕ *www.nestershome.com* Ⓜ *Queen streetcar 501; or Woodbine station, then bus 92.*

SHOES, HANDBAGS, AND LEATHER GOODS

Nature's Footwear. Established in 1978, this tiny, family-run shoe shop specializes in comfortable walking shoes. The store carries an impressive selection of styles, sizes, and widths by Birkenstock, Crocs, Keds, and Sperry Topsiders, as well as moccasins and Sorel and Kamik boots for winter. ✉ *1971a Queen St. E, at Waverley Rd., The Beach* ☎ *416/691–6706* ⊕ *naturesfootwear.com* Ⓜ *Queen 501 streetcar; or Woodbine station, then bus 92.*

THE DANFORTH

Often called Greektown, the Danforth is best known as a place to eat, and appropriately there's a fair amount of culinary retail to go along with the grazing. Carrot Common, just east of Chester subway, houses New Age businesses like the Big Carrot and its juice bar, yoga and massage studios, and a rock and crystal shop, along with a few independent boutiques.

FOOD AND TREATS

Big Carrot Natural Food Market. This large health-food supermarket carries good selections of organic produce, health and beauty aids, and vitamins. There's a vegetarian café on-site and freshly prepared foods for takeout. ✉ *348 Danforth Ave., at Hampton Ave., Danforth* ☎ *416/466–2129* ⊕ *www.thebigcarrot.ca* Ⓜ *Chester.*

HOME DECOR

IQ Living. This is a fun kitchen shop for those who take their cooking seriously. Every hue of Emile Henry ceramic cookware is available, as is the refined dinnerware by Sophie Conran and bright nesting bowls and utensils by the innovative Joseph Joseph. A huge selection of insulated lunch boxes and bags, including take-along bento boxes can be found, along with funky Popsicle molds and Sodastream machines. ✉ *542 Danforth Ave., at Carlaw Ave., Danforth* ☎ *416/466–2727* ⊕ *www.iqliving.com* Ⓜ *Pape or Chester.*

LESLIEVILLE

Head east to Leslieville, a slice of Queen East stretched between Carlaw and Greenwood, once noted for antiques and junk shops but now where hip clothing boutiques and brunch spots are the norm. Keep your eyes peeled as you trundle east over the DVP bridge; neighboring Riverside is catching up fast in terms of unique shops.

ANTIQUES

Fodor'sChoice
★

Gadabout. This antique shop is a rummager's paradise. The walls groan under 1950s salt and pepper shakers, snake skin handbags, costume jewelry, Hudson's Bay blankets, and racks of vintage clothing that range from the 1800s to the 1970s and an extensive section for men. You can rifle through the scores of carefully labeled drawers to find magicians' business cards, Nana Mouskouri specs, and creepy vintage curling irons. Display cases burst with curios—medicinal bottles, a collection of eggshell faced Japanese dolls, and a feng shui compass. ⊠ *1300 Queen St. E, east of Leslie St., Leslieville* ☎ *416/463–1254* ⊕ *www.gadabout. ca* Ⓜ *Queen streetcar 501; Greenwood, then bus 31 to Queen.*

ART GALLERIES

Arts Market. More than 50 artisans and purveyors display their wares in mini 4-by-4 spaces where vintage collections rub shoulders with meditation beads, hand-knit baby booties, mixed-media paintings, and rhubarb jam. ⊠ *1114 Queen St. E, east of Pape Ave., Leslieville* ☎ *647/997–7616* ⊕ *www.artsmarket.ca* Ⓜ *Queen streetcar 501; or Pape, then bus 72 to Carlaw and Queen.*

CLOTHING

Any Direct Flight. Sitting at the eastern edge of Leslieville, Any Direct Flight is worth the streetcar ride, if you're after retro-inspired yet contemporary designs for women. Its spacious, exposed-brick rooms have comfy couches encouraging leisurely browsing of its feminine yet slightly off-kilter collection of slouchy pants, sweater dresses, asymmetric tops, El Naturalista boots, and Sanita clogs. You can even mull over your clothing options at the in-store café. ⊠ *1382 Queen St. E, east of Greenwood Ave., Leslieville* ☎ *416/504–0017* Ⓜ *Queen streetcar 501; Greenwood, then bus 31.*

Bergstrom Originals. The wearability and quality of Christina Bergstrom's bold and bright designs is so evident that the items practically leap off the racks. Slip on an ankle-length dress in multicolor stripes, or an open-weave bright orange tunic, and you'll see what we mean. There's also a great selection of chunky heels by Fly London and El Naturalista. ⊠ *781 Queen St. E, east of Broadview Ave. at Saulter St., Leslieville* ☎ *416/595–7320* ⊕ *www.bergstromoriginals.com* Ⓜ *501 Queen streetcar; or Broadview, then 504 streeetcar to Queen.*

Doll Factory by Damzels. The Doll Factory has 1950s pin-up looks from Toronto designers Damzels in this Dress, including their own gingham and sailor-inspired numbers, and other rock 'n' roll retro designs from across the continent. Chunky heels and sweet polka-dot wedges are on the shelves, as are convertible high-waisted bikinis perfect for flattering those curves. Another branch can be found in Roncesvalles at 394 Roncesvalles Avenue. ⊠ *1122 Queen St. E, east of Pape Ave., Leslieville* ☎ *416/598–0509* ⊕ *www.damzels.com* Ⓜ *Queen streetcar 501; Pape, then bus 72 to Carlaw and Queen.*

WEST QUEEN WEST

West of Bathurst, Queen is packed with cool boutiques, slick interiors stores, and shoe shops galore. Even farther west, beyond Trinity Bellwoods Park, the cool quotient is stepped up, with mid-century modern antiques and cutting-edge galleries and a sudden flurry of big name designers—think Stussy, Fred Perry, and Tiger of Sweden—elbowing their way in among the quirky boutiques at Ossington.

ART GALLERIES

Fodor's Choice ★ Craft Ontario Shop. This shop, run by the Ontario Crafts Council, displays the best in Canadian crafts in the area. You'll find stunning examples of blown glass, fine woodwork, textiles, jewelry, and pottery—from earthy stoneware to contemporary ceramics. There's also a gallery of Inuit and indigenous art, including sculpture, beadwork, and prints. ⊠ 1106 Queen St. W , at Lisgar, West Queen West ☎ 416/921–1721 ⊕ www.craftontario.com Ⓜ Osgoode, then take 501 to Dovercourt; Ossington, then take 63 to Queen.

Stephen Bulger. This gallery focuses on historical and contemporary Canadian photography with a collection of 15,000 photos. The attached Camera screening room hosts free screenings on Saturday afternoon, while the gallery's bookstore focuses on photography. ⊠ 1026 Queen St. W, at Brookfield St., West Queen West ☎ 416/504–0575 ⊕ www.bulgergallery.com Ⓜ Osgoode, then streetcar 501 west; or Ossington, then bus 63 south.

BOOKS

Fodor's Choice ★ Type Books. A great but small independent bookstore, Type Books has a selection of carefully selected fiction and many hard-to-find authors, as well as shelves of graphic novels. The art and architecture section has pride of place at the front of the shop and the extensive children's area is in a bright spot up a few steps at the back. ⊠ 883 Queen St. W, at Trinity Bellwoods Park, West Queen West ☎ 416/366–8973 ⊕ www.typebooks.ca Ⓜ Osgoode, then streetcar 501 west; or Bathurst, then streetcar 511.

CLOTHING

Annie Aime. Bright comfy threads with a European aesthetic and a focus on sustainable production are the focus here. The current selection includes chunky knits from Icelandic brand Matthildur, breezy dresses by France's Cotelac, and Turkish-made deconstructed sweaters from Crea Concept. The eye-catching graffiti mural makes for a perfect fashion backdrop. ⊠ 42 Ossington Ave., West Queen West ☎ 416/840–5227 ⊕ www.annieaime.com Ⓜ Osgoode, then streetcar 501 west; or Ossington, then bus 63 south.

Fred Perry. Classic mod style from this iconic British clothing company fills the store, the only one of its kind in Canada. Originated by 1940s Wimbledon champion Fred Perry, the brand and its signature polo shirts have been associated with British youth culture for decades. ⊠ 964 Queen St. W, at Givins St., West Queen West ☎ 416/538–3733 ⊕ www.fredperry.com Ⓜ Ossington, then 63 bus south; or Osgoode, then 501 streetcar west.

Fodor's Choice
★

Gravitypope. This Canadian chain, frequented by dressers in the know, has an impressive selection that includes Paul Smith, Commme des Garçons, and Marni. Menswear and womenswear are on hand, but shoes are their specialty, with a massive selection of more than 2,000 pairs including See by Chloe, Camper, Hunter, Rag & Bone, and Doc Martens. ⊠ *1010 Queen St. W, at Ossington Ave., West Queen West* ☎ *647/748–5155* ⊕ *www.gravitypope.com* Ⓜ *Osgoode, then 501 streetcar west; or Ossington, then bus 63 south.*

I Miss You Boutique. Julie Yoo's immaculately restored picks in this upscale consignment shop include familiar names such as Pucci, Hermès, Dior, and Yves Saint Laurent. Fellas can head next door to I Miss You Man for vintage Versace button-downs, gently used Acne jackets, and Dior shades—all in near-mint condition. ⊠ *63 Ossington Ave., at Queen St. W, West Queen West* ☎ *416/916–7021* ⊕ *facebook.com/imissyouvintage/* Ⓜ *Queen 501 streetcar to Ossington Ave; or Ossington station, then bus 64 south.*

Victoire. This Ottawa-based boutique has its finger firmly on the pulse of Canadian fashion, stocking edgy cocktail dresses from Eve Gravel, cute sundresses from Birds of North America, and a treasure trove of jewelry and fun gifts. ⊠ *129A Ossington Ave., Ossington* ☎ *416/588–6978* ⊕ *www.victoireboutique.com* Ⓜ *Ossington, then 63 bus south.*

HOME DECOR

Morba. Mad for teak? This double-fronted shop is stuffed with Scandinavian furniture and lighting (especially white, papery Le Klint from Denmark), but there's loads of vintage pieces and retro knock-offs, too. A great place for gifts, Morba has a huge selection of quirky desk accessories, alarm clocks, and martini shakers for your friends stuck in the 1950s, plus a wonderful collection of colorful Scandinavian glass. ⊠ *665 Queen St. W, at Bathurst, West Queen West* ☎ *416/364–5144* ⊕ *www.morba. ca* Ⓜ *Bathurst, then streetcar 511; or Osgoode, then streetcar 501 west.*

Quasi Modo. Design classics such as Herman Miller lounge chairs and Noguchi lamps are just a sampling of the high-end design pieces you'll find here—there's not a knock-off in sight. There's also sleek modern homewares for the kitchen and bathroom as well. ⊠ *1079 Queen St. W, at Dovercourt Rd., West Queen West* ☎ *416/703–8300* ⊕ *www.quasimodomodern.com* Ⓜ *Osgoode, then streetcar 501 west; or Bathurst, then streetcar 511.*

Urban Mode. Modern and trend-oriented furniture and home decor at this West Queen West spot include the playful furniture designs of Blu Dot, along with sculptural fire pits from Modfire and bold Scandinavian creations from Muuto. ⊠ *145 Tecumseth St., at Queen St. W, West Queen West* ☎ *416/591–8834* ⊕ *www.urbanmode.com* Ⓜ *Osgoode, then streetcar 501 west; or Bathurst, then streetcar 511.*

GIFTS

Drake General Store. Only-in-Canada gifts like Mountie napkins, Hudson Bay Company wool blankets, totem-pole stacking mugs, super-soft Toronto-made Shared tees, and log-shaped pillows are tucked into every nook and cranny of this offbeat shop. Gifts here are a mix of fun, beautiful, and inexplicable: bike-shaped pizza cutters, passion fruit–coconut jam, fancy toiletries, and flamingo-shaped neon signs. ⊠ *1151 Queen St. W, at Beaconsfield Ave., West Queen West* ☎ *647/346–0742* ⊕ *www. drakegeneralstore.ca.*

JEWELRY AND ACCESSORIES

Lady Mosquito. Chunky necklaces in eye-popping colors cover the walls of this South American accessories shop. Bright felt brooches, dangly earrings, and embroidered handbags—all made from recycled or sustainable materials—don't have a hint of shabby about them. Cynthia Villegas chooses the work of Peruvian, Colombian, and Venezuelan artisans you'll see in the store, and she also creates many of the striking pieces herself, many made from the tagua seed of the Amazonian rainforest. ⊠ *1022 Queen St. W., at Ossington Ave., West Queen West* ☎ *647/637–9335* ⊕ *www.ladymosquito.ca* Ⓜ *Ossington, then bus 63 south; or Osgoode, then streetcar 501 west.*

Zane. This accessory boutique is the place to visit for offbeat but on-trend items. Find handbags by Rebecca Minkoff and local designer Opelle; fine luggage, including Rimowa hard cases; a great line of Karen Walker tortoiseshell sunglasses; and jewelry from indie designers like Jenny Bird and Giles & Brother. ⊠ *753 Queen St. W., at Euclid Ave., West Queen West* ☎ *647/352–9263* ⊕ *www.visitzane.com* Ⓜ *Osgoode, then 501 streetcar west; or Bathurst, then 511 streetcar.*

MUSIC

Fodor'sChoice **Rotate This.** Music buyers in the know come here for underground and inde-
★ pendent music from Canada, the United States, and beyond. It has CDs, LPs, some magazines, concert tickets, and other treats. ⊠ *186 Ossington Ave., at Rolyat, West Queen West* ☎ *416/504–8447* ⊕ *www.rotate.com* Ⓜ *Osgoode, then streetcar 501 west; or Ossington, then 63 bus to Dundas.*

SHOES, HANDBAGS, AND LEATHER GOODS

Heel Boy. A tried-and-true spot for cool and cute footwear for both sexes, Heel Boy stocks the most unique styles by well-known brands like Hunter, Ted Baker, Sam Edelman, Superga, and Dolce Vita, as well as on-trend bags and backpacks. ⊠ *773 Queen St. W, at Euclid Ave., West Queen West* ☎ *416/362–4335* ⊕ *www.heelboy.com* Ⓜ *501 Queen or 511 Bathurst streetcar.*

SPECIALTY GIFTS

Town Moto. True bikers and Sunday riders alike will love this crowded shop that has all types of gear for your bike lining the walls. Push to the back to find biker jackets, an impressive selection of helmets and goggles, and natty biker boots. There are posters and biker T-shirts, too. ⊠ *132 Ossington Ave., south of Dundas St. W, West Queen West* ☎ *416/856–8011* ⊕ *www.townmoto.com* Ⓜ *Ossington, then bus 64 to Argyle; St. Patrick, then 505 to Ossington.*

GREATER TORONTO

RONCESVALLES VILLAGE AND LITTLE PORTUGAL

The main drag in Roncesvalles Village, an upper-middle-class neighborhood near High Park, is lined with unique bookstores, clothing shops, restaurants and cafés, and vestiges of a once-dominant Polish community. Little Portugal, at Dundas West and Ossington, is evolving, with hip vintage stores and galleries popping up monthly.

ARTS AND CRAFTS GALLERIES

Wil Kucey Gallery. Work by contemporary and edgy emerging and mid-career artists are on display here. Owner/director Wil Kucey's taste for graffiti and street art is apparent in many of the shows, but the gallery also maintains a focus on historical Canadian artists. ✉ *1183 Dundas St. W, Little Portugal* ☎ *416/532–8467* ⊕ *www.wilkuceygallery. ca* Ⓜ *Ossington station, then bus 63 south; or 505 Dundas streetcar.*

Olga Korper Gallery. Many important Canadian and international artists, such as Lynne Cohen, Paterson Ewen, John McEwen, and Reinhard Reitzenstein, are represented by this trailblazing yet accessible gallery, which displays art from the 1960s on. It's a good place for contemporary collectors and art enthusiasts alike. ✉ *17 Morrow Ave., off Dundas St. W, Little Portugal* ☎ *416/538–8220* ⊕ *www.olgakorpergallery.com* Ⓜ *Dundas West, then streetcar east.*

CLOTHING

VSP. This spacious consignment store is where downtowners go to drop off last season's Marni, Alexander Wang, or Margiela, and where you can then grab it for a steal. Even more budget-friendly are the few vintage pieces mixed in with the designer selections. ✉ *1410 Dundas St. W, Little Portugal* ☎ *416/588–9821* ⊕ *www.vspconsignment.com* Ⓜ *St. Patrick, then 505 streetcar; or Dufferin, then 29 bus.*

YONGE AND EGLINTON

Jokingly called "Young and Eligible," this northerly nabe is a somewhat sterile but lively high-rise hot spot for chain stores, movie megaplexes, and Irish pubs.

CLOTHING: CHILDREN'S

FAMILY **Hatley.** This company began as a cottage business in rural Québec more than 25 years ago, with a line of aprons depicting cute farm animals. Now this mainly children's boutique is stocked with quirky, nature-inspired clothing covered in insects, animals, trees, and flowers—designs inspired by the Canadian wilderness. ✉ *2648 Yonge St., at Craighurst Ave., Yonge and Eglinton* ☎ *416/486–4141* ⊕ *www.hatleystore.com* Ⓜ *Lawrence or Eglinton, then 97 Bus.*

OUTDOOR EQUIPMENT AND CLOTHING

Sporting Life. The first off the mark with the latest sportswear trends, this is the place to get hip, outdoorsy labels like Barbour, Canada Goose, and Hugo Boss—or to snag snowboard gear and poll the staff for advice on where to use it. ✉ *2665 Yonge St., north of Eglinton Ave., Yonge and Eglinton* ☎ *416/485–1611* ⊕ *www.sportinglife.ca* Ⓜ *Eglinton.*

SIDE TRIPS FROM TORONTO

WELCOME TO SIDE TRIPS FROM TORONTO

TOP REASONS TO GO

★ **Niagara Falls:** The Falls' amazing display of natural power is Ontario's top attraction. See them from both the U.S. and Canadian sides.

★ **Shakespeare and Shaw:** A couple of long-dead British playwrights have managed to make two Ontario towns boom from May through October with the Shakespeare Festival in Stratford and the Shaw Festival in Niagara-on-the-Lake.

★ **Wineries:** The Niagara Peninsula has an unusually good microclimate for growing grapes; most of the more than 60 wineries have tastings.

★ **The Great Outdoors:** Ski at resorts north of Toronto; canoe backcountry rivers in Algonquin Provincial Park; hike or bike the Niagara-to-Lake-Huron Bruce Trail or the Niagara Parkway along the Niagara River.

★ **Edible Ontario:** Niagara-on-the-Lake and Stratford are both renowned for their skilled chefs who serve culinary masterpieces created with farm-fresh ingredients.

1 **Niagara Falls.** South of Toronto near the U.S. border, the thundering falls are an impressive display of nature's power.

2 **The Niagara Wine Region.** The temperate Niagara region bordering Lake Ontario is the ideal growing climate for all kinds of produce, including grapes. Wineries stretch along the shores of Lake Ontario south of Toronto to the pretty Victorian-style town of Niagara-on-the-Lake, at the junction of Lake Ontario and the Niagara River.

3 **Stratford.** An acclaimed Shakespeare Festival brings this rural town alive from April through October. Overwhelmingly popular, it has become Stratford's raison d'être, with a multitude of inns and locavore restaurants growing up around it. Frequent outdoor music and arts festivals color the squares and parks all summer.

4 **Southern Georgian Bay.** North of Toronto is a series of lakes and summer homes, ski resorts, and the small towns that serve them.

5 **Muskoka.** This area north of the city is known for its lakes and vacation cottages. Tackle the four-hour drive to Algonquin Provincial Park and you're rewarded with pristine forested land for canoeing, camping, and moose-spotting.

ONTARIO

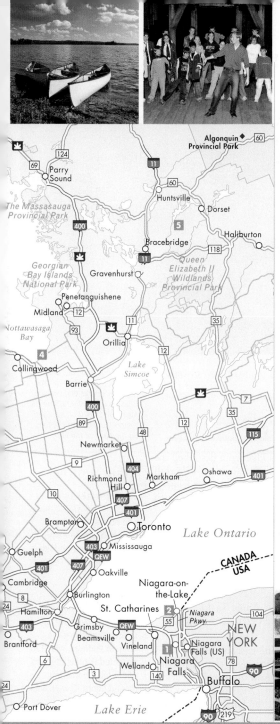

GETTING ORIENTED

Wedged between three Great Lakes—Ontario, Huron, and Erie—and peppered with thousands of smaller lakes, Southern Ontario is a fertile area of farmland, wineries, forests, and waterways. Within a two- to four-hour drive north, west, or southwest of Toronto are small towns, beaches, ski resorts, and rural farmland that feel light-years away from the city lights. Toronto sits at the eastern edge of southern Ontario, a region that makes up no more than 15% of the province but is home to nearly 95% of the population and most of its major attractions. Head north and you hit Muskoka and Algonquin, while heading west brings you to Stratford, and heading south–southwest to Niagara Falls and the Niagara Wine Region.

8

NIAGARA FALLS

Niagara Falls has inspired visitors for centuries, and the allure hasn't dimmed for those who want to marvel at this natural wonder.

(above) Niagara Falls is as dramatic by night as by day. (top right) Parks and walking trails surround the falls on the American side. (bottom right) Visitors get close to the falls on the Maid of the Mist.

Missionary and explorer Louis Hennepin described the falls in 1678 as "an incredible Cataract or Waterfall which has no equal." Nearly two centuries later, Charles Dickens declared, "I seemed to be lifted from the earth and to be looking into Heaven."

Countless daredevils have been lured here. In 1859, 100,000 spectators watched as the French tightrope walker Charles Blondin successfully crossed Niagara Gorge, from the American to the Canadian side, on a three-inch-thick rope. From the early 18th century, dozens went over in boats and barrels. Nobody survived until 1901, when schoolteacher Annie Taylor emerged from her barrel and asked, "Did I go over the falls yet?" Stunts were outlawed in 1912.

The depiction of the thundering cascades in the 1953 Marilyn Monroe film *Niagara* is largely responsible for creating modern-day tourism. And though the lights of the arcades, tacky souvenir shops, and casinos shine garishly bright for some, views of the falls themselves are unspoiled.

NIGHT LIGHTS

See **Fireworks Over the Falls** on Fridays, Sundays, and holidays at 10 pm from mid-May to early September (and on Friday during the Winter Festival of Lights).

Between early November and late January, the **Winter Festival of Lights** illuminates the Niagara Parkway, with 125 animated lighting displays and 3 million tree and ground lights. ⊕ *www.wfol. com.*

WAYS TO EXPLORE

By Air: National Helicopters. National Helicopters has 20-minute tours over the falls and wine country, plus romance and other specialty tours. ⊠ *Niagara District Airport, 468 Niagara Stone Rd., Niagara-on-the-Lake* ☎ *905/641–2222, 800/491–3117* ⊕ *www.nationalhelicopters.com* ✆ *C$149/person.*

Niagara Helicopters Ltd. This company does 12-minute sightseeing flights over the whirlpool, gorge, and all three falls, plus winery trips. ⊠ *3731 Victoria Ave., Niagara Falls* ☎ *905/357–5672, 800/281–8034* ⊕ *www.niagarahelicopters.com* ✆ *C$139/person.*

The **Whirlpool Aero Car** cable car crosses the gorge over the Niagara River whirlpool.

By Boat: The **Maid of the Mist** is an oldie but a goodie, and still pulls in huge crowds. Adrenaline-fueled Whirlpool Jet Boat Tours in Niagara-on-the-Lake plow headfirst into the Class-V Niagara River rapids on an hour-long ride.

By Bus: Double Deck Tours. Take an authentic, red London double-decker bus tour with Double Deck Tours. Fares include admission to Journey Behind the Falls, *Maid of the Mist,* and the Whirlpool Aero Car; the four-hour tour also includes the Floral Clock and Niagara Glen. Tickets and departures are next to the *Maid of the Mist* building. ☎ *905/374–7423* ⊕ *www.doubledecktours.com* ✆ *C$79.*

By Foot: Stroll the Niagara Parkway promenade, stand on the Table Rock Centre terrace, and walk over the Rainbow Bridge. The **White Water Walk** is the closest you'll get to the rapids from land; **Journey Behind the Falls** is a walk through tunnels behind the falls.

Cave of the Winds. Worth a border crossing, Cave of the Winds takes you 175 feet into the gorge to an observation deck less than 20 feet from thundering Bridal Veil falls. ■TIP➔ **You will get drenched; you are provided with a poncho and footwear for a reason.** ⊠ *Departures from Goat Island, Niagara Falls State Park, Niagara Falls* ☎ *716/278–1796* ⊕ *www.niagarafallsstatepark.com* ✆ *C$11.*

IN ONE DAY

If you have only a day in Niagara Falls, walk the waterfront promenade and go on a *Maid of the Mist* tour. (Plan for wet shins and shoes.) Also consider the Whirlpool Aero Car, a cable-car ride over the whirlpool, or the Whitewater Walk, to see the rapids up close. Dinner within view of the falls, which are colorfully lit at night, is a relaxing end to a full day.

THE AMERICAN SIDE

8

Canada has the superior views and a more developed waterfront, with better restaurants. In contrast, the American waterfront is lined with parks, ideal for hiking and picnicking. Because you're behind the falls here, rather than facing them, views are limited. Stick to Canada for most of your visit, but if you have more time, cross the Rainbow Bridge on foot to get close to Bridal Veil Falls on a Cave of the Winds tour from Goat Island.

WINE REGION KNOW-HOW

Ontario may not be famed for its wines— yet—but the Niagara Peninsula alone has around 75 wineries and has been producing wine commercially since the early 1970s. Four decades on, the region is coming into its own with some of the world's best wines of origin.

The position of the Niagara appellation, wedged between Lake Ontario and the Niagara Escarpment, creates a microclimate that regulates ground and air temperature and allows for successful grape growing (today more than 30 varietals) in an otherwise too-cold province. Winds off Lake Ontario are directed back by the escarpment, preventing cold air from settling. Heat stored in lake waters in summer keeps ground temperatures warmer longer into winter. In spring, the cold waters keep the grounds from warming too fast, protecting buds from late-spring frosts. Some say that the slightly colder climate means a more complex-tasting grape. Indisputably it *does* provide perfect conditions for producing some of the world's best ice wine.

WHAT'S IN A VQA

Canadian wine is regulated by the Vintners Quality Alliance, a government-sanctioned wine authority whose strict standards are on par with regulatory agencies in France and Italy. Many Niagara wineries proudly declare their vintages VQA; in fact, 65% of all VQA wines in Ontario are Niagara wines. To be deemed VQA is no small honor: wines must meet rigorous standards— including being made entirely from fresh, quality-approved Ontario-grown grapes (no concentrates) and approved grape varieties, passing laboratory testing, and approval by an expert tasting panel prior to release. Look for the VQA stamp on the label.

NIAGARA WINE TOURING BASICS

THE ONTARIO WINE ROUTE

Ontario Wine Route. Niagara wineries along the Ontario Wine Route are well marked by blue signs between Grimsby and Niagara Falls. ■ TIP➜ For a full map of the wine route, pick up the free Wine Country Ontario Travel Guide, updated annually and available at wineries and tourist attractions or directly from the Wine Council. ✉ *4890 Victoria Ave. N, Vineland* ☎ *905/562–8070* ⊕ *www.winecountryontario.ca.*

TIMING AND COSTS

Most wineries are open year-round, with limited hours in winter. Tastings begin between 10 and noon. Reservations may be needed for tours in summer.

Tastings usually cost C$1–C$2 per wine, or up to C$7 for more expensive wines. The larger wineries do regular public tours; at smaller operations you may be able to arrange a tour in advance. Tasting and/or tour fees are often waived if you buy a bottle of wine.

ORGANIZED TOURS

Crush on Niagara. Crush on Niagara wine-tour packages include overnight stays, meals, and winery tours. ✉ *4101 King St., Beamsville* ☎ *905/562–3373, 866/408–9463* ⊕ *www.crushtours.com.*

Grape and Wine Tours. Grape and Wine Tours runs day trips and one- or two-night wine-tour packages from Toronto and Oakville. Pickup and drop-off at Niagara-on-the-Lake and Niagara Falls hotels is included. ✉ *758 Niagara Stone Rd., Niagara-on-the-Lake* ☎ *905/562–4920, 855/682–4920* ⊕ *www.grapeandwinetours.com.*

Niagara Wine Tours International. Niagara Wine Tours International leads guided bus, van, and coach tours along the Wine Route and has bike rentals. ✉ *92 Picton St., Niagara-on-the-Lake* ☎ *905/468–1300, 800/680–7006* ⊕ *www. niagaraworldwinetours.com.*

Zoom Leisure. One of the most popular bike rental stores in the area because of its convenient location, Zoom Leisure has organized cycling/winery tours and custom-guided and self-guided tours. ✉ *431 Mississauga St., Niagara-on-the-Lake* ☎ *905/468–2366, 866/811–6993* ⊕ *www.zoomleisure.com.*

EVENTS

Niagara Wine Festival. The Niagara Wine Festival group organizes three big events in Niagara. The largest, with an annual half-million attendees is the eponymous, 10-day **Niagara Wine Festival**, in September, celebrating the grape harvest. The three-week **Niagara Ice Wine Festival**, in January, is a nod to Niagara's specialty, ice wine. The three-weekend **Niagara New Vintage Festival**, in June, is a wine-and-culinary event. ✉ *Montebello Park, 64 Ontario St., St. Catharines* ☎ *905/688–0212* ⊕ *www.niagarawinefestival.com.*

ONTARIO'S ICE WINES: SWEET SIPPING

Ontario is the world's leading producer of ice wine. It's produced from ripe grapes left on the vine into the winter. When grapes start to freeze, most of the water in them solidifies, resulting in a fructose-laden, aromatic, and flavorful center. Ice-wine grapes must be picked at freezing temperatures before sunrise and basket-pressed immediately. By nature ice wine is sweet, and when well made it smells of dried fruits, apricots, and honey and has a long, refreshing finish.

Vidal grapes are ideal for ice wine, due to their thick skin and resistance to cracking in subzero temperatures. The thin-skinned Riesling yields better results but is susceptible to cracking and ripens much later than Vidal.

Drink ice wine after dinner, with a not-too-sweet dessert, or alongside a strong cheese. Here in Niagara it also appears in unexpected places such as tea, martinis, chocolate, ice cream, French toast, and glazes for meat and seafood.

8

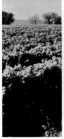

Updated by
Jesse Ship

The rush of 700,000 gallons of water a second. The divinely sweet, crisp taste of ice wine. The tug of a fish hooked under a layer of ice. Sure, the big-city scene in Toronto delivers the hustle and bustle you came for, but escaping the city can transport you to another world. The struggle is choosing which world to visit first.

There's Niagara Falls, acres of local vineyards in Niagara-on-the-Lake and the surrounding wine region, or the whimsical "cottage country," with its quiet towns, challenging ski slopes, and lakefront resorts. Or you can hit the outdoors on Bruce Trail, Canada's oldest and longest footpath, which winds from Niagara Falls to Tobermory 885 km (550 miles) north.

If superlatives are what you seek, the mesmerizing and deservedly hyped Niagara Falls, one of—or more technically, three of—the most famous waterfalls in the world, is Ontario's most popular attraction. Worth seeing at least once, it is truly beautiful (say what you will about the showy town behind it).

Oenophile trailblazers should consider Niagara's rapidly developing wine trail. The Niagara Escarpment, hugging Lake Ontario's western shores, is one of the most fertile growing areas in Canada. A lakeshore drive southwest of Toronto yields miles of vineyards and farm-to-table restaurants, culminating in the Victorian white-picket-fence town of Niagara-on-the-Lake, known for its amazing five-star restaurants and hotels and nearly-as-luxurious B&Bs.

Nourish your appreciation for the arts in and around Stratford. Two major theater events, the Stratford Festival and the Shaw Festival (in Niagara-on-the-Lake), have long seasons with masterfully orchestrated plays by William Shakespeare and George Bernard Shaw.

Both outdoors enthusiasts who want to rough it and soft-adventure seekers who yearn for a comfortable bed with the glow of a fireplace at night feel the lure of the nearly 3,000-acre Algonquin Provincial Park. Sunday drivers find solace near Georgian Bay and in the Muskokas, part of Ontario's lake-smattered cottage country.

PLANNING

WHEN TO GO

With the exception of destinations like wineries and ski resorts, June through September is prime travel season: Stratford and Shaw festivals are in full swing, hours of operation are longer for most attractions, the mist coming from Niagara Falls is at its most refreshing, and patios are open almost everywhere, not to mention the obvious abundance of water activities and amusement parks.

That said, there's fun to be had in wintertime as well. While Muskoka cottage country, Stratford, and some parks in Algonquin become inaccessible ghost towns between November and April (the time most resorts schedule renovations and maintenance), ski resorts and wineries offer many packages and activities. Enjoy tours on and tastings of one of Ontario's most prized exports during Niagara's Ice Wine Festival, or enjoy the Canadian winter by snowboarding, skiing, ice fishing, and snowmobiling. Travel around the holiday season to take in the beautiful decorations, lights, and special events.

GETTING HERE AND AROUND

AIR TRAVEL

Toronto's Pearson International Airport, 30 km (18 miles) north of downtown, is the obvious choice. Downtown Toronto's smaller Billy Bishop Toronto City Airport serves mostly Porter Airlines; it gets you Niagara-bound on the Gardiner Expressway in a matter of minutes. Hamilton International Airport is about halfway between Toronto and Niagara Falls. Buffalo Niagara International Airport is 30 miles from Niagara Falls, Ontario, but border crossings can add time to your trip.

Air Travel Contacts Billy Bishop Toronto City Airport. ☎ *416/203–6942* ⊕ *www.torontoport.com/airport.aspx.* **Buffalo Niagara International Airport.** ☎ *716/630–6000* ⊕ *www.buffaloairport.com.* **Hamilton International Airport.** ☎ *905/679–1999* ⊕ *www.flyhi.ca.* **Toronto Pearson International Airport.** ☎ *866/207–1690, 416/776–3000* ⊕ *www.torontopearson.com.*

CAR TRAVEL

You can get by without a car in downtown Niagara Falls and Stratford if you book a hotel close to the action.

Avoid Toronto-area highways during weekday rush hours (6:30 to 9:30 am and 3:30 to 6:30 pm). Traffic between Toronto and Hamilton might crawl along at any hour.

Ontario's only toll road is the east–west Highway 407, north of Toronto. It's expensive (22¢–25¢ per kilometer) and has no tollbooths; you will be billed via mail if the system has your state's license plate information on file.

The Ministry of Transportation has updates for roadwork and winter road conditions.

Car Contacts Ministry of Transportation. ☎ *416/235–4686, 800/268–4686* ⊕ *www.mto.gov.on.ca.*

8

PLANNING YOUR TIME

Toronto is a great base to begin your explorations of Ontario.

One Day: In a long day you could see a matinee at the Shakespeare festival, hit a ski resort north of Toronto, visit a few Niagara Escarpment wineries, or—with some stamina—see Niagara Falls. All these destinations require about four hours of driving time round-trip, not accounting for rush-hour traffic jams.

Two Days: A couple of days are sufficient to get a feel for Niagara Falls, Niagara-on-the-Lake, Stratford, or a Muskoka town or two. Alternatively, head up to Collingwood for an overnight snowboarding or skiing trip.

Four Days: You can decide between an intensive outdoorsy trip in the Algonquin area hiking, biking, camping, canoeing, and exploring; or, a relaxing tour of Niagara Falls and Niagara-on-the-Lake, with some time spent at spas and wineries, biking, and hitting culinary hot spots.

One Week: Combine Stratford and Niagara, or really delve into the Niagara region. (A week is probably too much for just Niagara Falls or just Niagara-on-the-Lake.) Alternatively, you could spend some serious time communing with nature in Algonquin Park and meandering through quaint Muskoka and Georgian Bay towns.

TRAIN TRAVEL

VIA Rail connects Toronto with Niagara Falls and Stratford. GO Transit, Toronto's commuter rail, has summer weekend service to Niagara Falls. Ontario Northland's Northlander line travels between Toronto and Bracebridge, Gravenhurst, Huntsville, and other northern points.

Train Contacts GO Transit. ☎ 888/438–6646, 416/869–3200 ⊕ www.gotransit. com. **Ontario Northland.** ☎ 800/363–7512, 705/476–5598 ⊕ www.ontarionorthland.ca. **VIA Rail.** ☎ 888/842–7245 ⊕ www.viarail.ca.

RESTAURANTS

The dining in Stratford and Niagara-on-the-Lake is enough to boost a whole other genre of tourism, as there are a number of outstanding restaurants thanks to the area's many chefs being trained at the area's reputable culinary schools, and impeccably fresh ingredients from local farms. Produce, meats, cheeses, beers, and wine are all produced in Ontario, and some restaurants even have their own gardens, vineyards, or farms. In the immediate areas surrounding Niagara Falls, the dining is a little more lackluster, as views, convenience, and glamour take precedence over food, but there are some great pubs and upscale restaurants to be found among the tourist traps. Reservations are always encouraged, if not essential.

HOTELS

Make reservations well in advance during summer and at ski areas in winter. Prices are higher in peak season and nearer to the tourist centers. In Niagara Falls, for example, hotel rates are determined by proximity to the falls. Taxes are seldom included in quoted prices, but rates sometimes include food, especially in more remote areas such as

Muskoka, where many resorts offer meal plans. *Hotel reviews have been shortened. For full information, visit Fodors.com.*

At the Cottage. Cottage rentals are available through local tourism boards or At the Cottage. ☎ 416/466–1452, 888/394–8884 ⊕ *www.atthecottage.com.*

BBCanada.com. BBCanada.com can help you locate a B&B and reserve a room. ☎ 800/239–1141 ⊕ *www.bbcanada.com.*

Federation of Ontario Bed & Breakfast Accommodations. A comprehensive B&B guide listing about 250 establishments is published by the Federation of Ontario Bed & Breakfast Accommodations. ⊕ *www.fobba.com.*

Camping, in campgrounds or backcountry, is popular in summer and early fall, especially in the provincial parks to the north of Toronto.

WHAT IT COSTS IN CANADIAN DOLLARS				
	$	$$	$$$	$$$$
Restaurants	under C$12	C$12–C$20	C$21–C$30	over C$30
Hotels	under C$125	C$125–C$175	C$176–C$250	over C$250

Restaurant prices are the average cost of a main course at dinner or, if dinner is not served, at lunch. Hotel prices are the lowest cost of a standard double room in high season.

VISITOR INFORMATION
Contacts Niagara Falls Tourism. ☎ 800/563–2557 ⊕ www.niagarafallstourism.com. **Ontario Parks.** ☎ 888/668–7275, 519/826–5290 ⊕ www.ontarioparks.com. **Ontario Tourism.** ☎ 800/668–2746, 905/754–1958 ⊕ www.ontariotravel.net. **Tourism Niagara.** ☎ 289/477–5344 ⊕ www.tourismniagara.com.

8

NIAGARA FALLS

130 km (81 miles) south of Toronto.

Niagara Falls has inspired artists for centuries. English painter William H. Bartlett, who visited here in the mid-1830s, noted that "you may dream of Niagara, but words will never describe it to you." Although cynics have called it everything from "water on the rocks" to "the second major disappointment of American married life" (Oscar Wilde)—most visitors are truly impressed. Missionary and explorer Louis Hennepin, whose books were widely read across Europe, described the falls in 1678 as "an incredible Cataract or Waterfall which has no equal." Nearly two centuries later, Charles Dickens declared, "I seemed to be lifted from the earth and to be looking into Heaven." Henry James recorded in 1883 how one stands there "gazing your fill at the most beautiful object in the world."

WHEN TO GO
Water-based falls tours operate only between mid-May and mid-September, and the summer weather combats the chilly falls mist. Fewer events take place in other seasons, and it's too cold in winter to linger

Clifton Hill's food, shopping, games, rides, and other attractions will keep the whole family entertained.

on the promenade along the parkway next to the falls, but it's much easier to reserve a window-side table for two at a falls-view restaurant. Clifton Hill and most indoor attractions are open year-round. At any time of year it feels a few degrees cooler on the walkway near the falls.

GETTING HERE AND AROUND

Niagara Falls is easily accessible by car and train from Toronto. VIA Rail and GO (summer only) trains serve Niagara Falls, both stopping at the main rail station, not far from the falls. The nearest airports are in Toronto, Hamilton, and Buffalo, New York. It is possible to use public transportation and cabs to get around, but a car is more flexible and is recommended. There is no public transport between Niagara Falls and Niagara-on-the-Lake, 20 km (12 miles) north.

The four- to eight-lane Queen Elizabeth Way—better known as the QEW—runs from the U.S. border at Fort Erie through the Niagara region to Toronto.

PARKING

In Niagara Falls, parking prices increase closer to the falls. It can be triple the price to park along the Niagara Parkway (C$25/day) than it is up the hill near Victoria Street (usually C$5/day). If you park up top, know that the walk down to the falls is a steep one. You might want to take a taxi back up, or hop aboard the Falls Incline Railway, a funicular that operates between the Table Rock Centre and Portage Road behind the Konica Minolta Tower. The trip takes about one minute and costs C$2.75 (day passes are available for C$7).

SHUTTLE

Available year-round, climate-controlled WEGO buses travel on a loop route on the Niagara Parkway between the Table Rock Centre and the Whirlpool Aero Car parking lot (9 km [6 miles] north) and as far north as Queenston Heights Park, 15 km (9 miles) downriver. A day pass, available from Welcome Centres and at any booth on the system, is C$6 per person per day (get the second day free from late October to mid-April). You can get on and off as many times as you wish at well-marked stops along the route, and buses pick up frequently (every 20 minutes).

BORDER CROSSINGS

Everyone—including children and U.S. citizens—must have a passport or other approved travel document (e.g., a New York State–issued "enhanced" driver's license) to enter the United States. Go to the Department of Homeland Security website (⊕ *www.dhs.gov*) for the latest information. Avoid crossing the border at high-traffic times, especially Friday and Saturday nights. The Canada Border Agency and the U.S. Customs and Border Protection list border wait times into Canada and into the U.S., respectively, online at ⊕ *www.cbsa-asfc.gc.ca/bwt-taf* and ⊕ *apps.cbp.gov/bwt*. Crossings are at the Peace Bridge (Fort Erie, ON–Buffalo, NY), the Queenston–Lewiston Bridge (Queenston, ON–Lewiston, NY), and the Rainbow Bridge (Niagara Falls, ON–Niagara Falls, NY).

DISCOUNTS AND DEALS

Pick up the free Save-A-Buck coupon booklet for discounts on various tours, attractions, and restaurants. ■TIP➔ **Many attractions have significant online discounts and combination tickets.** Bundled passes are available through the tourism board, at Welcome Centres (foot of Clifton Hill and Murray Hill, near *Maid of the Mist* ticket booth, Table Rock Centre), and at most attractions' ticket windows.

The **Clifton Hill Fun Pass** incorporates entry to six of the better Clifton Hill attractions (including the SkyWheel and the Midway Combo Pass rides) for C$25.95 plus tax. The Midway Combo Pass (C$9.99 plus tax) includes two indoor thrill rides: Ghost Blasters and the FX Ride Theatre.

The **Niagara Falls and Great Gorge Pass** (C$54.95; available mid-April–late October) covers admission to Journey Behind the Falls, *Maid of the Mist,* White Water Walk, and Niagara's Fury, plus a number of discounts and two days of unlimited use of both the WEGO buses and the Falls Incline Railway. It's available from Niagara Parks, as is the **Winter Magic Pass** (C$28; available late October–mid-April), which

8

NIAGARA FALLS: PAST AND FUTURE

The story begins more than 10,000 years ago as a group of glaciers receded, diverting the waters of Lake Erie north into Lake Ontario. The force and volume of the water as it flowed over the Niagara Escarpment created the thundering cataracts. Erosion has been considerable since then, more than 7 miles in all, as the soft shale and sandstone of the escarpment have been washed away and the falls have receded. Diversions of the water for power generation have slowed the erosion somewhat, spreading the flow more evenly over the entire crestline of Horseshoe Falls. The erosion is now down to 1 foot or less per year.

At this rate—given effects of power generation and change in riverbed composition—geologists estimate it will be some 50,000 years before the majestic cascade is reduced to rapids somewhere near present-day Buffalo, 20 miles to the south.

includes Niagara's Fury, the Butterfly Conservatory, Journey Behind the Falls, and discount coupons.

TOURIST INFORMATION

The main Niagara Falls Tourism center is on Robinson Street near the Skylon Tower.

Open June through August, Welcome Centres are run by Niagara Parks and have tickets for and information about Niagara Parks sights, including WEGO and Falls Incline Railway passes and the Niagara Falls and Great Gorge Adventure Pass. Welcome Centre kiosks are at the foot of Clifton Hill, foot of Murray Hill, and near the *Maid of the Mist* ticket booth; a Welcome Centre booth is inside the Table Rock Centre.

ESSENTIALS

Discounts and Deals Clifton Hill Fun Pass. ⊕ *www.cliftonhill.com.* **Save-A-Buck coupon booklet.** ⊕ *www.saveabuck.com.*

Transportation Contacts GO Transit. ☎ *888/438–6646, 416/869–3200* ⊕ *www.gotransit.com.* **Niagara Falls VIA Rail Canada Train Station.** ✉ *4267 Bridge St.* ☎ *888/842–7245.* **VIA Rail.** ☎ *888/842–7245* ⊕ *www.viarail.ca.* **WEGO.** ☎ *905/356–1179* ⊕ *www.wegoniagarafalls.com.*

Visitor Information Niagara Falls Tourism. ✉ *5400 Robinson St.* ☎ *905/356–6061, 800/563–2557* ⊕ *www.niagarafallstourism.com.* **Niagara Parks.** ☎ *905/356–2241, 877/642–7275* ⊕ *www.niagaraparks.com.*

EXPLORING

TOP ATTRACTIONS

FAMILY **Clifton Hill.** This is undeniably the most crassly commercial district of Niagara Falls, with haunted houses, more wax museums than one usually sees in a lifetime, and fast-food chains galore (admittedly, the Burger King here is unique for its gigantic Frankenstein statue towering above). For kids the entertainment is endless—especially kids who enjoy arcade games—and the SkyWheel is interesting for all ages. Attractions are typically open late (midnight–2 am in summer, 11 pm off-season), with admission ranging from about C$10 to C$16. One of the most popular attractions is the 175-foot **SkyWheel** (C$10.99) with enclosed, climate-controlled compartments. Next door, **Dinosaur Adventure Golf** (C$9.99) combines minigolf, ferocious mechanical dinosaurs, and an erupting minivolcano. The **Great Canadian Midway** is a 70,000-square-foot entertainment complex with arcade games, a bowling alley, air hockey, and food. **Ripley's Believe It or Not! Museum** is creepily fascinating, while **Movieland Wax Museum** has such lifelike characters as Harry Potter and Barack and Michelle Obama. The **Hershey Store** is 7,000 square feet of truffles, fudge, and the trademark Kisses, marked by a six-story chocolate bar at the base of the hill, on the other side of Casino Niagara. ⊠ *Clifton Hill* ☎ *905/358-3676* ⊕ *www.cliftonhill.com.*

Fallsview Casino Resort. Canada's largest gaming and resort facility crowns the city's skyline, overlooking the Niagara Parks with picture-perfect views of the falls. Within the 30-story complex are Canada's first casino wedding chapel, a glitzy theater, spa, shops, plenty of restaurants and, for the gaming enthusiasts, more than 100 gaming tables and 3,000 slot machines on one of the largest casino gaming floors in the world. The Las Vegas–style Avalon Ballroom showcases a wide array of talents, from Al Pacino to Jon Stewart. ⊠ *6380 Fallsview Blvd.* ☎ *888/325–5788, 905/371–7505* ⊕ *www.fallsviewcasinoresort.com.*

FAMILY
Fodor's Choice
★
Maid of the Mist. Boats have been operating for *Maid of the Mist* since 1846, when they were wooden-hulled, coal-fired steamboats. Today, double-deck steel vessels tow fun-loving passengers on 30-minute journeys to the foot of the falls, where the spray is so heavy that ponchos must be distributed. From the observation areas along the falls, you can see those boarding the boats in their blue slickers. ■**TIP**➜ Unless you cower in the center of the boat, your shoes and pants will get wet: wear quick-drying items or bring spares. ⊠ *Tickets and entrance at foot of Clifton Hill on falls side of Niagara Pkwy.* ☎ *905/358–0311* ⊕ *www.maidofthemist.com* ⊠ *C$19.75* ⊘ *Closed Nov.–Apr.*

FAMILY
Marineland. A theme park with a marine show, wildlife displays, rides, and aquariums—including a beluga whale habitat with underwater viewing areas where you can pet and feed the whale—Marineland is 1½ km (1 mile) south of the falls. The daily marine shows include performing killer whales, dolphins, harbor seals, and sea lions. Children can pet and feed deer at the Deer Park. Among the many rides are Dragon Mountain, the world's largest steel roller coaster, and Ocean Odyssey. ⊠ *7657 Portage Rd., off Niagara Parkway or QEW (McLeod Rd. exit)* ☎ *905/356–9565, 905/356–9565, 905/356–9565* ⊕ *www.marinelandcanada.com* ⊠ *C$42.96* ⊘ *Closed mid-Oct.–mid-May.*

Fodor's Choice
★
Niagara Falls. One of North America's most impressive natural landmarks, the falls are actually three cataracts: the American and Bridal Veil Falls in New York State, and the Horseshoe Falls in Ontario. In terms of sheer volume of water—more than 700,000 gallons per second in summer—Niagara is unsurpassed compared to other bodies of water on the continent.

On the Canadian side, you can get a far view of the American Falls and a close-up of the Horseshoe Falls. You can also park your car for the day in any of several lots and hop onto one of the WEGO buses, which run continuously to all the sights along the river. If you want to get close to the foot of the falls, the *Maid of the Mist* boat takes you near enough to get soaked in the spray.

After experiencing the falls from the Canadian side, you can walk or drive across Rainbow Bridge to the U.S. side. On the American side you can park in the lot on Goat Island near the American Falls and walk along the path beside the Niagara River, which becomes more and more turbulent as it approaches the big drop-off of just over 200 feet.

The amusement parks and tacky souvenir shops that surround the falls attest to the area's history as a major tourist attraction. Most of the gaudiness is contained on Clifton Hill, Niagara Falls' Times Square. Despite these garish efforts to attract visitors, the landscaped grounds immediately bordering the falls are lovely and the beauty of the falls remains untouched.

One reason to spend the night here is to admire the falls illumination, which takes place every night of the year, from dusk until at least 10 pm (as late as 1 am during the summer). Even the most contemptuous observer will be mesmerized as the falls change from red to purple to blue to green to white, and finally all the colors of the rainbow in harmony. ⊠ *Niagara Falls.*

Niagara Parks Botanical Gardens and School of Horticulture. Professional gardeners have graduated from here since 1936; 100 acres of immaculately maintained gardens are open to the public. Within the Botanical Gardens is the **Niagara Parks Butterfly Conservatory**, housing one of North America's largest collections of free-flying butterflies—at least 2,000 butterflies from 50 species around the world are protected in a climate-controlled, rain forest–like conservatory. ■ TIP➜ Between May and mid-October, for C$18.50 per person, you can tour the gardens in a horse and carriage. ⊠ *2565 Niagara Pkwy* ☎ *905/356–8119, 877/642–7275, 905/356–8554, 877/642–7275* ⊕ *www.niagaraparks. com* 🚗 *Parking C$5.*

FAMILY   **Skylon Tower.** Rising 775 feet above the falls, this is the best view of the great Niagara Gorge and the entire city. The indoor-outdoor observation deck has visibility up to 130 km (80 miles) on a clear day. Other reasons to visit include amusements for children, a revolving dining room, a gaming arcade, and a 3-D theater that lets you experience the falls up close. Tickets are sometimes as much as 50% off if purchased online. ⊠ *5200 Robinson St.* ☎ *905/356–2651, 800/814–9577* ⊕ *www. skylon.com* 🚗 *C$11.99.*

Whirlpool Aero Car. In operation since 1916, this antique cable car crosses the Whirlpool Basin in the Niagara Gorge. This trip is not for the faint-hearted, but there's no better way to get an aerial view of the gorge, the whirlpool, the rapids, and the hydroelectric plants. ⊠ *3850 Niagara Pkwy., 4½ km (3 miles) north of falls* ☎ *905/371–0254, 877/642–7275* ⊕ *www.niagaraparks.com* 🚗 *C$13.50* ☉ *Closed early Nov.–mid-Mar.*

Niagara Falls, Ontario

Rides on the *Maid of the Mist* have been thrilling visitors to Niagara Falls since 1846.

White Water Walk. A self-guided route involves taking an elevator to the bottom of the Niagara Gorge, the narrow valley created by the Niagara Falls and River, where you can walk along a 1,000-foot boardwalk beside the Class VI rapids of the Niagara River. The gorge is rimmed by sheer cliffs as it enters the giant whirlpool. ✉ *4330 Niagara Pkwy., 3 km (2 miles) north of falls* ☎ *905/371–0254, 877/642–7275* ⊕ *www.niagaraparks.com* ⌨ *C$10.95* ⊘ *Closed mid-Nov.–early Apr.*

WORTH NOTING

FAMILY **Bird Kingdom.** A tropical respite from the crowds and Las Vegas–style attractions, Bird Kingdom is the world's largest indoor aviary, with more than 400 free-flying birds and more than 35 exotic-bird species in the 50,000-square-foot complex. For creepy-crawly lovers, there are also spiders, lizards, and snakes—including a 100-pound python that you can hold. Check online for a schedule of feeding times. Parking is an additional $2 per half hour, but there's a public lot behind the building (on Hiram Street) that is $5 per day. ✉ *5651 River Rd.* ☎ *905/356–8888, 866/994–0090* ⊕ *www.birdkingdom.ca* ⌨ *C$16.95.*

Casino Niagara. Smaller and more low-key than Fallsview, Casino Niagara also has some older machines, but is well-equipped nonetheless. Slot machines, video-poker machines, and gambling tables for games such as blackjack, roulette, and baccarat fill this casino. Multisports wagering and off-track betting are available. Diversions from gambling are also offered. Within the casino are several lounges, a Yuk Yuk's comedy club, and an all-you-can-eat buffet restaurant. ✉ *5705 Falls Ave.* ☎ *905/374–3598, 888/946–3255* ⊕ *www.casinoniagara.com.*

OFF THE BEATEN PATH

Fort Erie Race Track. Beautifully landscaped with willows, manicured hedges, and flower-bordered infield lakes, the Fort Erie Race Track has dirt and turf horse racing, with the year's highlight being the Prince of Wales Stakes, the second jewel in Canada's Triple Crown of Racing. ⊠ *230 Catherine St., off QEW Exit 2, Fort Erie* ☎ *905/871–3200* ⊕ *www.forterieracing.com* ⊙ *Closed Sun., Mon., and Dec.–Apr.*

Journey Behind the Falls. This 30- to 45-minute tour starts with an elevator ride to an observation deck that provides an eye-level view of the Canadian Horseshoe Falls and the Niagara River. From there a walk through tunnels cut into the rock takes you behind thunderous waterfalls, and you can glimpse the back side of the crashing water through two portals cut in the rock face. ⊠ *Table Rock Centre, 6650 Niagara Pkwy.* ☎ *905/371–0254, 877/642–7275* ⊕ *www.niagaraparks.com* ▣ *Mid-Dec.–mid-Apr. C$11.25, mid-Apr.–Dec. C$15.95.*

Niagara Falls IMAX Theatre/The Daredevil Adventure Gallery. Get the human story behind the falls, from local native tribes' relationship with the waters to the foolhardy folks who went over the edge, with *Niagara: Miracles, Myths, & Magic* on the six-story IMAX screen. The Daredevil Adventure Gallery chronicles the expeditions of those who have tackled the falls and has some of the actual barrels they used on display. ⊠ *6170 Fallsview Blvd.* ☎ *905/358–3611, 866/405–4629* ⊕ *imaxniagara.com* ▣ *Movie C$14.50; exhibit C$9.28.*

FAMILY

Niagara's Fury. Learn how Niagara Falls formed over thousands of years on this 20-minute simulation ride. Standing on a mesh platform surrounded by an uninterrupted 360-degree viewing screen, you feel snow falling, winds blowing, the floor rumbling, and waves crashing as you watch glaciers form, collide, and melt, creating the falls as we know them today. ■ **TIP→** In certain spots you *will* get wet; ponchos are provided. ⊠ *Table Rock Centre, 6650 Niagara Pkwy.* ☎ *905/356–2241, 877/642–7275* ⊕ *www.niagaraparks.com* ▣ *C$14.25.*

8

WHERE TO EAT

Dining in Niagara Falls is still a bit disappointing because of the lack of sophistication that usually comes with a highly touristic area (especially when compared with the neighboring foodie paradise Niagara-on-the-Lake). A view of the falls and convenient location don't come cheap, so prices are rarely what one would consider reasonable. Thankfully, the landscape is slowly changing, and some falls-view restaurants, such as 21 Club, are hiring creative chefs who are stepping up the quality—though still at a pretty penny. But with views like these, it might be worth it.

$$$$
STEAKHOUSE

✕ **21 Club.** The best fine-dining-with-a-view in town, 21 Club plays up its casino locale without being kitschy. The tall-ceilinged, modern space is inspired by roulette, in a profusion of red, black, and gold, and juxtaposes the traditional steakhouse menu. More secluded seating areas wind around the perimeter next to huge windows overlooking the falls, on a raised, illuminated floor on a patio. The menu is seasonal, but you might start out with fresh oysters or roasted beet salad, then move on to Canadian or USDA Prime steak, Arctic char with warm potato salad, or a rack of lamb with parsnip puree and minted jus. The decadent chocolate mousse—with espresso and mocha *anglaise*—is a memorable dessert. Because 21 Club is accessible only via the casino floor, all diners must be at least 19. ⑤ *Average main: C$40 ⊠ Fallsview Casino Resort, 6380 Fallsview Blvd.* ☎ *905/358–3255, 888/325–5788* ⊕ *www.fallsviewcasinoresort.com/dining* ⊘ *Closed Tues. and Wed. No lunch* ⌲ *Reservations essential.*

$$$$
ITALIAN
Fodor's Choice
★

✕ **Casa Mia Ristorante.** Fresh, quality ingredients done simply and in generous portions are what make this off-the-beaten-path restaurant, about a 10-minute drive from the falls. A free shuttle service from Niagara Falls hotels whisks guests to this labor of love, owned and operated by the Mollica family. Modern Amalfi Coast–inspired decor brings a seaside terrace indoors, and it all feels miles, not minutes, away from the city's tourist attractions. To start, try a delectable *bresaola* (air-dried salted beef) served with arugula, Parmigiano-Reggiano shavings, and fragrant truffled dwarf peaches, drizzled with balsamic and truffle oils. Move on to tender pieces of shredded duck confit over linguine in a white-truffle–duck-broth reduction. A sommelier is on hand with suggestions from the 300-plus-label cellar. ⑤ *Average main: C$35 ⊠ 3518 Portage Rd.* ☎ *905/356–5410, 888/956–5410* ⊕ *www. casamiaristorante.com* ⊘ *No lunch weekends* ⌲ *Reservations essential.*

$$
AMERICAN

✕ **Edgewaters Restaurant.** Inside a former refectory building, this second-floor restaurant operated by Niagara Parks has a huge veranda overlooking the falls, across Niagara Parkway. Secondary to the view, the decor and menu are reflective of those in a diner—standard options of burgers, salads, pasta, and steaks served to small wooden tables. The location is prime and the patio is the perfect place to enjoy the view. Reservations are taken online, and you should make one if you want one of the coveted patio tables closest to the falls. Live amplified music often accompanies dinner in summer. ⑤ *Average main: C$17 ⊠ 6345 Niagara Pkwy., at Murray St.* ☎ *905/356–2217* ⊕ *www.niagaraparks. com/dining.*

$$
CANADIAN

✕ **Elements on the Falls.** Most tourists end up at the Table Rock Centre, where you can buy tickets for most of the attractions in Niagara Falls and peer over the brink of Horseshoe Falls. There are a fair number of fast-food restaurants—Burger Town, Tim Horton's, and a sushi takeout station—but upstairs, you can find casual fine dining in Elements on the Falls. The menu includes everything from seasonal Canadian fare, such as bison in wild-mushroom sauce and pork medallions with braised red cabbage, to Angus sirloin steak, which isn't terribly overpriced. The decor is simple but modern, and your meal can be enjoyed next to tall windows overlooking the falls or from the terrace. ⑤ *Average main: C$20 ⊠ Table Rock Centre, 6650 Niagara Pkwy., 2nd fl.* ☎ *905/354–3631* ⊕ *www.niagaraparks.com/dining.*

$$$
STEAKHOUSE

✕ **Lucky's Steakhouse.** Heavy soundproof doors insulate this classy 1920s-style steak house from the less glamorous and very loud Casino Niagara where it's located. Inside the intimate second-story dining room, all is quiet and comfortably chic, with gleaming hardwood floors, a floor-to-ceiling wine cabinet along one wall, semicircular leather booths, and music provided by some of the greats (Ella Fitzgerald,

Frank Sinatra) whose black-and-white portraits adorn the brick walls. Tall windows provide lots of light but, alas, only street views. The menu includes a wide range of choices and prices, from garlic-rubbed thin-crust pizza to surf and turf, but the house specialties are the chops and steaks: filet mignon, prime rib, T-bone, and more. ⑤ *Average main: C$30* ⊠ *Casino Niagara, 5705 Falls Ave., 2nd fl.* ☎ *905/374–3598, 888/325–5788* ⊕ *www.casinoniagara.com* ⊘ *No lunch. Closed Mon. and Tues.*

$$ ✕ **Napoli Ristorante e Pizzeria.** On busy Ferry Street, Napoli is a five-
ITALIAN minute drive from Clifton Hill but it's a local joint that manages to be both casual and refined. Sit in the back room if possible, where exposed-brick columns and black-and-white photos of Naples on the walls set the scene for the southern Italian pasta dishes and thin-crust pizzas. The extensive menu includes 10 pizzas with crisp, wafer-thin crusts and generous dollops of tomato sauce, and plenty of pasta dishes and hearty meat dishes to choose from. Start with a garlicky bruschetta before an entrée like homemade roasted sausage with baked polenta and rapini or fettuccine in a red-pepper-spiced oil-and-garlic sauce with ancho-vies, bread crumbs, and Pecorino. Wines are mostly Italian or from Niagara. ⑤ *Average main: C$16* ⊠ *5485 Ferry St.* ☎ *905/356–3345* ⊕ *www.napoliristorante.ca* ⊘ *No lunch.*

$$$$ ✕ **Skylon Tower.** The big draw here is the view from the **Revolving Dining**
AMERICAN **Room**: perched 520 feet above the Horseshoe Falls, it's simply breath-taking. And the atmosphere puts this restaurant above those serving similar cuisine in the area, drawing an eclectic crowd of couples in cocktail attire and families in casual clothes. The menu revolves as well; prime rib with horseradish sauce and chicken cordon bleu have made appearances. **The Summit Suite Buffet Dining Room**, an all-you-can-eat buffet restaurant one level up, doesn't revolve, but has comparable views for slightly less and serves a popular Sunday brunch. A reserva-tion at either restaurant includes free admission to the observation deck, which makes the prices a little easier to digest, considering the food is secondary to the view. ⑤ *Average main: C$55* ⊠ *5200 Robinson St.* ☎ *905/356–2651, 888/975–9566* ⊕ *www.skylon.com* ⊘ *Summit Suite closed Nov.–Apr. but open for Sun. brunch year-round* ⟶ *Reservations essential.*

WHERE TO STAY

A room with a view of the falls means staying in a high-rise hotel, usu-ally a chain. Hotels with falls views are clustered near the two streets leading down to the falls, Clifton Hill (and adjacent Victoria Avenue), and Murray Street (and adjacent Fallsview Boulevard), also called Mur-ray Hill. Families gravitate toward Clifton Hill, with its video arcades, chain restaurants, and *Maid of the Mist* docking at the end of the street. Murray Hill, where the Fallsview Casino is, is less ostentatious and closer to the falls.

Niagara Falls has plenty of B&Bs, but they're mediocre compared with those in Niagara-on-the-Lake, 20 km (12 miles) north. All the hotels we recommend here are within walking distance of the falls.

$ 🛏 **Country Inn & Suites.** If you're on a budget but not willing to stay at a
HOTEL dingy motor lodge, this seven-story hotel is probably your best choice.
Pros: low-cost parking; breakfast and high-speed Internet included;
within walking distance of Clifton Hill. **Cons:** no views; 15-minute
walk down to the falls. ⑤ *Rooms from: C$110* ✉ *5525 Victoria Ave.*
☎ *905/374–6040, 800/830–5222* ⊕ *www.countryinns.com* 🛏 *108
rooms* ⑩ *Breakfast.*

$$$$ 🛏 **Fallsview Casino Resort.** With the most coveted rooms and the best
HOTEL restaurants, shopping, gaming facilities, and views—all 35 stories over-
Fodor's Choice look the Horseshoe, American, and Bridal Veil falls thanks to its lofty
★   locale—Fallsview Casino Resort is *the* place to be in Niagara Falls.
Pros: the most glamorous address in Niagara Falls; great entertainment;
excellent fitness, spa, and pool facilities, amenities, and service. **Cons:**
pricey; rooms fill up fast. ⑤ *Rooms from: C$349* ✉ *6380 Fallsview
Blvd.* ☎ *905/358–3255, 888/325–5788* ⊕ *www.fallsviewcasinoresort.
com* 🛏 *374 rooms* ⑩ *No meals.*

$$$$ 🛏 **Great Wolf Lodge.** Instead of the usual casino-and-slot-machine ambi-
RESORT ence in other area hotels, you'll find a spectacular water park of 12
FAMILY slides, seven pools, water fort, outdoor hot tubs, and other fun water
facilities for the kids. **Pros:** great variety of water slides and facilities.
Cons: rooms are mostly open concept, so there is less privacy for the
parents. ⑤ *Rooms from: C$320* ✉ *3950 Victoria Ave.* ☎ *905/354–4888,
800/605–9653* ⊕ *www.greatwolf.com* 🛏 *406 suites* ⑩ *No meals.*

$$$ 🛏 **Sheraton on the Falls.** Just steps from the Niagara Parkway and *Maid
HOTEL of the Mist* ticket booth is this 22-story tower at the corner of Clifton
Hill, and it's the most polished option in that area. **Pros:** at the bottom
of Clifton Hill and very close to the falls; updated rooms; breakfast
overlooking all three falls is a great start to the day. **Cons:** no views from
rooms below sixth floor; expensive Wi-Fi and parking. ⑤ *Rooms from:
C$239* ✉ *5875 Falls Ave.* ☎ *905/374–4445, 888/229–9961* ⊕ *www.
sheratononthefalls.com* 🛏 *670 rooms* ⑩ *No meals.*

$$ 🛏 **Sterling Inn & Spa.** Unique among the chain options in Niagara Falls is
B&B/INN this boutique hotel in a converted 1930s milk factory—hence the bottle-
shaped building face. **Pros:** big rooms; free parking, Internet, and break-
fast; AG restaurant serves good locally sourced cuisine; noteworthy spa.
Cons: no views; north of Victoria Avenue opposite the top of Clifton
Hill, about a 20-minute walk to the base of Clifton Hill. ⑤ *Rooms from:
C$139* ✉ *5195 Magdalen St.* ☎ *289/292–0000, 877/783–7772* ⊕ *www.
sterlingniagara.com* 🛏 *41 rooms* ⑩ *Breakfast.*

SPORTS AND THE OUTDOORS

Niagara Glen. The 82.5-acre Niagara Glen nature reserve has 4 km
(2.5 miles) of hiking trails through forested paths that pass giant boul-
ders left behind as the falls eroded the land away thousands of years
ago. Some trails are steep and rough, and the Glen has an elevation
change of more than 200 feet. ✉ *Niagara Falls* ⊕ *www.niagaraparks.
com/nature-trails.*

Niagara Parks Commission. The Niagara Parks Commission has information on hiking and biking trails, local parks, restaurants, and the

Niagara Gorge. ⊠ *Niagara Falls* ☎ *905/371–0254, 877/642–7275* ⊕ *www.niagaraparks.com.*

Niagara River Recreation Trail. From Fort Erie to Niagara-on-the-Lake, this recreation trail is 56 km (35 miles) of bicycle trails along the Niagara River. The 29-km (18-mile) route between Niagara Falls and Niagara-on-the-Lake is paved. The trail is divided into four sections, each with site-specific history: Niagara-on-the-Lake to Queenston; Queenston to the Whirlpool Aero Car; Chippawa to Black Creek; and Black Creek to Fort Erie. ⊠ *Niagara Falls* ⊕ *www.niagaraparks.com/nature-trails.*

Ontario Trails Council. Ontario Trails Council has information and maps about hikes in the province. ⊠ *Niagara Falls* ☎ *877/668–7245, 613/389–7678* ⊕ *www.ontariotrails.on.ca.*

NIAGARA WINE REGION

Ontarians have been growing Concord grapes for (sweet) wine in the Niagara region since the 1800s, but experiments with European *Vitis vinifera* species between the 1950s and 1970s led to more serious wine production. Today, the Niagara Peninsula is Canada's largest viticulture area, accounting for nearly 80% of the country's growing volume. More than 60 wineries reside here, either north of St. Catharines spread out across the largely rural Niagara Escarpment, or south of St. Catharines, in close proximity to pretty, Victorian-tinged Niagara-on-the-Lake.

But wine tasting isn't the only game in the Peninsula. Niagara-on-the-Lake draws theatergoers to its annual Shaw Festival and food lovers to its unparalleled restaurants. The Niagara Escarpment is a prime Sunday-drive destination, with winding country roads, the charming town of Jordan, and a couple of diamond-in-the-rough restaurants.

8

NIAGARA-ON-THE-LAKE

15 km (9 miles) north of Niagara Falls and 130 km (80 miles) south of Toronto.

The hub of the Niagara wine region is the town of Niagara-on-the-Lake (sometimes abbreviated NOTL). Since 1962 this town of 14,000 residents has been considered the southern outpost of fine summer theater in Ontario because of its acclaimed Shaw Festival. As one of the country's prettiest and best-preserved Victorian towns, Niagara-on-the-Lake has architectural sights, shops, flower-lined streets and plentiful ornamental gardens in summer, quality theater nearly year-round, and some of the best chefs and hoteliers in the country.

WHEN TO GO

The town is worth a visit at any time of the year for its inns, restaurants, and proximity to the wineries (open year-round), but the most compelling time to visit is from April through November, during the Shaw Festival, and when the weather allows alfresco dining. Wine-harvesting tours and events take place in the fall and, for ice wine, in December and January. Be warned that the tiny town can get packed over Canadian

and American holiday weekends in summer: parking will be scarce, driving slow, and you might have to wait for tastings at wineries.

GETTING HERE AND AROUND

From Buffalo or Toronto, Niagara-on-the-Lake is easily reached by car via the QEW. NOTL is about a two-hour drive from Toronto, a bit far for just a day trip. From Niagara Falls or Lewiston, take the Niagara Parkway. There's no public transport in Niagara-on-the-Lake or to Niagara Falls, 15 km (9 miles) south.

Niagara-on-the-Lake is a very small town that can easily be explored on foot. Parking downtown can be nightmarish in peak season. Parking along the main streets is metered, at C$2 per hour. On most residential streets parking is free but still limited.

TOURS

Sentineal Carriages conducts year-round tours in and around Niagara-on-the-Lake. Catch a carriage at the Prince of Wales hotel or make a reservation for a pickup. The private, narrated tours are C$80 for 30 minutes, C$115 for 45 minutes, and C$145 for 1 hour (prices are per carriage).

Tour Contacts Sentineal Carriages. ☎ *905/468–4943* ⊕ *www.sentinealcarriages.ca.*

Visitor Information Niagara-on-the-Lake Chamber of Commerce and Visitor & Convention Bureau. ✉ *26 Queen St.* ☎ *905/468–1950* ⊕ *www.niagaraonthelake.com.*

WINERIES

Château des Charmes. Founded in 1978, this is one of Niagara's first wineries, and one of the two largest family-owned wineries in Niagara (Peller is the other). Originally from France, the Bosc family were pioneers in cultivating European varieties of grapes in Niagara. Wines here consistently win awards, and the winery is particularly known for its chardonnay and Gamay Noir Droit, made from a grape variety that was accidentally created through a mutation. The wine is proprietary, and this is the only winery allowed to make it. Château des Charmes is pioneering again and in the process of developing brand-new wholly Canadian grape varieties. ✉ *1025 York Rd.* ☎ *905/262–4219* ⊕ *www.chateaudescharmes.com* 🍷 *Tasting flights C$10; tours C$10–C$15.*

Frogpond Farm. Ontario's first certified-organic winery is a small, family-owned affair with exclusively organic wines. The setting is truly farmlike: sheep and guinea hens mill about outside while you taste. With only 10 varieties, all VQA and including a nice ice wine, you can become an expert in this label in one sitting. The wines are available on-site, online, and at selected restaurants in Ontario; many of the labels are available at the Liquor Control Board of Ontario (LCBO). ✉ *1385 Larkin Rd. (Line 6)* ☎ *905/468–1079, 877/989–0165* ⊕ *www.frogpondfarm.ca* 🍷 *Tastings free.*

Jackson-Triggs Niagara Estate Winery. An ultramodern facility, this famous winery blends state-of-the-art wine-making technology with age-old, handcrafted enological savvy, as evidenced by the stainless steel trough by the entrance. A multitude of tours, workshops, and events are

Niagara-on-the-Lake

Lake Ontario

Niagara
River

0 — 500 yards

0 — 500 meters

Queen's Royal Park

Golf Course

Royal George Theatre

Niagara Blvd.

Melville St.

Detater

Ricardo St.

Wellington

Prideaux St.

Byron St.

Front St.

Queen St.

Court House Theatre

Johnson St.

Gage St.

Picton St.

Queens

Shaw Festival Theatre

Niagara Parkway

Queens Parade

Lansdowne

Nassau St.

Dorchester St.

Butler St.

Centre St.

Brock

Baldwin Pl.

Simcoe St.

William St.

Mary St.

Gate St.

Victoria St.

Regent St.

King St.

Addison Ave.

Lakeshore Rd.

John St.

Mississauga St.

Anne St.

Peller Estates

Colonel Butler

Paffard St.

Chautauqua St.

Niagara Parkway

Promenade

Niven Rd.

Jackson Triggs

Hunter Rd.

Stratus

East-West Line

Niagara Stone Rd. (Hwy 55)

Concession 1

Frogpond Farm

Concession

TO
NIAGARA
FALLS

Inniskillin

KEY

🛈 Tourist
Information

8

offered. The hourly public tour is a great introduction to winemaking and includes three tastings and a mini-lesson in wine tasting. Its premium award-winning VQA wines can be sipped in the tasting gallery and purchased in the retail boutique. ✉ *2145 Niagara Stone Rd.* ☎ *905/468–4637, 866/589–4637* ⊕ *www.jacksontriggswinery.com* 🎟 *Tastings C$1 (C$5–C$7 ice wine). Tours C$5.*

Konzelmann Estate Winery. An easygoing winery with a friendly staff and sociable tasting bar, Konzelmann has garnered praise (and awards) from various authoritative sources like the *Wall Street Journal,* for its fruitier wines in particular, and it's known for high-quality ice wines, one of which made *Wine Spectator*'s top 100 wines list, the first Canadian wine ever to make the list. Konzelmann's vineyards border Lake Ontario, and the winery has a viewing platform with vistas of the vines and water. The retail shop is well stocked with wine-related gifts. ✉ *1096 Lakeshore Rd.* ☎ *905/935–2866* ⊕ *www.konzelmann.ca* 🎟 *Tours C$8–C$22.*

Stratus. Standing out from a vast landscape of single varietal wines, Stratus specializes in assemblage: combining multiple varieties of grapes to create unique blends. Established in 2000, and emerging on the Niagara wine scene in 2005, they continue to perfect what has traditionally been a recipe for disaster for winemakers. A fine example is the Stratus White, a mix of six grape varieties, that's complex and unlike anything you've ever tasted (in a good way). Sip all three assemblage wines (white, red, and ice wine) and a handful of single varietals in the modern glass-walled tasting room, installed in the world's first LEED-certified winery. ■TIP→ **Tours must be reserved in advance and can include cheese and charcuterie, or a beer-and-wine pairing with the craft brewery next door, Oast House.** ✉ *2059 Niagara Stone Rd.* ☎ *905/468–1806* ⊕ *www.stratuswines.com* ✉ *Tastings C$10 (4 wines).*

Trius Winery at Hillebrand. With more than 300 wine awards, this winery—one of Niagara's first and largest—produces many excellent varieties. Its reds (especially Trius Red and Trius Cabernet Franc) are some of the best in Niagara, consistently taking top prizes at competitions; the Trius Brut is another gold medalist. After the half-hour cellar and vineyard tour are three complimentary tastings. Another dozen themed tours and regular events include a seminar where you can blend your own Trius Red and an evening of chef-hosted meals at their terrific restaurant. ■TIP→ **Book in advance for tours.** ✉ *1249 Niagara Stone Rd.* ☎ *905/468–7123, 800/582–8412* ⊕ *www.triuswines.com* ✉ *Tastings C$2, C$5 (ice wine). Tours C$10–C$15.*

EXPLORING

FAMILY
Fodor's Choice
★

Fort George National Historic Site. On a wide stretch of parkland south of town sits this fort that was built in the 1790s but lost to the Yankees during the War of 1812. It was recaptured after the burning of the town in 1813 and largely survived the war, only to fall into ruins by the 1830s. Thankfully, it was reconstructed a century later, and you can explore the officers' quarters, the barracks rooms of the common soldiers, the kitchen, and more. Staff in period uniform conduct tours and reenact 19th-century infantry and artillery drills. ✉ *Fort George National Historic Site, 51 Queens Parade* ☎ *905/468–6614* ⊕ *www. pc.gc.ca/lhn-nhs/on/fortgeorge/index.aspx* ✉ *C$11.70 (C$5.90 parking)* ☉ *Closed Dec.–Feb. and weekdays in Mar., Apr., and Nov.*

Niagara Apothecary. Restored to look like a 19th-century pharmacy that opened here in 1869, the apothecary has glass-fronted walnut cabinets that display vintage remedies such as Merrill's System Tonic, which "Purifies the Blood and Builds up the System." Among the boxes and bottles is a rare collection of apothecary flasks. ✉ *5 Queen St.* ☎ *905/468–3845, 800/220–1921 off season and for group tours* ⊕ *www.niagaraapothecary.ca* ✉ *Free* ☉ *Closed Oct.–May.*

Niagara Historical Society & Museum. In connected side-by-side buildings—one the 1875 former Niagara High School building and the other the first building in Ontario to have been erected as a museum, in 1906—this extensive collection relates to the often·colorful history of the Niagara Peninsula from earliest times through the 19th century. ■TIP→ **During June, July, and August, the museum offers guided walking tours of the town (C$5) at 11 am on Thursday, Friday, and Saturday; and Sunday at 2 pm.** ✉ *43 Castlereagh St.* ☎ *905/468–3912* ⊕ *www. niagarahistorical.museum* ✉ *C$5.*

Queen Street. You can get a glimpse of the town's rich architectural history walking along this single street, with Lake Ontario to your north,

Niagara-on-the-Lake, in the heart of the Niagara wine region, has gained fame for its fine wines and food, beautiful setting, and the annual summer Shaw Festival.

and it is the core of NOTL's commercial portion. At the corner of Queen and King Streets is Niagara Apothecary. This high-style, mid-Victorian building was an apothecary from 1866 to 1964. The Court House is situated across the street. It became the Town Hall in 1862. Presently, it houses a small 327-seat theater during Shaw Festival. At No. 209 is the handsome Charles Inn, formerly known as Richardson-Kiely House, built in 1832 for Charles Richardson, who was a barrister and member of Parliament. ■TIP➔ The 10 or so blocks of shopping includes an olive-tasting room, upscale restaurants and cafés, designer-label boutiques, old-fashioned ice-cream parlors, and a spa. You could easily spend an entire day in this area. ✉ Niagara-on-the-Lake.

St. Mark's Church. One of Ontario's oldest Anglican churches, this was built in 1804, and St. Mark's parish is even older, formed in 1792. The stone church still houses the founding minister's original library of 1,500 books, brought from England. During the War of 1812, American soldiers used the church as a barracks, and still-visible rifle pits were dug in the cemetery. The church is open for concerts, lectures, and Sunday services only. ✉ 41 Byron St. ☎ 905/468–3123 ⊕ stmarks1792.com.

FAMILY **Whirlpool Jet Boat Tours.** A one-hour thrill ride, these tours veer around and hurdle white-water rapids that follow Niagara canyons up to the wall of rolling waters, just below Niagara Falls. Children must be at least six years old for the open-boat Wet Jet Tour and four years old for the covered-boat (dry!) Jet Dome Tour; minimum height requirements also apply. Tours depart from Niagara-on-the-Lake or Niagara Falls, Ontario (June–August only) and Lewiston, NY. ✉ 61 Melville St.

☎ *905/468–4800, 888/438–4444*
⊕ *www.whirlpooljet.com* 🖃 *C$61*
☉ *Closed mid-Oct.–mid-Apr.*

WHERE TO EAT

George Bernard Shaw once said, "No greater love hath man than the love of food," and Niagara-on-the-Lake, which hosts a festival devoted to the playwright, is a perfect place to indulge your epicurean desires. Many eateries serve fine produce and wines from the verdant Niag-

ara Peninsula, and the glut of high-end options fosters fierce competition. A number of inns and wineries here have restaurants. Especially in summer, make reservations whenever possible. Many restaurants serve dinner only until 9.

$$$$
INTERNATIONAL
Fodor's Choice
★

✕ **Hillebrand Winery Restaurant.** Niagara-on-the-Lake's first winery restaurant is still one of its best. After a complimentary winery tour and tasting, you can continue to indulge in the spacious, light-filled dining room with big double doors framing vineyards almost as far as the eye can see. The menu of locally inspired cuisine changes every six weeks. Tasting menus are available to try such culinary masterpieces as wild sockeye salmon with asparagus and fennel slaw, and Perth lamb pot pie with tomato-and-rhubarb terrine. Niagara strawberry shortcake is just one delicious dessert from the pastry chef that goes nicely with one of the in-house ice wines. ⑤ *Average main: C$38* ✉ *1249 Niagara Stone Rd., at Hwy. 55* ☎ *905/468–7123, 800/582–8412, 905/468–7123, 800/582–8412* ⊕ *www.triuswines.com* 🍴 *Reservations essential.*

$$
BRITISH

✕ **Olde Angel Inn.** You can request a Yorkshire pudding to accompany any meal at this tavern just off Queen Street, which should tip you off to its British leanings, played out further in the decor: a warren of rooms with creaky floors and worn (or well-loved, depending on how you see it) wooden tables and chairs, low ceilings and exposed beams, and convivial chatter throughout. In Ontario's oldest operating inn (it's believed to have opened in 1789) the Olde Angel sets out pub fare such as shepherd's pie, bangers and mash, and steak-and-kidney pie. Entrées change periodically but always include the house specialty, prime rib of beef au jus. Twenty-four domestic and imported (European) brews are on tap. ■TIP➜ **The pub has live music, ranging from Celtic to 1970s covers, on most nights of the week, beginning at 9:30.** ⑤ *Average main: C$15* ✉ *224 Regent St.* ☎ *905/468–3411* ⊕ *www.angel-inn.com.*

$$$$
EUROPEAN
Fodor's Choice
★

✕ **Peller Estates Winery Restaurant.** Frequently cited as the best restaurant in Niagara-on-the-Lake—an impressive feat in a town with so many excellent restaurants—Peller manages refinement without arrogance and has a superior view to its main competitor, Hillebrand. The stately Colonial revival dining room is anchored by a huge fireplace at one end and has windows running the length of the room overlooking a large patio and the estate vineyards. A menu of ever-changing expertly prepared entrées often weaves the Peller Estates wine into modern Canadian cuisine, such as the ice-wine lobster with basil cannelloni and

Peller Estates Winery, known for its award-winning Rieslings and ice wines, provides visitors an elegant experience, from winery tours to tastings to fine dining.

double-smoked bacon, or Ontario elk with cabernet-juniper sausage. Inventive desserts have included a honey-lemon soufflé with cardamom crème anglaise. $ *Average main: C$35* ✉ *290 John St. E* ☎ *905/468–4678* ⊕ *www.peller.com* ⌂ *Reservations essential.*

$$$ ✕ **Tiara Restaurant at Queen's Landing.** Niagara-on-the-Lake's only water-
CANADIAN front restaurant, the regal Tiara sits beside a marina with a view of the Niagara River beyond the sailboat masts. The elegant, amber-hued Georgian-meets-contemporary dining room is buttoned up but accented by a pretty stained-glass ceiling and near-panoramic windows that give nearly every table a water view. The outdoor tables next to the marina, however, are the ones to request to go with the exquisite French-influenced menu, which might include Ontario lamb duo—edamame-crusted chop and rosemary-rubbed broil with spearmint foam—and free-range roast chicken with spiced Niagara rhubarb. Round out the meal with homemade ice cream topped with seasonal berries. $ *Average main: C$25* ✉ *155 Byron St.* ☎ *905/468–2195, 888/669–5566* ⊕ *www.vintage-hotels.com* ⌂ *Reservations essential.*

$$$$ ✕ **Treadwell.** This brainchild of chef-owner Stephen Treadwell (formerly
CANADIAN of the prestigious Michelin-starred Auberge du Pommier), his chef de cuisine Matthew Payne, and his son, wine sommelier James Treadwell, Treadwell embodies the philosophy of farm-to-table. Sit down for dinner on the sidewalk patio or in the sleek dining room and indulge in pan-seared Lake Huron pickerel and wild mushroom tempura, or Cumbrae Farms pork tenderloin with organic quinoa and wild honey-glazed pork belly. A Sunday brunch favorite is lemon East Coast lobster on duck fat–fried bread with Monforte Dairy crumbled goat's cheese

and bacon. $ *Average main: C$33* ✉ *114 Queen St.* ☎ *905/934–9797* ⊕ *www.treadwellcuisine.com* ⌕ *Reservations essential.*

$$$
ECLECTIC
✕ **Zee's Grill.** For alfresco dining, it's hard to beat Zee's huge wraparound patio with heat lamps across from the Shaw Festival Theatre. More informal than most similarly priced restaurants in town, Zee's has a seasonal menu that brings panache to homegrown comfort foods, such as grilled swordfish with purple potato hash and buttered baby bok choy or beef strip loin with blue cheese–scalloped potatoes and whiskey shallot *jus*. Appetizers follow the same philosophy—elegant, yet whimsical—as represented by pulled pork poutine consisting of Cajun fries, 36-hour slow-cooked pork shoulder, and white cheddar cheese curds. $ *Average main: C$30* ✉ *92 Picton St.* ☎ *905/468–5715* ⊕ *www.zees. ca* ⊘ *No lunch Dec.–mid-Apr.* ⌕ *Reservations essential.*

WHERE TO STAY

In terms of superior lodging, you're spoiled for choice in Niagara-on-the-Lake and it's hard to go wrong with any of the properties within the town's historic center. Prices are high, but hotels sometimes offer significant deals online.

Niagara-on-the-Lake may be Canada's B&B capital, with more than 100 to its name. Their service and quality can rival some of the priciest hotels.

Niagara-on-the-Lake Bed & Breakfast Association. For B&B listings, contact the Niagara-on-the-Lake Bed & Breakfast Association. ✉ *Niagara-on-the-Lake* ☎ *905/468–0123, 866/855–0123* ⊕ *www. niagarabedandbreakfasts.com.*

$$$
B&B/INN
🏨 **The Charles Hotel.** An air of old-fashioned civility permeates this 1832 Georgian gem, with a nice location that's right on the main street. **Pros:** historic details with modern touches; highly lauded restaurant; impeccably decorated. **Cons:** some historic "quirks" like variable water temperature; some verandas are connected (i.e., shared with neighbors). $ *Rooms from: C$239* ✉ *209 Queen St.* ☎ *905/468–4588, 866/556–8883* ⊕ *www.niagarasfinest.com* ⇆ *12 rooms* ⦿| *Breakfast.*

$$$$
HOTEL
Fodor's Choice
★
🏨 **Harbour House.** The closest hotel to the waterfront in town is this luxurious and romantic boutique hotel with a contemporary-cottage theme just a block from the river. **Pros:** staff cater to every need; approachable luxury; full breakfast included. **Cons:** virtually no public spaces; no restaurant, gym, or spa on site; a few rooms without water views. $ *Rooms from: C$399* ✉ *85 Melville St.* ☎ *905/468–4683, 866/277–6677* ⊕ *www.harbourhousehotel.ca* ⇆ *28 rooms, 3 suites* ⦿| *Breakfast.*

$$
HOTEL
🏨 **Moffat Inn.** A central location on Picton Street, reasonable prices, and expert management make this 1835 stucco inn a real find. **Pros:** great location at a reasonable price; upscale linens; free Wi-Fi and parking. **Cons:** rooms small and not as posh as other area hotels; dated decor and worn carpets. $ *Rooms from: C$174* ✉ *60 Picton St.* ☎ *905/468–4116, 888/669–5566* ⊕ *www.vintage-hotels.com* ⇆ *23 rooms, 1 2-bedroom apartment* ⦿| *No meals.*

$$
B&B/INN
🏨 **Olde Angel Inn.** Though established in the late 1700s, this coach-house inn burned down during the War of 1812 and was rebuilt in 1816 (another casualty of that war, Captain Colin Swayze, is believed

to haunt the inn). **Pros:** excellent price at the heart of town; on-site English-style tavern. **Cons:** historic inn means poor soundproofing, which is a problem for rooms over the pub; dedicated parking for cottages only. $ *Rooms from: C$169* ✉ *224 Regent St.* ☎ *905/468–3411* ⊕ *www.angel-inn.com* ➥ *3 rooms, 2 2-bedroom suites, 2 2-bedroom cottages* ⦾ *No meals.*

$$$
HOTEL
Fodor'sChoice
★

🛎 **Pillar and Post.** A two-story hotel six (long) blocks from the heart of town, this building has been a cannery, barracks, and basket factory in its 100-plus-year history. **Pros:** exceptional staff; unaffected mix of historic and modern; cool spa and pool; free parking and high-speed Internet. **Cons:** not as central as some other hotels (a brisk 20-minute walk to Queen/Picton Street); no elevator to second-floor rooms. $ *Rooms from: C$250* ✉ *48 John St.* ☎ *905/468–2123, 888/669–5566* ⊕ *www.vintage-hotels.com* ➥ *122 rooms* ⦾ *No meals.*

$$$$
HOTEL

🛎 **Prince of Wales.** A visit from the Prince of Wales in 1901 inspired the name of this venerable hostelry that still welcomes the occasional royal guest or film star. **Pros:** nice spa; over-the-top-elegant public spaces; highly trained staff. **Cons:** some views of the parking lot; rabbit warren of corridors can be confusing; breakfast not included. $ *Rooms from: C$369* ✉ *6 Picton St.* ☎ *905/468–3246, 888/669–5566* ⊕ *www.vintage-hotels.com* ➥ *110 rooms* ⦾ *No meals.*

$$$
HOTEL

🛎 **Queen's Landing.** About half of the rooms at this Georgian-style brick mansion have knockout views of the fields of historic Fort George or the marina—ask for one when making a reservation. **Pros:** elegant, historic look; excellent service. **Cons:** breakfast not included; not actually historic. $ *Rooms from: C$250* ✉ *155 Byron St.* ☎ *905/468–2195, 888/669–5566* ⊕ *www.vintage-hotels.com* ➥ *142 rooms* ⦾ *No meals.*

8

$$$$
B&B/INN

🛎 **Riverbend Inn & Vineyard.** Surrounded by its own private vineyard, this beautifully restored, green-shuttered historic 1820 mansion is formal in style: it's fronted by a grand portico, and an enormous original 19th-century crystal chandelier greets you in the lobby. **Pros:** charming atmosphere, especially out on the patio if the weather permits; next to Peller Estates Winery. **Cons:** no elevators; far from central district. $ *Rooms from: C$295* ✉ *16104 Niagara Pkwy.* ☎ *905/468–8866, 888/955–5553* ⊕ *www.riverbendinn.ca* ➥ *21 rooms* ⦾ *No meals.*

$$$
HOTEL

🛎 **Shaw Club Hotel.** Clean lines, neutral colors, and modern elements like steel and glass give Shaw Club an edgy and hip vibe over its competitors, in a town that's largely Georgian or Victorian in style. **Pros:** hip cosmopolitan style unique in NOTL; ideal location just across the street from Shaw Festival Theatre; easygoing staff. **Cons:** small rooms; standard and annex rooms lack the wow factor of the rest of the hotel. $ *Rooms from: C$250* ✉ *92 Picton St.* ☎ *905/468–5711, 800/511–7070* ⊕ *www.shawclub.com* ➥ *30 rooms* ⦾ *Breakfast.*

$$$$
RENTAL

🛎 **Victorian Villas.** A breath of fresh air in Niagara-on-the-Lake, this lodging option offers ultramodern, beautifully appointed, and self-contained condolike properties right in the heart of the Queen Street shopping district. **Pros:** centrally located; in the heart of the action; renowned spa (Sanctuary) and restaurant (Treadwell), plus a Starbucks in the same complex. **Cons:** pricey; only 28 units, so they fill up fast.

⑤ *Rooms from: C$400* ⊠ *118 Queen St.* ☎ *905/468–4552, 855/988–4552* ⊕ *www.thevictorianvillas.com* ⇆ *28 units* ○| *No meals.*

NIGHTLIFE AND THE PERFORMING ARTS

Fodor's Choice **Shaw Festival.** Niagara-on-the-Lake remained a sleepy town until 1962,
★   when local lawyer Brian Doherty organized eight weekend performances of two George Bernard Shaw plays, *Don Juan in Hell* and
Candida. The next year he helped found the festival, whose mission
is to perform the works of Shaw and his contemporaries, including
Noël Coward, Bertolt Brecht, J. M. Barrie, J. M. Synge, and Anton
Chekhov. Now, the festival has expanded to close to a dozen plays,
running from April to October, including some contemporary plays by
Canadian playwrights, and one or two musicals (which are performed
unmiked). All are staged in one of four theaters within a few blocks of
one another. The handsome **Festival Theatre**, the largest of the three,
stands on Queen's Parade near Wellington Street and houses the box
office. The **Court House Theatre**, on Queen Street between King and
Regent streets, served as the town's municipal offices from the 1840s
until 1969, and is a national historic site. At the corner of Queen and
Victoria streets, the **Royal George Theatre** was originally built as a
vaudeville house in 1915. The **Studio Theatre**, the smallest of the four,
hosts mostly contemporary performances. The festival is one of the
biggest events in the summer. ■ **TIP→ Regular-price tickets cost C$35
to C$110, but discounts abound.** ☎ *905/468–2172, 800/511–7429*
⊕ *www.shawfest.com.*

SHOPPING

Niagara-on-the-Lake's historic Queen Street is lined with Victorian
storefronts housing art galleries; women's clothing stores; gourmet food
stores selling olives, marinades, and vinaigrettes; and tea and sweets
shops.

Greaves Jams & Marmalades. This shop has been making jams, jellies,
and marmalades from mostly local produce using family recipes, since
the company began in 1927. The spreads have no preservatives, pectin,
or additives. The brand has expanded into an operation with an online
store, and its jams are often served for afternoon tea in upscale hotel restaurants. ⊠ *55 Queen St.* ☎ *905/468–3608* ⊕ *www.greavesjams.com.*

▌EN
ROUTE
Harvest Barn Country Markets. There are many fruit stands and produce
markets along the streets of Niagara-on-the-Lake, but just outside of the
area is the mother lode that dwarfs the others. Harvest Barn Country
Markets, in a barn with a red-and-white-striped awning, sells regional
fruits and vegetables and tempts with its fresh-baked goods: sausage
rolls, bread, and fruit pies. After shopping for fresh and local ingredients, satisfy your hunger with lunch at the deli, or soup and salad bar,
and join locals at the picnic tables. ⊠ *1822 Niagara Stone Rd./Hwy. 55*
☎ *905/468–3224* ⊕ *www.harvestbarn.ca.*

THE NIAGARA ESCARPMENT

102 km (63 miles) southeast of Toronto and 41 km (25 miles) west of Niagara-on-the-Lake.

The Niagara Peninsula north of St. Catharines is known as Niagara Escarpment or the Twenty Valley, for the huge valley where the region's main towns of Jordan, Vineland, and Beamsville are. This area is much less visited than Niagara-on-the-Lake, and the wineries more spread out. Peach and pear trees, hiking trails, and long stretches of country road are the lay of the land. Aside from wine tasting, you can also visit the cute-as-a-button town of Jordan.

WHEN TO GO

Unlike Niagara-on-the-Lake, this area doesn't get overcrowded in summer, the ideal season for puttering along the country roads. Many restaurants, cafés, and shops have abbreviated hours between mid-September and late May. Most wineries do open for tastings in winter, but call ahead to be sure and to check on driving conditions, as some of these spots are on steep or remote rural roads.

GETTING HERE AND AROUND

Aside from booking a structured winery tour, getting behind the wheel yourself is the only way to visit the attractions in this region. This area is about 75 minutes from Toronto and 45 minutes from Niagara-on-the-Lake and is a feasible day trip.

VISITOR INFORMATION

Twenty Valley Tourism Association. ⊠ *4890 Victoria Ave. N, Jordan* ☎ *905/562–3636* ⊕ *www.twentyvalley.ca.*

WINERIES

Fodor's Choice ★ **Cave Spring Cellars.** On Jordan's Main Street, Cave Spring is one of the leading wine producers in Canada, with Ontario's oldest wine cellars, in operation since 1871. Go for the Riesling, chardonnay, and ice wine. It shares ownership with Inn on the Twenty and On the Twenty restaurant (next door) and produces custom blends for the latter. ■ **TIP→ There are public tours every day at 1:30 pm between June and September (only Friday and weekends the rest of the year).** ⊠ *3836 Main St., Jordan* ☎ *905/562–3581* ⊕ *www.cavespring.ca* 🍷 *Tastings C$1–C$4.*

Fielding Estate. Muskoka chairs by the cedar-framed entrance set the tone for the warm and charming winery within. Inside the modern West Coast–style cedar building with corrugated tin roof and massive stone chimney, Fielding has envious views of vineyards and Lake Ontario from huge picture windows and a big stone fireplace for chilly days. A young team—husband-and-wife owners and two winemakers—has been making quick strides here. The vineyard produces a low yield that enables flavors to be concentrated. ⊠ *4020 Locust La., Beamsville* ☎ *888/778–7758, 905/563–0668* ⊕ *www.fieldingwines.com* 🍷 *Tastings C$5 (3 wines); tours C$10.*

Tawse. Eco-friendly and partially geothermally powered, Tawse is so committed to producing top-notch pinot noir that it installed a six-level gravity-flow system to avoid overhandling the delicate grape. The investment seems to be paying off, especially considering they've been voted "Winery of the Year" multiple years at the Canada Wine Awards. The rural hillside winery is modern, its big stainless-steel vats visible from the tasting room. ■**TIP→ Don't leave empty handed because tasting fees are waived if you buy two or more bottles.** ✉ *3955 Cherry Ave., Vineland* ☎ *905/562–9500* ⊕ *www.tawsewinery.ca* 🍷 *Tastings C$8 (3 wines), tour $15.*

Vineland Estates Winery. One of Ontario's most beautiful wineries occupies 75 acres that were once a Mennonite homestead established in 1845. The original buildings have been transformed into the visitor center and production complex. Several tour and tasting options are available, including packages that include chocolate, ice wine, and specialty cocktails. The excellent restaurant on site serves lunch and dinner, and you can find a guesthouse and a B&B on the property. ✉ *3620 Moyer Rd., 40 km (25 miles) west of Niagara-on-the-Lake, Vineland* ☎ *905/562–7088, 888/846–3526* ⊕ *www.vineland.com* 🍷 *Tastings C$12 (3 wines plus tour).*

EXPLORING

Jordan Village. Charming Main Street Jordan, aka Jordan Village, is a small enclave of cafés and shops selling antiques, garden supplies, and artisanal foods. The Inn on the Twenty, the On the Twenty Restaurant, and Cave Spring Cellars are also here. Just a few blocks long, Jordan Village can be fully explored in a morning or afternoon. Home store **CHIC by Janssen** is worth a wander to gawk at items like Siberian fox throws, a bronze bear the size of an actual bear cub, and a $4,000 cedar canoe. **Irongate Garden Elements** is a favorite with gardeners. ✉ *Off QEW Exit 55 (Jordan Rd.); follow Jordan Rd. south 3 km (1.9 miles), take right onto 4th Ave.; follow signs to Cave Spring Cellars from here, Jordan* ⊕ *www.20valley.ca/site/shop.*

WHERE TO EAT

$$$$
EUROPEAN
Fodor's Choice
★

✕ **Inn on the Twenty Restaurant.** The huge windows framing the Twenty Valley conservation area are reason enough to dine at this restaurant, known as one of the best around Toronto, on Jordan's boutique-lined Main Street. Regional specialties and local and organic produce are emphasized on a seasonal menu that has included Wellington County boneless rib-eye steak served with mushroom-and-onion fricassee and bluecheese butter; and wild Huron trout with potato "mille-feuille" in spring leek cream. The dining room, reminiscent of the French and Italian countryside, is lovely, with a soaring ceiling, whitewashed exposed beams, and a view of the gardens. Cave Spring Cellars, which has a shop next door, provides many of the wines. ⑤ *Average main: C$32* ✉ *3836 Main St., off QEW Exit 55 or 57 (follow Cave Spring Cellars signs), Jordan* ☎ *905/562–7313* ⊕ *www.innonthetwenty.com* 🍴 *Reservations essential.*

$$$$
CANADIAN
Fodor's Choice
★

✕ **Restaurant@Vineland Estates Winery.** Exquisite progressive Canadian food and venerable wines are served by an enthusiastic staff on this bucolic property with three 19th-century Mennonite stone buildings. Sit on the large outdoor patio overlooking vineyards and Lake Ontario beyond or in the glassed-in restaurant, where many of the tables have a similar panoramic view. The menu is locally sourced and seasonal;

DID YOU KNOW?

Numerous waterfalls trickle along the Niagara Escarpment's beloved Bruce Trail. At more than 890 km (550 miles) long, it is the longest footpath in Canada.

tuna from Canada is rare-seared and blanketed with chorizo, corn green tomato relish, and pickled pole beans with mole. Carnivorous cravings are answered with venison haunch with heirloom beets, torchon, smoked cauliflower purée, and blackberry reduction. Desserts, like spiced pumpkin cheesecake served with mascarpone gelato, are the perfect demonstration of simplicity and innovation. $ *Average main: C$35 ⊠ 3620 Moyer Rd., Vineland* ☎ *905/562–7088, 888/846–3526* ⊕ *www.vineland.com* ☉ *Closed Mon. and Tues., Jan.–Apr.* ⚭ *Reservations essential.*

WHERE TO STAY

$$$$ ☷ **Inn on the Twenty.** Seven of the 24 suites in the main building of this
B&B/INN Main Street Jordan inn are 600-square-foot, two-story affairs, but the rooms to book—in nice weather at least—are the five ground-level suites with very private garden patios. **Pros:** large rooms; impeccably decorated; central location for the Twenty Valley. **Cons:** not as much to do in Jordan as in surrounding areas. $ *Rooms from: C$289* ⊠ *3845 Main St., off QEW Exit 55 or 57 (follow Cave Spring Cellars signs), Jordan* ☎ *905/562–5336, 800/701–8074* ⊕ *www.innonthetwenty.com* ⇨ *28 suites* ⱺ *Breakfast.*

SPORTS AND THE OUTDOORS

Bruce Trail. Canada's oldest and longest footpath, the Bruce Trail stretches 890 km (550 miles) along the Niagara Escarpment, with an additional 400 km (250 miles) of side trails. It takes in scenery from the orchards and vineyards of the Niagara Escarpment—one of Canada's 15 UNESCO World Biosphere Reserves—to the craggy cliffs and bluffs at Tobermory, 370 km (230 miles) north of Niagara-on-the-Lake. You can access the hiking trail at just about any point along the route; the main trail is marked with white blazes, the side trails with blue blazes. Northern parts of the trail are remote. ⊠ *Niagara Falls* ☎ *905/529–6821, 800/665–4453* ⊕ *brucetrail.org.*

STRATFORD

145 km (90 miles) west of Toronto.

In July 1953 Alec Guinness, one of the world's greatest actors, joined with Tyrone Guthrie, probably the world's greatest Shakespearean director, beneath a hot, stuffy tent in a quiet town about a 90-minute drive from Toronto. This was the birth of the Stratford Shakespeare Festival, which now runs from April to late October or early November and is one of the most successful and admired festivals of its kind.

Today Stratford is a city of 32,000 that welcomes more than 500,000 visitors annually for the Stratford Shakespeare Festival alone. But Shakespeare is far from the only attraction. The Stratford Summer Music Festival (July and August) is another highlight, shopping in the enchanting city core is a favorite pastime, and with more amazing restaurants than you could hope to try in one visit, dining out in Stratford could be a reason to return.

Stratford, Ontario

WHEN TO GO

The festival runs from mid-April through late October or early November. Most visitors choose their travel dates based on the play(s) they want to see. About half of the city's restaurants and B&Bs close off-season; the city is quiet in the colder months, but shops and art galleries stay open, hotels have reduced rates, and you'll rub elbows with locals rather than visitors.

GETTING HERE AND AROUND

Ontario's main east–west highway, the 401, which traverses the province all the way from Michigan to Québec, is the main route from Toronto to Kitchener-Waterloo; from there, Highway 7/8 heads to Stratford. Traffic-free driving time is about two hours. VIA Rail has daily service to downtown Stratford from Toronto's Union Station; the trip is about two hours.

Stratford is an ideal town for cruising via bicycle. Totally Spoke'd rents cruisers, mountain bikes, and tandem bikes (C$35–C$47/day; C$20–C$35/half-day).

ESSENTIALS

Bicycle Rental Totally Spoke'd. ⊠ *29 Ontario St.* ☎ *519/273-2001* ⊕ *www. totallyspoked.ca.*

Train Information Stratford Train Station. ⊠ *101 Shakespeare St.* ☎ *888/842–7245.* **VIA Rail.** ☎ *888/842–7245* ⊕ *www.viarail.ca.*

Visitor Information Stratford Shakespeare Festival. ⊠ *55 Queen St.* ☎ *519/273–1600, 800/567–1600* ⊕ *www.stratfordfestival.ca.* **Stratford Tourism Alliance.** ⊠ *47 Downie St.* ☎ *519/271–5140, 800/561–7926* ⊕ *www.visitstratford.ca.*

EXPLORING

Gallery Stratford. Regular exhibits of Canadian visual art and, in summer, of local artists' work are displayed here. ⊠ *54 Romeo St.* ☎ *519/271–5271* ⊕ *www.gallerystratford.on.ca* ⌂ *C$5* ⊙ *Closed Mon.*

Stratford Perth Museum. You can brush up on Stratford and Perth County history with permanent displays and changing exhibits that cover such topics as hockey in Stratford, the city's railroad, and the settlement of the area in the early 1800s. There are hiking trails and picnic areas on the property. ⊠ *4275 Huron Rd.* ☎ *519/393–5311* ⊕ *www.stratfordperthmuseum.ca* ⌂ *C$7.*

> ### STRATFORD WALKING TOURS
>
> The Stratford Tourism Alliance produces several themed, self-guided walking tours, such as Historic Downtown; Landmarks; and Shakespearean Gardens. Pick one up from the tourism office at 47 Downie Street, or for a more modern spin, download the tour podcasts from ⊕ *www.visitstratford.ca.*

WHERE TO EAT

For a tiny town, Stratford is endowed with an unusual array of excellent restaurants. Perth County is a locavore's dream of farmers' markets, dairies, and organic farms. The proximity of the Stratford Chefs School supplies a steady stream of new talent, and the Shakespeare festival ensures an appreciative audience.

$$$ ✕ **Bijou.** A husband-and-wife team, both Stratford Chefs School grads,
EUROPEAN   operates this small, self-professed "culinary gem." The chalkboard menu changes daily, and nearly everything on it is locally sourced. Two- or three-course prix-fixe dinners have French, Italian, and Asian influences; roast Muscovy duck wih mushrooms, beluga lentils, and carrot puree may be an option for your main course. For dessert, there might be a local ricotta cheesecake with seabuckthorn sauce and orange sorbet. The global dim sum Sunday brunch, with Asian small plate delicacies such as Korean braised beef cheek buns and spicy Chinese omelets, is a must-try. ■TIP➔ The small entrance, next to the Stratford Hotel, is easy to miss: to get here, cross the parking lot on Erie Street, or pass through Allen's Alley, off Wellington Street. ⑤ *Average main: C$27* ⊠ *105 Erie St.* ☎ *519/273–5000* ⊕ *www.bijourestaurant.com* ⊙ *Closed Mon. May–Oct.; no lunch Tues.–Thurs.; no lunch Sat. in Nov.–Apr.* ⌂ *Reservations essential.*

CLOSE UP

Bringing the Bard to Ontario

The origins of Stratford are modest. After the War of 1812, the British government granted a million acres of land along Lake Huron to the Canada Company, headed by a Scottish businessman. Surveyors came to a marshy creek surrounded by a thick forest and named it "Little Thames," noting that it might make "a good mill-site." It was Thomas Mercer Jones, a director of the Canada Company, who renamed the river the Avon and the town Stratford. The year was 1832, 121 years before the concept of a theater festival would take flight and change Canadian culture.

For years Stratford was considered a backwoods hamlet. Then came the first of two saviors of the city, both of them also Thomases. In 1904 an insurance broker named Tom Orr transformed Stratford's riverfront into a park. He also built a formal English garden, where flowers mentioned in the plays of Shakespeare—monkshood to sneezewort, bee balm to bachelor's button—bloom grandly to this day.

Next, Tom Patterson, a fourth-generation Stratfordian born in 1920, looked around; saw that the town wards and schools had names like Hamlet, Falstaff, and Romeo; and felt that some kind of drama festival might save his community from becoming a ghost town. The astonishing story of how he began in 1952 with C$125 (a "generous" grant from the Stratford City Council), tracked down Tyrone Guthrie and Alec Guinness, and somehow, in little more than a year, pasted together a long-standing theater festival is recounted in his memoirs, *First Stage: The Making of the Stratford Festival.*

Soon after it opened, the festival wowed critics worldwide with its professionalism, costumes, and daring thrust stage. The early years brought giants of world theater to the tiny town of some 20,000: James Mason, Alan Bates, Christopher Plummer, Jason Robards Jr., and Maggie Smith. Stratford's offerings are still among the best of their kind in the world—the next-best thing to seeing the Royal Shakespeare Company in mother city Stratford-upon-Avon, in England—with at least a handful of productions every year that put most other Canadian summer arts festivals to shame.

8

$ × **Boomer's Gourmet Fries.** The humble potato rises to become a star at
ECLECTIC Boomer's Gourmet Fries, equipped with a take-out window and a handful of stools at a counter. Toppings of every ilk can be found here, like veg chili, hickory sticks, and salsa. The imaginative pairings apply to burgers as well, with menu options like bruschetta and goat cheese and the "Parisienne" with Brie, grilled onions, and Dijon mustard. Fish-and-chips is done simply with cod. Try one of the many unique and delicious takes on a Canadian "delicacy," poutine; the traditional version is fries topped with cheese curds and gravy. ⑤ *Average main: C$12* ✉ *26 Erie St.* ☎ *519/275–3147* ⊕ *www.boomersgourmetfries.com.*

$$$ × **Pazzo Pizzeria and Taverna.** A corner of Stratford's main crossroads
ITALIAN is home to one of the city's best and most convivial Italian restaurants. Have a drink and people-watch at the bar or on the patio. The kitchen creates hearty regional Italian mains—like chicken scaloppine

with mushrooms, balsamic braised shallots, and wild arugula—and house-made pastas—such as seafood lasagna with smoked caccio-cavalo, lobster, shrimp crab, and tarragon cream—that make good use of locally sourced produce, meat, and sustainable fish. Downstairs, at the Pizzeria, go for the straightforward pasta dishes or the thin-crust pizzas. It's a popular meeting place after a play, the decor is soothing and modern, and the service is quick and friendly. $ *Average main: C$22* ✉ *70 Ontario St.* ☎ *519/273–6666* ⊕ *www.pazzo.ca* ☉ *Closed Mon.* ⌲ *Reservations essential.*

$$$$ ╳ **The Prune.** A converted 1905 house holds a number of charming
CANADIAN gray-purple dining rooms with white table linens surrounded by a tidy courtyard. Chef Bryan Steele, who is also senior cookery instructor at Stratford Chefs School, coaxes fresh local ingredients into innovative dishes with the best of what's available globally. Dishes change with the harvest but have included Lake Huron whitefish meunière with asparagus and cinnamon cap mushrooms; and spring risotto with Parmesan, crispy egg, and wild leek pesto. The owners proudly source their lamb from small family-owned Church Hill Farm, just 30 km (18 miles) away. The restaurant has a solid vegetarian selection, a knowledgeable sommelier on staff, and a strong wine list with many Ontario options. Desserts are made fresh for each meal by an in-house pastry chef. $ *Average main: C$40* ✉ *151 Albert St.* ☎ *519/271–5052* ⊕ *theprune.com* ☉ *Closed Nov.–mid-May and Mon. No lunch* ⌲ *Reservations essential.*

$$$$ ╳ **Rundles Restaurant.** At Stratford's top choice for sophisticated haute
EUROPEAN cuisine, the look is summery and modern; brick is exposed, windows
Fodor's Choice are unadorned and panoramic, and, with a theatrical flourish, flowing
★ white silk scarves hang from primitive stone masks. Diners have five to seven choices for each course (appetizer, entrée, and dessert) on the prix-fixe menu. Offerings change frequently, but regulars would protest the removal of the crisp and succulent confit of duck with braised eggplant, roast potatoes, and onions flavored with balsamic vinegar. $ *Average main: C$94* ✉ *9 Cobourg St.* ☎ *519/271–6442* ⊕ *www.rundlesrestaurant.com* ☉ *Closed Oct.–May and Mon. No lunch weekdays* ⌲ *Reservations essential.*

$$ ╳ **York Street Kitchen.** Locals come to this casual spot across from the
CAFÉ waterfront for the signature generously portioned and juicy sandwiches and, for dinner, homemade comfort dishes, such as meat loaf with Yukon Gold mashed potatoes or chicken gumbo. But breakfast (served daily) is a special treat; favorites are the French toast with homemade apple compote and the Mennonite sandwich with homemade summer sausage, cheddar, corn relish, and honey mustard on country white bread. A build-your-own sandwich menu is available for lunch and at the take-out window in summer. The bright dining room is decorated with vibrant-patterned vinyl tablecloths. $ *Average main: C$15* ✉ *24 Erie St.* ☎ *519/273–7041* ⊕ *www.yorkstreetkitchen.com.*

WHERE TO STAY

Stratford has a wide range of atmospheric B&Bs, motels on the out-skirts of downtown, and inns around the center. Room rates are discounted substantially in winter, sometimes by more than 50%.

Stratford Area Bed & Breakfast Association. The Stratford Area Bed & Breakfast Association conducts regular inspections of area B&Bs and maintains a list of those that pass muster. ⊠ *Stratford* ☎ *519/272–2961* ⊕ *www.sabba.ca.*

$$$
B&B/INN
🛏 **Avery House.** This 1874 Gothic Revival brick home transformed into an impeccably decorated B&B has an eclectic interior. **Pros:** continually updated; affable host; big breakfasts. **Cons:** communal dining and set breakfast time (9 am) not everyone's cup of tea; on a busy road; ground-floor unit's bathroom isn't directly en suite. ⑤ *Rooms from: C$189* ⊠ *330 Ontario St.* ☎ *519/273–1220, 800/510–8813* ⊕ *www. averyhouse.com* ⊘ *Closed Nov.–May* ➥ *6 rooms* ⦿*| Breakfast.*

$$
HOTEL
🛏 **Festival Inn.** Stratford's largest hotel—east of town and about 10 minutes by car from the theaters—offers a mixture of lodging types: motel rooms, suites with Jacuzzis, and a modern inn. **Pros:** fair prices; modern rooms; exceptional staff. **Cons:** slightly out of town on a commercial strip. ⑤ *Rooms from: C$145* ⊠ *1144 Ontario St.* ☎ *519/273–1150, 800/463–3581* ⊕ *www.festivalinnstratford.com* ➥ *169 rooms* ⦿*| Breakfast.*

$$$
B&B/INN
🛏 **Foster's Inn.** Two doors away from the Avon and Studio theaters, this brick building dates to 1906 and has a bit of history—it once housed the International Order of Odd Fellows, a fraternal organization that started in the United Kingdom. **Pros:** great deals in winter; excellent locale; free Wi-Fi. **Cons:** fills up fast in summer; sometimes a two-night minimum stay required. ⑤ *Rooms from: C$179* ⊠ *111 Downie St.* ☎ *519/271–1119, 888/728–5555* ⊕ *www.fostersinn.com* ➥ *9 rooms* ⦿*| No meals.*

$$
B&B/INN
🛏 **Queen and Albert B&B Inn.** A 1901 storefront, now bright blue with a striped awning, is the unique facade of this residential-neighborhood B&B, a 10-minute walk to Stratford's main shopping and eating strip. **Pros:** friendly host; large rooms; two rooms with a shared balcony. **Cons:** no elevator and only one ground-floor room, which has twin beds and is not as impressively decorated as upper-floor rooms. ⑤ *Rooms from: C$175* ⊠ *174 Queen St.* ☎ *519/272–0589* ⊕ *www.queenandalbert.com* ⊘ *Closed Nov.–Apr.* ➥ *4 suites* ⦿*| Breakfast.*

$$$$
B&B/INN
🛏 **Stewart House Inn.** The interior of this elegant 1870s home draws on the Victorian period but with modern conveniences. **Pros:** exceptional service; on-site outdoor pool; complimentary espresso available around the clock. **Cons:** not as central as some other inns; ground-floor Garden Room available only in summer. ⑤ *Rooms from: C$289* ⊠ *62 John St. N* ☎ *519/271–4576, 866/826–7772* ⊕ *www.stewarthouseinn.com* ➥ *6 rooms* ⦿*| Breakfast.*

$
HOTEL
🛏 **Swan Motel.** The original 1960s motel sign still marks this single-story tawny-brick motel 3 km (2 miles) south of downtown, behind which you'll find clean-as-a-whistle, albeit utilitarian, rooms at good prices. **Pros:** one of the best deals in town; warm hosts; on a private lot backed

8

The award-winning Festival Theatre, the largest of the Stratford Shakespeare Festival's four venues, has been staging great drama for theater lovers since 1957.

by farmland; outdoor pool. **Cons:** basic rooms with parking-lot views; not walkable to downtown; motor-lodge layout around a parking lot. $ *Rooms from: C$110* ✉ *960 Downie St.* ☎ *519/271–6376* ⊕ *www. swanmotel.ca* ⊘ *Closed Nov.–May* ⬩ *24 rooms* ⑩ *No meals.*

$$$
B&B/INN
The Three Houses. On a quiet residential street, this elegant and tastefully decorated trio of two Edwardian houses and one Victorian has been frequented by the likes of Kevin Spacey, Julie Andrews, and Christopher Plummer. **Pros:** star appeal; exquisite decorative taste; heated saltwater pool. **Cons:** irregular hours in winter; sometimes entire house is rented out to film crews. $ *Rooms from: C$225* ✉ *100 Brunswick St.* ☎ *519/272–0722* ⊕ *www.thethreehouses.com* ⬩ *6 suites* ⑩ *Breakfast.*

THE PERFORMING ARTS

Fodor's Choice
★
Stratford Shakespeare Festival. One of the two largest classical repertory companies in the world—England's Royal Shakespeare Company is the other—the Festival presents not only Shakespeare plays, but also works by other dramatists (including new plays) and popular musicals and musical revues in its four theaters.

The 1,800-seat Festival Theatre (55 Queen Street), with its hexagonal wooden thrust stage and permanent wooden stage set, is the largest and the oldest of the Festival's theaters—in its first incarnation in 1953 it was just a stage under a tent. The 1,100-seat Avon Theatre (99 Downie Street) has a traditional proscenium stage, while the Tom Patterson Theatre (111 Lakeside Drive) has a long, runway-style thrust stage and 480 steeply stacked seats. The petite Studio Theatre (34 George

Street E), with only 260 seats, is the go-to space for experimental and new works; built in 2002, it has a modern appearance and a hexagonal thrust stage.

Throughout the season, 12 to 16 productions are mounted, and at the height of the festival in July and August you may be able to choose from among eight performances. The Festival also offers numerous concerts, workshops, tours, lectures, and talks, such as Meet the Festival, where the public can ask questions of actors and artists. The festival has both matinees and evening performances (and many visitors do see two plays per day). Theaters are closed most Mondays. For tickets, information, and accommodations, contact the festival office directly. ⊠ *55 Queen St.* ☎ *519/273–1600, 800/567–1600* ⊕ *www.stratfordfestival.ca.*

> ### DISCOUNT TICKETS
>
> Regular Stratford Festival tickets are around C$55 to C$110, but there are many ways to pay less. Spring previews and some fall performances are discounted 30%. Savings of 30% to 50% can be had for students and seniors, and theatergoers aged 16 to 29 can buy seats online for C$25 for select performances two weeks prior. Also available are early-ordering discounts, rush seats, half-price Tuesdays, and family and group discounts.

Fodor's Choice **Stratford Summer Music.** For five weeks in July and August, Stratford Sum-
★ mer Music brings musicians—from string quartets to Mexican mariachi bands—to indoor and outdoor venues around town. Outdoor performances, like those sounding from a barge on the Avon River, are free. Series may include Saturday-night cabaret at the Church restaurant and classical-music lunches at Rundles. Some performances do sell out, so get tickets in advance. ⊠ *Stratford* ☎ *519/271–2101* ⊕ *www.stratford-summermusic.ca.*

SHOPPING

Downtown Stratford is a great place for daytime distractions and is utterly devoid of chain stores. Ontario Street alone is lined with quaint bookstores stocking great local reads, chocolatiers, myriad colorful housewares and women's clothing shops, and catch-all gift stores.

Stratford Festival Shop. In two locations (at the Avon and Festival theaters), this is the place for Shakespeare finger puppets, every Shakespeare play ever written, original costume sketches, soundtracks to the musicals, and Bard-themed children's books. Visit their online store if you missed the chance to go in person. ⊠ *Avon Theatre, 99 Downie St.* ☎ *519/271–0055* ⊕ *store.stratfordfestival.ca.*

Watson's Chelsea Bazaar. At this brimming curio shop you might find a cat curled up among the reasonably priced china, glassware, French soaps, kitchen gadgets, and other bric-a-brac. The Bradshaw family has owned a store at this location in various forms (it used to be a high-end china hall) since the 1800s. ⊠ *84 Ontario St.* ☎ *519/273–1790* ⊕ *www.watsonsofstratford.com.*

8

EN ROUTE	**St. Jacobs Farmers' Market.** Just outside of Waterloo, this biweekly farmers' market (Thursday and Saturday) features 100 vendors selling local produce, cheeses, baked goods, and meat. There are also hundreds of permanent indoor and outdoor booths (open every day) with home-made foods straight from the farm—preserves, pies, smoked meats, and cheeses—and flea-market fare like crafts and handmade furniture. ■**TIP→** Don't miss the fresh hot apple fritters, a made-to-order treat worth queuing up for. ⊠ *878 Weber St. N, Waterloo* ☎ *519/747–1830* ⊕ *www.stjacobs.com.*

SOUTHERN GEORGIAN BAY

150 km (90 miles) north of Toronto.

The southern shores of Lake Huron's Georgian Bay are home to water-front towns and beaches that are popular getaways for Torontonians in summer. Ski resorts—Blue Mountain is the most popular—draw city folk as well once the snow falls and become biking and adventure resorts in summer. The region's largest city is Barrie (population 130,000), on the shore of Lake Simcoe, originally a landing place for the area's aboriginal inhabitants and, later, for fur traders. Today it's a big-box-store-filled suburb and one of Toronto's farther-flung bedroom communities. More interesting are the quiet towns of Midland and Penetanguishene (also called Penetang by locals), occupying a small corner of northern Simcoe County known as Huronia, on a snug harbor at the foot of Georgian Bay's Severn Sound. These are docking grounds for trips to the Georgian Bay Islands National Park. To the west, the attractive harbor town of Collingwood, on Nottawasaga Bay, is at the foot of Blue Mountain, the largest ski hill in the province.

WHEN TO GO

After Labour Day and before Victoria Day weekend (late May), few tourist attractions apart from ski resorts are open.

GETTING HERE AND AROUND

Georgian Bay towns and attractions are west of Highway 400, either via Highway 26 toward Collingwood or well-marked off Highway 400 north of Barrie. These towns and regions are 2½ to 4 hours from Toronto and are generally long weekend or even weeklong trips from the city.

■**TIP→** If you are heading north of Barrie in winter, go with a four-wheel-drive vehicle. Resorts, especially, are usually well off the highway and may require navigating twisting backcountry routes.

ESSENTIALS

Tourism Information Georgian Bay Coastal Route. ⊕ *www.visitgeorgianbay. com.* **Visit Southern Georgian Bay.** ☎ *705/445–7722, 888/227–8667* ⊕ *www. visitsouthgeorgianbay.ca.*

PLANNING YOUR OUTDOOR ADVENTURE

The Ontario Tourism Marketing Partnership's website (⊕ *www.ontariotravel.net*) is a one-stop-shop for information on outdoor adventures from cycling to snowmobiling. It also publishes a free outdoor-adventure guide. The nonprofit Ontario Trails Council (*877/668–7245* ⊕ *www.ontariotrails.on.ca*) has information on every trail and trail sport in the province; click the Central tab for the Muskokas and Georgian Bay.

CAMPING

Peak season in Ontario parks is June through August. Reserve a campsite if possible, though all provincial parks with organized camping have some sites available on a first-come, first-served basis.

Ontario Parks. For detailed information on parks and campgrounds provincewide, to make campground reservations, or to get the *Ontario Parks Guide*, contact Ontario Parks. ⊕ *www.ontarioparks.com.*

FISHING

Ministry of Natural Resources. Fishing licenses are required for Ontario and may be purchased from Ministry of Natural Resources offices and from most sporting-goods stores, outfitters, and resorts. A C$9.68 Outdoors Card, good for three years, is also required for fishing beyond a day (Canadian residents always need the Outdoors Card). For non-Canadians, the most restrictive (i.e., cheapest) one-day fishing license is C$21.88 (C$12.95 for Canadians); eight-day and one-year licenses are also available. ☎ *800/667–1940* ⊕ *www.mnr.gov.on.ca.*

Go Fish Ontario (⊕ *www.gofishinontario.com*), operated by Ontario Tourism, is an excellent planning tool for fishing trips.

SKIING

Ski resorts with downhill runs are concentrated north and west of Barrie. The central Ontario region also has more than 1,600 km (994 miles) of cross-country ski trails.

Ontario Snow Resorts Association. Ski Ontario has information on the condition of slopes across the province. ☎ *705/443–5450* ⊕ *www.skiontario.ca.*

8

EXPLORING

Georgian Bay Islands National Park. A series of 63 islands in Lake Huron's Georgian Bay, the park can be visited only via boat. Organized boat tours with the park or private companies operate from the weekend closest to May 24 through mid-October, weather permitting. The only way to explore one of the islands on foot is to book a trip on the park's Daytripper boat, bring your own boat, or take a water taxi in Honey Harbour (contact the park for details).

The park's own boat, the Daytripper (C$15.70 June–early October), makes the 15-minute trip to Beausoleil Island, which has hiking trails and beaches, from Honey Harbour, 15 km (9 miles) north of Port Severn at Highway 400 Exit 156.

Two companies do cruises through the Georgian Bay but don't allow you to disembark on any of the islands. The 300-passenger *Miss Midland*, operated by Midland Tours (C$27), leaves from the Midland town dock and offers 2½-hour sightseeing cruises daily at 2 pm mid-May to mid-October. The company can arrange departures from Toronto, which includes time to explore the town of Midland. From the Penetanguishene town dock, Penetanguishene 30,000 Island Cruises takes passengers on Penetanguishene Harbour and the Georgian Bay islands tours, including 1½- and 2½-hour cruises of Penetanguishene Harbour and 3½-hour cruises of the 30,000 islands of Georgian Bay, on the 200-passenger *MS Georgian Queen*. Lunch and dinner cruises are available. Captain Steve, the owner and your tour guide, has operated these tours—a family business—since 1985. Cruises depart one to three times daily in July and August; less frequently (but usually Saturday, Sunday, and Wednesday) in May, June, September, and October.

✉ *Town and park welcome center: off Hwy. 400 Exit 153 or 156, Port Severn* ☎ *705/526–9804* ⊕ *www.pc.gc.ca/georgianbay* ◻ *C$5.80* ☻ *Closed early Oct.–late May.*

Huronia Museum. Nearly 1 million artifacts on native and maritime history are on display at the museum building, and there's also a replica Huron/Ouendat village. Visitors can expect contemporary art and extensive photography pieces, in addition to native art and archaeological collections. ✉ *549 Little Lake Park, Box 638, Midland* ☎ *705/526–2844, 800/263–7745* ⊕ *huroniamuseum.com* ◻ *C$10.*

Martyrs' Shrine. On a hill overlooking Sainte-Marie among the Hurons, a twin-spired stone cathedral was built in 1926 to honor the eight missionaries stationed in Huronia who were martyred between 1642 and 1649. In 1930, all eight were canonized by the Roman Catholic Church. ✉ *16163 Hwy. 12 W, Midland* ☎ *705/526–3788* ⊕ *www.martyrs-shrine.com* ◻ *C$4* ☻ *Closed mid-Oct.–mid-May.*

FAMILY **Sainte-Marie among the Hurons.** A Jesuit mission was originally built on this spot in 1639. The reconstructed village, which was once home to a fifth of the European population of New France, was the site of the first European community in Ontario; it had a hospital, farm, workshops, and a church. Workers also constructed a canal from the Wye River. A combination of disease and Iroquois attacks led to the mission's demise. Twenty-two structures, including two native longhouses and two wigwams, have been faithfully reproduced from a scientific excavation. Staff members in period costume demonstrate 17th-century trades, share native stories and legends, and grow vegetables—keeping the working village alive. ✉ *16164 Hwy. 12 W, 5 km (3 miles) east of Hwy. 93, Midland* ☎ *705/526–7838* ⊕ *www.saintemarieamongthehurons. on.ca* ◻ *Apr.–mid-May and mid–late Oct., C$10; mid-May–early-Sept., C$12* ☻ *Closed Nov.–Mar.*

FAMILY **Scenic Caves Nature Adventures.** Explore ancient caves, hike along craggy hilltop trails, get a thrill on zip-line rides, or brave the suspension footbridge, 25 meters (82 feet) above the ground with amazing views of the bay, 300 meters (985 feet) below. Hiking boots or sneakers are required. ✉ *260 Scenic Caves Rd., Collingwood* ☎ *705/446–0256* ⊕ *www.sceniccaves.com* ◻ *C$22.57* ☻ *Closed Nov.–late Apr.*

WHERE TO STAY

$$$$
RESORT
Fodor'sChoice
★

🏨 **Blue Mountain Resort.** The largest ski resort in Ontario, and only getting bigger, this huge property near Collingwood revolves around its brightly painted Scandinavian-style alpine "village" with several blocks of shops, restaurants, bars, a grocery, and a plaza with live music. **Pros:** just a skip and a hop from the pedestrian village where all shops and restaurants are located; wide range of accommodation; excellent skiing. **Cons:** Blue Mountain Inn needs renovation; other accommodations pricey in season. $ *Rooms from: C$400* ✉ *108 Jozo Weider Blvd., Blue Mountains* ☎ *705/445–0231, 877/445–0231* ⊕ *www.bluemountain.ca* ⇦ *Blue Mountain Inn: 95 rooms; Westin Trillium House: 222 suites; Mosaïc: 85 suites; Village Suites: 447 suites; Historic Snowbridge Mountain Homes: 150 units* ❒ *No meals.*

$$
RESORT

🏨 **Horseshoe Resort.** Modern accommodations at this lodge on a 1,600-acre property come in a variety of shapes and sizes: choose from two-level lofts, spacious hotel rooms, or condos. **Pros:** free Wi-Fi; fresh, modern rooms; never-ending list of on-site facilities. **Cons:** scenic but isolated location. $ *Rooms from: C$169* ✉ *1101 Horseshoe Valley Rd., Barrie* ☎ *705/835–2790, 800/461–5627* ⊕ *www.horseshoeresort.com* ⇦ *101 rooms* ❒ *No meals.*

SPORTS AND THE OUTDOORS

Most ski resorts have a multitude of summer activities, such as mountain biking, golf, and adventure camps.

Fodor'sChoice
★

Blue Mountain Resort. The province's highest vertical drop, 720 feet, is at Blue Mountain Resort. Ontario's most extensively developed and frequented ski area has 42 trails, 22 of which are available after dark for night skiing, served by high-speed six-person lifts; quad, triple, and double lifts; and magic carpets. Summer activities include a roller coaster, golfing, tennis, beaches, mountain biking, open-air gondola rides, and zip lines. ✉ *108 Jozo Weider Blvd., Blue Mountains* ☎ *705/445–0231, 416/869–3799 from Toronto* ⊕ *www.bluemountain.ca.*

8

Horseshoe Resort. One of the few resorts to offer snowboarding, tubing, snowmobiling, snowshoeing, and cross-country and downhill skiing trails and facilities is Horseshoe Resort, about an hour's drive north of Toronto, off Highway 400. The resort has a terrain park, competition-level half-pipe and 26 alpine runs, 15 of which are lit at night, served by six lifts and a magic carpet. The vertical drop is only 304 feet, but several of the runs are rated for advanced skiers. Winter sports is only half the fun. Treetop trekking, horseback riding, and other summer adventures are available as well. ✉ *1101 Horseshoe Valley Rd., Barrie* ☎ *705/835–2790, 800/461–5627* ⊕ *www.horseshoeresort.com.*

FAMILY
Mount St. Louis Moonstone. Skiers and snowboarders can take advantage of 40 runs at Mount St. Louis Moonstone, 26 km (16 miles) north of Barrie. The majority of slopes are for beginner and intermediate skiers, though there's a sprinkling of advanced runs. The resort's Kids Camp, a day-care and ski-school combination, attracts families. Inexpensive

cafeterias within the two chalets serve decent meals. ■TIP➜ **No overnight lodging is available.** ✉ *24 Mount St. Louis Rd., Off Hwy. 400 Exit 131, Coldwater* ☎ *705/835–2112, 877/835–2112* ⊕ *www.mountstlouis.com.*

MUSKOKA

Outcroppings of pink and gray granite, drumlins of conifer and deciduous forest, and thousands of freshwater lakes formed from glaciers during the Ice Age characterize the rustic Muskoka region north of Toronto. Called Muskoka for Lake Muskoka, the largest of some 1,600 lakes in the area, this region is a favorite playground of those who live in and around Toronto. Place names such as Orillia, Gravenhurst, Haliburton, Algonquin, and Muskoka reveal the history of the land's inhabitants, from Algonquin tribes to European explorers to fur traders. This huge 4,761-square-km (1,838-square-mile) swath of land and lakes is also referred to colloquially as cottage country. (In Ontario, "cottage" is broadly used to describe any vacation home, from a fishing shack to a near-mansion.) The area became a haven for the summering rich and famous during the mid–19th century, when lumber barons who were harvesting near port towns set up steamship and rail lines, making travel to the area possible. Since then, cottage country has attracted urbanites who make the pilgrimage to hear the call of the loon or swat incessant mosquitoes and black flies. A few modern-day celebrities are reported to have cottages here as well, such as Bill Murray and Steven Spielberg. For the cottageless, overnight seasonal camping in a provincial park is an option, as is a stay in a rustic lodge or posh resort.

TOURISM INFORMATION

Haliburton County Tourism. ☎ *705/286–1333, 800/461–7677* ⊕ *www.haliburtoncounty.ca.*

Muskoka Tourism. ☎ *705/689–0660, 800/267–9700* ⊕ *www.discover-muskoka.ca.*

GRAVENHURST

74 km (46 miles) north of Barrie.

Gravenhurst is a town of approximately 10,000 and the birthplace of Norman Bethune, a surgeon, inventor, and political activist who is a Canadian hero. The heart of town is the colorful Muskoka Wharf, with its boardwalk along the water, restaurants, steamship docks, vacation condos, and plaza that hosts festivals and a Wednesday farmers' market from mid-May to early October. Still, Gravenhurst is a tiny town and can be seen in a day or even an afternoon.

WHEN TO GO

As with everywhere in Muskoka, Gravenhurst comes alive in the summer months, with many attractions opening only after Victoria Day and closing between Labour Day and mid-October, as the weather dictates. Nevertheless, area resorts do plan winter activities—snowshoeing, sleigh rides, and the like—and restaurants are open (with shorter off-season hours) year-round.

GETTING HERE AND AROUND

From Toronto, take Highway 400 north, which intersects with the highly traveled and often congested Highway 11. Gravenhurst is about 70 km (40 miles) north of the junction on Highway 11. Driving time in good traffic is a bit over two hours. Ontario Northland buses and trains operate six days a week between Toronto's Union Station and downtown Gravenhurst; travel time is 2 hours 10 minutes.

ESSENTIALS

Transportation Information Ontario Northland. ☎ *800/461–8558* ⊕ *www. ontarionorthland.ca.* **Gravenhurst Bus and Railway Station.** ✉ *150 2nd St. S* ☎ *705/687–2301.*

Visitor Information Gravenhurst Chamber of Commerce. ✉ *685–2 Muskoka Rd. N* ☎ *705/687–4432* ⊕ *www.gravenhurstchamber.com.*

EXPLORING

Bethune Memorial House. An 1880-vintage frame structure, this National Historic Site honors the heroic efforts of field surgeon and medical educator Henry Norman Bethune (1830–1939), who worked in China during the Sino-Japanese War in the 1930s and trained thousands to become medics and doctors. There are period rooms and an exhibit tracing the highlights of his life. The house has become a shrine of sorts for Chinese diplomats visiting North America. ✉ *235 John St. N* ☎ *705/687–4261* ⊕ *www.pc.gc.ca/lhn-nhs/on/bethune/index.aspx* 🎟 *C$3.90* ⊗ *Closed Nov.–May.*

Muskoka Boat & Heritage Centre. Learn about steamboat history and technology in this museum with a rotating collection of historic boats that have included a 1924 propeller boat, a 30-foot 1894 steamboat, and gleaming wooden speedboats. ✉ *275 Steamship Bay Rd., Muskoka Wharf* ☎ *705/687–2115, 866/687–6667* ⊕ *realmuskoka.com* 🎟 *C$7.50* ⊗ *Closed Sun. and Mon. in late Oct.–mid-June.*

FAMILY **Muskoka Steamships Cruises.** In warm weather, cruises tour Muskoka Lake on historic and reproduction vessels. Excursions range from one to eight hours and include lunch and dinner cruises, sightseeing cruises, and themed trips, like the murder-mystery cruise and, for kids, a cruise with a magic show, a visit to a wildlife park, or pirate dress-up. The restored 128-foot-long, 99-passenger *RMS Segwun* (the initials stand for Royal Mail Ship) is North America's oldest operating steamship, built in 1887, and is the sole survivor of a fleet that provided transportation through the Muskoka Lakes. The 200-passenger *Wenonah II* is a 1907-inspired vessel with modern technology. Reservations are required. Learn about steamboat history and technology in the **Muskoka Boat and Heritage Centre** with a rotating collection of historic boats that have included a 1924 propeller boat, a 30-foot 1894 steamboat, and gleaming wooden speedboats. ✉ *185 Cherokee La., Muskoka Wharf* ☎ *705/687–6667, 866/687–6667* ⊕ *realmuskoka.com* 🎟 *Sightseeing cruises C$20–C$50; lunch and dinner cruises C$52–C$87* ⊗ *Closed weekends in Nov.–May.*

The Muskoka region north of Toronto is a popular destination for people wanting to escape the faster pace of city life.

WHERE TO EAT

$$ **CAFÉ** ✕ **Blue Willow Tea Shop.** The dozen or so petite tables are set with blue-willow-pattern china in this quaint restaurant serving traditional English fare on the Muskoka Wharf overlooking the bay. Afternoon tea—a three-tier platter of shortbread, scones with Devonshire cream, and savory finger sandwiches, plus a pot of tea per person—is served every day from 2 to 5 pm, for C$23. Other than tea, sandwiches, such as grilled bacon and Brie, quiches, and specials like homemade stews are offered for lunch. Popular items on the short dinner menu include baked fish and chips, prime rib with Yorkshire pudding, and classic bangers and mash. The attached shop sells loose leaf teas and other food items for your own tea party at home. $ *Average main: C$15* ⊠ *900 Bay St., Muskoka Wharf* ☎ *705/687–2597* ⊕ *www.bluewillowteashop.ca* ⊙ *Closed Sun. and Mon. in late Oct.–June.*

$ **CAFÉ** ✕ **Marty's World Famous Café.** Duck into this cozy café in the afternoon for what is possibly the best butter tart you've ever tasted. The chalkboard on the wall lists other home-cooked dishes like pies, quiche, and daily soups and sandwiches. Food and decor is simple, natural, and homey, just like the neighborhood. It's located outside of Gravenhurst in Bracebridge. $ *Average main: C$10* ⊠ *5 Manitoba St., Bracebridge* ☎ *705/645–4794* ⊕ *www.martysworldfamous.com.*

WHERE TO STAY

$$$ **RESORT** **FAMILY** 🏨 **Bayview-Wildwood Resort.** Seemingly remote but truly only a 20-minute drive south of Gravenhurst, this all-inclusive lakeside resort dates to 1898 and is particularly geared to outdoor types and families. **Pros:** great for families; casual atmosphere; free activities for kids. **Cons:** strict meal times; noisy cargo trains pass by day and night. $ *Rooms from: C$250* ✉ *1500 Port Stanton Pkwy., R.R. 1, Severn Bridge* ☎ *705/689–2338, 800/461–0243* ⊕ *www.bayviewwildwood.com* ⇄ *54 rooms, 16 cottages, 3 houses* ⊚ *All-inclusive.*

$$$$
RESORT
Fodor's Choice
★

⚏ **Taboo Resort, Golf and Spa.** A magnificent 1,000-acre landscape of rocky outcrops and evergreen trees typical of the Muskoka region surrounds this alpine lodge–style, deluxe resort. **Pros:** fantastic golf course; forest and lake views; excellent spa and restaurant. **Cons:** expensive; too easy to never leave the resort grounds. $ *Rooms from: C$289* ✉ *1209 Muskoka Beach Rd.* ☎ *705/687–2233, 800/461–0236* ⊕ *www.taboore-sort.com* ⇄ *101 rooms, 15 Cottage Chalets* ⊚ *No meals.*

SHOPPING

Muskoka Cottage Brewery. It's a real treat to visit this brewery, tasting room, and retail store for one of the most popular beers in Ontario, especially if you come for the free tour. While you're here, taste beers like the cream ale and Mad Tom IPA, or seasonal ales like summer weiss or double chocolate cranberry stout. It's half-way between Gravenhurst and Bracebridge, off Highway 11. ✉ *1964 Muskoka Beach Rd., Bracebridge* ☎ *705/646–1266* ⊕ *www.muskokabrewery.com.*

HUNTSVILLE

51 km (32 miles) north of Gravenhurst.

Muskoka's Huntsville region is filled with lakes and streams, stands of virgin birch and pine, and deer—and no shortage of year-round resorts. It is usually the cross-country skier's best bet for an abundance of natural snow in Southern Ontario. All resorts have trails.

WHEN TO GO

Summer is high season for vacationers in Huntsville, but the town is also ideal for cross-country skiing, ice fishing, and other backcountry winter adventures.

GETTING HERE AND AROUND

From Toronto, take Highway 400 north just past Barrie and then take Highway 11 north about 120 km (75 miles). Without traffic, the trip is about three hours. At least four Ontario Northland buses operate between Toronto's Union Station and Huntsville daily; travel time is four hours, and the station is in the north of the city, a short walk to Main Street.

From Gravenhurst, Huntsville is about 55 km (35 miles) north on Highway 11, a 45-minute drive.

ESSENTIALS

Transportation Information Huntsville Bus Station. ✉ *77 Centre St. N* ☎ *705/789–6431.* **Ontario Northland.** ☎ *705/789–6431, 800/461–8558* ⊕ *www.ontarionorthland.ca.*

Visitor Information Huntsville/Lake of Bays Chamber of Commerce. ✉ *8 West St. N* ☎ *705/789–4771* ⊕ *huntsvillelakeofbays.on.ca.*

WHERE TO EAT

$$$

CANADIAN

✕ **The Norsemen Restaurant.** Generations of devotees have returned to this lakeside restaurant in the wooded hills near Huntsville for the warm hospitality and modern Canadian cuisine with French flair, some of whom may even come by canoe or kayak. Built in the 1920s, the lodge became a restaurant in 1970 and is unabashedly rustic and homey: double-sided stone fireplace, locally harvested beams overhead, and oxbows over the doorways. Even the coffee is roasted in-house on a daily basis. Ask to be seated by the screened-in porch for a view of the lake to soak in the leisurely evening. Popular and enduring dishes include Ontario rack of lamb and prime rib with Yorkshire pudding. Round out the meal with fun and modern desserts like s'mores mousse and green-tea poached pear. The extensive wine list is a point of pride. $ *Average main: C$27* ✉ *1040 Walker Lake Dr., 2 km (1 mile) north of Hwy. 60* ☎ *705/635–2473, 800/565–3856* ⊕ *www.norsemen-walkerlake.com* ⊗ *Closed Nov. and Mon. year-round; Sun.–Thurs in Dec.–Mar.; Tues. in Apr.–June, Sept., and Oct.*

WHERE TO STAY

$$$

RESORT

▥ **Deerhurst Resort.** This deluxe resort along Peninsula Lake is a 780-acre, self-contained community with restaurants and lodgings to fit every budget and style, from weddings to corporate events. **Pros:** wide range of amenities; something for everyone. **Cons:** size can be overwhelming for some; busy check-in and checkout mean occasional waits. $ *Rooms from: C$219* ✉ *1235 Deerhurst Dr., just south of Rte. 60* ☎ *705/789–6411, 800/461–4393* ⊕ *www.deerhurstresort.com* ⇄ *400 rooms* ❏*No meals.*

$$

RESORT

FAMILY

▥ **Walker Lake Resort.** Rustic two- and three-bedroom cottages overlook Walker Lake at this resort, and many come with Jacuzzi tubs and fireplaces. **Pros:** very peaceful setting; lively and cheery restaurant. **Cons:** no TVs; cottages are by weekly rental only. $ *Rooms from: C$175* ✉ *1040 Walker Lake Dr., R.R. 4* ☎ *705/635–2473, 800/565–3856 in Canada* ⊕ *www.norsemen.ca* ⇄ *7 cottages* ❏*No meals.*

SPORTS AND THE OUTDOORS

Hidden Valley Highlands Ski Area. The ski area has 35 skiable acres with 13 hills and three quad lifts. It's great for beginner and intermediate skiers, with a couple of black-diamond runs for daredevils. ✉ *1655 Hidden Valley Rd., off Hwy. 60, 8 km east of town* ☎ *705/789–1773, 800/398–9555* ⊕ *www.skihiddenvalley.on.ca.*

ALGONQUIN PROVINCIAL PARK

35 km (23 miles) east of Huntsville.

WHEN TO GO

Most people go to Algonquin in the summer, but the many winter attractions—ice fishing, cross-country skiing, dogsled tours—make it a popular destination in cold months as well. The only time to avoid is the notorious blackfly season, usually sometime in May. The mosquito population is healthy all summer, so pack repellent, pants, and long-sleeved shirts. Algonquin Provincial Park can be done in a weekend,

ADVENTURE TOURS NEAR ALGONQUIN

If planning an Algonquin Park adventure seems daunting, leave it to the pros. Transport from Toronto, meals, and accommodations are included. You might, for example, do a multiday paddle-and-portage trip, catered with organic meals. Most companies have cabins, some quite luxurious, in Algonquin Park for tour participants; other tours may require backcountry tent camping.

Call of the Wild. Call of the Wild offers guided trips of different lengths—dogsledding and snowmobiling in winter, canoeing and hiking in summer—deep in the park away from the more "touristy" areas. The tour company's in-park Algonquin Eco Lodge is powered only by waterfall. A popular package is a four-day canoe trip and three days relaxing at the lodge. ⊠ *Algonquin Provincial Park* ☎ *905/471–9453, 800/776–9453* ⊕ *www.callofthewild.ca.*

Northern Edge Algonquin. Northern Edge Algonquin eco-adventure company provides adventurous learning vacations and retreats with themes such as moose tracking (via canoe), sea kayaking, yoga, shamanism, and women-only weekends. Home-cooked comfort food is local and organic; lodging ranges from new cabins to tents. ⊠ *Algonquin Provincial Park* ☎ *888/383–8320* ⊕ *www.northernedgealgonquin.com.*

Voyageur Quest. Voyageur Quest has a variety of adventure wilderness trips year-round in Algonquin Park and throughout northern Ontario, including a number of family-geared vacations. ⊠ *Algonquin Provincial Park* ☎ *416/486–3605, 800/794–9660* ⊕ *www.voyageurquest.com.*

Winterdance Dogsled Tours. Winterdance Dogsled Tours takes you on half-day, full-day, multiday, and moonlight dogsledding adventures in and near Algonquin Provincial Park. Canoe tours are available in summer, as are kennel visits with the sled dogs. ⊠ *6577 Haliburton Lake Rd., Haliburton* ☎ *705/457–5281* ⊕ *www.winterdance.com.*

but four days is the average stay; the park is huge and there's a lot of ground to cover.

GETTING HERE AND AROUND

A good four-hour drive from Toronto, Algonquin is most readily reached via Highway 400 north to Highway 60 east. The huge park has 29 different access points, so call to devise the best plan of attack for your visit based on your interests. The most popular entry points are along the Highway 60 corridor, where you'll find all the conventional campgrounds. If you're heading into the park's interior, spring for the detailed Algonquin Canoe Routes Map (C$4.95), available from the park's website. The visitor centers, at the park gates, or on the Highway 60 corridor, 43 km (27 miles) east of the west gate, have information on park programs, a bookstore, a restaurant, and a panoramic-viewing deck. ■TIP→ In winter, go with a four-wheel-drive vehicle.

Highway 60 takes drivers on a scenic route through Ontario's famed Algonquin Provincial Park.

EXPLORING

Algonquin Provincial Park. This park stretches across 7,650 square km (2,954 square miles), containing nearly 2,500 lakes, 272 bird species, 45 species of mammals, and 50 species of fish and encompassing forests, rivers, and cliffs. The typical visitor is a hiker, canoeist, camper, or all three. But don't be put off if you're not the athletic or outdoorsy sort. About a third of Algonquin's visitors come for the day to walk one of the 17 well-groomed and well-signed interpretive trails or to enjoy a swim or a picnic. Swimming is especially good at the Lake of Two Rivers, halfway between the west and east gates along Highway 60. Spring, when the moose head north, is the best time to catch a glimpse of North America's largest land mammal. Getting up at the crack of dawn gives you the best chance of seeing the park's wildlife. Park naturalists give talks on area wildflowers, animals, and birds, and you can book a guided hike or canoe trip. Expeditions to hear wolf howling take place in late summer and early autumn. The park's **Algonquin Logging Museum** (late-June–mid October, daily 9–5) depicts life at an early Canadian logging camp. ⊠ *Hwy. 60, main and east gate is west of town of Whitney; west gate is east of town of Dwight* ☎ *705/633–5572* ⊕ *www.algonquinpark.on.ca* ✉ *C$17 per vehicle.*

WHERE TO EAT

If you'd like wine with dinner, bring your own: park restrictions prohibit the sale of alcohol here.

$$$$
CANADIAN

✕**Arowhon Pines Restaurant.** A meal at this breathtaking, circular log-cabin restaurant in the heart of Algonquin Park is the highlight of many visits. A view of the lake is a great accompaniment to the food,

CLOSE UP

Camping in Algonquin Provincial Park

Algonquin Provincial Park.
Campgrounds, backcountry camping, and cabins are all available inside the park. Along the parkway corridor, a 56-km (35-mile) stretch of Highway 60, are eight organized campgrounds. Prices range from C$39 to C$51 depending on the location and whether you require electricity. Within the vast park interior, you won't find any organized campsites (and the purists love it that way). Interior camping permits are C$12 per person, available from Ontario Parks. Contact Algonquin Park's main number (705/633–5572) to learn about the guidelines for interior camping before calling Ontario Parks to reserve. In between the extremes of the corridor campgrounds and interior camping are the lesser-known peripheral campgrounds—Kiosk, Brent, and Achray—in the northern and eastern reaches of the park, which you access by long dirt roads. These sites do not have showers, and Brent has only pit toilets. The Highway 60 corridor campsites have showers, picnic tables, and, in some cases, RV hookups.

A bit less extreme than pitching a tent in Algonquin's interior but just as remote is a stay in one of the park-run ranger cabins (C$62–C$134 per person), which have woodstove or propane heat and, in some cases, mattresses and electricity. Four of the 13 cabins are accessible by car; the rest are reached by canoe, which can take from one hour to two days.

Reservations are required for all campsites, cabins, and for interior camping; call the Ontario Parks reservations line (888/668–7275 www.ontarioparks.com). ⊠ *Algonquin Provincial Park* ☏ *705/633–5572* ⊕ *www.algonquinpark.on.ca.*

8

but a towering stone fireplace in the center of the room is an attraction, too. Menu changes daily, but guests can expect hearty Canadian dishes with local and seasonal ingredients like Northern Ontario trout with sautéed potatoes and squash, rack of lamb scented with garlic and rosemary, or roasted loin of pork stuffed with apples and prunes. The menu always includes plenty of vegetarian options, and other diets are readily accommodated. Bring your own wine for no corkage fee. If you have kids in tow, take advantage of the early kids' dinner (5:30 pm) followed by a group babysitting service until 8 pm. ⑤ *Average main: C$75* ⊠ *Algonquin Provincial Park, near west entrance, 8 km (5 miles) north of Hwy. 60* ☏ *705/633–5661, 866/633–5661* ⊕ *www.arowhonpines.ca* ⊘ *Closed mid-Oct.–late May* ⚐ *Reservations essential.*

$$$$ ✕ **Bartlett Lodge Restaurant.** In the original 1917 lodge building, this small
CANADIAN   lakeside pine dining room offers an ever-changing prix-fixe menu of contemporary Canadian cuisine, which might kick off with fennel and mustard-rubbed pork belly and move on to pistachio and cherry-crusted Australian rack of lamb or the house specialty, beef tenderloin. Fish and vegetarian options, such as sweet-potato gnocchi with shaved Gruyère, are always available. Desserts, included with the meal, all made on-site, feature cheesecakes, some variation of crème brûlée (perhaps a chocolate-chili version), and homemade pie. ■TIP➔ **You must bring your own wine.** ⑤ *Average main: C$64* ⊠ *Algonquin Park, by boat from Cache*

Lake Landing, just south of Hwy. 60, Huntsville ☎ *705/633–5543, 866/614–5355* ⊕ *www.bartlettlodge.com* ⊗ *Closed late Oct.–mid-May. No lunch* ⚲ *Reservations essential.*

WHERE TO STAY

$$$$ ▦ **Arowhon Pines.** The stuff of local legend, Arowhon is a family-run **RESORT** wilderness retreat deep in Algonquin Provincial Park known for unpretentious rustic "luxury" and superb dining. **Pros:** all-inclusive swimming, sailing, canoeing, kayaking, hiking, and birding on a private lake in a gorgeous setting; excellent restaurant. **Cons:** limited cell phone service; pricey considering rusticity of cabins. ⑤ *Rooms from: C$251* ✉ *Algonquin Park, near west entrance, 8 km (5 miles) north of Hwy. 60* ☎ *705/633–5661, 866/633–5661 toll-free year-round* ⊕ *www.arowhonpines.ca* ⊗ *Closed mid-Oct.–late May* ⇥ *50 rooms in 13 cabins* ⑩ *All-inclusive.*

$$$ ▦ **Bartlett Lodge.** Smack in the center of Algonquin Provincial Park, this **RESORT** impressive 1917 resort is reached by a short boat ride on Cache Lake (just make your reservation and use the phone at the landing to call the lodge when you arrive), and one of only two that is inside the provincial park. **Pros:** completely quiet and peaceful; each cabin has its own canoe and porch. **Cons:** restaurant is expensive and only offers dinner (or picnic lunches); no phones or TVs in the cabins. ⑤ *Rooms from: C$200* ✉ *Algonquin Park, by boat from Cache Lake Landing, just south of Hwy. 60* ☎ *705/633–5543, 905/338–8908 in winter* ⊕ *www.bartlettlodge.com* ⊗ *Closed late Oct.–early May* ⇥ *12 cabins, 2 artist suites, 2 platform tents* ⑩ *Some meals.*

SPORTS AND THE OUTDOORS

Algonquin Outfitters. The most well-known outfitter in the area has multiple locations in and around the park, specializing in canoe trip packages and rentals, outfitting and camping services, sea kayaking, and a water-taxi service to the park's central areas. Stores are at Oxtongue Lake (the main store—near the west Highway 60 park entrance), Huntsville, Opeongo Lake, Bracebridge, Haliburton, and Brent Base on Cedar Lake. Visit their website and blog for updates on park conditions and other happenings. ✉ *Oxtongue Lake store, 1035 Algonquin Outfitters Rd., R.R. 1, just north of Hwy. 60, Dwight* ☎ *705/635–2243, 800/469–4948* ⊕ *algonquinoutfitters.com.*

Portage Store. If you plan to camp in the park, you may want to contact the Portage Store, which provides extensive outfitting services and guided canoe trips. It rents canoes and sells self-guided canoe packages that include all the equipment you need for a canoeing-and-camping trip in the park. Also available are bike rentals, maps, detailed information about routes and wildlife, and an on-site general store and casual restaurant. When you arrive, employees can help you brush up on your paddling and portaging skills. ✉ *Hwy. 60, Canoe Lake* ☎ *705/633–5622 in summer, 705/789–3645 in winter* ⊕ *www.portagestore.com.*

TRAVEL SMART
TORONTO

GETTING HERE AND AROUND

Most of the action in Toronto happens between just north of Bloor and south to the waterfront and from High Park in the west to the Beach in the east. It's easy to get around this area via subway, streetcar, and bus. Service is frequent.

Yonge Street (pronounced "young") is the official dividing line between east and west streets. It's a north–south street that stretches from the waterfront up through the city. Street numbers increase heading away from Yonge in either direction. North–south street numbers increase heading north from the lake.

▌ AIR TRAVEL

Flying time to Toronto is 1½ hours from New York and Chicago and 5 hours from Los Angeles. Nonstop to Toronto from London is about 7 hours.

Most airlines serving Toronto have numerous daily trips. Allow extra time for passing through customs and immigration, which are required for all passengers, including Canadians. The 2½-hour advance boarding time recommended for international flights applies to Canada. Pearson Airport has check-in kiosks for Air Canada flights, and Toronto Island Airport offers check-in kiosks for Porter, which cut back on time spent in line.

Brace yourself for the possibility of weather delays in winter.

All travelers must have a passport to enter or reenter the United States. U.S. Customs and Immigration maintains offices at Pearson International Airport in Toronto; U.S.-bound passengers should arrive early to clear customs before their flight.

Security measures at Canadian airports are similar to those in the United States.

Airline Security Issues Canadian Transportation Agency. ☎ 888/222–2592 ⊕ www.otc-cta.gc.ca. **Transportation Security Administration.** ⊕ www.tsa.gov.

NAVIGATING TORONTO

■ The CN Tower can be seen from most anywhere in the city except on very cloudy days. Remember its location (Front and John streets) to get your bearings.

■ Lake Ontario is the ultimate landmark. It's always south, no matter where you are.

■ The subway is the fastest way to get around. Stay at a hotel near a subway line to make navigating the city easier.

■ The streetcar and bus signs can be easy to miss. Look for the red, white, and blue signs with a black streetcar picture on electrical poles near street corners every five blocks or so along the route.

AIRPORTS

Most flights into Toronto land at Terminals 1 and 3 of Lester B. Pearson International Airport (YYZ), 32 km (20 miles) northwest of downtown. There are two main terminals, so check in advance which one your flight leaves from to save hassles. The automated LINK cable-line shuttle system moves passengers almost noiselessly between Terminals 1 and 3 and the Value Park Garage/Value Park Lot.

Wi-Fi Internet access is free in both Pearson terminals. There are several chain hotels at the airport.

Porter Airlines—which flies to destinations in eastern Canada and the northeastern United States, including Boston, Chicago, Halifax, Montréal, Newark, Ottawa, Québec City, and Washington, D.C.—is the only airline operating from Billy Bishop Toronto City Airport (YTZ), often called Toronto Island Airport. There are few amenities at this smaller airport, but the location provides easy, quick access to downtown Toronto. Free Wi-Fi is also available.

Airport Information Billy Bishop Toronto City Airport. ☎ *416/203–6942* ⊕ *www.toronto port.com/airport.aspx.* **Lester B. Pearson International Airport.** ☎ *416/776–9892* ⊕ *www.torontopearson.com.*

GROUND TRANSPORTATION

Although Pearson International Airport isn't far from downtown, the drive can take well over an hour during weekday rush hours from 6:30 to 9:30 am and 3:30 to 6:30 pm.

The most efficient way to get down-town from Pearson is the Union Pearson Express train (also referred to as the UP Express). The train connects Terminal 1 of Pearson with Union Station downtown, making stops at the Weston and Bloor GO stations. A trip from Pearson to Union takes only 25 minutes and costs C$12 for adults. Trains run every 15 minutes from 5:30 am to 1 am. Buy tickets at the termi-nal, or online at ⊕ *www.upexpress.com.*

Taxis to a hotel or attraction near the lake cost C$53 and have fixed rates to different parts of the city. (Check fixed-rate maps at ⊕ *www.torontopearson.com.*) You must pay the full fare from the airport, but it's often possible to negotiate a lower fare going to the airport from downtown with regular city cabs. It's illegal for city cabs to pick up passengers at the airport, unless they're called—a time-consuming process sometimes worth the wait for the lower fare. Likewise, airport taxis can't pick up passengers going to the airport; only regular taxis can be hailed or called to go to the airport.

GO Transit interregional buses transport passengers to the Yorkdale and York Mills subway stations from the arrivals levels. Service can be irregular (once per hour) and luggage space limited, but at C$5.35 it's one of the least expensive ways to get to the city's northern sections (or onto the subway line).

Two Toronto Transit Commission (TTC) buses also run from any of the airport terminals to the subway system. Bus 192 (Airport Rocket bus) connects to the Kipling subway station; Bus 58 Malton links to the Lawrence West station. Lug-gage space is limited and no assistance is given, but the price is only C$3.25 in exact change (*See Bus Travel*).

If you rent a car at the airport, ask for a street map of the city. Highway 427 runs south some 6 km (4 miles) to the lakeshore. Here you pick up the Queen Elizabeth Way (QEW) east to the Gar-diner Expressway, which runs east into the heart of downtown. If you take the QEW west, you'll find yourself swinging around Lake Ontario, toward Hamilton, Niagara-on-the-Lake, and Niagara Falls.

From Toronto Island Airport, an under-ground pedestrian tunnel with moving sidewalks connects the airport to the ter-minal at the foot of Bathurst Street. The airport also operates a free ferry from the Island to the mainland; both options take less than 10 minutes.

Porter Airlines runs a free shuttle from the ferry terminal/tunnel entrance to Union Station. The 510 Harbourfront and 511 Bathurst TTC streetcars also run past the Toronto Island Airport entrance, roughly a block to the north; from there, you can connect to the rest of the TTC system.

Contacts GO Transit. ☎ *416/869–3200, 888/438–6646* ⊕ *www.gotransit.com.* **Toronto Transit Commission or TTC.** ☎ *416/393– 4636* ⊕ *www.ttc.ca.* **Union Pearson Express.** ☎ *416/869–3300, 844/438–6687* ⊕ *www. upexpress.com.*

FLIGHTS

Toronto is served by Air Canada, Ameri-can, Delta, and United as well as more than a dozen European and Asian carri-ers with easy connections to many U.S. cities. Toronto is also served within Can-ada by WestJet, Porter, and Air Transat, a charter airline.

Airline Contacts Air Canada. ☎ *888/247– 2262, 514/393–3333* ⊕ *www.aircanada.com.* **Air Transat.** ☎ *877/872–6728, 514/906–5196* ⊕ *www.airtransat.ca.* **American Airlines.** ☎ *800/433–7300* ⊕ *www.aa.com.* **Delta Airlines.** ☎ *800/221–1212 for U.S. reservations,*

800/241–4141 for international reservations ⊕ www.delta.com. **Porter Airlines.** ☎ 888/619–8622, 416/619–8622 ⊕ www.flyporter.com. **United Airlines.** ☎ 800/864–8331 ⊕ www.united.com. **WestJet.** ☎ 888/937–8538 ⊕ www.westjet.com.

■ BOAT TRAVEL

Frequent ferries connect downtown Toronto with the Toronto Islands. In summer, ferries leave every 30 to 60 minutes for Ward's Island, every hour for Centre Island, and every 30 to 45 minutes for Hanlan's Point. Ferries begin operation between 6:30 and 9 am and end between 10 and 11:30 pm. Fares are C$7.50 round-trip.

Boat Information Toronto Islands Ferry. ☎ 416/392–8193 ⊕ www.toronto.ca/parks/island.

■ BUS TRAVEL

ARRIVING AND DEPARTING

Most buses arrive at the Toronto Coach Terminal, which serves a number of lines, including Greyhound (which has regular service to Toronto from all over the United States), Megabus, Coach Canada, Ontario Northland, and Can-AR. The trip takes 5 hours from Detroit, 3 hours from Buffalo, and 11 hours from Chicago and New York City. During busy times, such as around holidays, border crossings can add an hour or more to your trip as every passenger must disembark and be questioned.

Information on fares and departure times is available online or by phone. Tickets are purchased at the Toronto Coach Terminal before boarding the buses.

Some Canadian bus lines don't accept reservations, but Coach Canada and Greyhound Canada allow online ticket purchases, which can then be printed out ahead of time or picked up at the station. On most lines, there are discounts for senior citizens (over 60), children (under 12), and students (with ISIC cards). Purchase your tickets as far ahead as possible, especially for holiday travel. Seating is first-come, first-served; arriving 45 minutes before your bus's scheduled departure time usually gets you near the front of the line.

A low-cost bus company, Megabus, runs service to and from Buffalo, Niagara Falls, New York City, and Montréal. The further in advance tickets are purchased, the less expensive they are.

WITHIN TORONTO

Toronto Transit Commission (TTC) buses and streetcars link with every subway station to cover all points of the city. *See Public Transportation Travel.*

Bus Information Can-AR. ☎ 905/738–2290, 800/387–7097 ⊕ www.can-arcoach.com. **Coach Canada.** ☎ 800/461–7661 ⊕ www.coachcanada.com. **Greyhound Lines of Canada Ltd.** ☎ 416/594–1010, 800/661–8747 ⊕ www.greyhound.ca. **Megabus.** ☎ 866/488–4452 ⊕ ca.megabus.com. **Ontario Northland.** ☎ 705/472–4500, 800/461–8558 ⊕ www.ontarionorthland.ca. **Toronto Coach Terminal.** ✉ 610 Bay St., just north of Dundas St. W, Dundas Square Area ☎ 416/393–7911.

■ CAR TRAVEL

Given the relatively high price of gas, Toronto's notoriously terrible traffic, and the ease of its public transportation system, car travel is recommended only for those who wish to drive to sites and attractions outside the city, such as the Niagara Wine Region, Niagara Falls, and live theater at Stratford or Niagara-on-the-Lake. The city of Toronto has an excellent transit system that's inexpensive, clean, and safe, and cabs are plentiful.

In Canada your own driver's license is acceptable for a stay of up to three months. In Ontario, you must be 21 to drive a rental car. There may be a surcharge of C$10–C$30 per day if you are between 21 and 25. Agreements may require that the car not be taken out of Canada, including the U.S. side of Niagara Falls; check when booking.

CAR RENTAL

Rates in Toronto begin at C$30 a day and C$150 a week for an economy car with unlimited mileage. This does not include tax, which is 13%. If you prefer a manual-transmission car, check whether the rental agency of your choice offers it; some companies don't in Canada. All the major chains listed *below* have branches both downtown and at Pearson International Airport.

Contacts Alamo. ☎ 844/351–8648 ⊕ www. alamo.com. **Avis.** ☎ 800/331–1084 ⊕ www. avis.com. **Budget.** ☎ 800/472–3325 ⊕ www. budget.com. **Discount Car and Truck Rental.** ☎ 888/310–2277, ⊕ www.discountcar.com. **Enterprise.** ☎ 416/798–1465, 844/307–8008 ⊕ www.enterprise.com. **Hertz.** ☎ 800/654–3001 ⊕ www.hertz.com. **National Car Rental.** ☎ 800/227–7368 ⊕ www.nationalcar.com.

GASOLINE

Distances are always shown in kilometers, and gasoline is always sold in liters. (A gallon has 3.8 liters.)

Gas prices in Canada are higher than in the United States, but have dipped in recent years. The per-liter price is currently between C$1 and C$1.30 (US$2.92–$3.80 per gallon), but prices are always fluctuating. Gas stations are plentiful; many are self-service and part of small convenience stores. Large stations are open 24 hours; smaller ones close after the dinner rush. For up-to-date prices and where to find the cheapest gas in the city (updated daily), go to ⊕ *www.torontogas-prices.com.*

PARKING

Toronto has green parking-meter boxes everywhere. Parking tickets net the city C$50 million annually, so they are frequently given out. Boxes are computerized; regular rates between C$1.50 and C$4 per hour are payable with coins—the dollar coin, the two-dollar coin, and nickels, dimes, and quarters are accepted—or a credit card.

Parking lots are found under office buildings or on side streets near main thoroughfares. At select lots, parking fees can be topped up remotely through the city's Green P Parking App. Visit ⊕ *mobilepay. greenp.com* to learn more.

ROAD CONDITIONS

Rush hours in Toronto (6:30 to 9:30 am and 3:30 to 6:30 pm) are bumper to bumper, especially on the 401 and Gardiner Expressway. It's best to avoid travel during these times, particularly when coming into or leaving the city.

ROADSIDE EMERGENCIES

The American Automobile Association (AAA) has 24-hour road service in Canada, provided via a partnership with the Canadian Automobile Association (CAA).

Emergency Services Canadian Automobile Association. ☎ 416/221–4300, 800/268–3750 ⊕ www.caa.ca.

RULES OF THE ROAD

By law, you're required to wear seat belts and to use infant seats in Ontario. Fines can be steep. Drivers are prohibited from using handheld cellular phones. Right turns are permitted on red signals unless otherwise posted. You must come to a complete stop before making a right turn on red. Pedestrian crosswalks are sprinkled throughout the city, marked clearly by overhead signs and very large painted yellow Xs. Pedestrians have the right of way in these crosswalks; however, Toronto pedestrians rarely heed crosswalk signals, so use caution in driving along downtown streets. The speed limit in most areas of the city is 50 kph (30 mph) and usually within the 90–110 kph (50–68 mph) range outside the city.

Watch out for streetcars stopped at intersections. Look to your right for a streetcar stop sign (red, white, and blue signs on electrical poles). ■TIP➔ It's illegal to pass or pull up alongside a streetcar stopped at an intersection—even if its doors aren't open—as it might be about to pick up or drop off passengers. A red light by the streetcar doors indicates whether a passenger may still be getting on or off. Wait for the light to go off to proceed.

Ontario is a no-fault province, and minimum liability insurance is C$200,000. If you're driving across the Ontario border, bring the policy or the vehicle-registration forms and a free Canadian Non-Resident Insurance Card from your insurance agent. If you're driving a borrowed car, also bring a letter of permission signed by the owner.

Driving motorized vehicles while impaired by alcohol is taken seriously in Ontario and results in heavy fines, imprisonment, or both. It's illegal to refuse to take a Breathalyzer test. The possession of radar-detection devices in a car, even if they are not in operation, is illegal in Ontario. Studded tires and window coatings that do not allow a clear view of the vehicle interior are forbidden.

FROM THE UNITED STATES

Expect a wait at major border crossings. The wait at peak visiting times can be 60 minutes. If you can, avoid crossing on weekends and holidays at Detroit–Windsor, Buffalo–Fort Erie, and Niagara Falls, New York–Niagara Falls, Ontario, when the wait can be even longer.

Highway 401, which can stretch to 16 lanes in metropolitan Toronto, is the major link between Windsor, Ontario (and Detroit), and Montréal, Québec. There are no tolls anywhere along it, but you should be warned: between 6:30 and 9:30 each weekday morning and from 3:30 to 6:30 each afternoon, the 401 can become very crowded, even stop-and-go; plan your trip to avoid rush hours. A toll highway, the 407, offers quicker travel; there are no tollbooths, but cameras photograph license plates and the system bills you. The 407 runs roughly parallel to the 401 for a 65-km (40-mile) stretch immediately north of Toronto.

If you're driving from Niagara Falls (U.S. or Canada) or Buffalo, New York, take the Queen Elizabeth Way (QEW), which curves along the western shore of Lake Ontario and eventually turns into the Gardiner Expressway, which flows right into downtown.

Insurance Information Insurance Bureau of Canada. ☎ 844/227-5422 ⊕ www.ibc.ca.

▌PUBLIC TRANSPORTATION

The Toronto Transit Commission (TTC), which operates the buses, streetcars, and subways, is safe, clean, and reliable. There are three subway lines, with 65 stations along the way: the Bloor–Danforth line, which crosses Toronto about 5 km (3 miles) north of the lakefront, from east to west; the Yonge–University line, which loops north and south like a giant "U," with the bottom of the "U" at Union Station; and the Sheppard line, which covers the northeastern section of the city. A light rapid transit (LRT) line extends service to Harbourfront along Queen's Quay.

Buses and streetcars link with every subway station to cover all points of the city. Service is generally excellent, with buses and streetcars covering major city thoroughfares about every 10 minutes; suburban service is less frequent.

TICKETS

The single fare for subways, buses, and streetcars is C$3.25. An all-day unlimited use pass (valid from the start of service until 5:30 am the next day) is C$12. Discounts for single-ride tokens are available starting at three for C$8.70. Children under 12 ride for free on the TTC, while discounted tickets are available for students under 19 or seniors over 65 for C$2 each, or five for C$9.75 ▌TIP➔ On weekends and holidays, up to two adults and four youths under 19 can use the C$12 day pass—an excellent deal.

Tokens and tickets are sold in each subway station and many convenience stores. All vehicles accept tickets, tokens, or exact change, but you must buy tickets and tokens before you board. With tickets or exact change on the subway, you must use the turnstile closest to the station agent window and drop the ticket or money into the clear receptacle, whereas a token or swipecard can be used at any turnstile.

Paper transfers are free; pick one up from the driver when you pay your fare on the bus or streetcar or get one from the transfer machines just past the turnstiles in the subway, then give the driver or station agent the transfer on the next leg of your journey. Note that transfers are time-sensitive from your start point, and TTC staff knows how long it takes to get to your transfer point to prevent misuse. Be sure to keep track of your paper transfer or pass after you board TTC streetcars in order to show proof of payment. Failure to show your transfer or pass to a TTC fare operator on request could result in a minimum fine of C$235.

If you plan to stay in Toronto for a month or longer, consider the Metropass, a prepaid card that allows unlimited rides during one calendar week (C$42.25) or month (C$141.50).

TTC TICKET/PASS	PRICE
Single Fare	C$3.25
Day Pass	C$12
3 Token Pack	C$8.70
Monthly Unlimited Pass	C$141.50
Weekly Unlimited Pass	C$42.25

HOURS AND FREQUENCY

Subway trains run from approximately 6 am to 1:30 am Monday through Saturday and from 8 am to 1:30 am Sunday; holiday schedules vary. Subway service is frequent, with trains arriving every two to five minutes. Most buses and streetcars operate on the same hours as the subway. On weekdays, subway trains get very crowded (especially on the Yonge–University line northbound and the Bloor–Danforth line eastbound) from 8 to 10 am and 4 to 7 pm.

Late-night buses along Bloor and Yonge streets, and as far north on Yonge as Steeles Avenue, run from 1 am to 5:30 am. Streetcars that run 24 hours include those on King Street, Queen Street, College Street, and Spadina Avenue. Late-night service is slower, with buses or streetcars arriving every 30 minutes or so. All-night transit-stop signs are marked with reflective blue bands.

Streetcar lines, especially the King line, are interesting rides with frequent service. Riding the streetcars is a great way to capture the flavor of the city as you pass through many neighborhoods.

STOPS AND INFORMATION

Streetcar stops have a red pole with a picture of a streetcar on it. Bus stops usually have shelters and gray poles with bus numbers and route maps posted. Both buses and streetcars have their final destination and their number on both the front and back and side windows. The drivers are generally friendly and will be able to help you with your questions.

The free *Ride Guide*, published annually by the TTC, is available in most subways, with a less comprehensive "Lite" version available on buses, subway trains, and streetcars. The guide shows nearly every major place of interest in the city and how to reach it by public transit. The TTC's telephone information line provides directions in 80 languages.

Smoking is prohibited on all subway trains, buses, and streetcars, a rule that is strictly enforced.

Subway and Streetcar Information Toronto Transit Commission or TTC. ☎ *416/393–4636 recorded message, 416/393–4100 for lost and found, 416/393–4000 switchboard* ⊕ *www.ttc.ca.*

▮ TAXI TRAVEL

Taxis can be hailed on the street, but if you need to make an appointment (e.g., for an early-morning airport run) or if you're in a residential neighborhood, it's necessary to call ahead. Taxi stands are rare and usually only at hotels and at the airport.

Taxi fares are C$3.25 for the first 0.143 km and C25¢ for each 29 seconds not in motion and for each additional 0.143 kilometers. A C$2 surcharge is added for each passenger in excess of four. Minivan cabs for larger groups are often available, though if you order one through dispatch instead of hailing, a nominal fee to be agreed upon between passenger and driver will be charged (usually around $10). The average fare to take a cab across downtown is C$10–C$12, plus a roughly 15% tip, when the traffic is flowing normally. The largest companies are Beck, Co-op, Diamond, and Royal.

Ride-sharing app Uber is a popular and budget-friendly alternative to taxi travel in Toronto. Base rates for Uber rides start at C$2.50, with C$.80 added per kilometer and C$0.18 added for each minute spent idling. Other options within the app include UberXL, which uses SUVs and minivans, and UberPOOL, which allows you to share a fare with other riders for a low-cost option (though this system often means meandering and inefficient rides). Taking an Uber is generally safe, as penalties are harsh for ill-behaved drivers, but also exercise caution and make sure you're getting into the correct car. Though Toronto cabbies and Uber have enjoyed a bitter rivalry in recent years, many drivers for local cab companies also accept fares through Uber. Beware of surge pricing, which can significantly multiply the base rate during busy times.

▮TIP➔ Call 416/829–4222 to be connected to one of many taxi companies for free via an automated system.

Taxi Companies Beck. ☎ _416/751–5555, 877/883–2325_ ⊕ _www.becktaxi.com._ **Co-op.** ☎ _416/504–2667_ ⊕ _www.co-opcabs.com._ **Diamond.** ☎ _416/366–6868_ ⊕ _www.diamond-taxi.ca._ **Royal.** ☎ _416/777–9222_ ⊕ _www.royaltaxi.ca._

▮ TRAIN TRAVEL

Amtrak has service from New York and Chicago to Toronto (both 12 hours), providing connections between its own United States–wide network and VIA Rail's Canadian routes. VIA Rail runs trains to most major Canadian cities; travel along the Windsor–Québec City corridor is particularly well served. Amtrak and VIA Rail operate from Union Station on Front Street between Bay and York streets. You can walk underground to a number of hotels from the station, and there's a cab stand outside its main entrance.

Trains to Toronto may have two tiers of service: business class and reserved coach class. Business class is usually limited to one car, and benefits may include more legroom, meals, and complimentary alcoholic beverages.

To save money, look into rail passes, but be aware that if you don't plan to cover many miles, you may come out ahead by buying individual tickets.

VIA Rail offers two Canrail passes: the Windsor-Quebec City corridor and System, which covers the entirety of the cross-Canada rail system. The Windsor-Quebec City pass starts at C$299 for seven one-way trips in a 21-day period, while a VIA System pass starts at C$699 for seven one-way trips in a 60-day period. Both passes cover travel only in economy class.

Children under two travel for free in a parent's seat, and children up to 11 can get their own seat for roughly half the price of an adult ticket.

Major credit cards, debit cards, and cash are accepted.

Reservations are strongly urged for intercity and interprovincial travel and for journeys to and from the United States. If your ticket is lost, it is like losing cash, so guard it closely. If you lose your reservation number, your seat can still be accessed in their reservation system by using your name or the train you have been booked on.

GO Transit is the Greater Toronto Area's commuter rail. (It also runs buses.) The double-decker trains are comfortable and have restrooms.

Train Contacts Amtrak. ☎ *800/872–7245* ⊕ *www.amtrak.com.* **GO Transit.** ☎ *416/869–3200, 888/438–6646* ⊕ *www.gotransit. com.* **Union Station.** ✉ *65–75 Front St., between Bay and York Sts.* ☎ *416/366–7788* ⊕ *www.torontounion.ca.* **VIA Rail Canada.** ☎ *888/842–7245* ⊕ *www.viarail.ca.*

ESSENTIALS

■ BUSINESS SERVICES AND FACILITIES

FedEx Office—where you can fax, copy, print, and rent computers—has several locations in Toronto.

Contacts FedEx Office. ✉ *Sheraton Centre, 123 Queen St. W, Financial District* ☎ *647/255–1856.* **FedEx Office.** ✉ *Westin Harbour Castle, 1 Harbour Sq., Harbourfront* ☎ *647/288–1730.*

■ COMMUNICATIONS

INTERNET

Most hotels in Toronto offer free Wi-Fi, while some targeted at a business clientele will charge a nominal fee. Business-oriented hotels may also offer business lounges with computers available for guests' use. Independent coffee shops, as well as chains like Tim Hortons and Starbucks, generally offer free Wi-Fi for paying guests.

PHONES

The good news is that you can now make a direct-dial telephone call from virtually any point on earth. The bad news? You can't always do so cheaply. Calling from a hotel is almost always the most expensive option; hotels usually add huge surcharges to all calls, particularly international ones. Calling cards usually keep costs to a minimum but only if you purchase them locally. And then there are mobile phones, which are sometimes more prevalent than landlines; as expensive as mobile phone calls can be, they are still usually a much cheaper option than calling from your hotel.

When you are calling Canada, the country code is 1. The country code is 1 for the United States as well so dialing a Canadian number is like dialing a number long distance in the U.S.—dial 1, followed by the 10-digit number.

CALLING WITHIN CANADA

Local calls in Canada are exactly the same as local calls in the United States. Payphones (if you can find one, since most have disappeared from Toronto street corners) accept quarters (C50¢ for the first three minutes). Ask at your hotel whether local calls are free—there may be hefty charges for phone use. Buying a prepaid calling card or renting a cell phone may be worthwhile if you plan to make many local calls.

CALLING OUTSIDE CANADA

Calling to the United States from Canada is billed as an international call, even though you don't have to dial anything but 1 and the 10-digit number. Charges can be C$1 per minute or more on cell phones. Prepaid calling cards are the best option.

CALLING CARDS

Prepaid phone cards, which can be purchased at convenience stores, are generally the cheapest way to call the United States. You can find cards for as little as C$5 for eight hours of talk time. With these cards, you call a toll-free number, then enter the code from the back of the card. You can buy the cards online before you leave home.

MOBILE PHONES

If you have a multiband phone and your service provider uses the world-standard GSM network (as do T-Mobile, AT&T, and Verizon), you can probably use your phone in Canada. Roaming fees can be steep, however. And internationally you normally pay the toll charges for incoming calls. It's almost always cheaper to send a text message than to make a call as text messages have a very low set fee (often less than C5¢). Cell phone providers often offer packages for discounts on roaming that you can purchase before your trip, considerably lessening the cost; check with your provider to see what's available.

If you just want to make local calls, consider buying a new SIM card for around $10 (note that your provider may have to unlock your phone for this) and a prepaid service plan in the destination. You'll then have a local number and can make local calls at local rates. If your trip is extensive, you could also simply buy a new cell phone in your destination, as the initial cost will be offset over time.

Fido, a Canadian cell-phone company, sells prepaid SIM cards with monthly, weekly, and daily rates (local calling is C40¢-per-minute for daily packages) , but you have to go to a Fido store to buy and install the card. Gas chain Petro Canada and convenience store chain 7-Eleven may have the cheapest basic calling option, offering prepaid SIM cards with C25¢-per-minute calling rates.

Similicious, a Canadian start-up, offers prepaid SIM cards for travelers coming to Canada. Their plans last for one month from the activation date, and start at around C$35 (for a package that includes unlimited province-wide calls and 100 incoming texts). Other packages include up to 4 GB of data, unlimited calls to Canada and the United States, and discounts on international long distance rates. Order one online before your trip.

■ **TIP→** If you travel internationally frequently, save one of your old mobile phones or buy a cheap one on the Internet; ask your cell phone company to unlock it for you and take it with you as a travel phone, buying a new SIM card with pay-as-you-go service in each destination.

There are plenty of mobile-phone stores in downtown Toronto for renting phones. You can rent cell phones for as little as US$8 per day with Cellular Abroad, but buying the accompanying SIM card is mandatory and costs US$99.95 for a monthly plan. (The plan, however, is quite comprehensive, offering unlimited Canadian and U.S. calling and texting, plus 6 GB of data.)

Mobal rents mobiles and sells GSM phones with SIM cards (starting at US$29) that will operate in 190 countries. Per-call rates vary throughout the world. Planet Fone rents cell phones, but the per-minute rates are expensive.

Contacts 7-Eleven Speakout. ☎ 866/310–1023 ⊕ www.speakout7eleven.ca. **Cellular Abroad.** ☎ 800/287–5072 ⊕ www.cellular-abroad.com. **Fido.** ✉ Eaton Centre, 220 Yonge St., Dundas Square Area ☎ 416/597–1436 ⊕ fido.ca. **Mobal.** ☎ 888/888–9162 ⊕ www.mobalrental.com. **Petro Canada Mobility.** ☎ 866/788–3475 ⊕ www.mobility.petro-canada.ca. **Planet Fone.** ☎ 888/988–4777 ⊕ www.planetfone.com. **Similicious.** ⊕ www.similicious.com.

▮ CUSTOMS AND DUTIES

You're always allowed to bring goods of a certain value back home without having to pay any duty or import tax. But there's a limit on the amount of tobacco and liquor you can bring back duty-free, and some countries have separate limits for perfumes; for exact figures, check with your customs department. The values of so-called duty-free goods are included in these amounts. When you shop abroad, save all your receipts, as customs inspectors may ask to see them as well as the items you purchased. If the total value of your goods is more than the duty-free limit, you'll have to pay a tax (most often a flat percentage) on the value of everything beyond that limit.

Clearing customs is fastest if you're driving over the border. Unless you're pulled aside or traffic is backed up, you'll be through in a matter of minutes. When arriving by air, wait times can be lengthy—plan on at least 45 minutes. If you're traveling by bus, customs is a slow process, as all passengers must disembark, remove their luggage from the bus, and be questioned. Make sure all prescription drugs are clearly labeled or bring a copy of the prescription with you.

Visitors may bring in the following items duty-free: 200 cigarettes, 50 cigars, and 7 ounces of tobacco; 1.5 liters (or 53 imperial ounces) of wine, 1.14 liters (40 ounces) of liquor, or 24 355-milliliter (12-ounce) bottles or cans of beer for personal consumption. Any alcohol and tobacco products in excess of these amounts are subject to duty fees, provincial fees, and taxes. You can also bring in gifts of no more than C$60 in value per gift.

A deposit is sometimes required for trailers, which is refunded upon return. Cats and dogs must have a certificate issued by a licensed veterinarian that clearly identifies the animal and certifies that it has been vaccinated against rabies during the preceding 36 months. Certified assistance dogs are allowed into Canada without restriction. Plant material must be declared and inspected. There may be restrictions on some live plants, bulbs, and seeds. With certain restrictions or prohibitions on some fruits and vegetables—including oranges, apples, and bananas—visitors may bring food with them for their own use, provided the quantity is consistent with the duration of the visit.

Canada's firearms laws are significantly stricter than those in the United States. Regulations require visitors to have a confirmed "Firearms Declaration" to bring any guns into Canada; a fee of C$25 applies, which is good for 60 days. Non-restricted firearms—generally sporting rifles and shotguns—may be imported with a valid license. Restricted classes of firearms, including most handguns and semi-automatic firearms, require a special permit (Application To Transport) that must be obtained in advance, while others, including automatic weapons, are fully banned. All firearms must be declared to Canada Customs at the first point of entry. Failure to declare firearms will result in their seizure, and criminal charges may be made. For more information, contact the Canadian Firearms Centre.

> **DID YOU KNOW?**
>
> Though Canada is a bilingual country—it has two official languages, French and English—Toronto is the Anglophone center of Canada, and 99% of the people living here will speak to you in English. By law, product labels must also be in French, but you won't find French road signs or hear much French here.

Information in Canada Canada Revenue Agency. ☎ *800/959–8281 for international and nonresident inquiries* ⊕ *www.cra-arc.gc.ca.* **Canadian Firearms Centre.** ☎ *800/731–4000* ⊕ *www.rcmp-grc.gc.ca.*

U.S. Information U.S. Customs and Border Protection. ⊕ *www.cbp.gov.*

▌ ELECTRICITY

Canada's electrical capabilities and outlet types are no different from those in the United States. Residents of the United Kingdom, Australia, and New Zealand will need adapters to type A (not grounded) or type B (grounded) plugs. Voltage in Canada is 120, which differs from the United Kingdom, Australia, and New Zealand. Newer appliances should be fine, but check with the manufacturer and buy a voltage converter if necessary.

▌ EMERGENCIES

Like in the United States, the phone number for emergency services is 911. For a complete listing of emergency services, you can always check the Yellow Pages or ask for assistance at your hotel desk. The Dental Emergency Clinic operates from 8 am to midnight. Many branches of Shoppers Drug Mart are open until 10 pm, with some open 24 hours. Select Rexall drugstores are open until midnight.

All international embassies are in Ottawa; there are some consulates in Toronto, including a U.S. consulate. The consulate offers services between 8:30 am and noon by appointment.

Doctors and Dentists Dental Emergency Clinic. ✉ *1650 Yonge St., Greater Toronto* ☎ *416/485–7121.*

Foreign Consulates Consulate General of the United States. ✉ *360 University Ave., Queen West* ☎ *416/595–1700, 416/595–6506 emergency line for U.S. citizens, 416/201–4100 emergency line for U.S. citizens (after hrs)* ⊕ *ca.usembassy.gov.*

General Emergency Contacts Ambulance, fire, and police. ☎ *911.*

Hospitals and Clinics St. Michael's Hospital. ✉ *30 Bond St., fronting Queen St. East, Dundas Square Area* ☎ *416/360–4000* ⊕ *www.stmichaelshospital.com.* **Toronto General Hospital.** ✉ *200 Elizabeth St., Queen's Park* ☎ *416/340–3111* ⊕ *www.uhn.ca.*

24-Hour and Late-Night Pharmacies Rexall Pharma Plus. ✉ *777 Bay St., at College St., Dundas Square Area* ☎ *416/977–5824* ⊕ *www.rexall.ca* ✉ *63 Wellesley St. E, at Church St., Church–Wellesley* ☎ *416/924–7760.* **Shoppers Drug Mart.** ✉ *465 Yonge St., at College St., Dundas Square Area* ☎ *416/408–4000* ⊕ *www.shoppersdrugmart.ca* ✉ *388 King St. W, at Spadina Ave., Entertainment District* ☎ *416/597–6550* ✉ *390 Queen's Quay W, at Spadina Ave., Harbourfront* ☎ *416/260–2766.*

▌ HEALTH

Toronto does not have any unique health concerns. It's safe to drink tap water. Pollution in the city is generally rated Good to Moderate on the international Air Quality Index. Smog advisories are listed by the Ontario Ministry of the Environment at ⊕ *www.airqualityontario.com.*

HEALTH CARE

Consider buying trip insurance with medical-only coverage. In general, neither Medicare nor some private insurers cover medical expenses anywhere outside the United States. Medical-only policies typically reimburse you for medical care (excluding that related to preexisting conditions) and hospitalization abroad, and provide for evacuation. You still have to pay the bills and await reimbursement from the insurer, though.

Another option is to sign up with a medical-evacuation assistance company. A membership in one of these companies gets you doctor referrals, emergency evacuation or repatriation, 24-hour hotlines for medical consultation, and other assistance. International SOS Assistance Emergency and AirMed International provide evacuation services and medical referrals. MedjetAssist offers medical evacuation.

Medical Assistance Companies AirMed International. ⊕ *www.airmed.com.* **International SOS Assistance Emergency.** ⊕ *www.internationalsos.com.* **MedjetAssist.** ⊕ *www.medjetassist.com.*

Medical-Only Insurers International Medical Group. ⊕ *www.imglobal.com.* **International SOS.** ⊕ *www.internationalsos.com.* **Wallach & Company.** ⊕ *www.wallach.com.*

OVER-THE-COUNTER REMEDIES

OTC medications available in Canada are nearly identical to those available in the United States. In some cases, brand names are different, but you'll recognize common brands like Tylenol, Midol, and Advil. Nonprescription medications can be found at drugstores and in some grocery and convenience stores.

▌ HOURS OF OPERATION

Post offices are closed weekends, but post-office service counters in drugstores are usually open on Sunday. When open, hours are generally 8 to 6 or 9 to 7. There is no mail delivery on weekends. The Beer Store, which sells beer only, and the LCBO (Liquor Control Board of Ontario), which sells wine, beer, and liquor, are closed on holidays.

Most banks are open Monday through Thursday 10 to 5 and Friday 10 to 6. Some are open longer hours and on Saturday. All banks are closed on national holidays. Most have ATMs accessible around the clock.

As in most large North American urban areas, many highway and city gas stations in and around Toronto are open 24 hours, although there's rarely a mechanic on duty Sunday. Smaller stations close at 7 pm.

Toronto museums have an array of opening and closing times; it's best to phone ahead or check websites.

Most retail stores are open Monday through Saturday 10 to 6 or 11 to 7, and many now open on Sunday (generally noon to 5) as well. Downtown stores are usually open until 9 pm seven days a week. Some shops are open Thursday and Friday evenings, too. Shopping malls tend to be open weekdays from 9 or 10 am to 9 pm, Saturday from 9 am to 6 pm, and Sunday from noon to 5 pm, although many extend their hours pre-Christmas. Corner convenience stores are often open until midnight, seven days a week.

HOLIDAYS

Standard Canadian national holidays are New Year's Day, Good Friday, Easter Monday, Victoria Day (Monday preceding May 25), Canada Day (July 1), Civic Day (aka Simcoe Day in Toronto; first Monday in August), Labour Day (first Monday in September), Thanksgiving (second Monday in October), Remembrance Day (November 11), Christmas, and Boxing Day (December 26). In Ontario, Family Day (third Monday in February) is another statutory holiday.

▌MAIL

Canada's national postal system is called Canada Post. There are few actual post-office buildings in Toronto. Instead, many drugstores have post-office counters that offer full mail services. Check the Canada Post website for locations; a red, blue, and white Canada Post sign will also be affixed to the storefront. Post offices are closed weekends, and there is no mail delivery on weekends. During the week most post offices are open from 8 to 6 or from 9 to 7.

You can buy stamps at the post office, railway stations, airports, bus terminals, many retail outlets, and some newsstands. Letters can be dropped into red Canada Post boxes on the street or mailed from Canada Post counters in drugstores or post offices. If you're sending mail to or within Canada, be sure to include the postal code—six digits and letters. Note that the suite number may appear before the street number in an address, followed by a hyphen. The postal abbreviation for Ontario is ON.

Main postal outlets for products and services in the downtown area are the Adelaide Street Post Office; the Atrium on Bay Post Office near the Marriott, the Eaton Chelsea Hotel, and the Eaton Centre; and Postal Station "F," one block southeast of the major Bloor-Yonge intersection.

The Canadian postal system is almost identical to the U.S. system. To send regular letters within Canada, just ask for a letter stamp, which is C$1. Stamps for letters to the United States are C$1.20. Stamps for letters to countries other than the United States are C$2.50. Envelopes that exceed 30 grams (1 ounce) or are oversized cost incrementally more. Letter stamps are also sold in books of four or 10, or rolls of 50 or 100 for domestic and in books of six or rolls of 50 for international.

When sending mail other than a letter weighing less than 30 grams, take your envelope or package to a postal counter in a drugstore or to the post office to have it weighed and priced accordingly.

Mail may be sent to you care of General Delivery, Toronto Adelaide Street Post Office, 36 Adelaide Street East, Toronto, ON M5C 1J0.

Info Canada Post. ☎ *416/979–8822, 866/607–6301 in Canada* ⊕ *www.canadapost.ca.*

Main Branches Adelaide Street Post Office. ⊠ *31 Adelaide St. E, Financial District* ☎ *866/607–6301.* **Atrium on Bay Post Office.** ⊠ *595 Bay St., Dundas Square Area*

☎ 416/506–0911. **Postal Station "F"**. ✉ 663 Yonge St., Yorkville ☎ 416/413–4815.

SHIPPING PACKAGES
Customs forms are required with international parcels. Parcels sent regular post typically take up to two weeks. The fastest service is FedEx, which has 24-hour locations at University and Dundas and at Bloor and Spadina. "Overnight" service with Canada Post usually takes two days.

Express Services FedEx. ✉ 505 University Ave., at Dundas St. W, Chinatown ☎ 416/979–8447 ⊕ www.fedex.ca ✉ 459 Bloor St. W, at Major St., The Annex ☎ 416/928–0110.

▌MONEY

Unless otherwise stated, all prices, including dining and lodging, are given in Canadian dollars. Toronto is the country's most expensive city.

Prices here are given for adults. Substantially reduced fees are almost always available for children, students, and senior citizens.

ATMS AND BANKS
Your own bank will probably charge a fee for using ATMs abroad; the foreign bank you use may also charge a fee. Nevertheless, you'll usually get a better rate of exchange at an ATM than at a currency-exchange office or even when changing money in a bank. And extracting funds as you need them is a safer option than carrying around a large amount of cash.

▌TIP→ **PINs with more than four digits are not recognized at ATMs in many countries. If yours has five or more, remember to change it before you leave.**

ATMs are available in most bank, trust company, and credit union branches across the country, as well as in many convenience stores, malls, and gas stations. The major banks in Toronto are Scotiabank, CIBC, HSBC, Royal Bank of Canada, the Bank of Montréal, and TD Canada Trust.

ITEM	AVERAGE COST
Cup of Coffee	C$1.75
Glass of Wine	C$7–C$9
Glass of Beer	C$5–C$8
Sandwich	C$7–C$10
One-Mile Taxi Ride	C$2.80 (plus initial C$3.25)
Museum Admission	C$10–C$25

CREDIT CARDS
It's a good idea to inform your credit card company before you travel, especially if you're going abroad and don't travel internationally very often. Otherwise, the credit-card company might put a hold on your card owing to unusual activity—not a good thing halfway through your trip. Record all your credit-card numbers—as well as the phone numbers to call if your cards are lost or stolen—in a safe place, so you're prepared should something go wrong. Both MasterCard and Visa have general numbers you can call (collect if you're abroad) if your card is lost, but you're better off calling the number of your issuing bank as MasterCard and Visa usually just transfer you to your bank; your bank's number is usually printed on your card.

If you plan to use your credit card for cash advances, you'll need to apply for a PIN at least two weeks before your trip. Although it's usually cheaper and safer to use a credit card abroad for large purchases (so you can cancel payments or be reimbursed if there's a problem), note that some credit-card companies *and* the banks that issue them add substantial percentages to all foreign transactions, whether they're in a foreign currency or not. Check on these fees before leaving home so there won't be any surprises when you get the bill.

▌TIP→ **Before you charge something, ask the merchant whether he or she plans to do a dynamic currency conversion (DCC). In such a transaction the credit-card** processor (shop, restaurant, or hotel, not Visa or MasterCard) converts the currency and charges you in dollars. In most cases you'll pay the merchant a 3% fee for this service in addition to any credit-card company and issuing-bank foreign-transaction surcharges.

Dynamic currency conversion programs are becoming increasingly widespread. Merchants who participate in them are supposed to ask whether you want to be charged in dollars or the local currency, but they don't always do so. And even if they do offer you a choice, they may well avoid mentioning the additional surcharges. The good news is that you *do* have a choice. And if this practice really gets your goat, you can avoid it entirely thanks to American Express; with its cards, DCC simply isn't an option.

Reporting Lost Cards American Express.
☎ *800/297–8500 in U.S., 905/474–0870 within Toronto* ⊕ *www.americanexpress.com.* **Diners Club.** ☎ *800/234–6377 in U.S., 514/877–1577 collect from abroad* ⊕ *www.dinersclub.com.* **Discover.** ☎ *800/347–2683 in U.S., 801/902–3100 collect from abroad* ⊕ *www.discover.com.* **MasterCard.** ☎ *800/622–7747 in U.S. and Canada, 636/722–7111 collect from abroad* ⊕ *www.mastercard.com.* **Visa.** ☎ *800/847–2911 in U.S. and Canada, 303/967–1096 collect from abroad* ⊕ *www.visa.com.*

CURRENCY AND EXCHANGE

U.S. dollars are sometimes accepted—more commonly in the Niagara region close to the border than in Toronto. Some hotels, restaurants, and stores are skittish about accepting Canadian currency over $20 due to counterfeiting, so be sure to get small bills when you exchange money or visit an ATM. Major U.S. credit cards and debit or check cards with a credit-card logo are accepted in most areas. Your credit-card-logo debit card will be charged as a credit card.

The units of currency in Canada are the Canadian dollar (C$) and the cent, in almost the same denominations as U.S. currency ($5, $10, $20, 1¢, 5¢, 10¢, 25¢,

etc.). The $1 and $2 bill are no longer used; they have been replaced by $1 and $2 coins (known as a "loonie," because of the loon that appears on the coin, and a "toonie," respectively). The exchange rate is currently US77¢ to C$1, but, of course, this fluctuates often.

Even if a currency-exchange booth has a sign promising no commission, rest assured that there's some kind of huge, hidden fee. (Oh … that's right. The sign didn't say no *fee*.) And as for rates, you're almost always better off getting foreign currency at an ATM or exchanging money at a bank.

Google does currency conversion. Just type in the amount you want to convert and an explanation of how you want it converted (e.g., "14 Swiss francs in dollars"), and voilà. Oanda.com also allows you to print out a handy table with the current day's conversion rates. XE.com is another good currency conversion website.

Conversion sites Google. ⊕ *www.google. com.* **Oanda.com.** ⊕ *www.oanda.com.* **XE.com.** ⊕ *www.xe.com.*

■ PACKING

You may want to pack light because airline luggage restrictions are tight. For winter, you need your warmest clothes, in many layers, and waterproof boots. A scarf that covers your face is a good idea—winds can be brutal. In summer, loose-fitting, casual clothing will see you through both day and evening events. It's a good idea to pack a sweater or shawl for cool evenings or restaurants that run their air-conditioners full blast. Men will need a jacket and tie for the better restaurants and many of the nightspots. Jeans are as popular in Toronto as they are elsewhere and are perfectly acceptable for sightseeing and informal dining. Be sure to bring comfortable walking shoes. Consider packing a bathing suit for your hotel pool and a small umbrella.

■ PASSPORTS AND VISAS

Anyone who is not a Canadian citizen or Canadian permanent resident must have a passport to enter Canada. Passport requirements apply to minors as well. Anyone under 18 traveling alone or with only one parent should carry a signed and notarized letter from both parents or from all legal guardians authorizing the trip. It's also a good idea to include a copy of the child's birth certificate, custody documents if applicable, and death certificates of one or both parents, if applicable. (Most airlines do not allow children under age five to travel alone, and on Air Canada, for example, children under age 12 are allowed to travel unaccompanied only on nonstop flights. Consult the airline, bus line, or train service for specific regulations if using public transport.)

As of September 2016, non-Canadian citizens or permanent residents and non-U.S. citizens flying into Canada are now asked to acquire a temporary visa, called an Electronic Travel Authorization (or eTA), online through the Government of Canada website. The authorization costs C$7 and applications generally take up to 72 hours to approve (with most being approved in just a few minutes), but applications are still encouraged in advance in case of any unforeseen issues. After approval, the eTA is valid for six months. To learn more and apply, visit ⊕ *www.cic. gc.ca/english/visit/eta-start.asp*.

PASSPORTS

U.S. passports are valid for 10 years. You must apply in person if you're getting a passport for the first time; if your previous passport was lost, stolen, or damaged; or if your previous passport has expired and was issued more than 15 years ago or when you were under 16. All children under 18 must appear in person to apply for or renew a passport. Both parents must accompany any child under 16 (or send a notarized statement with their permission) and provide proof of their relationship to the child.

■TIP➔ Before your trip, make two copies of your passport's data page (one for someone at home and another for you to carry separately). Or scan the page and email it to someone at home and yourself.

If you're renewing a passport, you can do so by mail. Forms are available at passport acceptance facilities and online. The cost to apply for a new passport card and book (or a renewal) is $165 for adults, $120 for children under 16; renewals are $140. Allow six weeks for processing, both for first-time passports and renewals. For an expediting fee of $60 you can reduce this time to about six weeks. If your trip is less than six weeks away, you can get a passport even more rapidly by going to a passport office with the necessary documentation. Private expediters can get things done in as little as 48 hours.

U.S. Passport Information U.S. Department of State. ☎ 877/487-2778 ⊕ *travel.state.gov/ passport.*

U.S. Passport and Visa Expediters American Passport Express. ☎ 800/455-5166, ⊕ www.americanpassport.com. **Travel Document Systems.** ☎ 800/874-5100 ⊕ www.traveldocs.com.

■ RESTROOMS

Toronto is often noted for its cleanliness, which extends to its public restrooms. In the downtown shopping areas, large chain bookstores and department stores are good places to stop. If you dart into a coffee shop, you may be expected to make a purchase. Gas stations downtown don't typically have restrooms. Only a few subway stations have public restrooms; their locations are noted on the subway map posted above the doors in each car on the train.

■ SAFETY

Toronto is renowned as a safe city, but you should still be careful with your valuables—keep them in a hotel safe when you're not wearing them. Downtown areas are generally safe at night, even for women alone. Most of the seedier parts of the city are on its fringes. Nevertheless, areas east of Dufferin on Queen Street, College, or Bloor can feel desolate after dark, as can parts of Dundas Street.

Panhandling happens in Toronto, especially downtown. Jaywalking isn't illegal in Toronto and it happens frequently. Be alert when driving or walking—streetcars, jaywalkers, and plentiful bicyclists make downtown navigation somewhat hazardous.

■ **TIP→** Distribute your cash, credit cards, IDs, and other valuables between a deep front pocket, an inside jacket or vest pocket, and a hidden money pouch. Don't reach for the money pouch once you're in public.

Advisories U.S. Department of State. ⊕ *travel.state.gov.*

▌ TAXES

Toronto has a Harmonized Sales Tax (HST) of 13% (the combination of the former 5% national GST and the 8% provincial PST) on most items purchased in shops and on restaurant meals. (Be aware that taxes and tip add at least 30% to your food and beverage total when dining out.) The HST also applies to lodging and alcohol purchased at the Liquor Control Board of Ontario (LCBO). Prices displayed in LCBO stores include tax, so you won't see the extra taxes levied at the register.

▌ TIME

Toronto is on Eastern Standard Time (EST), the same as New York. The city is three hours ahead of Pacific Standard Time (PST), which includes Vancouver and Los Angeles, and is one hour behind Atlantic Standard Time, which is found in the Maritime Provinces. The Province of Newfoundland and Labrador is 1½ hours ahead of Toronto.

Timeanddate.com can help you figure out the correct time anywhere.

Time Zones Timeanddate.com. ⊕ *www.timeanddate.com/worldclock.*

▌ TIPPING

Tips and service charges aren't usually added to a bill in Toronto. In general, tip 15%–20% of the total bill. This goes for food servers, barbers and hairdressers, and taxi drivers. Porters and doormen should get about C$2 a bag. For maid service, leave C$2–C$5 per person a day.

▌ VISITOR INFORMATION

The website of the City of Toronto has helpful material about everything from local politics to public transit. The monthly magazine *Toronto Life* and the weekly alternative paper *NOW Magazine* list the latest art and nightlife events and carry information about dining, shopping, and more. Another site, ⊕ *toronto.com,* is one-stop shopping for nuts-and-bolts info like traffic or transportation, as well as for cultural events and links to a lot of other Toronto websites and blogs.

Written by locals, for locals, blogTO includes commentary on Toronto life and upcoming cultural events.

Official Websites Canadian Tourism Commission. ⊕ *www.canadatourism.com.* **City of Toronto.** ⊕ *www.toronto.ca.* **Ontario Travel.** ☎ *800/668–2746* ⊕ *www.ontariotravel. net.* **Tourism Toronto.** ☎ *416/203–2500, 800/499–2514* ⊕ *www.seetorontonow.com.*

Other Helpful websites Toronto Life. ⊕ *www.torontolife.com.* **Toronto.com.** ⊕ *www. toronto.com.* **NOW Magazine.** ⊕ *www.nowtoronto.com.* **blogTO.** ⊕ *www.blogto.com.*

INDEX

A

PHOTO CREDITS

NOTES

NOTES

NOTES

NOTES

NOTES

NOTES

NOTES

NOTES

NOTES

ABOUT OUR WRITERS

Toronto-based writer and editor Rosemary Counter moved downtown to study at the University of Toronto 15 years ago, and never left. Rosemary dabbles in every kind of writing she can—including health, news, relationships, humor and, her personal favorite, travel—and her work's popped up in *The New York Times*, *The New Yorker*, the *Guardian*, *Canadian Living*, and *Canadian Business*. She updated the Experience, Exploring, and Performing Arts chapters in this edition. Visit her at ⊕ *www.rosemarycounter.com*.

Natalia Manzocco spent her youth in Windsor, Ontario, trawling secondhand stores and having strong opinions about pizza before moving to Toronto to do more of the same. Currently the food writer at Toronto's alternative weekly newspaper, *NOW Magazine*, Natalia has written for the *National Post*, the *Toronto Sun*, *Metro* Canada, blogTO, the *Calgary Herald*, and more. She is also a vintage clothing dealer, musician, and the organizer behind Pink Market, Toronto's LGBTQ craft fair. This edition, she updated the Where to Eat, Where to Stay, Shopping, Nightlife, and Travel Smart chapters.

Writer and editor Jesse Ship found his calling while teaching English in Taipei. A Belgian national who grew up both in Toronto and Paris, it only made sense for him to pursue his passions in cultural and travel writing. If he's not out interviewing the latest experimental band or legendary DJ, he can be found at a screen monitoring or planning social media campaigns for media and entertainment companies. He updated the Side Trips from Toronto chapter this edition.

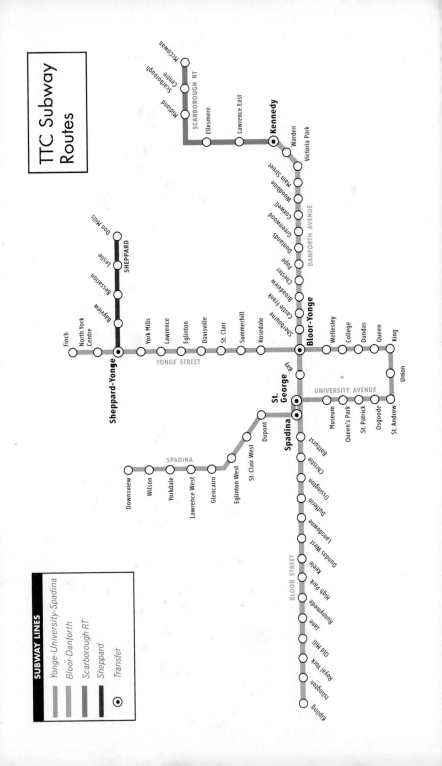

TTC Subway Routes

SUBWAY LINES

Yonge-University-Spadina
Bloor-Danforth
Scarborough RT
Sheppard
⊙ Transfer